CW00694861
KCLONIE
HOLY HOLY HOLY

S.C.E.G.G.S.

'Barham' by G. E. Peacock, 1845. Reproduced by S.C.E.G.G.S. Darlinghurst in 1988 from the original oil in the Dixson Galleries, State Library of NSW.

S.C.E.G.G.S.

A centenary history of Sydney Church of England Girls' Grammar School

Marcia Cameron

ALLEN & UNWIN

To Neil

First published 1994
Allen & Unwin Pty Ltd
9 Atchison Street, St Leonards, NSW 2065 Australia

National Library of Australia
Cataloguing-in-Publication entry:
Cameron, Marcia Helen.
S.C.E.G.G.S.: a history of Sydney Church of England Girls' Grammar School, 1895–1992.

Bibliography.
ISBN 1 86373 511 9.

1. Sydney Church of England Girls' Grammar School—History. 2. Anglican Church of Australia—Education—New South Wales—Darlinghurst. 3. Church schools—New South Wales—Darlinghurst—History. 4. Women—Education—New South Wales—Darlinghurst—History. I. Title. II. Title: Sydney Church of England Girls' Grammar School

376.99441

Set in 10.5/12 pt Baskerville by Graphicraft Typesetters, Hong Kong.
Printed by Kim Hup Lee Printing, Singapore

10 9 8 7 6 5 4 3 2 1

Endpaper illustrations by Kate Lonie, Sharon Bicknell and Claire Waterworth.

Foreword

Under the Public Instruction Act of 1880, the Church schools in New South Wales, many of which had been modelled on the English dame schools, became subject to government regulation. While some disappeared with this legislation others began a life which would take them through this century and beyond. The Sydney Church of England Girls' High School, as S.C.E.G.G.S. was first called, opened fifteen years after the Act on 17th July 1895 with one pupil, one teacher and a Headmistress, but also with the strong faith and clear vision of a handful of men and women. This same faith and vision have seen the school through a sometimes turbulent century of girls' schooling.

School histories abound nowadays. This history is different from those contemporary volumes. A history of S.C.E.G.G.S. it certainly is, but it is also a commentary on the influences which have made independent schooling what it is today. The reader can trace the influence of the Anglican Church, the developing role and status of teachers, and the increasing stature of girls and young women in society as they responded to the challenges which S.C.E.G.G.S. offered them.

Marcia Cameron, an Old Girl of S.C.E.G.G.S. Wollongong and now Chairman of the Board of S.C.E.G.G.S. Darlinghurst, has managed not only to capture some of that vibrant spirit and humour which is the essence of S.C.E.G.G.S., but she has identified and described those events which make S.C.E.G.G.S. unique in girls' education in this country. Two stand out in particular: the Council's evangelistic zeal in establishing branch schools throughout the state, and the consequent financial debacle which left Head School, Darlinghurst in a precarious financial position for almost a decade, even though it emerged from the crisis the stronger and the better in its management.

Some readers may baulk at Marcia Cameron's interpretation of sensitive subjects, which is simultaneously incisive, provocative and uncompromisingly honest. All will recognise some of their own history as they read this book.

I commend to you this history of the Sydney Church of England Girls'

Grammar School, illustrating the outstanding achievements of those who have created and supported an inner-city Anglican girls' school, a school which is set on a hill and will never be hidden.

Diana Bowman
Headmistress
S.C.E.G.G.S.

Contents

Illustrations

Tables and figures

Tables

Figures

Introduction

This account of S.C.E.G.G.S. Darlinghurst is the result of an invitation issued more than a decade ago. Miss Bowman asked me to write a new history of the school at a time when such a task seemed overwhelming. The process of interview, research, writing and rewriting has been a long one, and all the longer for having first submitted it as an MA thesis to the University of Sydney.

S.C.E.G.G.S. is a living organism, with the movement, life and infinite complexity of all living things. It is like a family, but again more complex because of the number of people who are part of it. The dimension of time, almost a century, makes attempts to define and describe S.C.E.G.G.S. at best like stills from a moving film. What one person sees as important may not be true of another. And so, while there are the 'facts'—dates, events, appointments, names and deeds—these are only some of the raw data of the school.

Every Old Girl or member of staff will have her own perceptions of S.C.E.G.G.S., each valid, each personal and each different. I stand on the outside, having been a pupil at a S.C.E.G.G.S. branch school, and many of the names and events I know about from my research, rather than knowing them first-hand. This history, which has tried to be a fair and balanced account of a remarkable school, will reflect my own background and views, just as any photograph must be taken from a particular place and focused on a particular subject. Because this is largely an account about people, there will be a mixture of the subjective and the objective.

It was a great advantage to have written it first as a university thesis. I had the benefit of the wisdom of my supervisor, Professor Kenneth Cable, who asked questions which made me think more clearly, and sent me into areas I might otherwise have neglected. The fact that it was first a thesis has made it into a particular kind of history. I have tried to keep a balance between the human interest of the S.C.E.G.G.S. story on the one hand, and drier, more academic considerations, necessary to an account which claims to be a credible history. The first two chapters are accordingly drier than what follows, because the main characters have not yet entered the scene and there is consequently little human interest. These chapters lay the foundation for the rest of the book. If you find them too difficult, leave them and go on to where the S.C.E.G.G.S. story proper begins.

The main sources of information have come from the school magazine, *Lux*, questionnaires and papers in the school archives, from what other people have written about education and schools and, very importantly, from interviews. The latter were a very enjoyable task. I met a number of Old Girls from Miss Badham's time, some of whom, sadly, have since died. I interviewed Old Girls and staff members from each of the four eras of the four Headmistresses' and although on nearly every occasion they expressed concern that they would have little to contribute, I came away with a transcript containing valuable information. The recollections of the older Old Girls were often amusing and very vivid. What impressed me about all the Old Girls, no matter what their vintage, was their confidence, their articulate speech and their independence of mind. There is undoubtedly a 'S.C.E.G.G.S. girl' who has been trained in her formative years to think for herself, to be confident of her own worth and to treat other people with courtesy and respect.

Faced with a mountain of data relating to S.C.E.G.G.S., how have I cut and ordered it to form this history? There were at least five main themes which I examined. I looked at what *shaped* the school: the people who influenced it, the location in Darlinghurst, its constitutional nature as founded by the Church of England Diocese of Sydney, external shapers such as economic factors, war and social changes. Other themes were: educational philosophy within S.C.E.G.G.S. and in New South Wales; the influence of Christian (and particularly Anglican) teaching in S.C.E.G.G.S.; the philosophy of expansion and its consequences as branch schools were set up; and, finally, the growth of a school tradition and unique characteristics which make S.C.E.G.G.S. the distinguished, distinctive school it is. I have not attempted to analyse in any detail the era of S.C.E.G.G.S. under the headship of Miss Bowman. I believe that is a job for my successor.

It has been a great privilege to be the author of this history of S.C.E.G.G.S. I have found the task even bigger than I first thought, and it took much longer to do than I imagined. My work of research and interviewing has increased my admiration for S.C.E.G.G.S. and I am very proud indeed to have been able to serve the school in this way. I *do* wonder who reads school histories, especially from beginning to end, but I believe that a good history is of great importance to a school because it sets down in writing what has happened and offers explanations as to why. Such information can only increase understanding for the whole S.C.E.G.G.S. community of our corporate identity, our values and our vision for the S.C.E.G.G.S. of the next one hundred years.

I am indebted to many people for their help and support. Among them are Miss Diana Bowman, Mrs Mary Maltby (tireless and utterly devoted archivist), Professor Kenneth Cable, and Bishop Donald Cameron, Registrar of the Diocese. A number of people helped by advising me in their various capacities. They include Dr Ray Nobbs, Dr Janet Scarfe, Mrs Anne Judd, Miss Joan Stevenson, Mrs Vashti Waterhouse, Mrs Heather Jones, Mr John Leslie Cameron and Miss Danusia Cameron. A special thank-you must go to my husband Neil for advice and encouragement, and to my family for their patience, interest and support.

Marcia Cameron
December 1993

— 1 —

Before S.C.E.G.G.S. began: education in New South Wales in the nineteenth century

SYDNEY CHURCH OF England Girls' Grammar School (S.C.E.G.G.S.) was founded in 1895. To understand the background to its establishment, it is helpful to start by examining the history of education in New South Wales from the early years of the nineteenth century, looking at the changes which occurred over this span of time. We shall then have some picture of what secondary education was like by 1895—what it offered, what it aimed to do, and where it was unsatisfactory. This will allow us to understand more clearly why the school was founded at all.

New South Wales began the nineteenth century as a colony in its infancy. Over the next one hundred years, its progress toward maturity involved great and dramatic changes socially, politically, economically and educationally. The sorts of changes which took place in education can be illustrated by the following three examples. While in 1788 all teachers had been *convict* women,[1] by 1900 the teaching population was equally balanced between males and females, and a significant number of the women were university or college graduates. The *control* of education also changed: up till the 1830s there was a virtual Anglican monopoly but this changed to a situation where, by 1900, the Roman Catholic system and the State Department of Education had both outpaced Anglican education. The *kind* of education available for girls changed too. The founding of the University of Sydney in 1850 marked the beginning of tertiary education in New South Wales and although its effects upon the education of women were not immediate, the long-term result was that the philosophy and practice of secondary education for girls altered. By the 1890s girls were offered subjects which had traditionally been taught only to boys, subjects designed to prepare them for entrance to university and a subsequent professional career. These subjects replaced or complemented the traditional ones for girls—the teaching of housewifely arts and artistic accomplishments.

Up until the last decade of the century, many people thought that secondary education was irrelevant. Employment was plentiful most of the time, and little or no education was required for most jobs. The pioneering days put emphasis on manual work and survival against the elements rather than on cultural pursuits and acquiring knowledge for its own sake. Elementary education was available through numerous private venture schools run by women, schools set up by the state (after 1848) and denominational schools. Secondary education was the preserve of the upper classes, and the curriculum was classical, based on Greek, Latin and mathematics. It was not designed to train young men and women for a career. When the first attempts were made by the Sydney Diocesan Synod in the late 1880s to establish high schools for girls, a number of people expressed deep frustration at the prevailing apathy of Anglican leaders towards such a venture.[2]

From 1788, the time of the Reverend Richard Johnson, the colony's first chaplain, Anglican church leaders took a strong interest in education—as did the early governors—because they valued education as a tool to improve the morals of the community. In the early days children learnt to read so that they could read the Bible and the catechism for themselves. But the early schools offered only an elementary education and the upper classes either went 'home' to England for their education, or were taught by their mother, or a governess or male tutor. The latter would have been an Oxford or Cambridge graduate who had emigrated to the colony.

When Thomas Hobbes Scott was appointed Archdeacon of New South Wales in 1824, he submitted a plan to the Colonial Office in London for the development of churches and schools in New South Wales. The purpose of his plan was to ensure that the Anglican church dominated education in the state. The scheme involved granting a substantial amount of land to the Anglican church which would finance primary schools and, in due course, central schools which would cater for 'higher attainments'.[3] His plans were only partially successful, for a number of reasons: other denominations—Roman Catholics, Methodists and Presbyterians—were also strongly vocal by that time, and not sympathetic to Anglican dominance in religion and education; lengthy land surveys delayed the grants; the 1825 economic depression in England, followed by a similar depression in the colonies from 1826 to 1828, led to the British Government limiting its financial assistance. Despite these setbacks, Anglican parochial elementary schools doubled from 17 to 36 between 1826 and 1829.

William Grant Broughton, the first Bishop of Australia, succeeded Archdeacon Scott. Like Scott, he fought to maintain Anglican supremacy in education and opposed Governor Bourke's attempts to establish a school system of education free from Anglican domination. The 1836 Church Act provided state aid to the major religious denominations and this was taken to mean educational aid as well. So from 1836 there were four competing systems of church elementary schools: Anglican, Roman Catholic, Presbyterian and Methodist. By 1848, when the state set up a National Board of Education, there were *five*.[4]

Bishop Broughton erred in his policy of opposing the plans of successive governors (Bourke, Fitzroy and Gipps) to establish a single educational system. A single educational authority would have been the most cost-effective solution to the problem of educating a population scattered thinly over the rural areas.

As it was, there was less finance available to establish new schools in needy areas. A Select Committee set up by the Legislative Council in 1854 appointed three commissioners to enquire into improving education in the colony. They visited 202 of the 217 state-aided elementary schools and their Final Report, submitted in 1855, showed that national schools were superior to the denominational schools, athough Anglican schools were slightly better than the other denominational schools. The commissioners' report was a damning indictment of elementary education in New South Wales, in particular of the denominational schools. It revealed that teachers were poorly equipped and poorly paid; the methods of instruction were mechanical and narrow; school buildings, especially in rural areas, were often unsuitable; schools were poorly furnished and equipped; and even in religious instruction pupils were said to be ignorant.[5]

The lasting contribution which Bishop Broughton made to education in New South Wales was his founding of The King's School, Parramatta, in 1832. Although it closed for five years from 1864, it is the oldest secondary school in the state. The Bishop founded two other secondary schools, The King's School Sydney and St James' Grammar School, but neither survived. The King's School Parramatta was designed to help create an educated wealthy gentry[6] and the curriculum was a modified version of the classical curriculum of English public schools. The boys were taught Greek, Latin, mathematics and a little geography, but not English literature, modern languages, music or the sciences.[7] Most dear to the Bishop's educational heart was that pupils acquire a thorough grounding in the Scriptures, Anglican doctrine and Church history.[8]

Apart from The King's School Parramatta, the Anglicans did not venture into secondary education until the 1880s. Just as rivalry had prompted school-founding fifty years earlier,[9] so again it was an awareness of being outstripped by other denominations which prompted the founding of Anglican secondary schools, including S.C.E.G.G.S. Darlinghurst, in the last decades of the nineteenth century.[10] In the meantime Sydney Grammar School had been founded in 1857 as a non-denominational school funded by government endowment. It became a model of a 'public school' in the Antipodes, and was the most important secondary school founded in mid-nineteenth century Sydney.[11] Established primarily as a feeder school for the University of Sydney, which commenced teaching in 1852, it excluded religious instruction and adopted the classical curriculum of the English public school. It aimed to provide a 'superior general, not professional education'.[12] While classics and mathematics were the nucleus of the syllabus, modern languages, history, geography, natural science, writing, drawing, French, dancing and gymnastics were also included. The syllabus was a contrast to the narrow King's School curriculum drawn up by Bishop Broughton.

By 1860 a debate had developed over the kind of curriculum suitable for secondary education. It was considered that what was appropriate for a pupil from the upper classes was not appropriate for a working-class child, because traditionally the upper-class son had been educated to equip him for social and political leadership. It was not intended that he should be trained for a specific type of work. Australia was lagging behind England here, for while England was moving away from a strictly classical curriculum, Australians such as Professor John Woolley, the first Principal of the University of Sydney and a member of the original Trust Board of Sydney Grammar School, were still saying: 'Education is not knowledge but the habit of thinking'.[14] Nevertheless a new influence on educational philosophy was the growing industrialisation of New South Wales. The expanding middle class demanded that their sons study commercial and scientific subjects. They sought a *practical* education which would prepare pupils for particular jobs.

Female education was an afterthought in such educational deliberations. Boys and girls received different elementary education and because the secondary course was dependent upon the foundations laid in elementary school, girls would not have been adequately prepared for some subjects offered to boys at secondary level. Girls' education was heavily biased towards needlework and the three Rs, and they spent much less time than the boys on mathematics and languages. The aims of education for women were not clear and ranged, in the late 1800s, from education for motherhood to academic excellence. For most, the home was the 'divine workshop' wherein a woman's destiny lay.

Catholic convent schools, which many Protestant girls attended, aimed to produce refined, accomplished, devout homemakers. The private venture schools (non-denominational private schools) which were, apart from private tutors or governesses, the only other avenue of secondary education for girls, did not aim at serious intellectual endeavour. They were open only to the wealthy, as their fees were prohibitively high. Both the convent schools and the private venture schools were designed, administered and organised entirely by women and were the trailblazers in the development of female education.[15]

In the second half of the nineteenth century, educational reform took place in three stages. First, in 1848, the plans which Bishop Broughton had done his best to sabotage came into effect—a National Board of Education was established. The Board organised a system of elementary state schools which existed alongside the four denominational systems under the Denominational Board. As Acting Secretary to the National Board, William Wilkins set up a system of inspectors and teacher training for the state schools.

Second, in 1866, under Parkes' Public Schools Act, elementary education in rural areas expanded following implementation of a plan to set up 'provisional' and 'half-time' schools. The Act also made it more difficult to establish a non-government school.[16] Ultimately this was a progressive step because the standards of the state system, which was stronger than the denominational system, were much higher and the denominational schools were forced to improve in order to compete.

Third, the Public Instruction Act of 1880 aimed to make education free, compulsory and secular, and it provided for the establishment of the first high schools. When state aid to denominational schools came to an end in 1882, many were forced to close. In reality state education was neither free, nor compulsory, nor secular, but elements of each were present. There was, as hitherto, provision for the teaching of religion in schools. Bishop Barker, Bishop Broughton's successor, did all he could to encourage religious instruction in state schools and, unlike the Roman Catholic Archbishop Vaughan, decided to work within the state system as well as through the church schools.

The University of Sydney, initially had little impact on the educational system. However, with the introduction of a matriculation examination in 1867, the admission of women to that examination in 1871, the widening of its courses to include science and law in 1882–83, and the admission of women to the university in 1881, it became a powerful influence on secondary education. Another influence was the growth of democracy in New South Wales. The granting of responsible government in the mid 1850s changed educational philosophy. From that time on a new duty of educationalists was to provide training for responsible citizenship, but only for males.

Before the 1880s there were few secondary schools in New South Wales. The Anglicans had The King's School and the Clergy Daughters' School (founded in 1856), and there was Sydney Grammar School. With the passage of the 1880 Act a great wave of school-founding began. In this decade St Andrews' Choir School (1885), a rejuvenated and reconstituted King's (1885), Sydney Church of England Grammar School (1889), Presbyterian Ladies' College Croydon (1888) and Methodist Ladies' College Burwood (1886) were founded along with the first schools of the great Roman Catholic system of education. These were St Aloysius (1879), St Joseph's College (1881) and Rose Bay Convent (1882), all the creation of Archbishop Vaughan in response to the establishment of a state system of education.

By contrast, the high schools established by the state did not prosper for the most part at this stage and two of the four high schools for girls (Goulburn Girls' High and Bathurst Girls' High, both opened in 1883) were forced to close mainly because high schools charged higher fees than Superior Public Schools. Nevertheless, the founding of the state high schools was very significant. These schools further extended secondary education for girls and raised standards in curriculum development and teacher qualifications.

Bishop Alfred Barry, Bishop of Sydney from 1884 to 1889, was the prime mover in the establishment of Anglican schools in the 1880s. He repeatedly promoted the idea that sound and thorough education of girls was important.[17] For him education was 'simple obedience to the law of God's providence . . . perhaps the chief need of a community, rapidly growing in material resources and breaking ground in every direction'.[18]

Above all, Barry wanted education to be *Christian.* By teaching the Christian faith as set out in the New Testament, the church would equip its young people to deal with the current problems of the age and to live as helpful members of their community. The church's duty was to carry on the work of instruction in Sunday Schools and through religious instruction in the public schools. Indeed he called it a 'sacred duty' and maintained that it was worth any labour and sacrifice to accomplish this task.[19]

Thus by 1890, although the churches had lost ground to the state in the field of elementary education, all the major denominations had established vigorous schools in which they could promote their religious teaching. There was still opportunity for religious instruction in the state system which Anglicans gladly utilised.

The area in which Sydney Anglicans were outpaced by the other denominations was in the establishment of secondary schools for girls. While they had established three boys' schools in the 1880s, a pressing need was the provision of Anglican schools for girls which would offer an academic curriculum. The Sydney Church of England Girls' Grammar School, opened in 1895, was a product of a century of development and metamorphosis.

— 2 —

Founding an Anglican school for girls

THE ESTABLISHMENT OF the University of Sydney was very important in changing attitudes to education in nineteenth century Sydney, because it generated a need for quality secondary education and provided a goal for pupils who completed high school, although not all secondary students aspired to a university education.

Amid much controversy educational opportunities for females had steadily extended, beginning with the right to sit for examinations set by the University in 1871 and, a decade later, to enrol there as students. State secondary education for girls had begun with the establishment of high schools for girls in Sydney, Bathurst and Goulburn in 1883. The opening of the University's Women's College in 1892 provoked a heated debate in the *Sydney Morning Herald* on the issue of women's rights to higher education. One letter writer (using the *nom de plume* Cutty Sark) thought it was a waste, stating 'women's brains are smaller and lighter than men's' and 'women do not need a university degree to run a household'.[1] An opposing view was that an intelligent and educated wife is a better companion for her husband.[2]

Clearly higher education for women was feared as potentially disruptive to the social order. Lower-class women would get ideas above their station and wives might challenge their husband's superior status. Women were seen as the moral guardians of the nation. An editorial in the Anglican newspaper the *Australian Record* stated, for example, 'It is of vast importance therefore, that the very best education, and this of course includes definite and religious instruction, should be given to her who is to become in the course of a few years the "angel in the house".'[3]

The new state high schools set up to implement the Public Instruction Act of 1880 made no provision for religious instruction in their curricula, except that clergy were permitted to visit the schools. In a lecture on religious instruction in high schools, James Hole said, 'It is to be regretted that our Education Act does not permit of our Special Religious Instruction [in] High Schools and Training Schools for teachers.'[4] By contrast, a program of religious instruction had been implemented in the state primary schools in the Diocese of Sydney, 21 000 out of a total of 45 000 Anglican children were given religious instruction by clergy, lay and employed scripture teachers. Had the Anglican church been free to extend its program of religious instruction into the new high schools, the need to provide Anglican secondary school girls with a Christian education would have been less pressing. The absence of such a program was a cogent reason for setting up an Anglican girls' secondary school.

Other denominations began to found girls' high schools after the Public Instruction Act. The Methodists founded the Methodist Ladies' College (MLC), Burwood in 1886 and the Presbyterians established the Presbyterian Ladies' College (PLC) at Croydon in 1888. Although the Clergy Daughters' School at Waverley (St Catherine's) dated back to 1856, its doors were open only to the daughters of the clergy. In his address to the Synod in 1886, Bishop Barry depicted the standards at St Catherine's as inferior to those of the girls' high schools in England, which offered what he called 'high class education'.[5] Regrettably no records of the early days of St Catherine's remain, but by 1894 it had been reformed. That year an advertisement placed in the *Australian Record* claimed that at St Catherine's '. . . the best features of the English and German High School System of teaching are combined with the advantages of a well-conducted Private School so as to give a thorough education with a decided religious training.'[6]

Sectarian rivalry was intense and it played as big a part as any other factor in the founding of S.C.E.G.G.S. Darlinghurst. The *Australian Record* editorial put it this way:

> *It seems strange that other religious bodies should be somewhat in advance of the Church of England in this matter. The Presbyterians have a large college at Ashfield, the Wesleyan Methodists have theirs at Burwood, and the Roman Catholics have theirs scattered all over the Colony, while the Church of England is content with St Catherine's. Why should members of our church be compelled to send their daughters to the colleges of other sects?*[7]

Even more worrying to some was the fact that Anglican girls were attending Roman Catholic schools. This was the case in a number of country towns, partly because of the reasonable fees charged for boarders. This particular matter was discussed at some length in the 1891 *Report to Synod on the Education of Girls in Connection with the Church of England:*

> *As to the religious effect of the education of members of the Church of England at a Convent School, it is not easy to speak in exact terms; but this can be said with certainty, that Church of England boarders at such schools are prohibited, except under very special circumstances, from receiving any instruction or even visitation from their own clergy, and also from attending the services of their own Church. They seem to be required also to attend certain services of the Roman ritual. The result that is likely to ensue in most cases will be, if not perversion to Romanism, ignorance of all religion except in forms that are horribly repellant, and a negative or hostile position taken up at the most impressionable period of life.*[8]

Girls' high schools, both state and independent, were now in existence. Their presence was a provocation for Sydney Anglicans to found their own girls' high school. The reality of the establishment and improvement of Anglican grammar schools for boys also stirred up the desire to provide a grammar school for the daughters of Anglicans.

This was the starting point of the 1891 *Report upon the Education of Girls in connection with the Church of England.*[9] The report was the work of a Select Committee chaired by the Rev. A. D. Langley (later Archdeacon of Cumberland). The Committee observed the fact that effective provision for educating boys had been made but nothing had yet been done for the 'higher education' of girls. At The King's School a new, reforming Headmaster, new buildings, and legislation which made the school responsible to the Synod, had contributed to the doubling of enrolments by 1888.[10] St Andrew's Cathedral Choir School (1885) and Sydney Church of England Grammar School, known as 'Shore' (1889) had been established. Both new schools had made steady progress. While there were about 50 pupils at the Cathedral school for most of the 1890s, at Shore enrolments had risen to 119 pupils by 1891.[11] The same report encouraged support for girls' education and promised that 'the actual necessary cost of establishing and working a high class school for girls may be set down as considerably less than in a similar institution for boys.'

Another reason for founding S.C.E.G.G.S. was to provide girls with the opportunity to pursue academic excellence in the context of an Anglican school. The first Principal of S.C.E.G.G.S. was to be none other than the daughter of the Principal of the University, Charles Badham. Although he died in 1884, his ideas strongly influenced his daughter Edith. His interest in education reached far beyond the University and in many of his speeches he used all the considerable force of his oratory to plead for education which teaches people to think for themselves. Education enabled a person to be clear-headed, to know how he or she arrived at a conclusion. It made good citizens: temperate, rational, sensitive adults. He believed that women should be given the same educational opportunities as men.[12]

The early 1890s were not economically propitious times for starting a new school. The worst depression Australia had experienced began in 1890 with the breaking of the boom which had begun as far back as the 1860s. The worst years of depression were 1892 and 1893, but there was little recovery before 1895. Added to this was the worst drought on record, which lasted from 1895 to 1903.

The depression was caused partly by an economic recession in Europe and America, and partly by financial overextension and overproduction in Australia during the boom years. Overseas capital during the boom years had seemed to be limitless and money had poured into the pastoral industry, buildings in the cities, and railway construction. More wool was produced than could be sold on the overseas market. By mid 1892, twenty Sydney-based land and building institutions had gone into suspension and banks fell 'like ninepins'.[13] By May 1892 there were only nine banks open in Australia. The resulting bankruptcies, liquidations and unemployment affected all sections of the community. The economic effects of the worst years of the depression continued long after the banks had reopened. Credit, in particular, was tight. Enrolments fell substantially at The King's School and Shore in 1896 and continued to do so until 1899 (see Table 2.1).[14] Bishop Saumarez Smith, the fourth Bishop of Sydney, noted in his Presidential Address to the Synod in September 1894 that 'the commercial depression has had somewhat of a lowering effect as to numbers.' Enrolments fell at the state high schools also. The Anglican committee for a girls' high school saw no hope for starting a school in their report of 1893: 'It is with much regret that the times have been so discouraging to any

Table 2.1 Enrolments at Anglican schools

	1891	1892	1893	1894	1895	1896	1897	1898
King's	116	113	102	102	87	72	82	93
Shore	118	139	141	124	130	126	112	94
St John's Darlinghurst (a parochial school)	525	532	509	406	382	394	245	189

new enterprise involving financial risk that it has not been found possible to put forth any scheme for the establishment of a High School for Girls in connection with the Church of England.'[15]

The kind of education girls received in Sydney in the nineteenth century did not change much until the 1880s. Before 1880 the privileged few of the upper and middle classes attended select ladies' academies or were taught at home by a governess or their mothers. Generally they were taught non-academic subjects. An advertisement for a school run by the Misses Dodd in 1843 offered:

> *... a thorough and expeditious knowledge of every indispensable branch of Education, with the useful branches of work, ornamental painting on Glass, Crystal Baskets, Tinting, Artificial Fruits, etc. Terms: Board and instruction in English Grammar, Writing, Arithmetic, Geography, History, Plain and Ornamental Needlework ... French, Music and Dancing, extra charges.*[16]

Convent schools offered the only systematic education in Australia for more than fifty years, with high standards and a tradition of excellent musical education. The curriculum was non-academic, nonetheless.

The aims of educators in the last two decades of the nineteenth century were not primarily academic. Religious and moral principles ranked as of first importance, followed by the training to become young ladies (or gentlemen). Academic training came next. Academic excellence and examinations were not popular with the parents of girls: they wanted their daughters to become well-groomed young ladies, not academic blue stockings. At this time women were destined to make a career in the home as wives and mothers: born to marry, in fact. This began to change when more women were compelled to enter the workforce as a result of the hardships arising from the depression of the 1890s. When women began to participate in the professions and commerce, academic and utilitarian subjects which would train them for a job became more popular. With the exception of the Superior Public Schools, 'Select' schools offering a 'superior' education for girls were for the wealthier sections of society and their attraction was social rather than academic.[17] The 'accomplishment' or 'social' subjects were modern languages such as German, French and Italian; and fine arts: music, painting, woodcarving, wax flower making, leatherwork, and the art of illuminating. In addition class singing, theory of music and harmony, elocution, dancing, gymnastics and callisthenics were often offered.

In addition to callisthenics and gymnastics in the physical education program, walking was a favourite form of exercise and good deportment was cultivated as an essential aspect of ladylike behaviour. 'Drill', which included marching in formation, emphasised discipline and precision. New sports were introduced in the 1890s: tennis, boating, cricket, croquet and swimming. These gradually replaced walking as exercise.[18]

Academic subjects were introduced into girls' secondary education after the admission of women to the University. The first state girls' high schools, as well as MLC Burwood and PLC Croydon, all had academic curricula similar to those of the boys' schools. The girls' schools were modelled on English public schools as were the boys' schools. The classical curriculum with modifications was taught. Latin and Greek were offered, but were generally not as popular as modern languages. The other main subject of the classical curriculum was mathematics but although mathematics was included in the girls' curricula, very often only those sitting for the University Examination took it. There were different requirements for boys and girls.[19] Despite opposition by many, science made its way into some girls' schools in the 1890s, geology, astronomy, botany and physiology being more popular than physics and chemistry.

The new secondary schools generally did not teach domestic science subjects.[20] The girls who attended such schools came from homes where domestic servants were employed to look after the cooking and housekeeping. Indeed domestic servants were at this time the largest class of wage-earning women in New South Wales. Secondary education was still a luxury for the middle and upper classes.

Some teachers in girls' high schools had had the benefit of teacher training and by the 1890s some had a degree but a great many did not. Many teachers based their ideas on English education and many were English.[21] Most schools had a very small staff. Bathurst Girls' High School had two teachers for all the subjects and Ascham's Headmistress, Miss Wallis, taught all but the specialist subjects when the school opened in 1886.[22]

By 1893, when plans to open S.C.E.G.G.S. were laid, there was an established tradition, albeit a short one, of academic education for girls which offered many of the same subjects offered to boys. However, there was an aim to educate girls to be well-bred and ladylike and this, together with daily religious and moral teaching, was considered more important than academic training. While boys were educated to be leaders, girls were to be wives and mothers exercising influence on the male leaders.

The establishment of S.C.E.G.G.S. can be traced back to the initiative of Bishop Barry. With a brilliant university record and a distinguished career in secondary education in England behind him, he had been Principal of Leeds Grammar School, Cheltenham College and King's College, London, and was the most scholarly leader the Sydney Diocese had had.[23] He was authoritarian by disposition, an able administrator and a forceful leader. It was to be expected that he would interest himself in education when he arrived in Sydney. He established new schools (notably St Andrew's Choir School and Shore), reorganised others and improved Moore Theological College. He also moved the College from Liverpool to its present site near the University of Sydney, so that working men could enrol for evening classes, students could undertake parochial work, and he could more closely supervise the College. Proximity to the University meant that theological training and secular education could be linked.

Barry's aggressive drive for Christian education was a response to what he perceived as the new and worrying secularism which threatened Christians in the 1880s. The teaching of the Bible was being attacked in popular lectures and meetings with sensational titles such as 'Christian Missions and Omissions'. Targets for criticism were alleged inconsistencies in the Bible, the Creation account in Genesis and the theme of judgment in the prophets.[24] Barry saw church schools and religious education in the state schools as the means whereby children could be taught a Christian value system. His language was the aggressive language of battle and mission: 'We must strive, any way and every way, so far as we may rightly do so, to make the education of the country, a Christian education. The Church . . . is false to her mission if she does not witness for Christ boldly in this truceless war.'[25]

In his presidential speech of 1885 he expressed a desire to see a new Anglican high school for girls established:

> *But while we hope thus in various ways to advance the right education of our boys, let me remind you that this is but half of our duty. No educational advance in England is more remarkable than that which has taken place of late for the sound and thorough education of girls, mainly through the action of the 'Girls' High School Company.' I hope ere long to see some corresponding movement here. That it is needed, I cannot doubt; that it would be easily self-supporting, I have full confidence; that it is a proper complement to all that is proper to do for the high religious education of our boys is obvious. Till recently the duty had been comparatively neglected in England. The success that has attended the attempt to repair that neglect may well encourage us here. By next year I trust I may be able to submit to you the announcement of some definite scheme.*[26]

In 1886 in his presidential address to the Synod, Barry referred once again to the higher education of girls. He dwelt on the improvements in the Clergy Daughters' School at St Catherine's Waverley. It had 'rapidly advanced under the able and kindly leadership of Miss Phillips', and was planning to admit girls other than clergy daughters. Their numbers would not exceed those of the daughters of the clergy, and there would probably be a total of 40 pupils. The main reason for this innovation seems to have been to make the school more financially viable. The plans for St Catherine's were definitely on a small scale compared with enrolments at the new boys' schools established by the Church of England up to the turn of the century. For example, within five years of its inception Shore had 140 pupils. Having praised St Catherine's for its 'admirable work', the Bishop repeated his desire to establish a number of 'schools of high class' for girls on the model of the 'Girls' High Schools' in England. The sooner the Church of England in Sydney started on this project, the better. The pressure of other work had prevented his acting personally to establish such schools; nevertheless the Bishop gave the enterprise his 'very cordial sanction and support'. Such a statement raises the query of the degree to which the Bishop's support was rhetorical rather than practical. There are no further references to the establishment of a good quality school for girls in the Bishop's subsequent presidential addresses. He left Australia in 1889 after six years.[27]

Lack of finance was the single most important reason that Sydney Anglicans were behind the other denominations in starting secondary schools for girls. The Roman Catholic convent schools depended on their middle-class Anglican pupils' fees to balance their budgets as their own flock was still too poor in most instances to pay adequate fees. The Presbyterians, with their rigidly centralised system, were wealthier than the Anglicans. There were rich individual entrepreneurs, but by contrast, the Diocese of Sydney was poor. There was no central fund, although some individual parishes were wealthy. While Shore had been established by the Synod grant of £30 900, derived from the sale of the St James' parochial school in the city,[28] there were no more windfalls to finance an Anglican girls' school.

In addition to financial considerations, there was also the fact that the driving force behind Anglican secondary education for girls was Bishop Barry. His departure marked a loss of momentum in the project. The facts that the Sydney Synod was composed entirely of men, and that education for girls was a contentious issue, also account for the long delay between Barry's initiative in 1885 and the actual establishment of S.C.E.G.G.S. a decade later. The theme of reports and presidential addresses is one of apathy, lack of finance, indifference, difficulties and neglect.

At the 1889 August Synod, Rev. A. W. Pain (for Rev. Dr J. C. Corlette) moved 'That the Synod refers it to the Standing Committee to consider what steps can be taken towards establishing a first-class High School for Girls in connection with the Church of England in this Diocese.' The motion was carried. (The Standing Committee is the body which meets as the executive when the Synod is not sitting.) At the same Synod the Sub-Committee re Girls' High School (as it called itself) presented a short report signed by Archdeacon Gunther, its chairman. The sub-committee did not hold out any hope that there would be funds available from the Diocese for the venture. The main content of the report was a recommendation that a church schools company be organised by interested persons and that members of the church take out shares in it. Any venture to establish a new school would benefit from the goodwill of the bishops of the church, which would confer status and the good name of the Anglican tradition.

Bishop Saumarez Smith's presidential addresses of 1890 and 1891 do not mention a first-class girls' school at all. The only mention of education by the new Bishop was in connection with religious instruction within the state school system. Like his predecessors he was aware of the immense potential for religious education that existed in the primary schools under the provisions of the Public Instruction Act. He spoke of 'culpable negligence' if Anglicans refused to go into the public schools to give religious instruction.[29]

In August 1891 a much fuller report from the 'Select Committee appointed to consider and report upon the Education of Girls in connection with the Church of England' was presented to the Synod by J. C. Corlette, a prominent churchman and Honorary Secretary of the Committee. He pointed out that nothing whatever had been done so far to establish a new Anglican girls' school. He dwelt at length on the lamentable contrast this made with the other Protestant schools recently established and the fact that many Anglican girls were actually attending Roman Catholic schools for want of their own. Since there existed successful private schools for girls in Sydney and in Armidale (the New England Ladies' College, opened in 1887, had had 'remarkable success'), a similar enterprise by the Church of England would most definitely succeed. There was certainly a demand for such a school. As to the difficult question of finance, he argued that the best solution would be some form of company, like the English Church High Schools Company, Limited. Schools in England were rarely under Diocesan control, so the concept was an unusual one in England. In Sydney, the attempt to implement the concept was through a company proposed in 1892, to be called 'The Church of England High Schools Company'.

Not one school, but many, were envisaged. These schools would be available to more than the wealthy and privileged, and would be located in smaller towns, thus effectively competing with the convent schools. Moreover girls' schools would cost less to run. Although he did not specify why, the reason was that salaries, the main expenditure in a school budget, were lower for female staff. The report ended with an exhortation for some decisive action, and for men with good business sense and expertise in public relations to 'carry this project onward to success'.[30]

In 1892 the Bishop commented in his presidential address: 'The movement in regard to high schools for girls has not gained much force. Perhaps it is because the need is not fully recognised, or because the scheme is not yet widely known. Dr Corlette, it will be seen, means to keep the subject alive.'[31] J. C. Corlette was secretary of the Girls' High Schools Committee. His report for 1892 looked again at the two main ways to fund the school: either by gifts, endowments and loans, or by the formation of a Church High Schools Company.[32] An attempt to make St Catherine's the centre of a network of church schools came to nothing because there appeared to be restrictions in the deeds of the school which limited its objectives to the education of clergy daughters. Also, it catered mainly for boarders because at that time Waverley, where it was located, was considered too far a journey from the city for day-girls to travel.

At the beginning of 1892 a statement concerning the establishment of a new high school for girls had been distributed. Of the 267 copies circulated, only 21 replies 'came to hand to testify to the interest felt in the subject'. How many of the 21 were women is unknown. A ray of hope was that twenty of the people who bothered to respond to Corlette's report were 'strongly in favour of pressing forward the establishment of such schools as were proposed'. The conclusion to this report was:

> *. . . that under present circumstances it was hopeless to attempt any new enterprise . . . this committee has therefore to report in short, with much regret that they have not as yet found any way of bringing the proposal committed to them to a practical issue . . . and that some way may be opened before long for effective work in the direction of removing this reproach, that the Church has done nothing in the way of providing High Schools for Girls.*[33]

The year, 1892, was the depth of the economic depression.

An editorial entitled 'Higher Education for Young Women' appeared in the *Australian Record*. It may well have been written by Ernest Beck, later the chaplain at S.C.E.G.G.S., and some of the arguments advanced the year before by Dr Corlette were employed. The embarrassment caused by other denominations' provision of girls' schools and, in particular, the fact that Anglican girls were attending convent schools—was a reason for prompt action, it maintained. An argument new to this particular campaign surfaced in the editorial, related to the influence that women had upon the well-being of society: 'We have to rely vastly on the religious education of women to secure a state of society which shall contribute to the good order, intelligence, honesty, virtue and physical well-being of the people . . .'[34]

The writer assumed that women would not want to take up careers and that a woman's idea of happiness centred on the home, not through involvement in public life. The intention was therefore not to train girls' minds to fit them for a profession or a job, but to mould their characters and to make them fit wives and mothers. Beck wrote to the *Australian Record* in November 1893 criticising the lack of interest shown by the church in the matter of educating girls: 'What we want in the matter is united effort and especially that each member of the Committee entrusted with this important scheme of establishing a school worthy of the Church of England should take up the work—not in a desultory manner, but with all his might, determined to make it a success.'

He was critical of parents who 'with a nonchalance born of pure apathy' were content to send their daughters to the nearest school regardless of its religious teaching; of the Diocese for letting the parochial schools 'drift away'; and of the Committee which was not putting the necessary muscle into its task.[35]

Corlette, who wrote most of the reports to the Synod of the Committee for Girls' Higher Education, and Beck were two men with a vision for a girls' school. Initially these two, with Barry, were the only zealous ones with a sense of purpose to establish it, although there were others who showed some interest in the project.

James Christian Corlette (1837–1900) was a cultivated churchman and a member of the privileged classes, but never held a top administrative position in the Sydney Diocese. He was born and educated in Stroud, New South Wales, and his father was the chief accountant of the prestigious Australian Agricultural Company. William Macquarie Cowper, later Dean of Sydney, was his tutor. He went to Camberwell in London, then to Exeter College, Oxford, where he graduated in 1861. In 1863 he gained his MA and was priested. In 1879 he gained his BD and DD but published very little. Back in Australia, he spent from 1863 to 1867 in the quiet rural parish of Jamberoo, then moved to St John's at Ashfield, a prosperous, middle-class church, where he remained until his death. He was an authority on the subject of church music, being precentor at the Cathedral from 1861 to 1880, and again from 1883 to 1884. His first wife, Sarah Isabella, died in 1863, and when he remarried in 1867 it was to Frances Manning, daughter of the Chancellor of the University and Judge of the Supreme Court. He was moderately High Church. In 1895 when S.C.E.G.G.S. was founded he was 57 years old and a man with considerable social and ecclesiastical prestige.[36] He was a member of the first committee which founded the school and a member of the school Council until his death in 1900.

Ernest Claude Beck (1858–1939) was the son of an agent on the Sandringham Estate in Norfolk. He was ordained in 1883 and came to Australia in 1885 at the invitation of Bishop Barry. He became Rector of St Clement, Mosman, in 1889, and while there served as military chaplain to the army batteries on the north side of the Harbour. In 1901 he went as chaplain to the Boer War and in 1902 he was appointed to the parish of St John, Darlinghurst. He became a Canon in 1911 and lived at St John's until he retired in 1923. According to P. Egan in his work on the history of St John's Darlinghurst, Beck was a 'traditional, prayerful high churchman'.[37] As such, his churchmanship differed from the majority of clergy of the Sydney Diocese, who were evangelicals, some of them—such as Archdeacon Langley and Reverend Arthur Pain—later becoming members of the school Council.

While he had not been a member of the Committee for the Girls' High School, Beck acted as secretary in the planning meetings held in 1895 before the school opened and was later appointed to the school Council where he was the Honorary Secretary. In 1895 he was only 37 years old, and so younger than his fellow clergy on the Council. He held the position for 33 years and rarely missed a meeting (except for his time at the Boer War in 1901).[38] He was chaplain of the school for 27 years.[39]

In his presidential address for 1893, the Bishop noted that the times were discouraging and a delay in proceeding with the matter of the girls' high school was inevitable. Nevertheless from this time real but tentative progress began. A draft prospectus was drawn up in September 1894 and at the Bishop's suggestion, the new committee was 'to avail itself of the co-operation of lady

Rev. Canon Ernest Claude Beck, school chaplain for 30 years and member of the S.C.E.G.G.S. Council for 33 years. He was one of the men whose vision and zeal was instrumental in the foundation of S.C.E.G.G.S.

consultees and others who may be interested . . .'[40] The Bishop personally selected the members of the Select Committee.[41] Its members were all men: Archdeacon J. D. Langley, Rev. W. Hough, Rev. Dr J. C. Corlette, E. I. Robson (Headmaster of Shore), E. R. Deas Thomson, and W. R. Beaver.[42]

At a meeting in November it was resolved to 'seek the advice and co-operation of a number of ladies who are known to be much interested in the subject of the higher Education of Girls.'[43] The coopting of women to advise the Committee was very significant. One advantage that women had was more time to devote to the practical issues connected with the work of the Committee. None of them was in paid employment, and some had servants to assist them in the house, so their time and energies could be fully devoted to the task. Undoubtedly some women had the cause of the education of their own sex close to their hearts, whereas for men the matter was a less urgent one. The impetus provided by the first women on what was the latest of a string of similar committees was what finally translated the dreams into reality.

Among the women mentioned who attended committee meetings were Miss Edith Badham, Mrs Catherine Selby and Miss Snowdon Smith. Mrs Selby, Beck's aunt and housekeeper, and Miss Snowdon Smith, sister of the Bishop, became faithful and longstanding members of the school Council. It was Edith Badham who, more than any other person, provided the energy and initiative for the new school. She was on every subcommittee, and her interest and involvement in the school covered every aspect of its formation, from the selection and furnishing of premises, to the fixing of fees and to drawing up a prospectus and constitution.[44]

Most of the information about the nine months' preparation time before the school was officially opened is contained in a small black exercise book. It is in Beck's graceful and readable handwriting, and inside the front cover are calendars for the years 1892 and 1893. Hence, the first school records were kept in a spare book he had handy, not something purchased specially with the consciousness that important events would be recorded.

The book begins with a resumé of the reports to the Synod concerning a girls' school from 1891. The report for September 1894 referred to the draft prospectus drawn up during the year and intended 'for private circulation only'. Its title was *Prospectus of the Church of England High Schools Company Limited.* The Company was to issue 15 000 shares at £1 each, and was 'being formed for the purpose of establishing and conducting High Schools for Girls, and if hereafter thought desirable, for Boys also.' The aim of such schools was 'a superior secular education' in addition to which there would be 'as an essential part of the School's curriculum, religious instruction in accordance with Prayer Book and Articles of the Church of England in Australia and Tasmania.' It was to be a school for children of the upper and middle classes and members of the Church of England were encouraged to take up shares because not only would they benefit from the cash dividends, they would also be supporting a school which would 'help to build up children . . . in the faith of their parents and forefathers.' The plan was to have a working capital of £1500 before the school commenced, and a balance sheet showed how the school could make an annual surplus of £150.

There followed a list of the names of the members of the Provisional Council and the Ladies' Committee. The Provisional Council comprised: the Most Rev. the Primate, President. Archdeacon J. D. Langley, Rev. Dr J. C. Corlette, Rev. A. W. Pain, Rev. W. Hough, Rev. E. C. Beck (Honorary Secretary), Mr E. R. Deas Thomson, Mr E. J. Robson, BA, Mr C. R. Walsh and Mr W. R. Beaver (Honorary Treasurer). On the Ladies' Committee were Miss Snowdon Smith, Mrs Cowlishaw, Mrs Delohery, Mrs Harrison, Mrs Barre Johnston, Mrs Langley, Mrs Read, Mrs Redman, Mrs Selby, Mrs Sharp, Mrs Yarnold, Miss French, Miss Hine, Miss Murray and Miss Robson. At the foot of the list was Miss Badham—Lady Principal.

Although the prospectus stated that Miss Badham was the Lady Principal, the black minute book recorded her formal appointment on 26 April 1895. The prospectus bears no date, but is referred to in the May 1894 Report to the Synod. Unless there was more than one prospectus, the formal appointment ratified an arrangement made a year previously and was for an initial period of six months.[45]

The Provisional Council first met on 22 November 1894. Old ground was traversed: another approach was to be made to St Catherine's to see if St Catherine's could be the centre of a girls' high school system. As Deas Thomson was a member of the Provisional Council and also Honorary Secretary for St Catherine's, it may have been his suggestion. Corlette, although absent, knew first-hand that nothing had come of a similar idea in 1892.

Predictably, at a meeting of the Council of St Catherine's with the Provisional Council, the result was 'that the Council of the Clergy Daughters' School could not at present entertain the idea of amalgamation with the High School

[Committee] but [would] be glad to meet them again, if the [Committee] were prepared with some definite scheme to submit to the Council.'[46]

It was resolved to call a meeting of invited, interested ladies. The meeting took place on 2 April 1895. Twenty-three interested women attended and a large number of women sent letters sympathetic to the scheme. Fifteen women were appointed to a committee, which included Edith Badham, and some later became members of the Council. With three exceptions, they are the same names as those appearing on the draft prospectus. There were three meetings in April, and a great deal was accomplished in this one month. The women were deputed to raise subscriptions, £500 being the target; the rental was promised for the first three years by a secret donor. The Lady Principal was formally appointed, a constitution was drawn up and the first Council formed.[47]

The ordinance entitled *Sydney Church of England Girls' High School Ordinance of 1895* was passed by the Synod on 2 October 1895—three months after the school had opened. Its purpose was 'to regulate the constitution of the Council of the Sydney Church of England Grammar School for Girls and to provide for the course of instruction to be imparted therein and for other matters in connection with the order and discipline thereof.'

It provided for a school Council consisting of the Bishop of Sydney as President *ex officio*, and of twelve members to be elected by the Synod of the Diocese of Sydney. Of the elected members three were to be clergymen, three laymen and six women. One clergyman, one layman and two women were to retire annually in rotation, but would be eligible for re-election.
Other provisions were:

1 Four members excluding the President or presiding member would form a quorum.
2 If any member other than the President were absent from three consecutive meetings without leave, the seat of the member would be declared vacant and could be filled by the Council.
3 Subject to the ultimate control of the Synod, the Council could determine the course of instruction and all matters in connection with the order and discipline thereof.
4 The Council was responsible for the management of the property and finance of the school.
5 The Council was to report at least annually to the Synod and submit a balance sheet with the report.

The provision for an equal number of men and women on the S.C.E.G.G.S. Council was remarkable for its time and may well have been unique. It seems to have been a recognition of the work women had done to bring the plans to found S.C.E.G.G.S. to fruition. Perhaps Edith Badham urged such a novel idea. It would fit with her strong commitment to women's education.

In a letter to Canon Beck,[48] the then Bishop, William Saumarez Smith, commended the Council for their choice of Edith Badham as Principal, praising her 'recognised ability, experience and educational enthusiasm'. He recommended that the school be commenced in July, before Synod met, and underlined his anxiety for the early establishment of the school: 'I consider that, under the special circumstances, it [would] be well to begin as soon as the Constitution of the School can be properly drawn out and agreed upon by the Committee, and sanctioned by myself, as Bishop, and President of Synod.' He ended: 'I rejoice in the hope by passing from the "theoretical" to the "experimental" of the formation of the High School for Girls we may be solving a problem which has long waited for practical solution. May God grant His favour and Blessing to the attempt.' There was no guarantee that the next Synod would approve the establishment of a school and there would possibly be more delays and obstructions. Far better to confront the Synod with a *fait accompli* which, in form and substance, was perfectly legal.

There was only one meeting of the Council in May. Miss Janice Bertha Uther was the first staff appointment.[49] She had graduated BA from the University the previous year.[50] Fees were fixed, arrangements regarding boarders, uniforms and a four-term year were made. A letter from the Bishop was tabled which approved the constitution. Another letter contained the resignation of Deas Thomson. No reasons were given.

In June it was obvious that more money had to be raised before the school could open. The ladies set to work to canvass more subscriptions and by 14 June there was £194 6s 0d in hand. More was promised and an anonymous 'Christian lady' promised £250 provided that an equal sum was raised by the Council.

A terrace house at 65 Victoria Street, Darlinghurst was chosen to be rented for three years as the school building. Edith Badham formed a subcommittee with other selected members of the Council to arrange for taking the house and furnishing it.[51]

Late in June a personal tragedy in the Badham family occurred. Robert Charles Badham, Edith's half-brother, died in Paris aged twenty-eight. His father, the Professor, had said of him: 'he is the only one who seems to have my own gift of learning rapidly.'[52] Edith wrote to the Council saying that she did not think she could now leave home to live at the school, but a week later another letter stated that she would abide by the original agreement and live at the school until Christmas. The minutes record that 'The Committee was very thankful to learn Miss Badham's decision,' presumably an understatement of their relief.[53]

The fortnight before the official opening in July was filled with further staff appointments: an art teacher, Miss Ethel Stephens; a dancing teacher and several music teachers, including one man, Mr Sydney. Despite the expressed wish of the Bishop for a quiet opening on 17 July, an advertisement was placed in the *Sydney Morning Herald*. At the top of the column of educational advertisements, and triple the size of the others, it read:

> *CHURCH OF ENGLAND HIGH SCHOOL FOR GIRLS, 65 Victoria Street, Darlinghurst.*
> *The Committee appointed by the Sydney Diocesan Synod to advance the formation of a Girls' High School wish to give notice that the SCHOOL will be OPENED by the Most Rev. the Primate THIS DAY 17th JULY at 2.30 p.m. Any interested in the establishment of the School are invited to be present.*
> *The object of the School is to supply a thorough Education based upon religious principles.*
> *Both Day Pupils and Boarders will be admitted.*
> *Prospectus &c, may be obtained upon application to the Lady Principal, Miss BADHAM; or to the Hon. Sec. Rev. E.C. BECK. St Clement's Parsonage, Mosman.*
> *ERNEST C. BECK,*
> *Hon. Sec.*

— 3 —

The beginnings and the Badhams

THE OPENING OF the school at 2.30 pm on 17 July 1895 was attended by an impressive number of church dignitaries: there were six bishops, one dean, two archdeacons, many clergy and lay men and women. The school population comprised only one pupil.

The *Australian Record* gave the following account of the occasion:

> *The Church of England High School for Girls was formally opened and dedicated by the Primate on Wednesday afternoon last, in the presence of a large number of friends and subscribers. The assemblage included the Bishops of Newcastle, Bathurst, Goulburn and Grafton and Armidale; the Dean of Sydney, Archdeacons Bode and Flower, Revs. Dr. Corlette, A. W. Pain, W. Hough, R. J. Read, and a large number of other clergy and laymen; also many ladies, who are well-wishers to the school. The premises are situated at 65 Victoria St Darlinghurst, and are particularly adapted to the purpose. The rooms consist of commodious schoolroom, drawing-room, dining-room, two balcony rooms, seven bedrooms, large balconies, and splendid kitchen arrangements. The 'furnishing committee' had worked hard to have everything ready for the time of opening, and the result of their labours was warmly commended.*
>
> *The Bishops were received at the entrance by the Lady Principal, Miss Badham, and the members of the committee; the company then adjourned to the spacious dining-room, where prayer was offered by the Rev A. W. Pain. The Hon. Secretary, the Rev E. C. Beck, who has worked with untiring energy in the movement, then explained the purpose of the school, and gave a detailed account of the way in which the committee, appointed by the Synod, assisted ably by a committee of ladies, had accomplished the work. A friend generously promised to pay the rent for three years; and a Christian woman who is warmly interested in religious education, but wished to remain unknown, gave, through the Dean, the amount necessary to make up £500 to start the school.*
>
> *The Primate then commended the school to all present as a Diocesan Institution, where the children of the Church of England would receive definite Christian training, combined with the highest secular education, under the able care of Miss*

65 Victoria Street, Potts Point, is now 55 Victoria Street. The school began here in July 1895 with one pupil and two teachers.

> *Badham and Miss J. Uther, BA. He then declared the school open, after a special dedicatory prayer.*
>
> *The company then dispersed to inspect the whole premises and to partake of afternoon tea, kindly provided by Miss Snowdon Smith (sister of the Primate).*[1]

The first pupil was Mary Watson whose father, a member of St Thomas' Church of England, North Sydney, was also a member of the Diocesan Synod.[2] It is likely that Mary's presence was a kind of symbolic goodwill gesture from a prominent layman. She had been attending Sydney Girls' High School up to this time, so she was receiving what would have been considered a good education there, albeit one with minimum religious instruction as part of the curriculum. Mary was later to recall that her first week at the school was long and lonely: she sat between Miss Uther and Miss Badham 'while they distilled knowledge into either ear all day.'[3]

The establishment of S.C.E.G.G.S. was not reported in the secular press. The whole subject of secondary education for girls was rarely publicly debated in letters to the editor, nor had it been the subject of an editorial in either the *Sydney Morning Herald* or the *Sydney Mail* in the decade and a half preceding the opening of S.C.E.G.G.S. Because there were numerous small educational establishments in Sydney—classes, dame schools and self-styled colleges for young ladies—one more school using a house for its premises and boasting a single pupil may not have been considered newsworthy, even though the

Mary Watson was the school's first pupil and attended from July 1895 to June 1896. She was the first Dux. Her married name was Mary Swift and she held a place of special honour. She did not send any of her three children to S.C.E.G.G.S. as they were all boys.

presence of the clergy in such impressive numbers might have indicated a new and promising educational venture.

The name Badham was a famous one in Sydney at the time. Edith Badham was well connected with the men and women of wealth and intellect in Sydney society as she was the daughter of the late Charles Badham, in his time Sydney's most eminent academic.

Charles Badham (1813–1884) was educated from the age of seven by Pestalozzi, a famous educationalist, then went as a King's Scholar to Eton. In 1839 he gained his Master of Arts from Oxford University. He was ordained Deacon of the Church of England in 1846, and Priest in 1848. He gained the degree of Doctor of Divinity in 1853, and an honorary Doctor of Letters from Leyden University in 1860. He was a considerable linguist, speaking German, French, Italian and Dutch, and had a magnificent command of English. Although he was highly regarded as a scholar, he did not secure a university teaching post in England and spent seven years in Europe, travelling, studying and meeting people.

On his return to England, he became Headmaster of three schools: the Grammar School at Southampton (1851), King Edward VI's Grammar School at Louth (1851) and Edgbaston Proprietory School (1854). He was an effective teacher, and a warm and devoted one, though capable of outbursts of bad temper. It was said of him that he 'had a natural taste for education' and 'a singular

Professor Charles Badham, Edith Badham's father.

power of imparting his knowledge and of attracting the minds of his pupils to the love and acquisition of it'.[4] During these years he published several books which were translations of Greek classics, and although slight in volume, they showed a very high standard of scholarship. A. E. Housman describes him as 'the one English scholar of the mid-century whose reputation crossed the Channel'.[5]

His religious views have been the subject of conjecture. A theological liberal, he could work easily with men of various ecclesiastical and theological opinions.[6] In Australia he never took out a licence to officiate as an Anglican clergyman. Here he found nobody else who shared his theological views: his was a form of liberal Anglican theology which simply did not exist in Sydney.

In 1867 he was appointed Professor of Classics and Principal of the University of Sydney, replacing Professor John Woolley, who had lost his life when the *London* sank. An orator, and prepared to speak strongly on issues which interested him, Badham became influential in the world beyond the University. He was involved in the establishment of the public high schools and, with Professor Morris Pell, Professor of Mathematics at the University of Sydney, comprised the Board of Examiners which conducted public examinations for the civil service and the matriculation. He engaged in evening lectures designed to offer further education for those employed during the day. Like his daughter after him, he clashed with the authorities in the Council of Education, strongly criticising inspectors and current teaching methods. In 1872, for example, in giving evidence to a civil service inquiry, Badham said he thought that the school system was 'much too mechanical . . . instruction in the public schools partakes largely of rote work and . . . there is very little exercise of the intellect.'[7]

Badham supported the admission of women to the University and in a commemoration speech delivered in 1872 he stated:

Edith Badham, S.C.E.G.G.S.' first Headmistress. Initially she agreed to be the school's 'Lady Principal' for six months but stayed on till her death, 25 years later.

> *As an academical body we shall be called upon one day or other to deal still more closely with the academical rights of the ladies . . .*
>
> *And now [the University of Sydney] avows its sympathy with the young women of this colony, who, hearing of the noble fields of labour which the female mind has opened for itself in Europe, are animated with the desire of following the example of their sisters . . . and we shall not only enable women to improve themselves but to be the cause of improvement in others.*[8]

The Professor stopped short of advocating the education of women for vocational or professional ends.[9]

At time of his death in 1884, Professor Badham was for many people the University personified. His scholarship and intellectual abilities were outstanding in a colonial city where the University was young and scholars were few. On the day of his funeral the Governor announced in a special issue of the *New South Wales Government Gazette* that government offices would be closed so that government officials could attend. Obituary notices in England and the Australian colonies paid him tribute.

Edith Annesley Badham was born at Louth, Lincolnshire, in December 1853, the eldest daughter of Charles and Julia Matilda (nee Smith). Her mother died in May 1856, having borne two more children, Charles and Herbert. Eighteen months later Charles Badham married Georgiana Margaret Wilkinson. She subsequently had seven children and outlived them all, dying in 1926.[10] The family lived first in Newtown, then in North Sydney (called Neutral Bay at that time). In 1879 the Professor moved into rooms at the University and the rest of the family moved to Faulconbridge. By 1883 Edith was keeping house for her half-brother Lewis at Tenterfield but, on the death of the Professor, the family sold their property at Faulconbridge and moved to 'The Nest' at Mosman. This house was to be an important part of the experience of the girls at S.C.E.G.G.S. in the Badham era. It was a stone convict-built house. Although the house is now demolished, the street in which it stood is still called Badham Avenue.

Before coming to Australia Edith went to school at Dinant, a fashionable resort in Brittany. She arrived in Sydney when she was fourteen years old and her father thereafter supervised her education. She became an able Greek scholar under the Professor's tutelage. In fact she corrected public examination papers for her father, though not eligible to attend the University. She was 28 years old when, in 1881, women were admitted to the University and by this time she may have felt she was too old to become a student there. After her father's death in 1884 she taught private students and continued with this work until she became Principal of S.C.E.G.G.S. at the age of 42.[11]

The fact that Miss Badham had never attended school in either England or Australia meant that she was without the ties of the old girls' network of the English schools, and she was alien to the traditions and lore (what little had developed) of such schools. She was not a product of the English educational system, its curriculum and its teaching methods. At the time this was unusual but not unique for headmistresses of Protestant schools.[12] One consequence was that she was never a traditionalist in her educational views but innovative, imaginative and something of an iconoclast; another was that she was at a disadvantage in not having English connections to draw upon for staff.

In appearance Edith Badham was small and unmistakably a gentlewoman. She spoke with a cultivated English accent. Her hair was a crinkled light brown, her skin fine, and her eyes very bright. She moved quickly and purposefully and around her tiny waist was always a belt from which hung an assortment of useful items: her mother's gold watch, glasses, money purse and sometimes a pencil.[13] She always wore a cross. Some of her first pupils still remember her clearly. The girls who became best acquainted with her were the boarders, and she was described by a former day-girl as 'fairly unapproachable'. She was greatly respected and sometimes feared. Her linguistic capabilities had their darker side in sarcastic speech, and she was known to have criticised a member of staff in front of the pupils on more than one occasion.[14] She was not a warm person, but on the other hand showed a deep commitment to her school and the girls in it. She strongly disapproved of a girl leaving S.C.E.G.G.S. to attend another school.

Her lessons were very exciting. Her concentration on the subject was almost electric. In classical Greek lessons her throwaway remarks of disgust directed against the editor of the text gave rise to classroom hilarity. (Her father often did the same.) She had little patience and her devastating wit must have made staff and pupils alike fearful of error. Her two dislikes were the Salvation Army and the Jesuits. Like her father, she was High Church. She knew her Bible very well and expected the girls to familiarise themselves with it.[15] Unlike her father, she was not a liberal. She seems to have had a much stronger faith than did her father in his latter years, but there is little direct reference to it in her writing or speeches. She probably considered her religious faith to be a personal and private matter. How she came to differ from her father in matters of faith is unknown. It is unlikely that her French school would have exercised such an influence. Friends, or the effect of a particular parish priest, or books she read, may account for her devoutness.

A paper she wrote for *Progress* in 1899 entitled 'The aims and objects of the CSU' (Christian Social Union) refers a number of times to Christ's teaching in the New Testament and her comments reveal mature understanding of the Christian faith. For example:

> *When ancient Christianity found itself face to face with slavery it did not proceed to invent an eleventh commandment to forbid its members under ecclesiastical pains and penalties to keep slaves; it set itself to educate the minds of the faithful until slavery became an impossibility. And so the Christian Social Union today sets up no theory of Government nor of the land question, nor over population, nor of arts and life . . . the CSU believes that there is but one solution of all our difficulties and that is the general acceptance of the Law of Christ, and its work is to train just its own members, and through them to train society at large, to apply that law to any departments of social life.*

Two other papers she published further indicate the quality of her erudition and her manner of thinking. In a speech entitled 'Women and Womanhood Suffrage', this educated, independent-minded woman opposed female suffrage.[16] 'I am here tonight to represent those women who do not want the suffrage and would not use it if they had,' she said. With sharp humour she said, 'It is scarcely fair to look at our own achievements through a microscope and those of men through diminishing glasses,' and by cogently reasoned analysis she argued convincingly for a point of view which nobody would take seriously in the 1990s.

Badham's attitude to the franchise was not an unusual one at the time. Many people had a limited view of the state: its function was to run public utilities like the railways. While a limited state did not mean a limited franchise, some women who supported the franchise for women, such as the Women's Temperance Union, were not interested in politics. They wanted women to exercise a *moral* influence on the community through the vote. Badham did not think the majority of women were fit by nature to vote or to govern, and their influence through family and home was far stronger than it would be through legislation. Both opponents and supporters of the vote for women were agreed on the importance of women's moral influence. Where it was most effective, and whether women possessed the necessary skills to enter the political arena, were the issues in the debate.

In a paper which she delivered to the Women's Literary Society, Badham chose to bend her learning to a mock-serious analysis of nursery rhymes. Her opening words were:

> *If the age in which we live is ever distinguished by posterity from other ages before or after it, it will probably be known as the Age of Seekers after Truth. It has laid down two axioms for general guidance, one is that everything has a meaning, the other that the more the meaning is obscure the more valuable and excellent it must be . . . But it has seemed to me that in the profusion of modern dark sayings we are generally somewhat neglecting the ancient oracles and particularly those mysterious runes which are vulgarly known as Nursery Rhymes.*

Although the humour is a little heavy at times, the paper is a glorious send-up of misapplied knowledge in the areas of etymology, theology, feminism and eschatology.[17]

There were many ways in which Edith Badham was like her father, and the daughter's debt to her father's influence was considerable. Their speeches and papers reveal both to have held strong opinions which were expressed forcibly and with a formidable use of English. Both were capable of great eloquence, although at times their love of words seems to modern ears to result in overstatement and pomposity. They shared a deep love for the classics, Greek in particular, and both spent their lives in the service of education where they displayed the abilities of true teachers. Both used their fine academic minds for the public good: they did not confine themselves to study and intramural pursuits but were public spirited and caught up in community activities in Sydney. Edith Badham's community activities included support for missionary work, for the Sydney City Mission, the Ashfield Babies' Home and Waverley Kindergarten College. Her membership of the CSU led to her active involvement in the founding of the District Nursing Association (DNA) in 1900. She was on the Executive from 1900–1905 and thereafter an annual subscriber until her death.

Edith Badham's views on education are to be found in a paper she wrote headed 'General Remarks', which contained some preliminary ideas for the Council prior to the opening of the school, and in her first Annual Report (September 1896). They provide a limited amount of information only, but it is impossible to ignore the profound influence her father's educational views had in the formation of her own, although it seems that she did not acknowledge them publicly.

Their views as to who should be educated and what they should learn were held in common. Both promoted the higher education of women. As for the kind of education which was desirable, the Professor believed that education should teach a person to think clearly and logically, that classical studies (in particular, Greek) were the means of achieving this, and that a gentleman was a person who had been educated in this way.[18] Edith Badham considered character training to be the most important part of education. 'All the learning of the Egyptians is as nothing compared with manners and character,' she said. 'We have set steadily before our eyes the maintenance of a good tone, and of that combination of simplicity, consideration for other people's feelings, and self-respect, which is the very highest form of good breeding.'[19]

Miss Badham referred in her first Annual Report to long-cherished educational theories of her own. She admitted that they were still being tested as they had only been implemented for a short time. She subscribed to the contemporary theory that by teaching Latin to small children, she would teach them to speak English well. She claimed that 'we teach no grammar here, save that of common sense and the Latin language.' Despite her intellectual and academic gifts, she was a very practical educationalist. She was concerned with the amount of education which would benefit young girls. She did not want them straining their eyes poring over books by gaslight, so she gave no homework. She did not want them to be given more information than they could absorb, so the only examination for which she decided to prepare her girls was the matriculation, because it required a proficiency in subjects which trained the mind and were the most difficult to cram. She claimed that scientific subjects were not included in the ordinary curriculum because they took up a great deal of time.[20]

Her father had had strong views on the sciences when it was first suggested that they be offered at the University. He thought of scientists as technicians or mechanics and did not consider that study of the sciences was real education.[21] In the 1890s scientific studies were regarded with suspicion by many parents, and although some girls' schools[22] taught science, chemistry and physics were rarely found, and biology presented difficulties, as the teaching of reproduction as a biological fact was strictly taboo. Shocked parents were known to have withdrawn their daughters from such classes.[23]

The divinity course consisted of the study of the Bible, the Book of Common Prayer and church history. The other subjects offered were: Latin (compulsory), classical Greek (when requested), English (language and literature), geography (physical and political), history (ancient and modern), mathematics (arithmetic, algebra, geometry) and modern languages (French language and literature with attention to French conversation) and 'drilling' (a form of physical exercise).[24] The aim was 'that a girl's facilities may be trained to the utmost, [that] she may be taught to derive the keenest enjoyment from intellectual and scientific pursuits'.[25]

A large range of extra subjects was to be offered, including modern languages (German and Italian), music (piano, violin, singing and theory of music), drawing, painting, dancing, botany, astronomy, geology, cookery, dressmaking and swimming. Whether these were taught would depend upon demand. The curriculum was tied to the University matriculation requirements which were coming under increasing criticism for their classical bias. Required were: English grammar and composition, Latin, algebra, geometry and two of the following (of which one must be a language): Greek, French, elementary chemistry and elementary physics.

Public examinations were unpopular with many parents. Dr J. Marden, Headmaster of PLC Croydon, said that the average number of pupils sitting for examinations was one in twenty.[26] Badham certainly promised that no girl should sit for the matriculation examination unless parents really desired it for their daughters.[27] Her stress on moral and religious education was in line with contemporary educational philosophy. Her inclusion of many of the 'accomplishment' subjects such as music and drawing was also usual in girls' education. By 1900 certain changes in secondary education were apparent: there was more emphasis on examinations (they provided a tangible measurement of achievement); more utilitarian subjects were being taught (commerce was introduced at the Convent of the Sisters of Mercy at Goulburn); schools were becoming more academically and less 'accomplishment' oriented.

In the boys' schools the curriculum based on Latin, Greek and mathematics had been modified by the introduction of the so-called liberal subjects. These included modern languages (French and German) and commercial subjects (bookkeeping, shorthand) as well as English, history, geography and science. It was a compromise curriculum, based on that of the English public schools but adapted to the colonial situation. The curriculum at Shore, for example, included all these subjects.[28] Girls' schools varied. At MLC Burwood the emphasis was on the 'accomplishments':

> *Whether primarily as an acceptance of the expectations of parents and other school authorities or as a reflection of his own attitudes, Prescott continued to stress the importance of the genteel accomplishments, and especially music, in the school's priorities. Subjects such as drawing, French conversation, needlework and letter writing occupied a significant place in the daily schedule.*[29]

By contrast Kambala, an independent girls' school at Rose Bay, offered a full range of academic subjects, plus some sciences and 'accomplishment' subjects.[30]

PLC Melbourne offered a similar course, with the addition of callisthenics. Sydney Girls' High School offered a compromise by including the practical domestic subjects of cookery and needlework with the usual liberal/academic/ accomplishment subjects.[31] S.C.E.G.G.S. offered a wide range of subjects in both the academic area and in the 'accomplishments'. Academic subjects, modern languages and religious instruction were available. By contrast with some of the other schools, there was no science in the curriculum, at least to begin with, although there was provision for it when the demand arose.

Although Edith Badham had not been formally trained to teach, she had some ideas well ahead of her time. Her desire to train girls in language conversation showed an emphasis which has only been formally present in high school language teaching since the 1970s. She carried this to the extent of organising the performance of Greek plays in the original as an annual event. Her love for learning meant that she gave practical consideration to the methods which would be most likely to promote this love in her girls. Her attitude was: 'If learning is not sufficient for its own reward it had better be given up altogether.'[32] The emphasis was always upon quality rather than quantity of knowledge.

What did she intend for her girls? For what end was she educating them? Like her father, she wanted girls to be given a first-class education and to have trained minds. Like him, she saw that the career of most girls would be marriage and motherhood. When asked at the end of her life whether any Old Girls had distinguished themselves, her reply was, 'Yes. Several of them have gained their university degrees, and many have married and have children.'[33] She provided opportunities for excellent education, but did not concede that this would lead to the question of what women would do with this asset. University courses and some of the professions were the next logical step, but she firmly held the view that a woman's highest duty and privilege was to be a wife and mother.[34] The emphasis at S.C.E.G.G.S. has always been on an academic education. The controversy over the right kind of education for women was over the best way to educate girls to become good wives and mothers. Some thought it was better to teach practical subjects such as cookery and dressmaking while others believed that because women were the nation's shapers of morality, it was necessary to train their minds. Edith Badham belonged to the latter school of thought.

— 4 —

Council decisions, 1895–1900

S.C.E.G.G.S. WAS THE first Sydney Anglican girls' school to be effectively governed by a council. Although St Catherine's Waverley had had a council since 1884, it was one in name only as it consisted of bishops from country areas who could not attend council meetings—in reality, Bishop Barry directed the school himself. The S.C.E.G.G.S. Council, on the other hand, was modelled on those of the English boys' public schools such as Uppingham and Rugby, and Cheltenham, a girls' public school. In Sydney, King's, Shore and St Andrew's Choir School had similar councils. S.C.E.G.G.S. differed from the small private schools (such as Abbotsleigh and Woodstock) which were owned and run by women, and also from the convent schools which were governed by the different Roman Catholic religious orders. S.C.E.G.G.S., like MLC Burwood and PLC Sydney, was governed by a council responsible to the church, a corporate institution rather than a private enterprise.

The plan promoted by the Prospectus of 1894, to form a limited liability company with shareholders, directors and annual dividends, had been abandoned. Instead, the school's finances depended on fees and gifts from benefactors. The Council, appointed by the Anglican Synod, was, as the 1895 Ordinance stated, to determine the course of instruction and manage the property and finances. There was the possibility that as finances and opportunities permitted, further schools might be established under the Council.

The composition of a school council and its relationship with the principal are of considerable importance to a school for its smooth running. Do council and principal trust each other? Who dominates the relationship: the council or the principal?

At a meeting of the provisional Council on 17 May 1895, a preliminary Ordinance to regulate the Constitution was passed and at the same meeting an agreement was made between the Council and the 'Lady' Principal.[1] The Ordinance dealt only with Council's composition and its duties with regard to the school finances, curriculum and related matters. The agreement spelt out further the rights and duties of both Council and Principal. The Council had the right to appoint the Principal. They were to fix the course of instruction after consultation with her, agree to the number of staff, fix salaries and fees, and be responsible for the property and the finances. In addition they were to appoint the examiners and regulate the conditions of entry to the school. The President was to have a casting vote when necessary.

The Principal was to have full direction of the teaching and discipline of the school. She was able to appoint and dismiss staff, subject to the approval of Council. There were special provisions for the dismissal of the Principal, should the issue arise, but no provision for the removal of an unsuitable member of Council.[2]

The areas of potential conflict were in the overlapping duties of Principal and Council in the matters of staffing and the content of instruction. Edith Badham made her views perfectly clear when she stated in her 'General Remarks' to the Council on her proposed curriculum:

> *The whole scheme is, of course, merely intended to be submitted to the Committee for discussion, but I should wish to enter a strong protest against any attempt to tie the hands of the Principal, whether myself or anyone else, more than is absolutely necessary. No woman who knows how to teach will consent to teach under minute direction.*[3]

The clergy on the first Council were Dr J. C. Corlette, Archdeacon Langley, the Rev. W. Hough and the Canon E. C. Beck.[4] These men were not homogeneous in churchmanship as Langley was an Evangelical and the others High Church in varying degrees. The man who remained on the Council the longest time was Beck. His churchmanship was agreeable to Edith Badham, and he later became school chaplain for nearly thirty years. The laymen were Mr E. I. Robson, Mr W. R. Beaver, Secretary of the Synod, and Mr C. R. Walsh, later the Diocesan Registrar. Both Beaver and Walsh were strong Evangelicals. All were men of good repute and status in the Diocese. The women were Miss Snowdon Smith, Miss French (step-daughter of the Dean), Mrs Selby, Mrs Hey Sharp (the wife of the Warden of St Paul's), Mrs Chadwick (described as 'an active church worker'), and Mrs Harrison (reputed to be keenly interested in S.C.E.G.G.S.).[5]

Beck, French and Selby were the most faithful attenders of Council meetings. The rest of the men on average attended fewer than half the meetings for the first year. Ernest Beck was the Secretary,[6] and W. R. Beaver was the Treasurer for the short time he was on the Council. He left in March 1897.[7] The Council met once a month at 4.00 pm at the school. Minutes of the meetings are brief. Initially small details of school life, some of which now seem trivial were discussed: the renting of a sewing machine, the purchase of a bathtub, and whether German should be an extra subject or part of the curriculum. Badham regarded the latter within her own province: it was an instance of teaching 'under minute direction'. After January 1896, her name is not on the list of those who attended meetings, although it is clear that she was sometimes present since she gave a report or made a strong statement on a particular issue. She may have attended part of the meetings, thus allowing the Council time to discuss in her absence private matters such as her salary or her housekeeping economies (always a problem).

When a serious matter had to be discussed by a small committee, three men were chosen: Robson, Beck and Docker (the new treasurer appointed in March

1897)[8] plus Edith Badham. When Archdeacon Langley was present he acted as Chairman, and because he was an archdeacon and Robson a headmaster, they were probably the most influential members of the Council. As time progressed, Mr Wilfred Docker showed himself to be invaluable to the Council because of his financial acumen and sound, reliable advice. The women on the Council were often among the most faithful attenders but they were rarely asked to become part of the significant subcommittees. It is likely that the combination of the weight of the clergy and other eminent men and their perception of the role of their own sex meant that the women did not dominate discussions.

The Depression of the 1890s meant that most schools had financial troubles: in the state schools teachers were retrenched and in most schools enrolments fell. A recurring theme of the Council meetings is the state of the school's finances. Dr Corlette had recommended in his Report to the Synod in 1894 that before the girls' high school was commenced, the Company should have £1500 in hand. In fact the school opened with about £680 in capital. Of this, £532 had been raised by subscription and £150 had been promised per year for the payment of rent. Amounts donated varied enormously: well over half the donations were amounts between one guinea and five guineas. Then there were seven donations of £10 and the remaining donations were for £25 or £30, with one very large donation (anonymous, but from a woman) of £300. The list of subscribers shows that of the 45 donors 24 were women.[9]

At the end of the first year the Report to the Synod showed receipts of £1251 and expenditure of £1145: a surplus of £106.[10] The following year there was a surplus of £6. The report stated: 'The financial affairs of the school have caused the Council no small amount of anxious thought.'[11] It was clear from the outset that the school could expect a struggle to balance its books. It was a losing battle to maintain a credit balance. The reasons given for the financial difficulties were the rapid expansion of the school population and the consequent costs of providing furniture, accommodation and equipment when the venture operated on a small capital base.[12] The Council accepted an offer from Edith Badham to donate the money she earned from her courses of public lectures on history and literature towards the salary of an assistant. Her first proposal had been to put this money towards a school library, but the library would have to wait for a while.

Fees had been set on a quarterly basis. They were as follows:

Day-girls, under 12	*£ 3*	*3*	*0*	*Day pupils (Luncheon)*	*£1*	*1*	*0*
Day-girls, over 12	*£ 4*	*4*	*0*	*Stationery (boarders)*	*£*	*5*	*0*
Boarders, under 12	*£16*	*16*	*0*	*Laundry (boarders) Summer*	*£2*	*2*	*0*
Boarders, over 12	*£18*	*18*	*0*	*Laundry (boarders) Winter*	*£1*	*1*	*0*
Church sitting (boarders)	*£*	*5*	*0*	*School Library*	*£*	*2*	*0*

For pupils who were sisters, a reduction of 10 per cent would be made for boarders and 5 per cent for day-girls. Boarders were to pay an entrance fee of £2 2s 0d in lieu of providing their own house linen. There were also additional subjects for which extra fees were charged, the cost for some extras amounting to as much as a day-pupil's full fee.[13] By comparison with other schools, the fees were neither exorbitant nor low. The records show that Sydney Girls' High School charged eight guineas per year in 1883;[14] Shore, fifteen guineas in 1889;[15] and S.C.E.G.G.S., sixteen guineas in 1895.[16]

The initial salaries of Miss Badham and her staff were not noted down in the minute book, but in January 1896 the Council decided to award Miss Uther a salary of £60 per annum, on the strong recommendation of Miss Badham. To Miss Badham herself, now permanent Principal, they awarded £100 per annum, plus a capitation fee (a sum paid for each pupil enrolled) of £1 per pupil. This would have made her salary £150.[17] It seems a generous salary when compared with her assistant's, but Miss Badham felt it was not enough, and at a special meeting the Council decided to award her £230 per year, by raising the capitation fees substantially.[18]

It was, by comparison with other principals' salaries, very low. For example, the salary of the Headmistress of Sydney Girls' High School was advertised as £400 per annum,[19] and that of E. I. Robson, the Headmaster of Shore, was about £800. This included £400 as salary and capitation fees of £5 per boarder, £2 for up to 200 day-boys, with £1 10s 0d for 200–400 boys: 'Bishopsgate', a large house in the grounds, formerly owned by the Dibbs family, was provided as his residence.[20]

The whole incident is instructive. On the one hand Miss Badham knew the school was short of cash, and to ask for a significant increase in salary was to add to the school's financial burdens. On the other hand, her living quarters and salary were below the standard of those of some other school principals. Many schools, however, would not have paid their principals the kind of salaries offered at Shore and Sydney Girls' High School. Many private venture schools and church schools were struggling to survive financially, and principals' salaries were tied to the schools' revenue.[21]

It is clear also that Miss Badham had a formidable manner of attack, and the members of Council were not prepared to risk putting the Lady Principal offside. It was the first clash of Council and Principal, and the Principal had won. Very likely Edith Badham saw her salary as a symbol of her worth: a high salary indicated her value and the Council's esteem. It is certain that she was very willing to help the school with the advance of a personal loan when funds were low. On this occasion she agreed to forego £50 of her salary on the understanding that it would be made good later on.[22] It is even possible that she was the anonymous woman donor who had given £300 in June 1895. Undoubtedly she liked to call the tune. She was prepared to be generous, but it was to be on her terms and she would not be taken for granted. The Council must have felt like one of her school classes at times like this.

The first school premises at 65 Victoria Street, Darlinghurst (since redesignated as 55 Victoria Street, Potts Point) had become inadequate by May 1896. The finances were a matter of concern as annual income stood at £360 and expenditure at £543 in May 1896.[23] It was estimated that fifteen more pupils were needed and the Principal was asked to look for alternative premises. The school had only one formal classroom, although perhaps one of the balconies or the seven bedrooms had also been converted into classroom space. As there were already seven boarders, there was very little room, and certainly none for expansion. There is no mention in the records of outdoor space for recreation. Because of the parlous finances and the lack of adequate facilities, it was clear that an alternative venue would be necessary.

In June 1896 'Chatsworth', a house in Macleay Street, Potts Point, was chosen. It would cost £250 per year to rent, in addition to rates of £30 per annum. It was leased for two years and 65 Victoria Street was successfully sublet. The school's first prize-giving was held at Chatsworth and it must have been a very happy occasion. Chatsworth represented tangible growth and a measure of success in the S.C.E.G.G.S. venture. In her first Annual Report, Miss Badham

Chatsworth, the second location of S.C.E.G.G.S., was on the corner of Wylde and Macleay Streets, Potts Point. The school was here from July 1896 to December 1900, and then moved to Barham.

said of it: 'The position of the building, commanding a magnificent view of the harbour, the tennis court, boathouse and swimming baths are many inducements to parents to render patronage to an institution which has all the requirements of an ideal home for girls.'[24]

Chatsworth is no longer standing, but a photograph shows it to be an imposing building of two storeys, with a grand entrance portico and upper verandahs edged with iron lace. The grounds extended to the water and there were large shady trees and a big garden. It must have been infinitely more desirable to schoolgirls than the cramped conditions of the Victoria Street terrace. Minnard Crommelin was a boarder at Chatsworth. She recalled:

> *Chatsworth had been very much over-decorated. The woodwork was cedar and beautiful when untouched by paint. The Ball room floor was parquet of native woods, and with great mirrors on both sides of the long room—with candelabra lighting the curved tops—a lovely effect of long vistas was obtained. It was beautiful—even if the red plush upholstery of the musicians' gallery was a little tawdry . . . and the mythological figures of gods and goddesses upon the painted ceiling seemed in danger of coming to earth.*[25]

The Council's homework assignment over the Christmas holidays of 1897 was to consider how the work of the school could be extended. No details of discussion leading up to this are recorded, but in the light of subsequent events it seems that there were two concerns. The more pressing one was, yet again, a shortage of space. Beck's report to the Synod of 1897 stated that there were now 74 pupils.[26] Numbers were such that Chatsworth was no longer big enough for the school population. Related to that was the idea of establishing an extension school, one thought being to retain the boarders at Chatsworth while the day-girls attended school at some other site.

The problem of adequate accommodation had three possible solutions, the Council decided the following January:

1 To purchase Chatsworth. It was worth between £7000 and £13 500. The Archbishop advised strongly against buying Chatsworth as it was too risky financially. He was, however, willing to contemplate the purchase of Chatsworth if the interest on the purchase money did not exceed the present rent paid. The disadvantage of Chatsworth was that it would need more buildings, and its advantage was its marvellous harbourside location.
2 To retain Chatsworth on a lease and open a day school elsewhere.
3 To purchase a new site.

For almost two years the question of the school's future location was debated. Chatsworth's lease was not renewable and there were lengthy negotiations with its owner, Mrs Wangenheim. By November 1899 Miss Badham was very concerned as to how to handle further applications for admission to the school, there being no further space for new pupils at Chatsworth. Numbers had risen to 92 by 1898.[27] There had also been an offer, from a Mrs Wallis, for S.C.E.G.G.S. to buy her school at Darling Point for £2000, as she was shortly leaving for England.[28] The offer from Mrs Wallis was the first of many similar ones and although not taken up, the idea of establishing new branch schools, or taking over an existing school, was of great importance in the history of S.C.E.G.G.S. over the next sixty years.

The Council's deliberations about a new school site ended with a special Council meeting held on 5 January 1900. The purpose of the meeting was to discuss the advisability of purchasing a property named Barham in Forbes Street, Darlinghurst. By the time the meeting took place, Barham had been sold for £3750 to a Mr Davis. Despite this, it was resolved to enquire if Davis would accept an offer.

Edith Badham's opinions on Barham were initially negative: she considered the locality fatal to the prospects of the school.[29] However, when Docker had completed negotiations for the purchase, she changed her mind. The minutes state:

> *She had carefully inspected Barham with a view to purchase and adapting it to our requirements and she was much struck with the capabilities of the place. She had gone there much prejudiced but on inspection her objections were entirely removed and she thought the site was admirable for a Day School and when the additions were made she did not think that the parents of boarders could raise any objections.*[30]

The Barham purchase showed Docker's value as a leading member of the Council in his persistence in acquiring the property despite the headstrong Principal's opposition, and despite the fact that the purchase price of £4500 was an extra £750 over what they had initially hoped to pay. It was still a much smaller financial commitment than the purchase of Chatsworth would have been.

A loan was arranged with the Commercial Banking Company of Sydney and

S.C.E.G.G.S. girls and staff at Chatsworth, 1898. Reading from left to right: back row: *Joan Twynam, Muriel Brown, Lucy Palmer, Rebe Wight;* 4th row: *Doris Barnett, Lily Williamson, Ruth Bannister, Gladys Lee, Leila Richardson, Jeanie Ranken, Ruth Oliver, Ethel Rankin, Mary Truman, Brenda Lee, Grace Capper, 'Docey' Alice Allen, Edith Hinton, Doris Salenger, Meg McPhillamy, Mary Ballantyne (sitting), Irene Holmes;* 3rd row: *Ruth Amos, Florence Wallach, Stella Herring, Vivian Jackson, Nellie Amos, Mary Stephens, Gwen Paterson, Lily Christian, unknown, Myra Brown, Dorothy French, Violet Black, Margery Smithers, Ettie Wallach, Millicent Forbes;* 2nd row: *Miss Rae Sweetland, Vera Le Patourel, Fraulein Fast, Miss Grace Horrocks, Miss Walker, Miss J. Uther, Miss Badham, Miss Constance Wilson, Miss Gilfillan, Miss Ilma Wilson, Miss E. Palmer;* front row: *Stella Wallach, Eva MacNeil, Constance Stephens, Leila McPhillamy, Margaret McIntyre, Dorothy Airey, Muffie Barton, Doris Arnheim, Kathleen Stephens, Dorothy Farran, Christina MacNeil, Alison McPhillamy, Freda Arnheim, Millie Nathan.*

a further £4000 borrowed from the National Mutual Life Association for building work. H. O. Jackson, Badham's brother-in-law, drew up plans for the proposed buildings and on 4 October 1900 the foundation stone was laid. The church dignitaries arrived in much the same numbers as at the 1895 opening of the school, but this time there were nearly 100 pupils.

Barham, its name differing by only one consonant from Badham, is a character in its own right in the history of S.C.E.G.G.S. The house has always been the central building on the site, the nerve centre of administration and the location of the Head's office. Though crowded by the many other buildings which have since sprung up on the school site, and disfigured by additions tacked on, the original house remains a living connection with the distant days of S.C.E.G.G.S.

Barham was built in 1833 for Edward Deas Thomson and was occupied for most of the time from 1840 until 1884 by the Deas Thomson family.[31] Edward

Barham in 1901, the location of S.C.E.G.G.S. since that time.

Deas Thomson was an eminent man in colonial society. He was one of the Select Committee which drafted the Constitution for New South Wales and a member of the Legislative Council from 1837 to 1856. At various times he had been Colonial Secretary, Registrar of Records and a member of the Executive Council. He occupied a position second only to the Governor, holding office in the time of Governors Bourke, Gipps, Fitzroy and Denison. He was connected by marriage to both the Bourke and the Macleay families. In 1833 he married Anna-Maria, second daughter of Sir Richard Bourke and one of their daughters married Sir William Macleay of Elizabeth Bay House. Deas Thomson was knighted in 1874. He was a member of Wentworth's Select Committee to enquire into the establishment of a university in Sydney, was a member of the first Senate of the University and became Chancellor in 1865, a position he resigned through ill health in 1878, only a year before his death. He was thus connected with Edith Badham's father, Charles Badham.

As Principal, Charles Badham had had long and close contact with Deas Thomson—in particular, through their joint work to foster a bursary scheme. Deas Thomson gave £1000 to found a scholarship and during his time as Chancellor, more than £25 000 was received for bursaries and exhibitions.[32] A portrait and bust of Deas Thomson are housed in the Great Hall of the University to commemorate his work. On his death in 1879 Parliament adjourned and he was mourned by the whole state.

A great judge and lover of horses, Deas Thomson was for many years President of the Australian Jockey Club, of which he was a founding member. During his residency at Barham, the house was surrounded by a garden of daphne, camellia, heliotrope, mignonette and violets. Vegetables from the kitchen garden won prizes at the Sydney Agricultural Show.[33]

Subsequent occupants of Barham were Colonel K. Snodgrass, who lived there between 1834 and 1836 and was Acting Governor of New South Wales from December 1837 to February 1838. In 1885 Deas Thomson's three daughters sold Barham to E. D. S. Ogilvie for £9000. Mr Ogilvie was a member of the Legislative Council from 1863 to 1889 and lived at Barham for a short time with his wife and daughters. From 1886 to 1890 Ogilvie leased Barham to Mrs Louisa Ellis for a school called Newnham High School for Girls. No information has so far come to light about this school. Professor T. T. Gurney leased Barham from 1893 to 1896 then, after Ogilvie's death, it was sold for £3500 to James Frederick Harvey MLA, JP.[34]

Hence up to 1900 Barham had been home to the wealthy and powerful, and had been connected with the Badham family and with education before it became the home of S.C.E.G.G.S. In addition E. R. Deas Thomson, son of the original owner, had been a member of the provisional Council set up in 1894 to found S.C.E.G.G.S. Prices paid for the purchase of Barham prior to 1900 varied considerably,[35] and the low price in the mid 1890s was possibly due to the impact of the Depression.[36]

Barham was built to command a sweeping view over the once beautiful Woolloomooloo Valley, its front facade facing what is now Bourke Street. It was designed by John Verge as a freestanding Georgian villa and built of rendered handmade bricks. The verandahs are flagstones with blocks of freestone and the solid foundations and large cellars are also stone. An 1845 painting of Barham by G. E. Peacock and an illuminated testimonial presented to J. F. Harvey in 1898 containing a fine miniature of Barham provide a vivid impression of Barham as the prestigious villa of a wealthy man. A circular drive swept up to the stone front steps, and well-kept lawns, shrubs and leafy trees surrounded the house. The spacious grounds contained stables (the site of the present gymnasium) and the house stood alone, stately and with no other building to be seen. The 1845 painting shows Barham surrounded by a freestanding trellis or balustrade, but by 1898 the trellis had been replaced, according to the miniature, with a verandah supported by posts and enclosed to the left of the steps. The steps were then covered by a latticework porch.[37]

John Verge was a talented and fashionable architect. His career spanned the brief period from 1830 to 1837 and in that time he designed 75 buildings, of which fourteen still stand. His more famous houses include Tusculum, Potts Point; Camden Park House, Menangle; and Elizabeth Bay House. Of Verge's work, Clive Lucas said:

> *Verge's work is comparable to English work of the period and shows none of the provincial traits, either in conception or finish, found in the work of his contemporaries. His buildings are complete; they are three dimensional forms containing interior suites of rooms that are a joy to pass through. The finish of his best work is without equal. Whether it be in stone, waxed cedar, stucco, plaster or iron, it is superbly detailed and executed. That he is so good is a mystery, for his background does not suggest any training or indeed strong influences which would lead him to create such buildings in an antipodean wilderness.*[38]

However Lucas dismisses Barham as one of Verge's lesser works:

> *It is a straightforward design with two adjacent fronts, facing north and west. There are French doors with stone architraves and entablatures to the ground floor and, above, wide windows (formerly shuttered) beneath broad eaves. The verandahs are perhaps early additions, for they cut across the friezes of the door architraves.*

The garden at Barham. Although pavement and buildings now cover most of the garden and the lily pond has vanished, the Moreton Bay figtree still dominates the grounds.

> *They are, however, well detailed with incised, tapering posts and vandyked valence, and are reminiscent of the verandahs added by Verge to nearby Goderich Lodge.*
>
> *The entrance doorway has an attractive fanlight, but the sidelights are cramped owing to the narrowness of the entrance corridor. Indeed the planning, proportioning and interior detailing of Barham are rather pedestrian. Although Verge supervised the construction, there is little of his characteristic elegance.*
>
> *Barham is, nevertheless, an important and pleasant house, although without the evidence of the ledger only the stone architraves of the French doors indicate Verge's hand. It is unfortunate that the house has been disfigured by additions and by the insensitive enclosure of the verandahs.*[39]

Although Verge was an excellent architect, he lost interest in his business. He obtained a land grant of 2500 acres in the Macleay area, downstream from the present town of Kempsey, and devoted himself to his property Austral Eden, on which he built a succession of houses, none of which survives. He died in 1861 aged seventy-nine.

Darlinghurst was a distinctive and very mixed locality during the nineteenth century. Some notable Sydney identities lived there, among them J. H. Challis, Sir William Manning, Sir Charles Nicholson (associated with the University), Walter and Eliza Hall (public benefactors) and Bishop Saumarez Smith. The southern end of the suburb contained the gaol (occupied from 1841 to 1914), the Female School of Industry nearby, and the Victoria Barracks, which encouraged the presence of brothels and grog shops.[40] The growing pressures of population had turned Woolloomooloo into a slum area by 1900, so that

Darlinghurst was divided between the mansions of the upper class at its northern end, and the poorer residents at the southern end. Because of its proximity to the city and the development of an efficient tram system to the eastern suburbs, Darlinghurst was a highly urbanised area by the beginning of this century. Barham was located among the mansions on Darlinghurst Hill, at the northern end. The Barham site has always been a mixed blessing. Its advantages are its centrality and proximity to transport, so that it has always attracted pupils from a wide area of Sydney. Its disadvantages are its small site and its location in Darlinghurst: an area which has become steadily less salubrious over the years.

In order to reduce the debt incurred by the purchase of Barham, 56 feet (about 17 metres) of land along the Bourke Street boundary of Barham was sold in 1901 for 13s 0d per front footage (see map B.)[41] The sale was regrettable as it significantly reduced the area of the school site. Opportunities to increase the site came in the 1930s, and again in the 1970s, but despite attempts on these occasions to purchase additional land for the school, S.C.E.G.G.S. in 1990 stood on substantially the same land it owned after the 1901 sale. Consequently, siting buildings, housing staff and pupils, and providing adequate sporting and recreational facilities have been a continuing problem for Principals and school Council.

Soon after S.C.E.G.G.S. moved to Barham, a large entrance porch on the south side was built.[42] The building stood quite separate from Barham. It had a very attractive staircase with a fine wooden balustrade and the high ceiling, arch and well-made architraves were a suitable addition to the school for well-bred young ladies.

— 5 —

School life, 1895–1900

S.C.E.G.G.S. was a school for young ladies. Those who attended it were from the privileged classes in Sydney, but wealth alone was not a guarantee of acceptability. The most acceptable young ladies were those whose fathers were squatters, professional men, or part of the church hierarchy. There was a strong view that gentlemen did not engage in trade, but a distinction was drawn between those engaged in wholesale trade and those who sold over the counter. The former were more acceptable.[1] Sarte Russell, an Old Girl, stated that there were very few 'ordinary' girls at S.C.E.G.G.S. in its first years. The Archbishop of Sydney and the Governor-General sent their daughters to S.C.E.G.G.S., as did Sir Edmund Barton, Australia's first Prime Minister. Old Girls recall that Lady Honor Ward, daughter of the Earl of Dudley, had special lessons with Lila Wright, the daughter of the Archbishop.[2] These girls seemed to have had a separate timetable and did not eat with the other girls as a rule. A questionnaire distributed to Old Girls reveals that fathers' occupations were varied. There were four solicitors, and one of each of the following: timber and shipping agent, bank teller, surveyor, dispensing chemist, importer, civil engineer, company secretary, journalist, company director, stock and station agent, gentleman of leisure, wool broker, merchant, company representative and doctor (see Appendix 2, Table E). Titles such as 'company representative' and 'merchant' could well have been euphemistic.

Miss Badham herself was of Sydney's upper class. Her friends included the Macleay family, and her stepmother, Georgiana, took an active part in the social life of Sydney, entertaining Prince George (later George V) and his brother Albert to afternoon tea when they visited the Australian colonies. In today's terms, Miss Badham seems to have been guilty of favouritism on the basis of a parent's social status.

From the beginning the school enjoyed a good reputation as a superior educational establishment. The Badham name was a guarantee of academic excellence and the Old Girls maintain it was considered the best school in Sydney. Even allowing for hyperbole, the fact is that people withdrew their daughters from other schools to send them to S.C.E.G.G.S. and the socially prominent were prepared to support it. Class feeling in the 1890s was such that upper- and some middle-class parents preferred not to send their daughters to the recently established Sydney Girls' High School as girls from the lower classes attended. Girls' secondary education tended to be valued for its social rather than its educational benefits.[3]

The aim of the founders of the school was to establish a school of high quality for girls. This concept included not only quality academic education but also the training of young ladies. This in turn depended upon the families from which the girls came. Since only girls from families of the upper classes were acceptable at S.C.E.G.G.S., cultural, moral and religious values, social attitudes and a consciousness of social superiority were mutually reinforced.

Upper- and middle-class mothers did not go to work. When a woman married she ran the household (with servants to do the housework), and her time was occupied with her family, social engagements and voluntary work. No mothers of this generation had received any tertiary education, and there was no allowance in the social scheme of things for a mother to pursue any role except that of homemaker. Married women of the upper classes did not go out to work, and this remained the case until World War I, when the shortage of men drew some women into the workforce. Questionnaires filled in by Old Girls who were at S.C.E.G.G.S. before 1914 reveal that for the most part they also received no tertiary education, and after leaving school occupied themselves with sport, handiwork, housekeeping and voluntary work.[4]

A characteristic of S.C.E.G.G.S. from the beginning to the present time has been its wide catchment area. Between 1895 and 1900, day-girls came from Bondi, Botany, Darlinghurst, Drummoyne, Gordon, Hunters Hill, Mascot, Mosman, North Sydney, Rose Bay, Stanmore and Woollhara. The boarders came from Coffs Harbour, Bowral, Brisbane, Carcoar, Grafton, Orange, Wagga Wagga and Wallerawang. Travel to school for boarders was by train, except that one girl caught a coastal steamer. Many of the day-girls caught the tram to school, and the rest caught a ferry or a train (see Appendix 2, Table D).

The school opened with Mary Watson, aged fifteen, as its solitary pupil. Mary later recalled being on her own with two teachers for the first week; thereafter numbers grew steadily. By October 1895 there were twelve pupils: ten day-girls and two boarders. By the following July, there were 49 pupils, including seven boarders. Although the Prospectus does not indicate at what age girls were eligible to attend the school, they would have been at least twelve years old as S.C.E.G.G.S. was founded as a high school. Numbers continued to rise until, in August 1898, S.C.E.G.G.S. had 100 pupils. It is not clear how long the Council paid Badham a capitation fee, but it was probably discontinued after numbers rose to a satisfactory level. The notion of capitation fees was by this time an old-fashioned one, having its origin in the fact that a resident mistress paid for the board of her charges out of her own pocket and was reimbursed by the capitation fee.

Very little information survives on school life before 1900. However, the letters that one pupil wrote have survived. Although not concerned with lessons or the quality of teaching generally, they otherwise provide a great deal of information about the life of a S.C.E.G.G.S. boarder at that time. Kate Waddy wrote to her friend Elsie from July 1899 to August 1900. She turned seventeen while at the school, and her first letter from S.C.E.G.G.S. begins:

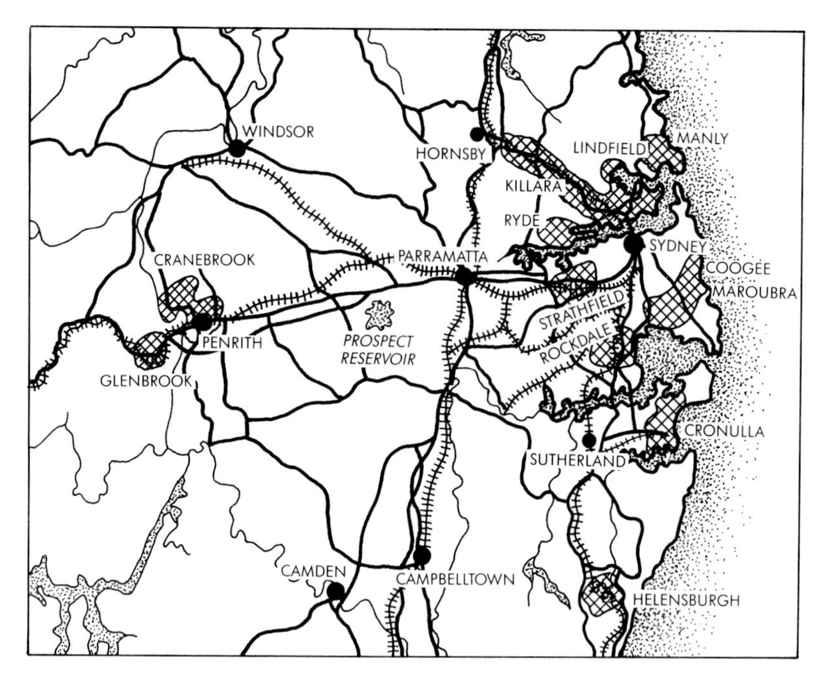

Map of Sydney, showing the wide catchment area for the school population.

'I am settled at "prison" at last, I do not like it very much. The first week was awful. I got terribly homesick and all the rest of it, but I am a bit better now.'[5]

She could not have found life dull as in her first week she went to the Shore sports, a picnic at Balmoral, a football match with a young man named Gar (either her brother or her cousin, later the well-known cricketer Edgar Waddy), her first rowing outing and a tea and concert in aid of St James' Church. Her comment was: 'We have been out nearly every evening since I came here,' and it would appear that there was a great deal more social activity and freedom to come and go from school than is generally allowed boarders today. There was no homework, so there was more time for relaxation.

Further outings are mentioned in Kate's letters. There was a concert at the Town Hall when a Maori prince sang and played. She heard the organ, which she enjoyed greatly. There was a walk to the Botanic Gardens, and a picnic afternoon tea at Bondi. She and some other boarders took a billy and boiled it on the beach, went for a paddle, were drenched by a wave and returned to the school on top of a bus at 9.00 pm. There were shopping expeditions up William Street. On another occasion the girls went to Mrs Badham's home in Mosman, 'The Nest', for magic lantern slides and singing. They often played tennis with young men who invited them to dances. There are many references to males, with a regretful tone that King's boys were seen on the Harbour and at sporting events, but Kate did not know their names. The letters were not censored, which surprised Kate. She commented: 'No one reads the letters here. They don't even ask who they are from!'

On rowing she wrote: 'We went out rowing for the first time on Thursday afternoon. It was lovely. I took a pair of oars and then steered for a while. It was grand. We went round the men-of-war. You should have seen the middies on the "Royal Arthur". They ran and got their telescopes and looked at us, then took off their caps and grinned.'[6]

Rowing was not always possible: 'We have only been out rowing about four times this quarter. The weather has been bad and the harbour rough.' The girls also went swimming twice a week. At the age of seventeen, Kate was still learning how to swim. She recorded: 'I can't manage to kick my legs about and keep my arms going, at the same time.' She hoped she would be able to swim before Christmas.

Another boarder who was at S.C.E.G.G.S. a decade after Kate Waddy remembers what they wore: 'A few of the very, very up to the minute ones wore stockings, but all our bathing suits were neck to knee, or just below your knee, and they all had skirts and we all had bandanas which we tied round our bathing caps and a great big bow in front.'[7]

Sundays were different from the rest of the week. The girls went to church at least once, and there was half an hour of hymn-singing in the drawing room, followed by prayers and supper. Miss Badham read to the girls in the afternoon: 'I fell asleep in the drawing room this afternoon while Miss Badham was reading to us. I was sound asleep once, but Miss Badham didn't notice me. I wasn't the only one who was nodding.'[8] There were prayers three times on Sunday and, in addition, the boarders had to learn the collect for the day.[9] Sundays were also letter-writing days and the times when boarders were most homesick. Kate Waddy writes: 'Have you been riding lately? I expect you go out every day for a ride about the paddocks. I wish I was up there. Do you remember the Friday we went up to the top paddock. Didn't we have fun riding back?'[10]

At the beginning of 1900 Kate, another boarder and two teachers ('governesses', as they were called then) moved out of 'Chatsworth' (the second location of the school) into other rooms. Kate rather liked the experience: 'It seems as if Pearl and I are day-scholars, coming down every morning (by ourselves) and going back at night with a teacher.'[11]

A matter of great concern to all was the Boer War. Kate wrote 'We hardly speak of anything else here, but the war. A little is quite enough for me although I have a cousin there.'[12] The following March, 1900, she reported:

> *I went to see the Bushman's contingent off on Wednesday. The 'Atlantican' was anchored near Clark Is. and on the Thursday morning at 6.30 we got three boats and rowed round it and the 'Maplemore' which was near Garden Is. Miss Badham said I could wish them luck, so I called 'We wish you all luck and hope you come back safely'. They took off their caps and said 'thank-you' about half a dozen times. Some of our girls had relations on board and Miss B. said they could speak to them.*[13]

School life for boarders and day-girls seems to have been pleasant, although strict standards of behaviour and religious conduct were observed. There was an absence of academic pressure and a refreshing liberty about school life and what the boarders were permitted to do. There were about seventeen boarders and the school was small enough for each girl to be an individual and to feel herself an important person in the school community, known by both staff and pupils. The fact that their school building was a large and attractive house set in spacious grounds made S.C.E.G.G.S. feel more like a home than an educational institution. Compared with today's priorities, the whole S.C.E.G.G.S.

venture seems a little amateurish, with its relaxed organisation of boarders' outings and the boating program, and in educational policies.

It was widely recognised that educational standards were generally low in the secondary schools and in 1892 a Teachers' Association was formed. Most of its members were from church or private schools, although state school teachers were invited to join. The Association tried to remedy existing faults in the educational system and in many ways laid the foundations for the reforms which were to occur in the next decade. Many teachers in private-venture schools had no formal teacher training, and for the most part those who came from England were likely to be more highly qualified than those born in Australia. The most common type of teacher training was the pupil–teacher system, introduced in the 1850s by William Wilkins and continuing until 1905. Fort Street Model School trained only a few teachers annually: in 1887 entrance was restricted to the ten best passes in the pupil–teacher examination. Opportunities for women to be trained were scarcer than for men, because the Council of Education preferred male teachers.[14] The establishment of Hurlstone Training College for Women in 1883, with Caroline Mallett as its first Principal, increased the opportunities for women to be trained to teach. Caroline Mallett, an energetic and well-educated Englishwoman, had been on the staff of Whitelands Training College in London before taking up her post in Australia. Hurlstone College was closed in 1906 when Sydney Teachers' College was established.

In 1894 a scheme for teacher training at the University of Sydney was devised by Miss Harriet Newcomb, an Englishwoman. She arrived in Australia in 1897 and with Margaret Hodge, another Englishwoman, opened Shirley School in 1900. This school is described by Noelene Kyle in *Her Natural Destiny* as the school representing most clearly the innovation and vision of the first decade of the twentieth century.[15] A Teachers' Registry was established by private individuals as a kind of genteel employment agency. This gave a measure of support to governesses or teachers exploited by their employers. Women in particular had suffered exploitation in terms of salaries, teaching conditions, isolated teaching posts in the bush and opportunities for promotion. The *Australian Teacher* was the magazine of the Teachers' Registry.

The main weaknesses in the state education system by 1900 were: the lack of sufficiently trained teachers, the dominating effect of the University matriculation requirements on the curricula, the lack of carefully graded courses based on sound educational principles, and the comparatively poor results achieved by school leavers.[16]

Many teachers still employed rote learning. The students' heads were crammed with facts instead of being trained to think clearly. Badham was opposed to this teaching method and stated that her educational aim was 'that a girl's faculties may be trained to the utmost'.[17] At S.C.E.G.G.S. the original staff members would not have been trained to teach. It is unlikely, however, that they would have taught by rote. In subjects such as mathematics and French, there was probably much use of repetition in order to drill basic facts such as tables and verb endings into pupils' memories. However, as the Principal was likely to wander into a class and listen to the lesson, it is reasonable to suppose that she would have put a stop to any teaching methods she disliked. Old Girls recall her correcting a teacher in front of the class.[18]

The teachers' personalities made a strong impact on the girls, especially when the school and classes were small. Old Girls' accounts of their teachers are often detailed and vivid. The relationship with the teacher frequently determined how well a girl performed in her subject: a well-liked teacher would motivate girls to try to work hard and to please her, and vice versa.

Teaching was a genteel occupation for single or widowed women and after women were admitted to the university, teaching remained one of the only means of support and one of the few career opportunities open to young women graduates. The teachers at S.C.E.G.G.S. mostly lived at the school in spartan conditions and with little privacy or personal space. Their salaries were about £50 per annum, plus board, with a rise of £10 per annum for some. There was no state system of awards and each salary was determined by the school Council.

Thus when Miss Langley began teaching at S.C.E.G.G.S. in 1900, she commenced on an annual salary of £70, yet another new staff member was paid only £40.[19] Teaching staff were paid higher wages than domestic staff. While information about salaries of staff at other girls' schools is not available,[20] staff at some of the boys' schools were receiving up to and above £200 per annum. At Sydney Grammar School, for example, fifteen members of staff were receiving over £200.[21]

Miss Janet B. Uther was referred to as a 'visiting teacher', meaning she did not live at the school. When she became Mrs Swain in 1901, she left S.C.E.G.G.S. The other staff mentioned in an undated early prospectus are Miss Wheatley Walker, teacher of music and sister of Mrs Garvin, who was Head of Sydney Girls' High School; Miss Ethel Stephens, drawing and painting; Fraulein Fast, German; and Miss Beatrice Howard, dancing. The minutes of 16 July 1895 record four other part-time music teachers.

Most of the staff stayed at S.C.E.G.G.S. for more than five years. Some married: Hilda Robson (sister of Ernest Robson, Headmaster of Shore) became Lady Garran, Miss Synge became Mrs Benson, and Grace Horrocks became Mrs Rayment. Staff members left when they married. Two staff members, Miss Howard and Miss Stephens, stayed for over twenty years. Miss Howard perforce resigned when she was detained in England during World War I.[22] Miss Stephens was the daughter of Professor W. J. Stephens, the first Headmaster of Sydney Grammar School. In 1916 she painted Edith Badham's portrait to mark the school's twenty-first year and had another painting hung in a salon in Paris in 1921. She was an important portrait painter and the University of Sydney has a number of her portraits of professors in their collection. Her work also hangs in the Art Gallery of New South Wales. In addition she was a crack shot with a rifle and in 1913 hit fourteen bullseyes in a competition. She left S.C.E.G.G.S. because of illness in 1917. Miss Badham described her as a good friend.

School discipline was allied to the inculcation of ladylike behaviour. The bell would ring and all girls would assemble. Miss Badham would enter the room, mostly beginning, 'It has come to my notice . . .', while the girls would await in trepidation the news of a misdemeanour. On one occasion a girl was advised by Miss Badham either to bathe or go and see a doctor because there must have been something quite wrong—in fact, she had worn perfume to school.[23] Another Badham disciplinary technique (albeit one common to most schools) was to require girls to write 'lines'. Evelyn Olding, when found running around the playground noisily, was summoned by Miss Badham and directed to write out 'I must not behave like a wild animal' several times, in French. Miss Badham supplied her with the French.[24]

Dressmaking and cooking classes began in May 1896 and a sewing machine was hired for use in the classes. Because there was no homework, and because most girls did not intend to go on to university after school, there was not much pressure to achieve, for staff or girls. At a Council meeting in 1897 Edith Badham strongly urged that the girls take independent examinations, and in 1899 she reported that the whole school would be examined by an independent examiner the following year. In 1900 two girls sat for their matriculation but failed to pass all their mathematics papers.[25] In consequence Miss Badham increased the amount of time spent on mathematics and announced that Mr Newbury would spend more time teaching mathematics. Later she decided that Newbury would *examine* but not *teach* mathematics.

Evelyn Olding recalls that while she was a pupil at S.C.E.G.G.S., her father rang Miss Badham and asked if his daughter could be prepared for the Junior examination (taken after four or five years' secondary schooling). Miss Badham's reply was: 'But why?' The father was a little nonplussed but said he wanted to advance his daughter's education. 'Oh,' said Miss Badham, 'I don't think that is a good idea, unless you think she is frightfully clever?' As her father did not think she was 'frightfully clever', the whole subject was dropped and Evelyn continued with the more ladylike pursuits of music, painting and dancing.

Evelyn could remember only two girls being encouraged to seek tertiary education while she was at school.[26] Perhaps Badham wanted only the brighter students to sit for the public examinations, since mediocre results would reflect badly on the school. Evelyn attended a girls' school in England, interrupting her time at S.C.E.G.G.S. She had the impression that the English school was far more concerned with education than was S.C.E.G.G.S.[27] Notwithstanding these impressions, S.C.E.G.G.S. could boast in 1902 of its first graduate from the University. Her name was Nellie Amos.

Badham's reluctance to promote academic ambition is striking. Regarded as a fine scholar, and with her connections to the University, it could have been expected that she would foster scholarship in more of her students than she did. Similarly one would expect her to have supported educational opportunities for young women at the University, but records from the archives of the Women's College show that she was not involved in its foundation in 1892. Her name does not appear on the list of members of the Ladies' Committee which worked to raise funds to establish the College, nor was her name on the list of subscribers. By contrast, her stepmother was both a member of the Ladies' Committee and a subscriber.

From time to time S.C.E.G.G.S. Council minutes hint at a certain amount of stinginess and also a lack of financial acumen on Badham's part. Unless she was an anonymous donor, she did not subscribe to S.C.E.G.G.S., so that a lack of financial support did not necessarily indicate a lack of interest. In 1892 she was not yet caught up in her work at S.C.E.G.G.S. and, leading woman scholar as she was, her support for the cause of women in tertiary education might have been expected. She did not apply for the position of Principal of the Women's College, although a number of applicants were teachers. Perhaps she did not do so because she did not have a degree.

There are two possible reasons for her unexpected and strange attitude to university education. First, she was an unmarried woman who regarded herself as a classicist, even a kind of sage, and it was a jealously guarded position of honour to which only a select few were permitted to aspire. Second, since she thought it proper that most girls would marry and bear children, she probably believed that education beyond a certain point would not benefit future housewives. It would create a tension between the roles of wife and mother on the one hand, and career woman on the other.

The new genre of girls' private schools, of which S.C.E.G.G.S. was an example, was modelled on the boys' schools, which in turn had drawn heavily on the English public school model. Thomas Arnold, Headmaster of Rugby from 1828 to 1852, had wrought a transformation in the public school system. His aim was to make Christian gentlemen of his pupils and his conviction was that education has above all a moral function. The ideal school was a Christian community and he fostered a close rapport between teachers and scholars. Two people carried his ideas further: Edward Thring, Headmaster of Uppingham from 1853 to 1887, and Frederick William Sanderson, Headmaster of Oundle from 1892 to 1922. Both men recognised that boys are individuals rather than simply members of a community, and both were firmly committed to character training. As the nineteenth century became increasingly secular, Arnold's ethic of godliness was replaced by an ethic of manliness. In *Barker College: A History*, Stuart Braga wrote: 'The "Christian gentleman" was not necessarily one who communicated regularly and said his prayers. He was a man of honour, with high principles of service to his fellows and his country, who believed in fair play and sportsmanship.' This type of education came to value sport highly and to place sportsmanship above scholarship.[28]

In Australia A. B. Weigall developed the public school tradition at Sydney Grammar School. Clifford Turney in his book *Grammar, A History of Sydney Grammar School 1919–1988*, stated that Sydney Grammar School soon became a striking exemplar of the Arnoldian public school tradition.[29] Turney wrote:

> *His Headmastership saw the development of such aspects as organised sport, a School Magazine, prefect system, Cadet Corps, school colours and uniform. All these he regarded as important agents in the development of a desirable tone and corporate spirit in the school, and as being contributory to his general objective of moulding the character of his pupils.*[30]

In time S.C.E.G.G.S. was to adopt these and other traditions, except, of course, the cadet corps.

Basic to an identity is a name. 'S.C.E.G.G.S.' was not the original name chosen. Initially the school was to have been 'Church of England High School for Girls', which would have produced the unpronounceable initials C.E.H.S.G. At a meeting of the Council on 30 August 1895 it was resolved that the name should be 'The Sydney Church of England Grammar School for Girls'. For years the initials for the school were C.E.G.S., pronounced 'sea eggs'.[31] The inclusion of the word 'grammar' placed S.C.E.G.G.S. in the English public school tradition, and at the same time, by removing the word 'high', distanced it from the state schools. The school motto was chosen in 1896 by the Bishop. It was *Luceat lux vestra*, 'Let your light shine', and was taken from the text Matthew 5: 16: 'Let your light so shine before men that they may see your good works and glorify your Father who is in heaven.'

At the June 1896 meeting of the Council, the Principal was asked to attend to the composition of a school crest. The school badge is a traditional shield surmounted by a mitre, with the school motto underneath the shield. The symbols displayed are an oil lamp representing knowledge, a distaff for industry (of a domestic kind) and the stars of the Southern Cross. Thus Christian faith, hard work and scholarship define the school's values and all in a distinctively Australian location, the latter represented by the Southern Cross.

The first edition of the school magazine was produced in 1900. Called *Lux*, it was issued four times a year. The publication of *Lux* is invaluable to an

The school badge.

understanding of the growth of school tradition and corporate spirit. Before 1900, source material is mostly limited to Council minutes and interviews with Old Girls. The information in *Lux* indicates that Miss Badham strove to create in her school a sense of each individual's worth and she strongly encouraged past students and staff to maintain links with the school. From 1990 *Lux* always devoted a section to Old Girls' news, including letters, marriages, births, careers and holidays.

At school Miss Badham was far better known by the boarders than the day-girls, and maintained a dignified and somewhat forbidding presence for staff and pupils. One Old Girl[32] recalls her vacating her bedroom for a sick boarder to use. The same Old Girl recalls being allowed to play with Miss Badham's pet tortoise as a reward for good behaviour. Such personal touches contributed to the intangible and indefinable compound which constitutes 'school spirit'.

An early prospectus stated: 'A simple uniform is worn by all pupils of the school. DAY PUPILS: blue serge (winter). Blue serge skirt, with striped blue and white print blouse, or entire dress of blue and white striped prints (summer), sailor hats with school hatbands.'

Full school uniform was still uncommon in girls' schools of the period. There was no set school uniform as such, so long as it was navy and white. Girls wore navy skirts and white blouses and jackets, or navy frocks with detachable white collars. The style was left up to the individual pupil, whose mother would arrange for a dressmaker to make the garments. The only variations to the navy and white were all-white frocks for tennis and, for speech day, all-white voile frocks with lace collar and cuffs. If a girl were in mourning for a close relative, she was allowed to wear mourning (all-black) for a three-month period.[33]

The sport promoted was rowing. Rowing uniforms included floppy blue crushed linen hats and silk blouses with red or blue ties to distinguish boating teams. Miss Badham believed that it was an essential exercise for women. When the school moved to Chatsworth there was a boatshed and boats for the girls to use. After the move to Barham in 1900, the girls caught a ferry to Mosman and walked across the headland to Sirius Bay, where they hired rowing boats. There would be five or six boatloads with a teacher in charge of every boat. During the time of Ruby Bulkeley, who left in about 1912, there were rowing examinations conducted annually by a master at Shore, 'Chops' Hall. At least one other girls' school, Ascham, offered rowing as a sport.[34] Tennis, athletics, physical culture, cricket and basketball were offered. A gymnasium was erected at Chatsworth[35] and, the grounds being extensive, physical culture, basketball and cricket would have been taught on the school site.

There were no prefects because Miss Badham did not like the idea of girls disciplining girls. Instead there were 'pioneers', girls who were like prefects in that they had privileges but, unlike prefects, no responsibilities. Their own room, situated to the left of the front steps, was known as 'Valhalla'—a suitable name for the abode of the goddesses of school life.[36] Other esoteric names became part of S.C.E.G.G.S. school lore as the years passed: 'Siberia', 'Bondi' and 'The Strand' were names for various places in the school. The boarders' experiences and customs contributed significantly to building up school folklore and school tradition.

In its first five years, S.C.E.G.G.S. had grown to nearly 100 pupils. Its curriculum catered for the moral education of young women rather than providing a strongly academic emphasis, although this was available for those whom Badham considered bright enough to take up the challenge. It was a school with social prestige, a finishing school for many, and for some a means of entry to the University. These first years witnessed the establishment of traditions which gave the school a corporate identity both within and beyond the school boundaries.

— 6 —

Expansion, 1900–1912

FOR S.C.E.G.G.S., THE period up to 1914 was one of expansion, challenge and vitality, and in New South Wales generally it was a period of prosperity, expansion and urban growth. There were 92 girls enrolled in 1900[1] and the numbers grew steadily thereafter. A kindergarten and junior school were opened in 1900, and this would have accounted in part for the increase in numbers (see Table 6.1). During this time three branch schools were established and a number of offers came to take over existing schools. All plans and opportunities were hampered by a shortage of funds. Since the school did not have a capital base, every venture was hazardous. There was a constant tension between providing even reasonable facilities for pupils and staff, and expanding the educational operation further.

The first branch school was established at Bowral in 1906 with fifteen pupils, two of whom were boarders.[2] In 1905 Miss Swinson had offered her school, a 'Girls' Grammar School' in Bowral, to the S.C.E.G.G.S. Council because she was returning to England.[3] Miss Badham supported the idea of taking the school on as a branch school, and so the school was purchased for £150. Miss Langley became the first Principal, but was replaced by Miss Constance Smith at the end of 1906. By April 1906 the school had moved to 'Woodbine' in Bowral, a site which the Council subsequently bought. Boys under ten were admitted as well as girls, and soon the school had 26 students. Its numbers stayed at about that level until 1911 when, with 34 pupils, it was full. It was never to be a financially viable school. Beck reported to the Synod in 1906: 'The Council entered upon the undertaking with some misgiving because of the financial burden thereby incurred' but concluded that it was 'perhaps the most important event in the school year'.[4]

In 1910 a suggestion was noted that a branch school at North Sydney be opened.[5] Miss Badham was very enthusiastic because it would save the girls who lived on the North Shore the ferry journey across the Harbour. Miss Nona Dumolo, Miss Badham's First Assistant, was willing to undertake the management of the school 'at her present salary'. Christchurch Hall could be

Table 6.1 Enrolments at S.C.E.G.G.S. Darlinghurst, 1900–11

Year	Total	Boarders
1900	92	28
1904	90	25
1905	106	27
1906	100	N/A
1907	N/A	N/A
1908	130	N/A
1909	127	31
1911	130	43

leased for 30s 0d per week. The following February the school opened with sixteen pupils. Numbers grew satisfactorily, so that there were already 50 pupils by October 1912.[6] The North Sydney S.C.E.G.G.S. was the most successful of the branch schools in terms of its educational standards, financial viability and longevity. Of it Beck reported in 1912: 'The Council has every reason to believe that the standard of teaching is very high.' Already two Old Girls were attending the Kindergarten Training College at Waverley, and one was enrolled in pharmacy at the University of Sydney. In the ensuing years the main problem was accommodating the number of pupils attending the school.

In 1910, at the same Council meeting where the idea of the North Sydney school was mooted, a letter was received from the Rev. Edward Owen in which he suggested a branch boarding school at Hunters Hill. At that time the Council decided it could not entertain such a proposition. However, in April

'Endersley' at 30 Viret Street, Hunters Hill, was a branch school of S.C.E.G.G.S. from 1912 to 1915.

Table 6.2 Branch school financial statements, 1912–14

Date	Hunters Hill	North Sydney
November 1912	£981 debit	N/A
April 1913	£1147 debit	£40 credit
March 1914	£1102 debit	£220 credit
April 1914	£1177 debit	N/A
July 1914	£1149 debit	£123 credit
September 1914	£1145 debit	£84 credit

Note: few records were kept of the Bowral finances
Source: S.C.E.G.G.S. Council minute book, vol. 4, September 1915

1912 Miss Wight started a school in Hunters Hill, Binstead Girls' Grammar School, and the impression prevailed that it was a branch school of S.C.E.G.G.S. After obtaining a prospectus, Miss Badham communicated with Miss Wight, who agreed to alter the prospectus 'so as to preclude any mistaken view that the school was under the Council's management'. Miss Wight's eagerness to be affiliated with S.C.E.G.G.S. indicates the quality of S.C.E.G.G.S.'s reputation. Further letters from Rev. Owen and Hunters Hill residents strongly urging that a branch school be opened persuaded the Council to go ahead and 'Enderslea' was leased. In this way the S.C.E.G.G.S. third branch school was opened at Hunters Hill in 1912.[7] Miss Galloway, formerly Principal of the Girls' Grammar School at Goulburn, was appointed Principal, with the strong support of Badham.[8] With regard to Miss Wight's school, the Council hoped that friction between the two schools might be averted and in July 1912 Miss Wight invited S.C.E.G.G.S. to purchase her school, even though it had only been operating for three months. The offer was rejected and Binstead closed in 1917, because of Miss Wight's poor health.[9] The Hunters Hill branch of S.C.E.G.G.S. (which, like the North Sydney school, was also opened so that local girls did not have to make the trip across the Harbour to Head School) had a short career, for it closed in 1915.[10] It always operated at a loss (see Table 6.2).

It was necessary to clarify the relationship of the branch schools to Head School. The first step was the decision at the Council meeting in July 1912 that the Headmistresses of all the schools would meet quarterly to discuss and arrange the school work generally, so that some uniformity in standard might be maintained. The following November Edith Badham requested that the relationship between Head and branch schools be clearly defined and in August 1913 the relationship was drawn up by a constitution. The Principal of Head School had full direction of the teaching and discipline of all of the schools, subject to the Council's approval. Each branch school Headmistress was directly responsible to the Council and could appoint staff in consultation with the Principal. The Council reserved the right to consult with the Principal in matters relating to the branch schools. All branch schools were to follow the same syllabus as that at Head School. The Headmistresses did not enjoy equal status with the Principal. Staffing and the curriculum at branch schools were dependent upon the Principal's views.[11]

The tight finances of the S.C.E.G.G.S. operation meant that the Council had to devote an extraordinary amount of attention to detail. The Headmistresses appeared hamstrung by their financial limitations. Thus, for example, Miss Galloway at Hunters Hill requested Council's permission to buy more spoons, forks and fertiliser in August 1913. Miss Smith's school at Bowral suffered from chronic water shortages and inadequate heating, lighting and desks.[12]

Miss Galloway and Miss Badham did not get on well. By April 1914 Miss Badham had asked to be relieved of any further responsibility with regard to the Hunters Hill school as Miss Galloway persistently ignored her and declined to use the agreed text books.[13] The question arose whether the Hunters Hill school should be closed down. One parent, Mrs King, transferred her three daughters from the school to Head School. Beck summed up the situation in the 20th Annual Report to the Synod:

> *This school has been the source of much anxiety to the Council, as it has not progressed so well as anticipated when it opened. At the present moment, indeed, it is being carried on at a loss. This is due to various reasons, especially, perhaps to the situation of the school, which is not as prominent as may be desired, and the distance from town which makes it most difficult to secure an adequate staff of efficient visiting teachers. It would certainly appear that there is no opening for a Boarding School at Hunter's Hill, and no great support even of a large Day School.*[14]

The school closed at the end of 1915 and Miss Galloway started her own school, 'St Albans', in Hunters Hill in January 1916. This school continued until 1935 when it became financially unviable.[15]

There were at least six other schools in operation in Hunters Hill when the S.C.E.G.G.S. branch opened.[16] Pressure from the Rev. Edward Owen (Rector of All Saints', Hunters Hill from 1900 to 1925) and other influential residents seems to have persuaded the school Council against its better judgment to open a branch there. Attendance at its best was about 50 pupils, which was better than Bowral, and not significantly behind North Sydney when it first opened. The very poor shape of the finances cannot be easily explained. Miss Galloway and Badham disliked each other, and possibly the subservient role that was the Headmistresses' lot under Miss Badham irked one who had enjoyed independence as a Principal in her previous school. The S.C.E.G.G.S. enterprise did not have room for two strong-minded and autocratic women.

Miss Badham revealed her views on branch schools in her Principal's Report of 1913:

> *Personally I hope we shall not have any more branches for some time to come. Four schools can meet comfortably four times a year, and even Bowral can be managed within the compass of one day, but if we had five schools, it would take a mathematician to arrange the time of meeting, and if we all had to go, say, to Leura, or Orange, or Uranquinty, in addition to our present peregrinations, we should have very little time left to do our proper work.*[17]

The S.C.E.G.G.S. venture with branch schools was extraordinary. No other school in Sydney attempted to set up a network of branch schools as S.C.E.G.G.S. did. When the school was still struggling financially, the Council took on the further liability of *three* more schools in the short space of six years.

The whole business of the branch schools seems to have been basically *ad hoc*. There was no strategic plan whereby S.C.E.G.G.S. would systematically expand its operation as funds and opportunities permitted. The S.C.E.G.G.S. Council could not be said to have been aggressively expansionist. It seems simply that as opportunities and pressures arose, each case was determined on its merits and a decision taken. The implications for S.C.E.G.G.S. were very serious, but it is doubtful if these were appreciated by the Principal and the Council.

Synod was not consulted, as far as the records indicate. By establishing the branch schools, the S.C.E.G.G.S. Council was enlarging its powers and altering its mandate to govern a single school. It is clear, however, that a network of schools was probably acceptable to the Synod, for this was part of the vision of Beck and Corlette in the days before S.C.E.G.G.S. was founded. Thus, in the 1892 Report of the Girls' High Schools Committee, Corlette had reported communicating with St Catherine's: 'for the purpose of ascertaining whether the Council of that Institution would entertain the idea of affording in some way a centre from which a system of Girls' High Schools for the church generally might be started'.[18]

More significant still had been Beck's report to the Synod in September 1895. After reporting the opening of S.C.E.G.G.S. the previous July, he had added the words:

> . . . *the Committee desire to express their conviction that the Church may look forward hopefully to a useful future for the school thus successfully launched, and they trust that the present movement* may in time lead to the opening of other Church of England Schools for Girls in Sydney and elsewhere. *(author's emphasis)*[19]

Beck no doubt hoped that S.C.E.G.G.S. was the first of a wave of similar schools. As a founding member of the Council who rarely missed a meeting, a member of all significant subcommittees, Secretary of the Council, and member until after Badham's death, Beck's encouragement of the branch schools is undoubted. He seems to have been a quiet man, persistent and conscientious in any duties he took up, and he must have found a ready and very active co-visionary in Badham. Her own energy, strong personality and brilliance were ready for new challenges by 1906, after ten years of consolidation at S.C.E.G.G.S., and in Beck she would have had all the support and encouragement she needed for the venture. The first opportunity had come with Miss Swinson's offer of her school at Bowral.

There is no record of the Synod's reaction to the plans to found further schools like S.C.E.G.G.S. which Corlette and Beck had mooted in the 1890s. A decade later membership of the Synod would have altered considerably and again nothing is known of Synod's views on the branch schools. Synod Ordinances drawn up in these years make no mention of the changed structure of S.C.E.G.G.S. Archbishop Saumarez Smith, who died in 1909, had rarely attended Council meetings. His successor, Archbishop Wright, attended Council meetings reasonably often[20] and his wife became a member of the Council in 1915.[21] By the time they were involved with S.C.E.G.G.S. therefore, the branch schools were a *fait accompli.* In 1917 the Archbishop showed considerable interest in the matter of a Certificate of Title relating to the North Sydney branch but there is no indication whatsoever that the issues of relative rights and powers of Synod and the Council were ever considered. At a time when many private schools were closing, the branch school venture was something of a gamble.

A wave of reform had meanwhile swept through the state system of education, initiated by the New South Wales Director of Education, Peter Board, upon his appointment in 1905. The Leaving Certificate replaced the old matriculation examination in 1913 and educational standards became much stricter. This may explain in part why the S.C.E.G.G.S. Council was approached a number of times to take over small schools, as it did, for example, at Bowral. Private schools were closing not only because of financial stress but because of the related problem of educational standards now expected by the Department of Education.

One long-term consequence of the founding of the branch schools was the financial drain on the Head School: Bowral, in particular, siphoned off resources and the result was that Head School was always in a state of near-penury. The other consequence was the workload imposed on the Council. Although there were subcommittees from the Council for each school, they were mainly concerned with housekeeping matters. The Council simply could not deal with four schools as well as it could with one, nor could there be that concentration of interest and concern for each school which would ensure the proper support and advice to which its Headmistress was entitled.

The branch school venture was unsystematic and not properly thought through. It was a response to pressure from groups or individuals, and sometimes it was the status of the pressure group, rather than any genuine educational market it represented, that won the Council's support. Empire-building was tempting and exciting and the Council took on too much too soon.

Apart from those which were acted on, there were at least four approaches to the S.C.E.G.G.S. Council between 1908 and 1914 to take over or found a school. In 1908 the Rev. Howard Lea of Dubbo requested the establishment of a branch school at Dubbo.[22] The Council decided to enquire further from the Bishop of Bathurst and nothing further came of this proposal. In 1911 a Miss Armstrong of Summer Hill enquired whether the Council would like to purchase a well-established school in a good suburb.[23] In 1914 a Miss Carter was anxious to dispose of her school at Mosman and she thought it might be advantageous for S.C.E.G.G.S. to purchase it, amalgamating the North Sydney school with it.[24]

The most tempting offer came in 1911 when Miss Clarke proposed that S.C.E.G.G.S. take over her school, Abbotsleigh, at Wahroonga.[25] The school had large grounds and 139 pupils. The S.C.E.G.G.S. Council was very interested indeed. They chose Miss Ruth Jarrett as its prospective Headmistress, obtained the Archbishop's approval, and decided to offer up to £7000. Miss Clarke refused the offer and there the matter ended.[26] The disappointment generated by this outcome may well account for the decision in 1912 to open the Hunters Hill branch. There is no doubt that Abbotsleigh would have been a tremendous asset to S.C.E.G.G.S., changing its ethos and nature drastically. In time the Head School might well have moved to Wahroonga. A North Shore student population with a significant number of wealthy parents would have meant facilities and opportunities which have never been within S.C.E.G.G.S.'s reach. The school population would have been more conservative and less socially diverse. The large grounds would have given sporting and recreational facilities never available on the Barham site. On the other hand, a single council responsible for Abbotsleigh and S.C.E.G.G.S. would have created intolerable tensions. There would have been too much work for one council to handle effectively, and there would have been pressures stemming from differences of tradition and expectation at each school.

As Head School increased its numbers, the need for further buildings became steadily more pressing. From 1900 until 1911 more buildings were planned and built as finances permitted. Gymnastics lessons were conducted in the Victoria Street Markets and then moved to St John's Darlinghurst Church Hall in 1904. A gymnasium on-site was one desire of the Council. In 1908 a 'hospital' was built after about three years' planning, financed by proceeds from lectures Miss Badham gave and money raised by the Old Girls. The 'hospital' must have consisted of a couple of rooms at the most. Not very useful as it happened, it was demolished after Miss Badham's time.

By 1907 Beck reported that the school was too full for comfort. Finances would not yet permit any building work, and only piecemeal renovations and furnishing were possible. A refrain from Miss Badham at many Council meetings was the request for more room: for classrooms, bedrooms and space for the matron. The expedient of enclosing the verandah provided dining room space in 1909. Four classrooms were built in 1910, and although no records or building plans exist, they would have been an extension of the 1901 building, running parallel with Barham and forming a courtyard between the two buildings.

The pressures on Badham and the Council caused by shortage of finance and rooms resulted in some rather strained Council meetings. Badham was so desperate for further bedrooms that she personally approached a Miss Eadith Walker, a well-known philanthropist, for a guarantee of £500 so that the new bedrooms might be built at once.[27] Miss Walker had replied that she was willing to lend money on this occasion but that she must never be approached again. At the September meeting of the Council a letter from Miss Badham was read 'in which she expressed her views at length as to what she deemed advisable', and she followed this up by a strongly worded plea in person. After a great deal of discussion the Council nevertheless decided to defer further extensions until 1910. Badham asked the Council what she should say to Miss Walker and the Council directed her to thank Miss Walker for her kindness but to say that the Council had no occasion for availing itself of such a guarantee.[28]

It was the first recorded time that Badham had not gained her way with the Council. Her involvement of Miss Walker was a kind of lever, a desperate attempt to get the Council to act. It was symptomatic of a tension between the Head and the Council on matters requiring action. Projects and issues of great concern to the Principal can be maddeningly slowed down or thwarted by the Council bureaucracy, composed as it often is of individuals for whom the school is only a part-time interest and who are more concerned with financial stability than with what may be educationally desirable.

In October 1910 the Council decided to build two additional storeys onto the classroom block erected the year before. The lower storey would in the future be used as an assembly hall, though ultimately it was to be a chapel, and the storey above would contain more dormitories. The voting was close: Docker, Bellingham, Christian and MacCallum were in favour, and Selby, Street and Beck against.[29] Badham had strongly recommended this particular plan. Beck announced in his Sixteenth Annual Report to the Synod that no more buildings would be required.[30]

Lux and reminiscences of Old Girls provide colourful details of life at S.C.E.G.G.S. in the first decade of the twentieth century. School excursions were frequent: to Bondi by tram, to the National Park where they hired ten rowing boats, and geology excursions with Miss Jarrett to Prospect, Manly, Wollongong and Mt Victoria. One pupil wrote to the editor of *Lux*:

> *At the breaking up festivals we generally have a French play. Although these are rather popular amongst the girls, I would venture to suggest that we should have an English one occasionally. There is a lot of hard work in the French plays. First,*

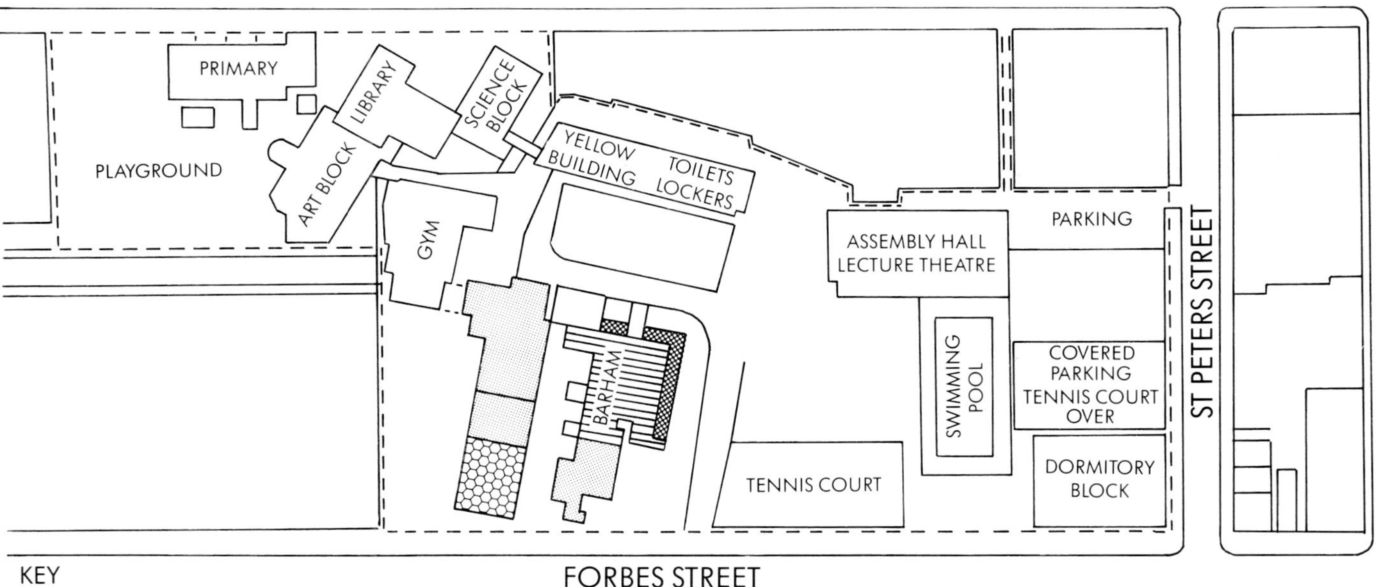

Plan of the school site, showing buildings erected between 1833 and 1911.

'Trachiniae' a Greek play by Sophocles, was performed on 27 and 28 September 1912. It was spoken in Greek by Grace Newbery as Queen Deanire, maidens Dulcie Cook, Freda Mowle, Jean Duff, Lilias Robson Scott, Gwendoline Marshall and Marjorie 'Poppy' Sawkins.

> *we have to learn the text, then have our pronunciation corrected; then comes the ordeal of rehearsing before the school, and learning how to act our parts; and, lastly, the eventful night. Could we not have one of Shakespeare's plays instead?*[31]

Miss Badham's views on Greek plays deserve to be quoted:

> *Last November, for the second time in our life we gave a representation of Lewis Campbell's metrical rendition of the Trachiniae of Sophocles. The first time we gave it the daily papers exhausted themselves in commendation; this time on the whole the play was much better presented, yet the papers, with the exception of the* Church Standard, *whose critic had the advantage of understanding Greek, did not seem quite sure what they ought to say about it. One gentleman apparently thought it ought to follow the lines of modern melodrama and fell foul of it because it failed to do so . . . Next time we have a Greek play, I hope it will be all in Greek, with English chorus. It would be too much to expect the gift of song and a knowledge of Greek in the same person. But I suppose our next effort will be a French play. There are no Latin ones suitable for girls.*[32]

Dorothea Baltzer, an Old Girl, remembers the Greek plays. She described them as 'very amateurish'. It was hard for girls to stand up and talk in a foreign language in front of their contemporaries. Marjorie Hesslein, another Old Girl, recalls that Miss Badham used the same costumes year after year. It was always just a simple tunic with a girdle around the middle: 'They were all the same length, so that on the short children there were huge folds over the top of the girdle and they came down past their knees, and on the big girls the tunics were very short.'[33] Distribution Day was held in June and marked the conclusion of the school year. (The practice of ending the school year in the middle of the calendar year followed the English pattern.) There were some remarkable prizes: one for popularity and another for neatness.[34] Generally the prizes were distributed by the Archbishop or a woman of note such as Lady Chelmsford, the Governor's wife. There were prizes for proficiency in essay writing, general knowledge, and for the individual subjects. There were also prizes for Prayer Book, tennis, sculling, fencing and physical culture.

Ascension Day was very important as an annual tradition at S.C.E.G.G.S. The first one was held at Chatsworth to welcome the Old Girls back to the school. It was a festival which took over the whole day, and an occasion when past and present girls and staff joined together in various activities. At the Ascension Day celebrations of 1906, for example, there was an early service at the Cathedral, another service at 11.00 am at St John's Darlinghurst, some performances which included the mad hatter's tea party scene out of *Alice in Wonderland* (so successful it had to be repeated later), 'an exhibition of skirt dancing', followed by a potato race in which some of the staff entered. There was singing, including 'frequent repetition of the National Anthem', and lastly dancing. At the close of the afternoon 'there were prolonged cheers for Miss Badham, for the King, for the school, and for many other less important persons and things'.[35] Old Girls sent a telegram of apology if they were unable to come to Ascension Day in Miss Badham's time.

Following English convention Miss Badham frequently used the church calendar. She expected the Old Girls to know when Ascension Day would fall each year and named the terms in ecclesiastical language: for example, the last term in the calendar year was Michaelmas term. The boarders remember her Lenten fast of bread and water. Being High Church she observed Lent strictly,

Miss Badham's bedroom, now the Latin room. The bed was so high that she had to stand on a box to climb into it.

and prohibited eating before taking communion at the Cathedral on Ash Wednesday. There was always the possibility that one of the girls would faint on the long walk.

Ruby Bulkeley, a boarder, thought that a lot of the religious observance at S.C.E.G.G.S. in those days was dry and rules-orientated. Instead of making Christianity a revelation about relationships, the girls learnt a lot about not doing things because they were wicked, and there seemed to be a great many regulations to observe, especially in Lent and Advent. There was strong emphasis on honesty. Ruby Bulkeley came from a small private school in Wallerawang and was struck by this one day early in her time at S.C.E.G.G.S.:

> *We were all gathered together for the after-luncheon service and there was the most awful uproar going on, and we were supposed not to talk, you see, when we went there. The Headmistress just walked in and said, 'Stand up the girls who were talking', and to my astonishment half the room stood up and I thought, 'What madness is this?', and I jolly soon learnt that you didn't get out of things, you had to admit if you did it. But it seemed a most extraordinary thing when they all stood up.*[36]

Detentions were the punishments most commented upon in *Lux*. There was a satirical comment in June 1905 on the 'attempt to crush any demonstration of affection among the girls, by putting the offender down for detention'. Another complaint was that detentions were too long:

> *It is quite natural that our teachers should keep us in: when we do not know our lessons, we naturally expect to be punished; but it is too much when we are only allowed to eat our lunch in the space of ten minutes, go straight back to work without any fresh air between times, and expected to take as much interest in the afternoon lessons as we would otherwise. It is bad for our health, and affects mine considerably.*[37]

Other complaints were the cockroaches in the desks, too much homework (there is no evidence as to when it was introduced) and a scarcity of chairs. 'A Lay of the Old Remove', subtitled 'The Battle of the Chairs', by 'Camauley' presented the case in *Lux* in 1906:

> *The Removites' brows were sad*
> *The Removites' speech was low,*
> *And darkly looked they toward the door,*
> *And thought they heard the foe.*
> *For the Battle of the Chairs*
> *Had begun at school that day,*
> *And Remove had firmly settled*
> *That the Hoii they would slay.*
> *Then out spake fair-haired Maudie*
> *(And at talking she is great),*
> *'To every girl upon this earth*
> *Death cometh soon or late;*
> *And how can one die better*
> *Than facing fearful odds,*
> *For the glory of her class, girls,*
> *And to prove that we're not clods.'*
> *'Put both chairs in the background*

With all the speed ye may;
I, with two more to help me,
Will hold the foe in play.'
Thus spake the dauntless Doris,
And all the rest chimed in,
'Ay, all we girls will try to-day
To keep the chairs and win.'
Then out spake gallant Dophius,
A Bondian proud was she,
'Lo I will stand at thy right hand
And hold the chairs with thee.'
And out spake strong Lorninius,
Of Scottish blood was she,
'I will abide by thy left side,
And hold the chairs with thee.'
They scarcely all were settled
When in rushed every foe,
Remove cried, 'Vaincre ou mourir,'
The Fifth all shouted 'Ho!'
Poor Maudie was o'ertumbled,
But up she rose again,
And though they all fought fiercely
Not one of them was slain.
Then in came Miss La Traille,
Who said the fight must cease,
And though they grudged it sorely
They were forced to make a peace.[38]

Lunch in the hall had its detractors:

> *Lunch was dreadful. We had to have it there, and it was terrible. All those girls sitting on forms and the smell of mandarins and bananas and oranges and tomatoes, especially on a hot day—it was very, very trying. And everybody sitting around and munching sandwiches. I had to get permission to go into the garden to eat mine. I couldn't take it.*[39]

The boarders were also critical of lunch:

> *Luncheon was always the same: shredded lettuce with egg and tomato on top and a variation of corned beef, roast beef or roast lamb. They always knew what they were going to get. This was always followed by a hot stodgy pudding and custard. The girls at each table took turns around the table to say grace for the whole table and invariably there would be an argument of 'I said it yesterday!' 'No you didn't!' 'I did!' 'It's your turn', etc. until a 'Hush, hush, quiet gels!' command came from the high table.*[40]

Mary Beith said she thoroughly enjoyed boarding: 'Our aim was to get to the cubicles on the top floor. You'd arrived when you got a cubicle and also when you sat at Miss Badham's table.'[41]

Until 1905 sport seems to have been for the boarders only. This served to drive a wedge between boarders and day-girls. Tennis for day-girls began in 1905. Boating continued until Badham's death in 1920. Other sports were

The boarders' sitting room in c.1910.

basketball and physical culture. Hockey was introduced in 1911 but not long afterward Nessie Wynter was hit in the face with a hockey stick, losing two front teeth, and Miss Badham banned the game as being far too rough and unladylike.[42]

It is difficult to assess the quality of the staff and recollections of Old Girls are subjective. Some teachers were thought eccentric, and others such as Miss Scroggie, Miss Capper and Miss Noad were well-liked. A remarkable feature of the S.C.E.G.G.S. staff is the number who became heads of other schools: Miss Ruth Jarrett went to Brisbane Girls' High School in 1909, Miss Nona Dumolo to the North Sydney branch of S.C.E.G.G.S., Miss Murray to New England Grammar School in 1913 and Miss Langley and Miss Smith to the Bowral branch. This may have indicated a high standard of teaching at S.C.E.G.G.S.

The other indicator of standards is equally inconclusive: examination results. They show the calibre of the staff in part only because examination results depend as much upon the calibre of the students themselves as that of their teachers. Although the consensus among the Old Girls is that S.C.E.G.G.S. was highly regarded as an educational institution, about 1910, examinations results were not noteworthy (see Tables 6.3 and 6.4). It is not known whether S.C.E.G.G.S. girls sat for the Senior examinations prior to 1913.

Judged by its public examination results, S.C.E.G.G.S. offered similar educational standards to Ascham, and higher than Kambala and Rose Bay Convent in the Junior examinations. These schools were the closest geographically. MLC Burwood and PLC Croydon had significantly more successful candidates in the Senior and Junior examinations and they were therefore at that time the most academically successful of the girls' private schools up to 1914. St Catherine's poor academic reputation of the 1880s was no longer deserved.

Table 6.3 Senior examination results, 1897–1913

School	1897	1902	1906	1909	1913
MLC	4	3	3	5	N/A
PLC	1	3	1	1	3
Kambala	—	—	—	—	—
SGHS	4	3	7	16	—
Ascham	—	—	—	—	—
St Catherine's	1	—	—	—	—
S.C.E.G.G.S.	—	—	—	—	1
Rose Bay	—	—	—	1	3
Abbotsleigh	5	1	—	—	2

Source: Manuals of Public Examinations, University of Sydney Archives

Table 6.4 Junior examination results, 1897–1914

School	1897	1903	1907	1910	1914
MLC	7	9	9	10	—
PLC	9	4	7	8	—
Kambala	—	—	—	—	—
SGHS	28	20	28	47	—
Ascham	—	1	2	2	6
St Catherine's	1	—	2	2	1
S.C.E.G.G.S.	—	3	4	4	—
Rose Bay	—	—	—	—	—
Abbotsleigh	1	1	6	2	—

Source: Manuals of Public Examinations, University of Sydney Archives

The school which stands out is Sydney Girls' High School, which was preparing up to ten times as many successful candidates as S.C.E.G.G.S.

Few girls at this time had academic aspirations and S.C.E.G.G.S., like the other girls' private schools, was as much a finishing school as an educational establishment aiming at academic excellence. Changes in the state system of education under the direction of Peter Board, changing expectations as a result of World War I and the advent to S.C.E.G.G.S. of some very bright students were to alter this situation in the last decade of Miss Badham's reign.

The school was examined annually and a report submitted to the Principal and Council. C. H. Hodges, Headmaster of Shore until 1909 and Council member (1901–11) examined the school in English, history, geography, Latin and French in 1911. His conclusions were:

> *The work of the higher forms was in most cases extremely satisfactory . . . the papers sent in by the little girls gave evidence of careful and thoughtful teaching and learning . . . The general impression I have received from my examination is that there is good, honest, steady effort and progress being made throughout the school.*[43]

— 7 —

The last decade of Edith Badham 1912–1920

THE PROCESS OF improving education in New South Wales had not ceased with the 1880 Instruction Act. The demand for further educational reform gathered momentum after 1900 and significant and lasting change took place under Peter Board, Director of Education from 1905 to 1922. In this period the entry of the state into secondary education broke the monopoly which had been exercised by the church and private schools.

In 1902 a Royal Commission had been set up to report on education in New South Wales, following extensive criticism of the state educational system which had included teachers' poor pay, poor teaching methods, the crippling effect of examinations on good teaching, inadequate teacher training, state school fees, absence of secondary school curricula, lack of supervision of private schools and lack of coordination of state ones.[1] The two Commissioners appointed were G. H. Knibbs and J. W. Turner. Their massive report was in three parts: Primary Education (1903), Secondary Education (October 1904) and Technical and Other Education (December 1904). In addition, Peter Board, at that time an inspector of schools, produced a twelve-page *Report with Regard to Primary Education in Other Countries.* Conferences were held in 1904 to discuss the first part of the Knibbs–Turner Report, but at these conferences Board's Report proved more influential. In it he advocated a return to old educational principles which were currently in vogue in England and Scotland.

A wave of reform began in 1905 with the appointment of Board as Director of Education and continued until 1916. In 1906 Sydney Teachers' College, which was coeducational, replaced the Fort Street Training School and the Hurlstone Training School. A Diploma in Education course was introduced in 1911, in association with the University of Sydney. This was a twelve-month postgraduate course of professional training for those intending to be secondary school teachers. The first new state high school for nearly twenty years was established at Newcastle, and by 1911 there were eight high schools (compared with two in 1905). In 1910 state secondary education was reorganised: fees were abolished and curricula drawn up for high schools, junior technical, junior commercial and domestic science schools.

Of great significance was the establishment of three new examinations: the Qualifying Certificate (at the end of the primary school course), the Intermediate Certificate Examination (at the end of two years of secondary school), and the Leaving Certificate Examination (after four years of secondary school). The Leaving Certificate was accepted by the University in lieu of the old matriculation examination, and it was based on a broader curriculum and on organised progression of subject matter. The Board of Examiners comprised representatives from both the Department of Education and the University. The first syllabus for high schools, drawn up by the lecturers at Sydney Teachers' College in 1911, was a compromise curriculum as it provided for a cultural education augmented by vocational subjects.[2] The first Leaving Certificate Examination was held in 1913.

The Bursary Endowment Act of 1912 provided for able students from poor families to be educated at state and private schools and at the University. Private schools wishing to offer bursaries had to be registered, which meant that inspection by officers of the Department of Education was mandatory. The Public Instruction (Amendment) Act of 1916 required registration of all private schools.

The effect of these reforms on private education was considerable. The new high schools provided competition with private schools. Now state education was free and the curriculum more extensive. State high schools increased in popularity so that in the year between 1910 and 1911 enrolments at these schools doubled. By the end of 1911 there were 2293 boys and girls attending them.[3] Raised standards meant that some private schools failed to qualify for registration and the number of non-denominational schools dropped dramatically from 339 in 1908 to 186 in 1918. Enrolments fell from 8604 to 6986. However, while there were fewer schools, they were larger.[4]

Edith Badham expressed her views on the reforms by the Department of Education in 'Registered Schools and the Syllabus', part of her Report read at the annual prize-giving for 1914. This work is a masterpiece of witty analysis and reveals not only how the reforms affected a corporate school like S.C.E.G.G.S., but what Badham's own educational theories were by 1914.

The Report begins:

> *At the beginning of last year, 1913, we were registered under the Department of Public Instruction, and undertook to follow, more or less, the syllabus put forth by that body, and to prepare our pupils for the Intermediate and Leaving Examination. To this end we remodelled our Time-Table to include all the subjects required by the Department for all pupils. We were not overwhelmed with admiration for the Junior and Senior—nothing in this life is perfect—and we were willing to try a new venture, even though we stared at some of the regulations laid down for us . . .*
>
> *We have never sent a large proportion of our girls up for Public Examinations; the parents generally do not care for it, and I have not, hitherto, thought the matter warranted any kind of pressure. But our aim has always been that the Girls in V should be up to the Junior standard, and that VI should do the work required for the Senior and Matriculation Honours . . . Latin has always been taught throughout the school, and Greek, when we could persuade anyone to learn it. The Cooper Classical Scholar[5] at the University matriculated from this school in November, 1912, with great distinction in English, French, Latin and Greek, and with second-class honours in Mathematics. Though we have only sent a small*

number to the University, yet at any time those girls who wished to matriculate, could do so without any dislocation of Classes or Time-table.[6]

Miss Badham stated that she and other Heads of church schools had written to the Department of Public Instruction to demand relief from what she termed 'an intolerable system'. All church schools would suffer under a special disadvantage because as there was no provision for religious instruction in the new syllabus, time had to be taken from other subjects to make room for it.

Edith Badham continued:

It is only right that I should explain why I object to this system and wish to be rid of it. First and foremost, the whole course is abominably overloaded . . . If the powers that be think it absolutely necessary that everyone shall learn a little about everything, instead of a good deal about a few things, could they not arrange that the weak subjects should be taken at a preliminary standard, and the others at a more advanced grade?

Far too many books had been set, she maintained, and many of them ill-chosen. In English, for example, books such as *Tom Brown's Schooldays* and *Treasure Island* were books to be read, she believed, as a pastime, not textbooks for an examination: 'If the Director of Education really wanted to make them unpopular, he could hardly have gone a better way to work.' Some of the most valuable parts of the set books had been omitted from the editions recommended by the Department, and notes had been added which Badham described as 'sometimes obscure and sometimes merely silly'.

Criticism of the Latin and French courses included poor choice of textbooks. About Greek she said:

The statement 'that progress in this subject will be rapid because the classes will be small' (unless we are to understand that in other subjects the classes are too large), suggests a curious piece of reasoning. It is as though one should say that the progress of a class is in inverse ratio to its size, or that because 25 pupils can assimilate a certain amount of Greek in a given time, five pupils will assimilate five times as much . . .

These notes go on to say that the study of Greek is only a means to an end. Quite so, and we imagined that that end was a knowledge of Greek, but this, it seems, is a mistake—the true end is to understand exactly what is meant by a hydro-aeroplane.

Edith Badham strongly argued against lowering standards to make university entrance easier. She particularly disliked the weakening of language requirements and the strengthening of mathematics:

There is too much of everything except Latin, and more Mathematics than anything.

. . . has anyone the right to insist that Mathematics shall be the intellectual foundation on which every boy and girl among us must build, and shall also form by far the largest part of the superstructure. To quote the words of Pope, describing the empire of Dullness:—

'Beneath her foot-stool Science groans in chains,
And Wit dreads exile, penalties and pains.
There foam'd rebellious Logic, gagged and bound,
There stript fair Rhetoric languish'd on the ground.

* * *

Mad Mathesis alone was unconfined,
Too mad for mere material chains to bind,
Now to pure space lifts her ecstatic stare,
Now running round the circle finds it square.'

But our boys and girls to-day are so busy with Conic Sections and the Differential Calculus, and Sines and Co-sines, etc., etc., that they have no time to wander along the pleasant path of wit and wisdom. The humanities must give place to Mechanics, and the children of the present day must take all their Literature, ancient and modern, English and Foreign, from dreary grammars and mutilated text-books, which seem to have been prepared after the fashion of pemmican, to get the largest amount of mental pabulum into the smallest possible compass, or as though the Department—

'thought, like Otaheitan cooks,
No food was fit to eat till they had chewed it.'

... To quote Pope once again, the old truth stands—

'The proper study of mankind is man.'

Miss Badham went on to speak of education for girls. Despite all the 'nonsense talked about the "Rights of Women" and the "Higher Development" of her nature, the fact remains that her highest and happiest destiny is to be a wife and mother; and any scheme of education which unfits women for their natural place in life cannot be good'.

The modern young woman was not necessarily an improvement on the Victorian woman. The latter was accomplished in domestic economy, languages, painting and wrote 'exquisite English'. She valued self-control as highly as self-expression. By contrast, the modern young woman:

... has been, perchance, overloaded with Mathematics, and decorated, with heads and tails of Physiology and Botany and Geology, and second-hand trimmings of a little Language and Literature. An overcrowded brain must seek some relief, so the product of our modern system devotes her holidays to strenuous exercise, hockey and tennis and golf, till, as a friend of mine said the other day, 'she has made her body as tough as her mind.'

Miss Badham stated that abolition of fees in the state system was of little significance, since any student of Sydney Girls' High unable to pay fees in the past had had them waived. She further claimed that, despite the wording of the 1912 Bursary Endowment Act, bursaries were only valid for state high schools, so that if a S.C.E.G.G.S. girl gained a bursary, she could not use it at S.C.E.G.G.S. This was, in fact, not the case.

The Report concluded with a declaration that the criticisms were meant for the system, not individuals. Indeed, she said:

As a School, we have met with courtesy from the officials from the Director downwards; the alarming Inspector turned out to be a most pleasant and sympathetic man, and we should offer no objection to his inspecting this school at any time. It is not inspection we object to, it is Dictation as to what we shall teach and how we shall teach it, with the consequent result of the lowering of our standards in all language classes, which is obvious both to our examiners and to ourselves at the close of this our 19th school year. 'Luceat Lux Vestra' is our motto, and we should prefer to keep our lamps trimmed.

'Registered Schools and the Syllabus' shows Miss Badham still holding fervently the same educational ideals she had had twenty years earlier, influenced by her father's educational theories. Hence she had a strong preference for a classical education and its product: a woman or man of refinement, wit and clarity of thought. She was still unwilling to push many girls towards examinations and tertiary education, and she trained them to be good wives and mothers rather than career women. Her criticism of the new syllabus is important for two reasons. First, it reveals that education in Australia was still in its infancy. The establishment of an *Australian* education meant that appropriate Australian content had to be included in subjects like English literature and modern history. A local culture was barely recognisable in 1914, so that cultural reserves were meagre. The educational issue was part of Australia's search for a national identity. The experiences of the Anzacs in World War I were to contribute richly to Australia's sense of identity.

It is a pity that the lecturers from Sydney Teachers' College, who drew up their makeshift syllabus, did not consult experienced and brilliant educators like Edith Badham in their daunting task. The syllabus would have been both more sophisticated and more practical had such advice been sought and implemented.

The reforms engineered by Peter Board produced a crisis for schools like S.C.E.G.G.S. In the state system, secondary schools were henceforth streamed along academic and vocational lines. The high schools offered academic work for those intending to proceed to the University or colleges. Other secondary schools, often only extending to Intermediate level, offered more practical subjects. Hence Miss Badham's comments on the lack of weight on the accomplishment subjects and her criticism of the burden of academic content thrust upon secondary pupils. Edith Badham had to decide what course S.C.E.G.G.S. would pursue. Would it provide a strictly academic curriculum, or offer a broader range of subjects? Would Miss Badham encourage more pupils to take up tertiary study or continue to train her girls to be good wives and mothers?

A prospectus for S.C.E.G.G.S. and the two branch schools, published in about 1916, provides some clues. It is clear from the North Sydney branch section that the course was fairly strongly academic. It was:

. . . a sound general course, including English, Latin, Greek (optional), French, Mathematics, History, Botany (optional), Geology (optional) and Geography. Geography is only taught in the upper classes to those who do not learn Latin. Needlework only in Lower School.

The pupils . . . enter the Four Years' Course prescribed by the Department of Public Instruction.

In its prospectus Head School listed the extra subjects, which included piano (taught by at least four visiting teachers), violin, singing, drawing and painting, French, German, dancing, physical culture and fencing. Leaving Certificate results published in *Lux* show that a classical academic curriculum was still offered. It consisted of mathematics, Latin, Greek, English and history, as well as geography, German, French, botany and geology. Miss Badham's solution was to continue to offer a broader education than that available to high school pupils in the state system. In addition to the academic subjects taught

Playing tennis, 1907–1908. From left*: Laura Haydon, Doris Rook, Bell Dugan, Eileen O'Connor.* Below*: The tennis A team, 1915. Note the initials S.C.E.G.G.S. on the blazer pocket.* From left*: Sadie Carr, Lella Trindall, Gwen Scott, Marjory Hesslein.*

in accordance with the state requirements for registration, a range of accomplishment and practical subjects were also offered for those girls who did not intend to proceed to tertiary education. In essence, Badham's fear was that the state would dictate educational policy to her.

World War I dominated Australian life in the years from 1914 to 1918. Its impact was felt more keenly in the boys' schools than the girls', because of the great drain on manpower which the war exacted. Many Old Boys served as soldiers. Some were killed and others wounded, and in addition there was a drastic shortage of male teachers because many teachers, actual or prospective, went to the war also. Honour boards in boys' schools bear witness to the losses sustained by school communities. By 1918 the Headmaster of The King's School claimed that as many Old Boys were on active service as had been turned out over a twenty year period.[7] Australia had the highest casualty rate of any Empire army.[8]

In the editorial of *Lux*, October 1914, Edith Badham spoke of the significance of the war for S.C.E.G.G.S. The immense support for the Imperial cause in Australia generally is demonstrated:

> *It is impossible just now to think, or speak, or write of anything but the war, the war of which many have said, for years past, that it must come and that when it comes it will be the most dreadful war that the world has ever seen. And now we are in the midst of it . . . It is quite unnecessary to say anything about the justice of our cause. We all know that we are fighting, not only to fulfil our most sacred obligations and to crush an unscrupulous and barbarous tyranny, but to preserve our own Empire and the liberty for which it stands.*
>
> *Some of you have already said good-bye to those you love, and are watching anxiously for tidings from day to day; others must do so in the near future; if it is a brave man who goes to fight for his country, it is no less a brave woman who helps equip her man for the fight, and sends him forth with smiles and words of hope. And those who are not called upon for this supreme act of self-sacrifice can help their country, as you are doing, by working for the soldiers and for those whom the war has plunged into poverty, and by giving all they can spare to the different War Funds.*[9]

The war became a major preoccupation for S.C.E.G.G.S. Most teachers and pupils had brothers, husbands, fathers and fiancés on active service. *Lux* published a list of all men engaged in the war who were connected in some way with the school. By 1918 the list contained nearly 500 names and a further list of those killed contained 102 names. The war left no family untouched: everyone suffered the loss of relatives or friends.

S.C.E.G.G.S.'s contribution to the war effort was to raise money for the Belgian and War Chest Funds: by July 1915, £165 had been collected. The Old Girls lent strong support to the school in the fundraising, and the girls knitted kits for the Shore volunteers. Sewing classes were devoted to making garments for the Belgian Relief Fund. Various fundraising entertainments were organised, such as the Lantern Entertainment where slides were to be exhibited by lantern: admission was 1s 0d for adults and 6d for schoolboys, schoolgirls and children.

At least two S.C.E.G.G.S. Old Girls volunteered for active service. Joan Twynam went to the front as a nurse in 1915 and was present at the Allied landing at Gallipoli. *Lux* comments: 'We hope she will write to us and that her letters will escape the Censor's kind attention.' Olive Kelso King drove her own motor car in the services of the wounded in the north of France, then in Serbia.

There was a strong link with Shore school. The first two Headmasters of Shore, E. I. Robson (1889–1900) and C. H. Hodges (1900–1910) served on the S.C.E.G.G.S.' Council. Many girls had friends and brothers at Shore. The first issue of *Lux* after the outbreak of the war contains this note: 'We wish heartily to congratulate the Church of England Grammar School on the number of its Old Boys who have joined the volunteers to the war, and to offer our sympathy for the death of Captain Brian Pockley, though at the same time we, like everyone else, are full of admiration at the manner of it.' B. C. A. Pockley was the first Australian officer killed in the war and of him Sherington says: 'His death symbolised what would become a growing concern—the loss of so many men of promise in the rising generation.'[10]

The girls and women of S.C.E.G.G.S. were mostly spectators of the war. In an anonymous short article, 'Play up! Play up! And play the Game', in *Lux* in 1915, the difficulty of this passive role was explored:

> *. . . But there is another warfare, another game—a siege warfare without music or tattoo of drums, a game without exultation or racing of the blood where the 'Play up' bugle call reaches but hardly.*
>
> *To live among the grey things, the necessary things, the commonplace things, without heartsickness, to play the game up to the hilt every moment of it, never to lose courage but to face the threadbare tasks with fresh courage and quiet gaiety every morning—this also is a game which calls for endurance and self-control and pluck . . . Remembering how schoolboys throughout the world are carrying the rules of their school games with them into the battle, may we take heart and play our lesser game of commonplace, not altogether unlike the way in which they are playing the great game of Empire!*[11]

The social repercussions of the war meant that many of the women Miss Badham had trained to be wives and mothers remained single because of the number of men killed in the war. Nearly 60 000 Australian men had died. Dorothea Baltzer, an Old Girl, stated: 'When the war was over . . . there was not the chance of marrying, and then people began to think, "Oh, why should I just wander around?" ' She remembers girls who had formerly spent their time going to dances and amusing themselves socially, now joining the workforce. Her father had always employed male clerks and typists before the war, but with the shortage of men during and after the war, women gradually took over the clerical work.[12]

The war affected relationships in another way. Fraulein Fast, the German teacher at S.C.E.G.G.S., died in April 1916. She had only three pupils at the time and German was discontinued. Shortly after there were complaints at the North Sydney branch about the presence of three German girls at the school. Parents threatened to withdraw their daughters if the girls remained. Miss Dumolo recommended that the girls be allowed to stay. She said that they were particularly nice girls and she had observed no difficulty in the school. The next month, however, Mrs Weinlig wrote to say that her daughters would shortly be leaving Australia.[13] This was in accordance with government policy.

Marjorie Hesslein recalled the announcement that war had begun:

> *I can remember Miss Badham coming at about lunchtime, I suppose, coming back from town and she called all the girls—there weren't so very many . . . There was a big gum tree, I can just see it all, a gum tree below the main house and the school classrooms, and it was all rough, just where the new buildings were, and Miss*

The staff 1917. Back row: *Miss Nesbitt, Miss Dorothea Flower, Miss Maria Skinner, Miss Lily Ward, Miss Margaret Elliott, Miss Fanny Smith, Miss Eleanor Watson, Miss Stella Scroggie;* front row: *Miss Millicent Harwood, Miss Elsie Capper, Miss Florence Wood, Miss Emma Noad, Miss Edith Badham (Headmistress), Mr Wilfred Docker (Hon. Treasurer), Rev. E.C. Beck (Chaplain, Hon. Secretary), Madame Laura Dunn, Miss Bertha Pasley, Miss Charlotte Gilfillan, Miss Ellie Smith.*

> *Badham read out the paper, because that was the only way we could hear that England was at war, and she had just brought the paper home.*[14]

In 1915 on the first day of term, the school was taken to College Street to see the route march of the First Australian Expeditionary Force. *Lux* commented: 'The splendid Light Horse, the no less fine Infantry and Artillery, the bands and the Colours formed a sight which none of us will ever forget.' Marjorie Hesslein remembers the troops marching past the school:

> *The troops would go from their camps to Moore Park or the Showground and they'd stay the night for two days or so before they left and then they'd march down, at about five o'clock in the morning from the Showground down Bourke Street to Woolloomooloo, where they'd board the ships and we'd wake up and hear the band playing, and if any relations of any of the girls—I remember the Shields' brother was one—and we went down there, we were allowed to run down, and it was very exciting in the mornings, you know, on the cold mornings going down and seeing them all. And really we didn't realise what it was, you know, when you think about it now, how terrible it was.*[15]

Other reminders of the war were the letters (reprinted in *Lux*) from Old Girls in England and Europe which described wartime conditions. Marjorie Hesslein saw the prisoners of war from New Guinea marched up Forbes Street to Darlinghurst gaol.[16] Opposite the school Rose Hall became a convalescent home for returned soldiers. The death of Lord Kitchener affected Miss Badham deeply. Mary Beith, a boarder at the time, remembers: 'We were all sitting in the annexe and she got the paper and found out that he was dead. And she was in a towering rage. We didn't see her for days after that.'[17]

In her Annual Report of 1916, Edith Badham dwelt at length on the loss of Kitchener. After announcing that his portrait would be hung in the Main Hall opposite the picture of King Edward VII, she spoke of his religion. Her remarks give some insight into her own kind of faith:

> *We have heard that he was a religious man, with the only kind of religion that is really worth anything—the kind that moulds the whole life, and that sees in duty 'the Godhead's most benignant grace.' But which of us would have suspected that his favourite hymn was 'Abide with Me'.*[18]

During the war, many bereaved people pressured clergy to pray for their dead. Sydney Anglican clergy for the most part did not do so as they regarded the practice as unscriptural.[19] Badham's solution was to pray for the dead in classical Greek. The war certainly heightened religious awareness as people faced death and bereavement: it was a period of unparalleled self-analysis for the church.[20] Twice *Lux* printed prophecies about the Antichrist by a certain sixteenth century French monk named Brother Johannes. The prophecies were published under the title: 'Kaiser Antichrist'. Although *Lux* could not vouch for their authenticity, the prophecies proved immensely popular, causing 'a profound impression'. Support for the war cause had become a kind of religious sentiment. In her Annual Report for 1916, Miss Badham said: 'We are all sharing in a common anxiety, a common grief and a common glory, and it is some comfort to know even in the midst of deep distress, that so many are joined in sorrow and sympathy, and that so many will share in the joy with which our returning heroes will be welcomed back to us.'

The Council minute books reveal the financial strains imposed by the war. In September 1914 the Council deferred raising school fees 'in view of the existing crisis'. A parent applying for a fee reduction in February 1916 was told that the Council was not likely to make any concession as, on account of the war, it had refrained from raising the school fees. The Head School and the North Sydney branch had decided that the girls would forego their prizes, receiving certificates instead, and the money saved would be given to the Patriotic Fund. Salaries were below those for staff at other schools.[21] The Council wanted to make extensive additions at the three schools, but said that 'in these days of high prices and much unrest it is felt necessary to proceed with the greatest caution'.[22] However, the fees of one girl, Olga Palmer, were to be reduced (not waived) because the brother who had been paying her fees had been killed in action.[23]

In line with other corporate schools, enrolments had risen. This was partly a result of Peter Board's reforms, which had caused the closure of many independent schools. At Head School there were 119 enrolled in 1914 and 161 in 1917. By 1917 the North Sydney branch had 133 pupils.[24] The schools were overcrowded and building was imperative. The S.C.E.G.G.S. Council was approached in 1918 to take over two more schools: a private school in Beecroft and 'Meriden' at Strathfield.[25] Both offers were rejected.

Two factors explain the Council's apparent reluctance to expand the S.C.E.G.G.S. empire. First, finances did not permit it. The Council's reply to the Beecroft proposal was that it could not be entertained at the moment. In the case of Meriden, the Council 'regretted that in view of its present financial obligations it was unable to entertain the proposition'.[26] Finances were tight for a number of reasons. The Bowral school never ran at a profit and its finances were a continual source of concern. Inflation had pushed up salaries while the Council endeavoured to keep fees down. During the war years urgent building and maintenance work at the school had been postponed and required attention. On top of this, the influenza epidemic for 1919 meant that in February there was no money to meet costs because many fees had not been paid.[27]

Second, in addition to financial considerations, the Council and its Principal were old and tired. The strains of the war years, the deaths of some Council members and the age of the others, and the deteriorating health of the Principal meant that by the end of the war S.C.E.G.G.S. was in the doldrums.[28]

Five people had been on the Council since its inception: Docker, Beck, French, Christian and Selby. By 1915 this amounted to twenty years' service. Most Council members were not recent appointments. Ill health, old age and death were the sad refrain of the years until 1920. In 1910 Hodges had resigned because of ill health, and was soon to be confined to a wheelchair. Mrs Selby resigned in 1915 because of ill health; Mrs Christian was widowed in 1918 and died a few months later; Mr Docker died in 1919.[29]

Docker's last months on the Council were not entirely happy. In a disagreement with the Council over the decision to pay Mr Russell, a solicitor, legal fees for his work, Docker tendered his resignation, stating that he regarded the Council's action as a want of confidence in himself as Treasurer and also as a personal slight. He then withdrew from the meeting.[30] It seems to have been the action of a man who was old and set in his ways, and who was accustomed to having his own way on Council. As Treasurer he had never charged the Council fees, and he did not see why Russell should not be solicitor in an honorary capacity. The increased financial strains imposed by the war may have meant that Russell needed to charge for his legal services. The Council accepted Docker's resignation 'with very great regret' and the Secretary was instructed to inform Docker that '. . . the Council has the deepest appreciation of his valuable and unstinted services rendered to the school for so many years, has always had, and still has, the most undoubting confidence in him, and trusts he may see his way clear to remaining in office.'[31] Docker came back to the Council but died two months later.[32]

Miss Badham was also seriously ill from March 1918 until her death in May 1920. She missed many Council meetings and her contributions were no longer those of a Principal in her prime: she raised a number of housekeeping matters, for example, and also proposed that a chapel be erected in Docker's memory. Her acerbic wit had not disappeared though. Of Marjorie Hudson, a student who held a scholarship (then called an exhibition), she said, 'Her work was very good but her character was just the reverse.'[33]

The epidemic of pneumonic influenza which swept the country in 1919, killing 11 500 people, added to the school's burdens. Beck reported:

> *. . . the work of the Grammar School has been seriously interfered with; attendance of pupils has been uncertain, the enrolment has diminished, and the actual teaching has been carried out under great difficulties; however it is a matter for congratulation that the school has not suffered more than it already has. In order that the girls should suffer as little as possible, the school year was divided into three terms instead of four.*[34]

Badham's comments on the epidemic appeared in her last annual report:

First annual Old Girls' Union Dinner, held 17 July 1917 in the Barham dining room.

> *Then 1919 brought with it pneumonic influenza with all the trouble, confusion and anxiety which came in its train. What with the demands of the Board of Health, and the changes made by the Board of Education in their endeavour to meet the case, we did not know from one day to another what we were going to do. We attended an august meeting convened by the Minister for Health arrayed in shirt sleeves and a mask. The weather was hot. We also wore the regulation strip of muslin across our noses and mouths, the principal effect of which was to produce a most un-Christian feeling towards the powers that be . . . We instituted correspondence classes, and all the time we had to keep the school going for the sake of the faithful few—mainly the examination girls—who worked all through with a wholeheartedness which some people cynically ascribed to their having nothing else to think about! They were mostly boarders or temporary boarders; their conduct was splendid, and considerably lightened our labours; but I must confess that the conversation of VIA at my own table at meal times, was so learned generally, and especially so classical, that I began to wonder how long I should be able to rise to the occasion.*[35]

The epidemic caused delays in the payment of school fees and the Council had to seek to meet expenses by a £1000 overdraft. There were no external examinations for the S.C.E.G.G.S. girls in 1919 because of the epidemic, and fewer prizes were awarded. None of the girls or staff seems to have died, but several were dangerously ill, one girl lost a brother and others nursed the victims.

In the twilight years of the Badham era, there is one encouraging and significant area of achievement: the quality of the Old Girls and their support for the school after they left S.C.E.G.G.S. The strength of the Old Girl network and the calibre of its individuals was largely the work of Edith Badham. The earliest copies of *Lux* show Badham's deliberate policy of cultivating the Old Girls. There was always an Old Girls' section in *Lux* which gave news and described Old Girls' functions. The first Old Girl's wedding was described at length in 1900[36] and in 1901 it noted that the first Old Girl to enrol at the University, Nellie Amos, had completed her second year there.[37]

Travel, trips from country properties into town, bereavements, marriage and babies constituted most of the news. In addition to the Old Girls' Notes, Miss Badham referred to the Old Girls often in Annual Reports, in editorials and in the occasional open letter. One written in 1904 shows the ways Badham kept in contact with the Old Girls. Ascension Day had been the traditional day for the Old Girls to gather for a picnic. Invitation cards would be sent out and this had led at times to some being overlooked. Edith Badham outlined her plans for future gatherings:

> *For the future I propose to have a Garden Fete, here in the School Garden, every Ascension Day, from 2.00 pm till 6.00 pm. We shall try to provide different kinds of amusement, and shall always give notice, both of the Fete, and of the hours for the Cathedral Service . . .*
>
> *In the next place, I am going to give up being 'at home' to receive the Old Girls on the first Tuesday in each month. I have given up all kinds of invitations in order to be 'at home' and the numbers who generally come vary from two to none . . . in future, I wish to set aside two afternoons during the year, the SECOND THURSDAY in August, and the SECOND THURSDAY in November, on which I hope that all the Old Girls will meet here.*[38]

A grandchildren's party was recorded in *Lux* in 1918: 'The lily pond was a great attraction, especially as some of the younger guests were informed that crocodiles lurked in its depths.'[39]

An Old Girls' Union was formally established in 1909 when a president, secretary and treasurer, and executive committee of five members were elected for the first time.[40] The president was Miss Badham (until her death in 1920), and the annual subscription was 3s 0d per year. Of this, 2s 0d went to pay for four copies of *Lux* and the remaining 1s 0d to a general fund from which the Old Girls awarded an annual prize for English literature, and from which gifts could be made to the school. A frame for a portrait of Edward VII was their first purchase. Old girls' unions were not unusual in Sydney girls' schools. The S.C.E.G.G.S. one was to prove unusually active and immensely useful to the school in later years.

The Old Girls' Union was an important part of the S.C.E.G.G.S. tradition by the end of Miss Badham's time. Miss Badham had encouraged her Old Girls to maintain contact with the school and by 1906 they had engaged in their first fundraising exercise. This was to raise money towards building the school hospital.[41]

Fundraising efforts during the war meant that a common purpose bound the S.C.E.G.G.S. community, past and present, together. Edith Badham said in her 1915 Report: 'I think if anything had been needed to draw our Old Girls' Union more close to us, the war would have been the means of doing that.'[42] There was no organised parent body such as a ladies' auxiliary to raise money or foster community bonds in the school and between school and the wider community. The Old Girls' Union performed these functions for S.C.E.G.G.S.

The east side of Barham showing the lily pond, c.1910.

Old Girls came back to the school as teachers, the earliest being Ruth Murray Prior and Ida Horrocks. Each had been Dux of her year. The great majority of Old Girls travelled, helped keep house, and finally married. A few went to the University and were successful in other non-domestic endeavours. For example, in 1910 Freda Du Faur was the first woman to climb to the top of Mt Cook, the highest peak in the Southern Alps in the South Island of New Zealand. In 1912 she was the first alpinist to ascend Mt Tasman, the second highest peak in the Southern Alps. Miss Badham was proud of her:

> *Miss Du Faur writes with an arresting simplicity, which usually marks the doers of fine things, of toilsome and prolonged climbs, in the teeth of bitter wind, over the fields when not only each step, but even grip holes for the fingers must be cut with the axe. We hope to make arrangements for publishing the ascent of Mt. Tasman, with some illustrations, in the next number of* Lux.[43]

Freda Du Faur published an account of her exploits in an entertaining book, *The Conquest of Mount Cook and other Climbs*, published in 1915. It was republished in 1975. The Visitors' Centre at Mt Cook has a life-size wax model of her standing with ice-pick in her right hand and rocks towering behind her. She has a determined face, not unlike Edith Badham's, and is wearing a white blouse with lace insertions, navy skirt and ornamented belt. These were the clothes she set out in for her climbs. Once out of sight of civilization, she wore more suitable mountaineering gear. The model was taken from a photograph of Du Faur which is part of a display of early mountaineers of Mt Cook.

She was the kind of woman Edith Badham would have been proud to have

Freda du Faur was the first woman to ascend Mt Cook and the first alpinist to ascend Mt Tasman. She was at school from 1896–1898. (Courtesy Canterbury Museum, Christchurch, New Zealand)

educated as she was a woman of character and real independence of spirit. She had a goal which she pursued until it was gained. In addition she was a gentlewoman, although frustrated by the conventions of the times. On arrival at the Hermitage, Mt Cook, she expressed her intention of climbing Mt Sealy:

> *Mount Sealy requires a bivouac . . . as I was a girl, travelling alone, the women in the house considered themselves more or less responsible for my actions. As soon as I announced, when asked, that I was going to climb Mount Sealy alone with a guide, I found myself up against all the cherished conventions of the middle-aged . . . they assured me in all seriousness that if I went out alone with a guide I would lose my reputation.*
>
> *The fact that the guide in question was Peter Graham, whose reputation as a man was one at which the most rigid moralist could not cavil, made no difference . . . One old lady implored me with tears in her eyes not to 'spoil my life for so small a thing as climbing a mountain'. I declined gently but firmly to believe that it would be spoilt, and added, with some heat, I'm afraid, that if my reputation was so fragile a thing that it would not bear such a test, then I would be very well rid of a useless article.*
>
> *. . . I sought out Graham and told him that the female population was holding up hands of horror, and asked what we were going to do about it. He suggested a compromise in the shape of taking a porter with us.*

On the Mt Sealy climb:

> *The chaperon, weighted with rucksack, was depressingly slow and stolid, and eventually got left far behind . . . At first Graham, who led, turned round every minute or so to show me a hand or foot hold, or to give me a pull with the rope on what he considered a difficult bit. He evinced considerable surprise when he usually discovered me at his heels without the proferred assistance . . . By the time we reached the summit I was left severely alone to do as I pleased, and all the attention was directed to the porter, who was a novice on rock, and consequently rather unhappy. He was short in the limbs (and breath), and had visibly not been intended by nature for a mountaineer. As I watched his struggles it was borne upon me that I was not the only victim being offered up on the sacred altar of the conventions.*

Upon reaching the summit the chaperon slept off his exertions while Du Faur raised the possibility with Graham of climbing Mt Cook. During the difficult descent:

> *. . . the porter, who was nervous, slipped, lost his footing, and slid away down the slope. In less time than it takes to tell my axe handle was jammed in a crack with the rope around it, and the porter brought to a standstill before Graham had time to reach me. He exclaimed 'Where did you learn that?' 'I didn't learn it; I knew it—by instinct, I suppose', I answered, quite as surprised as he was . . . Meanwhile the porter, dangling on the rope, looked reproachful that we should discuss such a detail while he was so uncomfortable.*[44]

After describing her return from her ascent of Mt Cook the same year, Du Faur commented:

> *Superstitions die hard, and being perfectly well aware that the average person's idea of a woman capable of real mountaineering or any sport demanding physical fitness and good staying power, is a masculine-looking female with short hair, a loud voice and large feet, it always gives me particular pleasure to upset this pre-conceived picture. In the year of grace 1910 a love of fresh air exercise is not a purely masculine prerogative, fortunately, and should be quite easily associated with a love of beauty and personal daintiness, which the last generation deemed impossible except to the type of woman to whom personal adornment is the one serious pursuit in life . . . Consequently, I strolled out to dinner in my prettiest frock, and so supported was able to face the hotel full of curious strangers and the toasts and congratulations that were the order of the evening.*[45]

On her pioneering achievements she wrote:

> *Fortunately in this world, the wonder of one day is taken as a matter of course the next; so now, five years after my first fight for individual freedom, the girl climber at the Hermitage need expect nothing worse than raised eyebrows when she starts out unchaperoned and clad in climbing costume. It is some consolation to have achieved as much as this, and to have blazed one more little path through ignorance and convention, and added one tiny spark to the ever-growing beacon lighted by the women of this generation to help their fellow-traveller climb out of the dark woods and valleys of conventional tradition and gain the fresh, invigorating air and wideview-point of the mountain-tops.*[46]

Other Old Girls from Badham's time who achieved fame included Dorothy Gordon, the radio personality known as 'Andrea'; and Midge Caird, who married Michael Bruxner (sometime Minister for Transport and Deputy Premier of New South Wales), like many Old Girls made famous because of their husbands who became well-known. Margaret Henderson attended the Melba Conservatory in 1919 and *Lux* records that Dame Nellie Melba was so impressed with her voice that she offered her six months' training.

Ethel Turner's daughter, Jean Curlewis, was one of the two outstanding scholars of Badham's era. In 1915 she matriculated with first class honours in French and English and second class honours in Latin, obtaining A's in Italian and history. She did not go on to the University, but wrote *The Ship That Never Set Sail*, a book published in 1921. It was followed by three other novels which were boys' adventure stories. They sold poorly and Jean Curlewis was hampered by the inevitable comparisons drawn with her famous mother. She died in 1930, aged 31, and although she had undoubted literary talent, she did not live long enough to develop it into a mature adult style.[47]

In 1915 Grace Newbery, who had been an outstanding scholar at S.C.E.G.G.S., gained her BA with first class honours in classics and the University Classical Medal. Subsequently she attended Oxford University where her achievements were described as brilliant. She does not seem to have taken up a career but instead married and lived as a farmer's wife.

J. L. Rankin, whose poems and articles appeared in early numbers of *Lux*, published a book of poems in 1912. Miss Badham reviewed it thus: 'Her poems vary widely, and range through all kinds of themes, from the simplest to the most complex, but they convey the impression of one who has an idea, and seeks to express it in verse, not of one who, stringing hymns together, hunts round for an idea to set amongst them.'[48]

In her Annual Report of 1918 Edith Badham reviewed the growth of S.C.E.G.G.S. over the previous 23 years. She made a personal appeal that the school not be known as 'Miss Badham's School':

> *Miss Badham has no school, and never, at any period of her life, wished to have a school. If this is my school then . . . all sense of unity is lost . . . Everyone who knows anything of schools knows also that the most desirable asset that any school can have is that quality that is called* esprit de corps, *tradition or atmosphere . . . We are, even now, not very old as a School, only twenty-three years old, and it would have been hard to develop a strong tradition in that time: but we are a Church School, and our tradition goes back for 1900 years . . .*[49]

She went on to say that she was only a steward and that shortly it would be time for her to give an account of her stewardship. There would be other stewards to take up the work. By now she was fighting severe ill health and memories of some Old Girls who were new to the school in about 1920 were of a very frail old lady sitting in the sun in a wheelchair. During this time Miss Noad, the Headmistress, ran the school.

The qualities for which Edith Badham was remembered were her quick mind and tongue, her tenacity and vehemence when promoting her views, her outspokenness, her warmth, generosity and impulsiveness.[50] Although she was not possessive about S.C.E.G.G.S., the school was nonetheless her creation. What had been a temporary appointment of six months had become 25 years of dedicated work. The school was her family to rear and nurture. Her literary

Senior girls in 1917: class VIB. Back row from left (standing)*: Enid Norton, Alex Trindall, Liska Woodhouse, Mary Sinclair;* middle row (seated)*: Lillian King, Olive Mette, Gwendolyn Scott, Lilian Cannan, Maie Baum, Marjorie Wylie;* front (sitting on floor)*: Josephine Seaton*

talent, her fierce love and her creative ability she concentrated on her high-class school for girls.

Her 25 years at S.C.E.G.G.S. had achieved a great deal. Under her headship the school was firmly established, with 190 girls enrolled in 1920. The school had a very good reputation for Christian standards, quality academic education and its emphasis on training pupils to become young ladies. Some S.C.E.G.G.S. girls had made their mark at the University, many others made significant contributions to the community. Badham's high standards were a model for both staff and girls.

The school was so stamped with her personality that her successor's task was an unenviable one. The effect of her death 'in the saddle' produced a sort of Badham cult which automatically generated hostility to the next Principal.

— 8 —

Dorothy Wilkinson's first decade, 1920–1930

EDITH ANNESLEY BADHAM died on 17 May 1920. The Council of May 1920 recorded 'its profound sense of loss at the death of Miss Badham, first Principal of S.C.E.G.G.S.'. Whilst Council members, especially the older ones, may have felt lost with the removal of the school's key figure, they must not have been taken by surprise, as Miss Badham's ill health had pointed to her imminent retirement or death. They appointed a subcommittee the same afternoon to consider all matters relating to the appointment of a new Head. Mrs MacCallum, Mrs Street, Beck and Cowper formed the subcommittee.[1] Advertisements were to be placed in the *Herald*, the *Telegraph*, the two church papers (the *Australian Church Record* and the *Church Standard*), the Melbourne *Argus*, the Queensland *Courier* and newspapers in South Australia, Western Australia, Tasmania and New Zealand. The new Principal had to be a communicant member of the Church of England and was asked to furnish references, her age and when she would be able to commence as Principal.

By September there were thirteen applications for the position and a shortlist of five was chosen: Miss Bevington, Miss Ironside, Miss Dumolo (of the North Sydney branch), Miss Lenthall and Miss Wilkinson. Only Miss Wilkinson and Miss Bevington were interviewed.[2] Because Miss Wilkinson was living in Launceston, Miss Williams, Principal of the Women's College, was invited to give her opinion on Miss Wilkinson's qualifications. The Council found her information valuable and invited Miss Wilkinson to Sydney to be interviewed by the Council. Miss Wilkinson was given to understand that this did not necessarily mean that she would be appointed Principal.

As it turned out, in October the Council offered her the position and she accepted promptly.[3] She appointed Miss Noad to choose any staff necessary for the new year and when she left her school in Launceston, her mother took charge there with a salaried head to carry on the schoolwork.

Dorothy Irene Wilkinson was born on 22 May 1883. She was 37 years old when she became Principal of S.C.E.G.G.S. She had been born in England, in

Miss Dorothy Irene Wilkinson, Headmistress 1921–1947.

Up Holland, Lancashire. Her father, Christopher Wilkinson, was recruited by Bishop Montgomery in 1889, and emigrated to Tasmania to be Rector of the parishes of Wynyard, Burnie and St Leonards. In 1895 he became Headmaster of Launceston Church Grammar School, where he remained for 22 years. In 1896 Dorothy was sent back to England for her secondary education to a school called Casterton, at Westmoreland, in the Lakes District.

Casterton is famous as the school Charlotte Bronte attended, and as the original model for the terrible 'Lowood' of *Jane Eyre*. It was a school for the daughters of clergy and its historian argues that Lowood was not an accurate picture of the Casterton attended by Charlotte Bronte.[4] When Dorothy Wilkinson was a pupil, Miss Williams, who had become Headmistress two years earlier, had eased the severity of the discipline, encouraged academic excellence and fostered music through concerts, choirs and organ recitals. She raised the status of sport, especially cricket, tennis and hockey, leasing ground for games fields and organising inter-school matches.[5] Dorothy Wilkinson was a good student, gaining the Royal Society's Medal for Physical Geography in the Senior Cambridge Examination[6] and gaining a Second Class Pass overall. She was a fast runner and played hockey at school and later at university.

She returned to Tasmania in 1900 and helped her mother run the boarding house at Launceston Church Grammar School. At some stage she became involved with teaching her father's junior pupils. In 1912 she gained her Diploma of Education and, the following year, her BA from the University of Melbourne. For a short time after that she taught at Church of England Grammar School in Melbourne, returning in 1915 to start her own school, Broadland House, in Launceston. In 1920 she gained an MA from the University of Melbourne.

The original Broadland House, situated in Elizabeth Street, had been a private school belonging to Miss J. C. Hogg. Miss Hogg sold her school and lent her building to Miss Mary Hogg and Miss H. Middleton. When Miss Hogg and Miss Middleton moved the school from Elizabeth Street to its present site in Lyttleton Street in 1915, Miss J. C. Hogg was annoyed and asked Dorothy Wilkinson to start another school in the Elizabeth Street building. It was called the Church of England Girls' Grammar School, Broadland House. Soon there were two educational institutions calling themselves Broadland House.[7] In the space of six years, Dorothy (also known as Doris) Wilkinson had built her school into a financially sound institution, 200 pupils strong.[8]

When her father retired from Launceston Church Grammar School (LCGS) in 1918, Miss Wilkinson's parents came to live with her at the Broadland House school. It is clear from the scanty information available that Dorothy Wilkinson, like Edith Badham, was strongly influenced by her father. He is described in Rait's LCGS history as 'pre-eminently a scholar, and was firm, dignified and impersonal but with a very kindly bearing and manner. He was greatly loved by all the boys, and his courtesy and kindness, probity and uprightness, made him loved by all. He was one of the "Grand Old Man" type of headmasters.'[9] While dissimilar in some aspects of personality, father and daughter shared a common love of schools, not simply teaching in them but running them. There was a very strong bond between Dorothy and her father, until his death in 1929. Mrs Wilkinson was similarly deeply involved in schools: as matron and house manager at LCGS and later at the Elizabeth Street Broadland's. Father, mother and daughter were all remembered for their warmth and love for people.

Dorothy Wilkinson was a contrast to Edith Badham. Impulsive, warm, frank, spontaneous and utterly disregarding of personal dignity, she must have seemed an unsuitable successor for those seeking a replacement in the Badham mould. She 'half-ran' instead of walking, her hair was often untidy and even in a formal photograph (taken at the opening of the gymnasium wing in 1925) she is turning to talk to somebody behind her. She was described as completely unselfish, acting out her deep Christian faith in a concern for other people and in this she was both sensitive and wise.

A short note about her in *Lux* was prophetic, if understated:

> *We are fortunate in having seen our new Principal, and having seen her, we feel that we are fortunate. We gathered from her little address to us that her watchword will be 'forward'. Construction, not destruction, will be her aim. To quote her own words, we must make the school worthy of the soul of the great woman who was its first Principal. Other Principals will come and be forgotten, but the name of Miss Badham will sound like a clarion through the ages, and to quote her own words, 'We must make the school worthy of the ideals she laid down for it.'*[10]

The language here is cool, not warm. The implications of a Wilkinson 'constructive' policy are a threat to the Badham ways: an intimation of change (and decay). Miss Wilkinson's diplomacy and graciousness are evident in the diplomatic manner in which she praised Edith Badham. The strongest statement by the author of the note—'other Principals will come and be forgotten'—is that Miss Badham is of such stature that her headship will dwarf subsequent ones. A daunting welcome to the new incumbent.

Nearly twenty years later, Dorothy Wilkinson spoke of her first impressions of S.C.E.G.G.S.:

> *I shall never forget my first sight of the school, and the hopeless feeling of institutionalism, of bricks and mortar, which overpowered me and made me remember my own little school in Launceston, and the love and sunshine waiting for me there. And so I faced my first Council meeting, presided over by the kindly Bishop Co-adjutor, then Archdeacon Darcy-Irvine. 'No one could see visions and dream dreams there,' I told them. Yet within 48 hours I had burnt my boats, gripped by the problems and possibilities of this School.*[11]

On 2 March, the Old Girls held a welcome function for the new Principal. In her speech Miss Wilkinson raised the Old Girls' hackles by observing that many things were wrong with S.C.E.G.G.S. She stated that the school should be moved from the Darlinghurst site, giving as her reasons the unsavoury locality, the cramped grounds, and the necessity for up-to-date classrooms and teaching facilities. It did not matter that she had planned a weekly 'at home' to get to know the Old Girls better; nor that she had included them in her plans for future expansion. She completed her implicit criticism of her predecessor's work by concluding: 'The school is what it is in spite of its limitations.'[12]

Mrs W. Sharland, author of the 1955 S.C.E.G.G.S. history as well as a member of staff and a good friend of Dorothy Wilkinson, remembered the issues clearly:

> *Well, the Badhamites . . . she [Wilkinson] told me, 'When I came to the school I realised that things had been left to slide.' They had to because Miss Badham was in no physical condition to look after them. So [Wilkinson] said, 'Those were the first things that I had to cope with. 'Well, the minute she started changing anything, the Badhamites, you see, just made themselves as unpleasant as they possibly could, and I think they really gave her hell. But she went on. She realised things had to be done in spite of all this frightful opposition from the Badhamites, as they were called, and she had a very, very difficult start, because there was all this opposition to everything in the way of what they thought, you see, was casting aspersions on their beloved headmistress.*[13]

Miss Wilkinson was soon nicknamed 'Stick', short for 'Sticky Beak', because she seemed to be everywhere, finding out all she could about the details of the school. It was a term of abuse at the beginning, but the name remained, and later on people thought of it as a term of endearment. It came to mean one who 'stuck by' people, someone dependable. Mrs Sharland described her thus:

> *She was completely sui generis. It's very hard to describe, isn't it? Completely sincere, and her own individuality all the time, and didn't care two hoots for other people's opinions. I mean, unless they were worth listening to. But criticism and that sort of thing, unless it was well-informed, would just pass over her. And absolutely devoted to the girls, of course. She used to call the boarders her dear noisy boarders. I don't think she had any feeling of, the word isn't superiority, but I*

mean, being as Headmistress and they being girls . . . [She was] without any sort of personal . . . the word isn't dignity, but, for example, she'd wash her hair and she wouldn't mind at all the girls seeing her, you know, all loose, hanging drying.[14]

There is no information about Dorothy Wilkinson's educational views when she came to S.C.E.G.G.S., unlike Badham, who spelt out her objectives prior to starting S.C.E.G.G.S. The changes Miss Wilkinson proposed were mostly to do with the school's physical environment. Her other concern was for good relationships to the extent that people later claimed that she not only had an extraordinary memory for names but also for character and personality.[15] She was primarily a practical person rather than an academic, despite her MA.

There was minimal change in the composition of the Council and the teaching staff in Miss Wilkinson's first year. Miss Noad, the First Assistant, on the staff since 1913, resigned soon after Miss Wilkinson's arrival, and three more staff left at the end of 1921.[16] Two Council members resigned: Archdeacon Darcy-Irvine and R. G. I. Dent, but the stalwarts remained. In addition, there was now a representative of the Old Girls' Union on the Council: Mrs Lilian Sargood,[17] the Old Girls' Union president. The Council minutes for November 1920 record that two Old Girls could now be appointed by their Union to represent the Old Girls on the Council.[18] This had happened as a result of the Council's desire to forge stronger ties between the Old Girls and the Council.[19] The Council seems to have lent Miss Wilkinson their support and the minutes give no hint of difficult relations between Principal and Council.

Even before Miss Wilkinson took up her position at S.C.E.G.G.S., in the November Council meeting of 1920, the matter of the school's location was raised and the possibility of removing the school was aired. This must have been precipitated by her stated views on its existing location. Two properties on the market—Kambala at Bellevue Hill, and Grantham at Potts Point—were considered as alternative sites. Kambala was rejected, but the Treasurer was requested to secure an option over Grantham. Further investigation showed that Grantham was beyond S.C.E.G.G.S.'s pocket, on the market at £21 000 with the additional expenses of heavy rates and new buildings.[20]

In June 1921 Mrs Street, with Miss Wilkinson and the female members of the Council, inspected the school thoroughly and presented a report which recommended increased accommodation, bedroom renovations and new furniture. By September the first renovations had been carried out to Miss Wilkinson's satisfaction and further additions and renovations were planned at an estimated cost of £4000.[21]

The arrival of Dorothy Wilkinson with her enthusiasm, human warmth and energy brought a great many changes to S.C.E.G.G.S. The school population almost doubled in her first decade as Head,[22] the curriculum was widened and school life became richer with the introduction of new activities and organisations.

Enrolments increased dramatically: there were 190 girls enrolled in 1921, 225 by December 1921, 270 by February 1924, and 330 by February 1926—an increase of 73 per cent in five years. The 1920s were a period of apparent prosperity and expansion and in schools generally there was a great deal of building activity and an increase in the student population. Miss Wilkinson must be given her due as presiding over such growth, and she was responsible for the building work which made increased student numbers possible. The first building program was completed by 1921 and consisted of much-needed renovations and increased accommodation for the boarders.[23] In July 1923 Miss

Wilkinson presented the Council with a new scheme for a building on the site of the hospital.[24] In it would be a gymnasium and recreation room, classrooms and a laboratory. This was completed in 1925.[25]

The growth of the school population emphasised the limitations of the small Darlinghurst site: the hospital, erected less than twenty years earlier, was demolished to build the new block. Undoubtedly it occupied an ideal position because of its proximity to existing classrooms. The buildings at S.C.E.G.G.S. have needed careful planning so that no space is wasted and maximum use is made of all available land.

Dorothy Wilkinson's reservations on her arrival about the location of S.C.E.G.G.S. were probably for two reasons. Not only was space for buildings and sporting activities limited, but Darlinghurst had become a slum area, where criminal gangs roamed the streets. In February 1924 a thief had entered some of the bedrooms and stolen money and shortly after that, two more break-ins were reported. Bars were fitted to the windows.

The number of times the Council minutes mention available land indicates that it must have been contemplating moving the school from the Darlinghurst site. Thus in 1923 Morven Garden School, Gore Hill, was 'for disposal'. Miss Wilkinson was keen to pursue this, though whether as a branch school or as a replacement site for Head School is unclear. The scheme to acquire it proved 'beyond the Council's present capabilities'. It was not until April 1929 that the school paid the balance of its mortgage to the Church Property Trust, thus being clear of debt. Other sites available over the years were:

- St Hilda's Grammar School, Cremorne (1923), where there was insufficient room for expansion[26]
- Four properties at the corner of Forbes Street and St Peter's Street, at an estimated price of £2500. The Council decided that they were of no real value to the school[27]
- Land at Carlingford[28]
- Land at Mona Vale[29]

The Mona Vale and Carlingford sites were probably regarded as too far away. Although the North Sydney branch school had moved to 'Toongarah', Waverton, in 1917, there was regular review of moving the North Sydney school again, and in 1926 the Council was very interested in a property at Wollstonecraft called Chip Chase.[30] Nothing came of this, nor of a property known as Carlver, up for sale in 1929 for £6000.[31] The North Sydney branch enrolments climbed steadily from 140 in 1926 to 170 in 1930, so the problem of accommodation was a continuing one. There was a change of Headmistress in 1922 when Miss Dumolo resigned from the headship of the North Sydney Branch, after a total of 23 years at S.C.E.G.G.S.[32] She had built up her school into a respected and thriving establishment of over 100 girls and left to become Headmistress of the New England Grammar School, Armidale. Miss Ida Slack BA, First Assistant at Ravenswood, became the new Headmistress at the North Sydney branch.[33]

As in Badham's time, there were numerous requests to take over existing private schools, all of which were refused. The schools included: Miss Turner's school at Strathfield (1921); Morven Garden, Gore Hill (1923); Mrs Connoly's school, Westwood (1925); Brighton College, Manly; and a boys' college at Killara (1926).[34]

The existence of the other branch schools accounts for the Council's

Table 8.1 Bowral financial statement, 1922–28

	1922 £	1923 £	1924 £	1925 £	1926 £	1927 £	1928 £
Income	3783	4124	4429	3940	2526	2642	1904
Expenditure	3550	3900	4000	3720	2800	3100	2185
Profit	233	224	429	220			
Loss					274	458	281

Source: S.C.E.G.G.S. Council minute book, vol. 6, 1921–1931

conservatism in these years. Bowral had always been a small school and a financial liability to Head School.[35] Its continuing existence probably explains why the North Sydney branch did not change to a bigger site and why the Council decided that Head School could not afford to purchase one of the attractive properties for sale. More telling than dropping income and annual loss was the capital advanced from the funds of Head School, which amounted to £2923 by 1927. Although this was offset by the sale of Commonwealth bonds in 1930, Bowral still owed Head School almost £1500.[36]

The Bowral venture had never been a great success. When first opened, it had the attraction of being a country school where the air was healthy and bracing, as opposed to the city, traditionally the home of disease, pollution and foul smells. By the 1920s sanitation, efficient garbage disposal, paved streets, and active municipal councils had changed cities from deathtraps into low-risk locations. No longer was it necessary or desirable to send delicate daughters to the country for their education. Because Bowral was not a big town it was inadequate as a catchment area for the school. There were many small schools in the district but most of them closed down over time. The great survivor was Frensham, which offered a distinctively different kind of education under Winifred West and attracted pupils for that reason. (In her opening remarks in *Fifty Years at Frensham*, Esther Tuckey stated of Frensham: 'The experimental approach is characteristic.'[37])

The Headmistresses at the Bowral branch, Miss Constance Smith and her successors, were isolated from the other two S.C.E.G.G.S. schools by distance, and the minutes record various attempts to make stronger links between Bowral and Head School. For example, Mrs Laidley (a member of the Council) recommended in 1922 that periodic visits to the school be made by Council members, or that a local Ladies' Auxiliary be formed.[38] In 1925 Miss Smith asked that a closer investigation of the school, its needs and work, be made by the Council.[39] She resigned early the following year, after twenty years' service to S.C.E.G.G.S. Although the records give little indication of her character or personality, it is clear that she soldiered on in her lonely capacity at Bowral, struggling to make the school a success, often conscious that the Council was not sufficiently concerned with the Bowral branch except that it was a drain on financial resources. Her successor was Miss Muriel Hammond, previously Headmistress of Tamworth Church of England Girls' School.[40] During Miss Hammond's first five years as Head, the matter of the Bowral branch absorbed the Council's attention almost exclusively.

In 1925 the churchwardens of Saint Simon and Jude Church of England, Bowral, proposed to the Council that monies they had set aside for a Church of England school for boys be diverted towards S.C.E.G.G.S. in view of the acquisition of the Tudor House property by the church authorities. The (unstated) plan seems to have been that the school would move from 'Yerenbah' to a bigger site. The S.C.E.G.G.S. Council accepted the offer gratefully and pointed out that a further £10 000 would be needed for the furtherance of this scheme.[41]

By August 1927 Miss Hammond had tabled a long report on the condition of the school and the Council decided to hand over control of the Bowral property to a local Council on certain conditions. If it did not prove possible to implement Miss Hammond's proposals, the Council decided it would close down the school at the end of the year. The precipitating factor seems to have been the proper supervision of some building work at 'Yerenbah'. The Council should have closed the school down, but it was loath to do so in view of all the work Miss Smith had put into it, and because of pressure from the local residents to keep it open. A local committee was formed which was responsible for the Bowral branch, but still under the S.C.E.G.G.S. Council. For a time there was a fresh burst of enthusiasm to save the school: 'keen interest' was shown by local people, and the visit of the Governor's wife, Lady de Chair, and visits from members of the Council were all 'greatly appreciated'.[42] In 1929 the Council bought a property at Moss Vale on the main southern highway, and £6000 was to be spent on buildings and renovations. The Forbes Street property was mortgaged for £8000 as security.[43]

The Bowral (now Moss Vale) troubles did not end there. Enrolments sank from 70 (1921) to 35 (1930). There was considerable dissatisfaction with Miss Hammond, expressed both by the parents and the Council, and the Council considered accepting her resignation. The Council resolved:

> *. . . that a letter be sent to Miss Hammond expressing the entire dissatisfaction of the Council in view of the number of children being withdrawn from the school and the alienation of sympathies on the part of parents as evidenced by the various letters received from them. Also, with the appointment of what appears to be additional members of the teaching and domestic staff without the sanction of the Council, involving in expenditure beyond the present income.*[44]

By November 1930 there were nineteen boarders and nine day-girls, and the list of further expenses for the Moss Vale school continued: a metal road costing £600, a tennis court, farming implements, levelling of the playing fields and a horse and cart.[45]

As the Darlinghurst school's population grew, its social character changed. From being a school for the daughters of the gentry in the 1890s, under Miss Wilkinson no such class bar seems to have existed. A survey of parents' occupations shows a social mixture which has continued ever since. Fathers' occupations covered a very wide range: from barristers, graziers, doctors, clergymen and lawyers to a poultry farmer, taxi driver, bank teller and commercial traveller. In addition, the school catchment area was enormous. Its central urban location and the excellent transport system meant that it was accessible from most points of the compass. A large proportion came from the eastern suburbs because there was an efficient tram network to this area. The population there doubled in the 1920s. The most common form of transport to school was tram (see Table 8.2).

Another notable and early change under Dorothy Wilkinson was the emphasis on sport. Dr Clubbe, a resident of Forbes Street, Darlinghurst, was asked whether his paddock could be used as a sportsground.[46] The girls played baseball there and he lent it rent-free to the school until he sold it in 1925.

Table 8.2 Means of transport used to attend S.C.E.G.G.S.

	1920s %	1930s %	1940s %
Tram	47	42	39
Ferry	21	20	10
Bus	10	10	25
Train	13	14	16
Walked	3	17	5
Car	4	5	5
Trolley-bus	0	3	10

Note: Some girls travelled by more than one form of transport
Source: figures taken from survey of Old Girls (See Appendix 2)

There is no longer any mention of boating, but S.C.E.G.G.S. reintroduced hockey from the beginning of 1921, using a field at Sydney Grammar School. Soon afterwards, S.C.E.G.G.S. girls were playing tennis on Grammar's courts. A sportsmistress was engaged for four afternoons a week, and by June 1922 the girls began to use the sportsground at Rushcutter's Bay. The two tennis courts were repaired and a third built subsequently.

Miss Wilkinson introduced netball and hockey soon after her arrival, and coached the hockey team herself. She saw this as a way to get to know some of the girls.[47] Eurythmics were introduced in 1923 (after the school witnessed an impressive display by Frensham) and cricket in 1924. The timetable was altered to make Monday afternoons sports afternoons. *Lux* now had a picture of sporting equipment on its front page. S.C.E.G.G.S. had enjoyed some sporting successes in inter-school competitions during Miss Badham's time. For example, in 1916 the school had won the inter-school tennis and swimming cups.[48] The increased emphasis on sport brought success in the inter-school competitions during Wilkinson's first decade. In 1921 Enid Charlton (sister of Andrew 'Boy' Charlton) won the inter-school swimming cup; in 1927 both the hockey and netball teams won the premiership, and in 1930 S.C.E.G.G.S. tied with Ascham to win the All Schools Swimming Carnival.[49] Considering the pronounced lack of sportsgrounds and facilities at the school, these were proud achievements.

A house system was established in 1926. Miss Wilkinson wrote:

> *Enthusiasm, both in work and sport, is sure to wax even keener than it has done this year, and we look forward to much friendly rivalry between the houses. The all-important question of names has been decided, and the choice of calling each house after one of our great pioneers has met with universal approval throughout the school.*[50]

The houses were:

Badham: Named for Edith Annesley Badham, first Principal of the school, 1895–1920. Crest: a gold shield with a red cross, the cross charged with five five-pointed stars. Motto: *Virtu astra petit.* Colours: red and gold.

Barton: Named for Sir Edmund Barton, first Prime Minister of the Commonwealth, 1901–1904. Father of Muffie Barton (Mrs David Maughan), second president of the Old Girls' Union. Crest: red shield with silver fesse indented. Colours: red and white.

Beck: Named for Rev. Canon E. C. Beck, first Secretary of the school Council,

The house shields.

1894–1927, Chaplain, 1901–1927. Crest: blue shield, three gold fishes. Colours: yellow and blue.

Christian: Named for Lily Christian (Mrs Sargood), active member of the Council and first Old Girl president of Old Girls' Union. Crest: red shield with black cross crosslet. Colours: red and black.

Docker: Named for Wilfred Docker, Treasurer of the school Council, 1896–1919. Crest: blue shield, black bridge. Colours: black and blue.

Langley: Named for Bishop Langley (second Bishop of Bendigo), keen founding member of the school Council. Crest: gold shield, three roundels green. Motto: *Fide sed cui vide.* Colours: yellow and green.[51]

The house system, copied from the boys' schools, which had copied them from the English public schools was a feature of many girls' secondary schools by the 1920s.[52] It helped to generate school spirit and sporting enthusiasm. In addition it encouraged good conduct and was intended to form part of the process by which character was formed.

Along with increased sporting activity and the house system went the establishment of the prefect system. Miss Wilkinson announced:

> *We have now Prefects, Probationers, and Form Captains. The Prefects are allowed special privileges and a special badge and blazer; one and all are proving themselves of great service, and we hope we are stepping forward towards the goal of self-government, which has been set before us by so many great English Schools.*[53]

Many new clubs were formed in Miss Wilkinson's first year: the Girl Guides, a Debating Club, a Christian Club called 'Heralds of the King', a Dramatic

Old Girls and students assemble for Ascension Day, 10 May 1923.

Society, and a Camera Club. They began with a flourish but some, like the Debating Club, did not last for long.

Regular lunchtime musical recitals began. These became a feature of S.C.E.G.G.S. in Miss Wilkinson's time and gave the girls the opportunity to hear live performances and explanations about the music.[54] It was a unique musical education. The musical tradition was also fostered in other ways. In 1923 Frederick Mewton, organist at St Andrew's Cathedral, wrote suggesting he be director of music at S.C.E.G.G.S.[55] He was appointed on a temporary basis for six months and proved a valuable addition to the staff. He remained with S.C.E.G.G.S. until his death in 1926. His contribution to S.C.E.G.G.S. music was noted in an obituary in *Lux*:

> *. . . the music staff had learned to depend on him for advice or assistance . . . undoubtedly Mr Mewton's influence for good on the musical side of school life was very great. The marked improvement in the standard of instrumental music and the singing of the choir at some of our special services in the chapel bear witness to his ability and interest . . .*[56]

The two other staff members remembered in connection with music are Miss M. Spencer and Miss I. Horrocks. They were labelled 'the musical twins' by the girls and spent over 40 years teaching music at S.C.E.G.G.S. Ida Horrocks was Dux in 1900 and returned in 1921 to teach music. She retired in 1966. Miss Spencer was at S.C.E.G.G.S. from 1917 till 1968. Miss Horrocks played the piano for the choir and Miss Spencer conducted. The choirs trained by Miss Spencer performed well, winning first place in the British Musical Society's inter-school competition in 1928 and 1929.[57]

An outstanding woman who joined the staff in 1921 was Mrs Nellie Griffin. She stayed at S.C.E.G.G.S. for twenty years. Sir David Griffin, her son, described her as a brilliant woman of many parts. She went to Europe at the age of sixteen to study art because of exceptional ability to draw and paint. She was an outstanding linguist, speaking German fluently, and later at the university of Sydney was the first woman ever to graduate with honours in both Latin and Greek. She could speak and write Attic Greek fluently. In addition she was an excellent sportswoman. She was at one time captain of the New South Wales women's hockey team, played tennis for the University and was the New South Wales women's champion at golf. When at S.C.E.G.G.S., she still played golf in the Royal Sydney A Grade Team.

She taught at Sydney Girls' High until sometime after her marriage in 1914, when being a married woman disqualified her from holding a position in a government school. The girls loved her because of her warm personality, sharp intellect and astonishing ability at games. Often when she arrived at school in her large Willys-Knight, there were girls waiting to meet her. Many Old Girls speak of her influence on their school life. Her classes were of an extremely high standard. If girls could not cope, they had to give up the subject. She was not prepared to bother with girls who were, in her words, 'stupid'.[58]

There was a slight change in the curriculum under Miss Wilkinson. All the subjects available in Miss Badham's day were continued. In addition, zoology and physiology were offered up to Leaving Certificate standard, and chemistry was taught up to the Intermediate Certificate. The extra subjects included dancing, elocution, physical culture, drawing and painting, piano, violin, bookkeeping, shorthand and typing, needlework, French, Spanish and Italian conversation. Miss Beatrice Ogilvie, the sportsmistress, also took remedial work.[59] In the Badham tradition S.C.E.G.G.S. provided a diversity of education which was not available to school pupils attending state schools.

Peter Board's reform of secondary school education had been in effect a piece of social engineering. At the end of sixth class children sat for two statewide examinations, the High School Entrance Examination and the Permit to Enrol Examination,[60] which streamed them into academic or non-academic education. In the state school system a child's examination performance at the age of eleven normally determined his or her career because there were only two types of secondary school, one offering an academic curriculum and the other, a technical one. A child who showed new aptitude in secondary school could alter her/his education and future career prospects only by changing school.

In the 1920s the new principles of secondary education laid down under Peter Board were consolidated. In 1922 S. H. Smith replaced Board as Director of Education, and although maintaining the main features of Board's system, he was more conservative and favoured a more formal approach to education, with increased emphasis on basic subjects. Thus diversity of subjects and freedom of teachers were more restricted.[61] The syllabi became more prescriptive, and the required textbooks were essential reading if a pupil wished to pass the examinations.

Secondary courses were fairly stable and did not change much until the 1940s. There was little interest in educational theory, and what there was had been imported. There was usually a time-lag effect, and educational theories were likely to be discounted as being unsuitable for the inhabitants of a young country who wanted a practical education.[62] Neo-Herbartian theory was favoured with its emphasis on moral training and citizenship.[63] Curricula now showed less emphasis on the classics and increased emphasis on the sciences.

In 1918 the secondary course was extended from four years to five, and

Table 8.3 Occupations of girls leaving high and intermediate high schools, 1921

Occupations	428
Stayed at home	1137
Further education	617
Total leavers	2182
Occupations:	
Professional	60
Public Service (typists and clerks)	24
Commercial (clerks, typists, shop assistants)	280
Dressmaking, millinery, tailoring	45
Factory hands	5
Miscellaneous	14

Source: J. Milburn, Girls' Secondary Education in NSW 1880–1930, MA thesis, University of Sydney, 1965, pp. 172–3

some limits were imposed with regard to Leaving Certificate requirements. The maximum number of papers a Leaving Certificate candidate could take was reduced to ten, and a candidate's number of subjects was to be not more than seven and no fewer than six. These reforms eased the burdens on Leaving Certificate candidates and redressed some of the problems Badham had criticised.[64] The Intermediate Certificate became an important document for those seeking employment and the number of candidates for the Intermediate Certificate Examination increased after 1925 when pupils in technical and domestic science schools were permitted to sit for it also.

S.C.E.G.G.S. girls acquitted themselves well in examinations. Miss Wilkinson reported to the Council that in 1921, and again in 1922, five girls gained exhibitions to the University. In 1923, 32 out of 35 passed the Intermediate Certificate and 10 out of 12 passed the Leaving Certificate. In 1925, 45 out of 48 girls passed the Intermediate Certificate and 16 out of 18 passed the Leaving Certificate. Unlike Miss Badham's policy a decade earlier, girls were encouraged to sit for examinations and to proceed to tertiary education.

In Edith Badham's time (1895–1920) 30 girls attended the University of Sydney. It is likely that not all these completed their degree. Most enrolled in Arts, although there was one in Architecture, one in Medicine and one in Science. In Miss Wilkinson's first decade (1921–1930) 79 girls attended the University and although the majority enrolled in Arts, ten enrolled in Science and a few others in Medicine and Architecture. Times had changed. More women were now entering the workforce, more completed secondary studies and more went on to tertiary education (see Table 8.3).[65]

Dorothy Wilkinson's first decade at S.C.E.G.G.S. saw significant changes in the school Council. From November 1924 Miss Wilkinson was invited to be present at Council meetings, not just attend part of the time. The next year the Headmistresses of the two branch schools were also invited to attend. The minutes show that they generally attended the meetings thereafter. It must have been an encouragement to the branch Heads, in particular, to be included in Council business as they were now enabled to contribute to discussion, give advice or a different point of view as the ones actually at work at the coalface. The 'we/they' dichotomy which would inevitably arise from Head School's position vis-a-vis the branch schools was also thereby reduced. The branch heads were now accorded more status than previously and it was very likely at Miss Wilkinson's suggestion that this course was adopted. Another mark of the branch schools' enhanced status was the Council decision in February 1921 that they should each have their own prospectus.

The most noteworthy change in Council membership was the retirement of Canon Beck in 1925. The minutes record:

> *The resignation was accepted with expressions of the most profound regret and appreciation of Canon Beck's devoted services to the school since its inception and the wish was expressed that he would see his way to continue as Honorary Chaplain. Mr Cowper acting as Hon. Sec. was requested to convey the following resolution which was duly carried unanimously to the Rev Canon Beck: 'That in accepting Canon Beck's resignation from the Council the members desire to place on record their deep regret at the loss of the valuable services so cheerfully given as Honorary Secretary extending over a period of 31 years since the establishment of the school and congratulate him on the practical interest he has taken in the course of education. In addition his very practical help as Honorary Chaplain for nearly a quarter of a century during which his influence on all those with whom he came in contact has left lasting impressions and endearing memories.'* [66]

Some other changes were that two Council members acquired titles. Although Beck always referred to Mrs MacCallum as 'Mrs' MacCallum in the minutes, she was in reality Lady MacCallum by the time he retired. Similarly, Mrs Street became Lady Street when her husband, the Chief Justice of the Supreme Court, was knighted in 1928.

Mrs Selby, a former Council member, died in 1922. She had been Beck's housekeeper and in her memory Beck donated £100 for the Catherine Selby Prize, to be awarded annually, at the Principal's discretion, to the best 'all round' girl at Head School. It has the reputation of being the most coveted prize offered at S.C.E.G.G.S.

Mrs Sargood, the first Old Girl representative on the Council, proposed the building of a chapel as a memorial to Edith Badham. The idea of a school chapel had first been mooted by Edith Badham as a suitable memorial to Wilfred Docker shortly after his death, but the Council did not pursue the matter. At a special meeting in December 1921 Beulah Bolton, for the Memorial Fund Committee, read out her version of the Council's attitude to such a project: 'That as the Council considers a School Chapel unnecessary and undesirable the Memorial Committee shall, subject to the approval of the contributors, hold the money contributed to the Edith Annesley Badham Fund in trust . . .' Archbishop Wright was present at the meeting and after discussion the less offensive words 'impractical at the present juncture' were substituted for 'unnecessary and undesirable.' He had the reputation of a peacemaker.

The time was not yet ripe for a Badham Memorial Chapel. Wilkinson had enough trouble with the Badhamites without the added threat of a Badham shrine and its acolytes in the heart of her school. By 1925 it was a different matter. A letter from the Old Girls requesting that the Council sanction the conversion of the assembly room into a chapel and that the Archbishop be asked to license fully the chapel met with Wilkinson's cooperation, Council approval and the Archbishop's sanction.[67] The Old Girls were to pay for all the necessary alterations. The oak-panelled chapel was Dedicated on Ascension Day, 9 April 1926, by Archbishop Wright. The occasion marks a high point in the S.C.E.G.G.S. collective memory. It represented the fulfilment of Edith Badham's heartfelt wish and it has continued to be a very important focal point for all generations of the school community, representing as it does the strong and distinctively Anglican emphasis on the Christian faith in the S.C.E.G.G.S. educative process.

The school chapel. Originally built in 1901 as an assembly hall, the chapel was dedicated 9 April 1926. Sketch by A. Warner.

Dorothy Wilkinson's first decade as Principal of S.C.E.G.G.S. had been one of considerable change. By widening the curriculum to include more subjects, by a stronger emphasis on sport, by the introduction of clubs and weekly concerts and the introduction of the house system, Miss Wilkinson provided a richer educational experience for S.C.E.G.G.S. girls. The school grew physically as the enrolment doubled and major building projects were completed. The emphasis on academic excellence continued, with significantly more girls sitting for the Leaving Certificate and completing tertiary studies. The school became less socially exclusive as girls from a wide range of social backgrounds attended. The atmosphere was a warmer one: Miss Wilkinson was both respected and approachable. Her spontaneity and kindness made it a school where every person was valued, regardless of ability.

It had been a difficult decade for Miss Wilkinson in many respects. Although she had achieved a great many goals with the support of Council and staff, she had had to contend with the Badhamite opposition during her first five years at the school. Her father died in 1929, and that bereavement, coupled with the burden of the Bowral/Moss Vale branch worries, may explain the illness she suffered at that time.[68] She was given a month's leave of absence. Her whole term as Principal was hard, because the next decade was that of the Great Depression, and the following one was dominated by World War II.

— 9 —

S.C.E.G.G.S. in the 1930s

THE WALL STREET Crash in October 1929 marked the beginning of the Great Depression. This intensified a recession already evident in the Australian economy, making a bad situation worse. For S.C.E.G.G.S., as for practically every other institution, the 1930s was a period of managing to survive in the face of economic crisis. It was the second depression in 40 years the school had had to contend with and, as in the 1890s, over much of the decade the Council struggled on with a debit bank balance. It was in these years that the two branch schools proved to be millstones around the Head School's neck and the consequences of the decision to keep the branch schools open had a permanent and harmful effect on the Forbes Street school.

As in all private schools, enrolments fell between 1930 and 1932 (see Table 9.1).[1] The worst years were from 1930 to 1934. After that the enrolments recovered and leaped ahead at the Head School, until there was a record number of 450 pupils in 1938. The Moss Vale school seems to have suffered less than the other S.C.E.G.G.S. schools and the enrolment gradually improved. The North Sydney school steadily declined in numbers and in 1938, when the other S.C.E.G.G.S. schools showed encouraging growth, there were no new pupils at all. Boarding schools suffered during the Depression years. At Shore boarders dropped from 320 in 1930 to 281 in 1931. At Kambala the 27 boarders in 1930 dropped to ten in 1931. In 1932 Miss Wilkinson reported fewer boarders at S.C.E.G.G.S.[2] Conversely enrolments grew in the state high schools. At North Sydney Girls' High School numbers grew from 257 in 1930 to 294 in 1934.[3] Some pupils crossed from the private schools to the state high schools and, since there were fewer jobs, more students stayed at school, especially because education at state schools was now free. External examination candidates rose, as did enrolments at the University.

For a short time S.C.E.G.G.S. was in the happy position of owing nothing to creditors and showing a healthy profit as well. This occurred in April 1929 (before the Wall Street Crash), when the school Council authorised payment of the balance owed to the Church Property Trust and the Treasurer announced

Table 9.1 Enrolments at independent schools, 1928–39

School	1928–29	1930	1931	1932	1934	1936–39
S.C.E.G.G.S.	340	340	310	300	340	450 (1938)
Moss Vale branch	54	28	43	61	72	76 (1936)
North Sydney branch	150	161	120	N/A	N/A	125 (1939)
PLC Sydney	206	180	144	165	182	262 (1938)
Knox	287	320	81	250	211	231 (1936)

Note: For the years 1936–39, one year only is selected for each school in the table
Source: A Nobbs, *Kambala: The First Hundred Years 1887–1987*, Globe Press, Sydney, 1987, p. 69

a credit balance of £4041. Soon afterwards the new site for the Bowral school was purchased at Moss Vale and with this financial commitment S.C.E.G.G.S. entered upon a long period of financial difficulty. The Moss Vale property cost £12 090, while buildings and other work cost a further £13 858, making a total of £25 948.[4]

While Head School was operating at a profit, the branch schools were losing money year after year.[5] When the branch schools' accounts showed a marginal improvement, it was sometimes because the Head School had injected funds into their accounts as, for example, in 1935, when Head School lent the Moss Vale school £1134. In addition there were overdrafts from the bank to meet operating costs. For example, in 1938 the Council borrowed £4600 from the Bank of New South Wales and the following year a further £3000.

From time to time a question mark hung over the future of both branch schools. In 1930, serious concern was expressed about the state of the Moss Vale finances. As the years passed, however, the Treasurer became more optimistic about the school, saying in 1933:

> *Miss Hammond is deserving of the highest praise for her untiring efforts to pull the school out of a serious difficulty. Her confidence in the future is now being rewarded as the estimated increase in income for the current year should be in the vicinity of £800, which provided no additional heavy expenditure is incurred, should considerably assist the general finances of the three schools . . .*[6]

The prospects of the North Sydney branch were not hopeful: 'The North Sydney School is still a worry. Only 93 pupils are on the fee sheet this year and losses are certain unless an appreciable increase in numbers occurs during the year.'[7] And again in 1935: 'Always a financial problem, the accounts this year disclose a loss . . . I cannot foresee any marked improvement in the finances for the current year.'[8]

In July 1936 Archbishop Mowll suggested that the school be closed down at the end of the year. As enrolments fell between 1930 and 1934, the income from fees dropped. In addition to this, there was a plethora of parents' requests for reduced fees because of financial problems. Collecting fees became difficult and there were some bad debts. One Moss Vale parent paid his fees in kind: eight pigs one year, and cows the next. A range of measures was introduced to cope with the financial crisis during the Depression years. Staff salaries were reduced: those of the teaching staff by 15 per cent (a voluntary sacrifice, although 10 per cent was mandatory throughout the state) and those of the domestic staff by 20 per cent. Miss Wilkinson offered to reduce her salary by £100, an offer that was gratefully accepted. Retrenchments were spoken of. Partial restoration of salaries began only in 1937.[9] In fact, these financial

The Moss Vale branch school. Founded in 1906 at Bowral, the school moved to Moss Vale in 1931. It closed in 1974.

measures were harsh, even mean, when compared with the general situation in the community. Prices dropped 15 per cent in these years, so the school stood to gain rather than lose, since fees were cut by only 7.5 per cent when in fact 10 per cent was normal in many schools.

There was to be strict supervision of the use of the gas stove and the radiators, with fines for negligence. The tuckshop was run differently, with a saving of £90 per annum. Housekeeping, especially the quantity of meat and milk, was affected by the economies. In order to drum up enrolments advertisements were placed in *Country Life* to promote the North Sydney school and Miss Hammond visited country towns to advertise the Moss Vale branch. From the beginning of 1931 the Moss Vale property held holiday camps to generate more income. The first holiday camp was pronounced a great success and £100 was raised.[10] It was good publicity in addition. Whatever venture Moss Vale engaged in, whether moving site or setting up a farm or becoming a holiday camp, there were continual requests for more money.[11]

In 1931 the City Council advised the school that it was liable to pay £800 for two years' arrears of municipal rates. This was a great blow to the S.C.E.G.G.S. Council. The Council viewed their unfortunate position as the result of negligence on the part of the Education Department. The matter dragged on for years, with the Archbishop meeting the Minister of Education in July 1936 to set the facts before him.[12]

Two other financial matters before the Council indicate the effects of the Depression on S.C.E.G.G.S. In 1938 the minutes note that the Docker estate had become bankrupt and the school's solicitors, Maxwell and Boyd, were instructed to refrain from communicating any further with the creditors of K. B. Docker's bankrupt estate. So ended the Docker connection with S.C.E.G.G.S. The other matter occurred the following year, subsequent to the death of Maxwell. The Council was surprised to be billed for costs for Maxwell's legal services. The costs were all the more surprising in view of his frequent absences from Council meetings, due to ill health.

Various schools approached S.C.E.G.G.S. as a prospective purchaser during the Depression years, but as in the previous decade these approaches were rejected by the Council. Brighton school at Manly seems to have been seriously considered in 1933, but was finally rejected because it was too small and would not operate at a profit.[13] Milton Grammar School at Killara came on the market in 1935 but at a point of time when the school finances were £2477 in debt.[14] Besides, two other properties, Loyola and Rose Hall, were far more attractive properties currently under consideration by the Council.[15] In November 1936 the Trustees of Cremorne Girls' School requested the Council to consider amalgamation with the North Sydney branch. A number of problems, including the North Sydney debit balance of £2412, meant that the offer was never seriously considered. Possibly the step of amalgamating two unsuccessful schools seemed an unacceptable gamble.

The most important decision the Council made in the 1930s was a decision about the purchase of a property. It decided the fate of the future of S.C.E.G.G.S. and its branch schools. It stated a commitment to the continuation of the branch schools at the expense of Head School. It was a statement of faith in the future of the branch schools but it demonstrated a lack of foresight with which S.C.E.G.G.S. has had to live ever since. The property was Rose Hall. The 1934 February minutes record that it was up for sale at £20 000. In 1929 it had been on the market for £45 000. The drop in land values caused by the Depression gave S.C.E.G.G.S. the opportunity to purchase, and Miss Wilkinson was very keen to acquire it. The February issue of *Lux* carried this story:

POSSIBILITY OF BIG DEVELOPMENT AT HEAD SCHOOL

The Rose Hall Property, opposite the school in Forbes Street (one acre and three-quarters, belonging to the Red Cross), is still up for sale. As this will probably be the last opportunity of acquiring in this neighbourhood, open land for playing fields and for up-to-date buildings, it is most desirable that this property be acquired by us.

Although our numbers are back to normal (340) and the promise for next year is excellent we have not yet our full complement of boarders; consequently our income is smaller than of yore. In addition to the Head School, the School Council has several properties, including two branch schools; it cannot therefore at present consider any new proposition, however desirable. His Grace the Archbishop and other members of the Council individually are most interested and enthusiastic about extending the School.

First and foremost, Rose Hall would mean fresh air and exercise. (I need not waste your time by emphasising the benefits of playing fields on the spot.)

Now as to the land itself—the whole block—which includes St Peter's Rectory and Upton Court Flats, is a rough triangle. The property under consideration is a five-sided piece of land with access to Forbes Street, Clapton Place and Farrell Avenue . . . It runs in terraces, the lowest of which, with a retaining wall at the Forbes Street and St Peter's Lane end give us a rectangular hockey field . . . Diagonally with the help of a corner we should get a 100 yard track for running. On the remaining highest terrace it should be possible to construct three tennis courts, leaving room for a Junior School, lawns and garden. Colonel Vernon, our School Architect has already got to work on a possible scheme . . . there is little doubt that unless the School Council or some other body can accept this responsibility, our last chance of expanding on this present site will be lost and we shall be overshadowed by huge flats. We have a wonderful stand here, and I believe we have a big work still to do. Day girls have in the last few years come to us regularly from Manly and beyond, from Springwood and Lawson, from Sutherland and Cronulla, from Hurstville and Hunter's Hill. We are essentially metropolitan.[16]

As Miss Wilkinson pointed out in her article, the branch schools reduced the possibility of purchasing Rose Hall. The reality was that S.C.E.G.G.S. was still paying back the loan on the Moss Vale property (the Forbes Street property was mortgaged for £8000 as security)[17] and while Rose Hall was under consideration, several properties in North Sydney were being investigated as alternative sites for the North Sydney school. On 13 May 1936 the choice was put before the Council: either an alternative site for North Sydney, or Rose Hall could be purchased—but not both.

The Council had looked at various options for the North Sydney branch. They included closure (1936), amalgamation with the Cremorne Grammar School (it was to close in 1939), or purchase of a larger site. From 1933 onwards Miss Slack, Headmistress of the North Sydney branch, wanted to move from the Toongarah school site. The Harbour Bridge had been opened in 1932 and since then there had been a definite increase in traffic on the Pacific Highway. In addition the climb up the hill from North Sydney station and the movement of population further up the 'line' were all, according to her, contributing factors to the school's drop in enrolments. Advice from local residents confirmed her in this opinion.

Loyola was considered at intervals from 1933 until 1937, when 'Standish' was investigated. Priced at £6000 compared with the £12 000 asked for Loyola, Standish seemed an ideal site on ten acres of land at Greenwich. It was purchased in 1937 and the Bank of New South Wales lent the Council £16 000. A second mortgage was placed over the Forbes Street property.[18]

The Council abandoned plans to purchase Rose Hall. In her Principal's Report for 1936, Miss Wilkinson stated: 'Though the ABC have shattered our dream of acquiring Rose Hall they have also shattered the nightmare of flats.'[19] The Council's decision not to purchase Rose Hall was very important indeed. It was a large site exactly opposite Head School, and therefore conveniently close. Priced at £20 000 it was just within the Council's reach, and would have been undoubtedly possible had either the North Sydney branch or the Moss Vale branch been closed down and the property sold. Never would the land be within S.C.E.G.G.S.'s grasp again, and it was a site which would have added immeasurably to the very small parcel of land on which Head School stood. Head School was the only school which had consistently prospered and the purchase of the land would have been a huge encouragement to Miss Wilkinson and also a vote of confidence in her ability to continue to make the school prosper. A disinclination to make the hard decision to close the unprofitable branch schools, cost what it would in disappointment and criticism, showed a lack of statesmanship. It was the kind of decision made by people who want to please everybody and end by pleasing nobody. Perhaps the Council unconsciously took advantage of Dorothy Wilkinson's Christian grace and self-abnegation.

The flats Miss Wilkinson feared would encroach on the school were becoming more common in the 1930s. Until then they had been the holiday abode of the rich, generally in seaside suburbs like Bondi. Now they were recognised as a cheap form of housing and the Darlinghurst area was an obvious place to build them, with its advantageous proximity to the city. Miss Wilkinson possibly disliked the idea of the size of the buildings which would house flats, and also

Table 9.2 Financial statement for the three schools, 1930–38

	1930 £	1931 £	1932 £	1933 £	1934 £	1935 £	1936 £	1937 £	1938 £
Head School	—	—	1561	180	—	1604	1927	2712	2032
Moss Vale	1800 (loss)	—	—	—	3218 (loss)	—	200	100 (loss)	1398 (loss)
North Sydney	—	—	—	—	—	124 (loss)	2412 (loss)	2911 (loss)	1025 (loss)

Source: S.C.E.G.G.S. Council minute book, vol. 7, 1931–40

the quality and quantity of the flats' inhabitants. Nonetheless, flats were erected on the north-east corner adjoining the school site and in time were to be purchased by the school for use as a boarding house and named, ironically, 'Wilkinson House'.

In the 1930s the three schools were competitors. Each demanded money to be spent on upkeep and new buildings. Moss Vale had required new buildings as soon as the school moved in 1929, and by 1936 had spent more than £5000 on further buildings. Extra classrooms and alterations were required at Standish when the North Sydney school moved there in 1939. At Head School Old Girls remember the strictest economy in painting and general refurbishing. The leap in enrolments at Head School after 1934 may have generated more cash, but it gave rise to a critical shortage of space. This was the case at the branch schools as well. There is a note of desperation in Miss Wilkinson's requests to the Council for solutions to the problem of accommodation. In June 1936 there was an urgent request for more classrooms; in October 1936 Miss Wilkinson stated that the enrolments were good: would the Council please lease or buy St Peter's Rectory; in November 1936 she requested instructions as to how to cope with the Junior school threatening to overflow the classrooms.[20] The following year St Peter's Rectory was used for the Junior school. It was at first leased and later purchased by S.C.E.G.G.S. Space was so short that the Council discovered that Miss Wilkinson had moved out of her bedroom to provide another dormitory.[21]

By 1939 World War II had imposed a new set of financial constraints. The Treasurer's comment on the financial situation in 1940 sums up the situation neatly: 'The disappointing numbers at North Sydney must result in the school sustaining a heavy loss. This, together with the deficiency at Moss Vale means that the surplus revenue from the Head School will be wholly absorbed in meeting these losses, and in consequence leaving no funds for extraneous expenditure.'[22]

It was discouraging for Miss Wilkinson to see her school suffer because of the demands of the branch schools. They had the grounds which Head School so desperately needed, and yet somehow with all their resources they were second-rate academically and a continual curb on Miss Wilkinson's plans and visions. She admitted to being old and tired in a report for Council in April 1940:

> *I would like leave to investigate the possibility of flooring and lining at my own expense, a room in the roof of top floor. This year I could get back to my old room, but I feel I am too old and often too tired to stand the legitimate racket of youngsters all round me. But of course, we are using the room and next year I should probably have to move again.*[23]

Boarders' crocodile on the way back to school from church at St John's, Darlinghurst, 1937.

An indication of her generous nature is her offer in August 1939 to have her salary reduced to the amount paid her in the Depression. The Council was unwilling to accept the offer.[24]

The branch school finances were not the only concern for the Council. The Headmistresses also caused worry in different ways. Miss Slack left the North Sydney branch school in 1934, having been Headmistress for eleven years, to take up an appointment as Principal of Sydney Kindergarten and Preparatory Teachers' College. By the time she left, the school was no longer preparing candidates for the Leaving Certificate.

Her replacement was Mrs Arundel, who had served as a temporary Headmistress at Moss Vale in 1934 during Miss Hammond's absence. Although Mrs Arundel seems to have been a very efficient and practical Headmistress, her term at North Sydney was clouded by what the Council termed 'her domestic situation'. She had three children who were young enough to need a nursemaid in 1934 and her husband was absent, it seems, because of his job. It is not clear what the problem really was. However, it meant that in November 1937 the Council communicated to her that she was to regard her appointment as temporary. The minutes state that Mrs Arundel 'fully understood the circumstances prompting the action'.[25]

A Miss Gilham was invited to become the new Headmistress when the school moved to Standish, but nothing further came of this. Through 1938 Mrs Arundel asked for extensions of her term as Headmistress and applied for the job when the position was advertised. There was some excitement on the Council relating to the appointment, as the Archbishop was absent in England and was to interview a prospective applicant there. He had cabled: 'Miss Enderby St John's School Invercargill recommended by Headmistress St Andrews Scotland and am interviewing Cheltenham Thursday Will Cable Result.' The promised cable did not arrive.[26]

The Council was strongly in favour of appointing Mrs Arundel, but hesitated to do so without the Archbishop's sanction. The Secretary was accordingly instructed to send him the following cable: 'Feeling of Council in favour Mrs Arundel awaiting result of your interviews.' At the next meeting on 9 November

1938, Mrs Arundel advised that she was obliged to give an answer to Miss Knox, Headmistress of PLC Pymble, that very day by 2.00 pm, and she was accordingly chosen as Headmistress of the school she had run for the last five years.[27]

The move to Standish and the appointment of a Headmistress began a period of prosperity for the North Sydney school. Enrolments rose and the future seemed bright. In November 1940 Mrs Arundel requested the Council that the school no longer be regarded as a branch school. Unfortunately for her school and Head School, the North Sydney finances could not permit such a step with the responsibilities independence would entail.

At Bowral, from 1930 until her final departure in 1937, Miss Hammond was an unsatisfactory Headmistress. The first of a series of resignations from Miss Hammond came in April 1930. Miss Hammond succeeded in offending the parents, the local people and her own staff. On one occasion the Council decided to ignore her letter of resignation completely, stating 'that the letter be treated as if it were not written'.[28] Compassion for her difficult personality and recognition of some good work she had done for the school prevented their dismissing her. The Council meeting of 8 November 1937 is memorable for the fact that the decision was taken to dismiss two Headmistresses. Mrs Arundel was henceforth to regard herself as temporary (as described above) and, as for Miss Hammond, it was unanimously resolved that:

> *Following upon the serious matters mentioned in the reports before the meeting, that the resignation of Miss Hammond as headmistress of the Moss Vale School be asked for, and that she be paid a sum equal to six months' salary and in addition, provided she leaves Australia for England before the end of the year, the cost of her fare be paid by the Council. Miss Hammond be asked to continue on as headmistress until the end of the present term. It be further resolved to invite Miss Steel MA to act as headmistress until a new appointment is made.*[29]

It was not easy to make Miss Hammond leave. The Council increased its offers of financial assistance but 'regretfully' confirmed its decision. Lady MacCallum tried to persuade the Council to postpone the resignation for a year, then spoke with Miss Hammond to persuade her to hand in her resignation. Her grievance was that she had not been given an opportunity to speak to the Council. In one of a series of November meetings the Council invited her to speak to them, which she did briefly. She clearly did not intend to resign and the Council had decided to refer the matter to their solicitors when 'Miss Hammond unexpectedly returned to the room and addressed the meeting at some length.' After this the legal notice terminating employment was sent to her and all offers of financial help were withdrawn. In the new year Miss Steel took up her duties as acting Headmistress and by May 1938 she was appointed as Headmistress 'in view of the very satisfactory work carried out by her'.[30]

One very evident effect of the branch schools was the time and attention they demanded of the Council. An Executive was formed in May 1936 to attempt to handle some of the matters for the Council to consider. The Executive Minute Book is still available. The first members of the executive were Dr McDouall, Lady MacCallum, Mrs Maughan, H. B. Cowper and Archdeacon Johnstone.[31] In 1939 the Council was expanded to include four new lay members. Those elected were Professor Holme, Dr Stephens, Miss B. S. Long and Mr J. Scarvall. Despite these changes, the volume of school matters requiring the Council's attention made it impossible to give due attention to the particular needs of each school. Miss Wilkinson and Head School required more support from the Council than was actually given.

Over the decade there were other changes in the Council. Archbishop Wright died in 1933 and his successor, Howard Mowll, chaired his first Council meeting in March 1934. He took a very active interest in S.C.E.G.G.S., chairing most meetings thereafter. This was a most unusual practice for the Archbishop of Sydney. Mrs Mowll was also appointed to the Council and the following year replaced Mrs Maughan on the Executive Committee.

Miss French resigned in June 1932. The minutes record: 'The Council place on record the consistent and faithful service rendered by Miss French to the school since its inception, and regrets the consequential severance of the last remaining link with the original Council.'[32] A quiet and reliable member of Council, she had served on it for 37 years. Another resignation came from Lady Street, a much more active member. She resigned on a number of occasions, but rather than let her go, she was retained as a member of Council even if she could no longer attend meetings. She sent in a final resignation in March 1936 and this one was accepted with regret. Shortly after, her daughter-in-law, Mrs K. Street, was appointed to the Council. Archdeacon Langley resigned in June 1941, having replaced Beck as Honorary Secretary. One practical result was that his successor, Archdeacon Johnstone, saw to the typing of the minutes, which made them completely legible for the first time. Beck died in 1939, bequeathing S.C.E.G.G.S. £1000.[33]

One of the most active, respected and generous members of Council was Lady MacCallum. There is little doubt that her title added weight to her opinions and that the school liked the association with those of her class and the prestige attending it. Nevertheless, she was undoubtedly a strong-minded and capable woman in her own right. She took, rightly or wrongly, a particular interest in the branch schools, acting as negotiator in difficulties with the Headmistresses and contributing financial support as well. It is likely that her active support was the main reason the branch schools were not closed down in the 1930s. Thus in 1931 she undertook to pay the salary of an additional staff member at Bowral, bought two draughthorses for the Moss Vale farm and later paid for two workmen's cottages there. With her husband, Sir Mungo, she contributed substantially towards the cost of the new buildings at Moss Vale in 1935; and in 1939 gave £50 towards the classroom block at Standish. The minutes refer to her 'valuable contribution in debates'. Although she lost the sight of one eye in 1935, had a motor accident in 1938 and lost her husband in 1942, she returned after each misfortune to the Council meetings. Perhaps the Council thought her days on Council were ending when, in 1936, they presented her with an illuminated brochure prepared by the Archbishop, Cowper and Archdeacon Johnstone. The notion of preparing such a token of the Council's appreciation was received 'with much enthusiasm'. Clearly she added warmth, vigour and the encouragement of her solid commitment to S.C.E.G.G.S. at the Council meetings she attended.

In his autobiography *Plankton's Luck*, Lady MacCallum's grandson Mungo painted her as a formidable, dominating woman, respected but not loved.[35] He referred to her 'clench' in family relationships and her 'iron hand' in imposing her will. She was German, born Dorette Peters, and though she always spoke English in Sydney, she thought in German all her life.

When war was declared in 1914, she was on holiday in Germany with her husband Mungo, fatigued from all her voluntary work which included presiding over the Infants' Home at Parramatta, the University Settlement and the National Council of Women. The MacCallums managed to leave Germany and get to England, but their situation in Sydney on their return was an uncomfortable one: a well-known man married to a well-known woman who was German. In addition they had always shown a particular love for Germany. Publicly and privately they were regarded as aliens during the war period.[36]

Mrs MacCallum had joined the S.C.E.G.G.S. Council in 1907, and throughout the war she attended Council meetings regularly and was active in debate and committee work. She was not present at the two Council meetings where anti-German sentiments were aired[37] but the effects of the war were discussed at other Council meetings at which she was present.[38]

This difficult decade was the midpoint of Miss Wilkinson's term as Principal. Although in education generally there was little change, for S.C.E.G.G.S. it was a time of solid achievement, and even some innovation. It is clear that Dorothy Wilkinson tirelessly spent herself for her beloved school and the people in it. Mrs Sharland recalls that Miss Wilkinson had no outside interests:

> *She didn't have the time. No. I mean this was typical of her—we used to go down to Collaroy quite a lot because we used to rent a cottage down there belonging to friends, and she was staying with us, and she used to go like smoke the whole term long, always on the go, so I used to make her rest and that sort of thing. But terribly difficult to do. And I remember taking her out her early morning cup of tea. Well the bed had a high thing at the top and the bottom, and then a flat bit on the top of each pillar. Blow me if she wasn't sitting up in bed with a pot of ink here on this thing and writing away. I said, 'Now what are you doing?' And so she said, 'Oh, just getting the Sunday School lessons ready.' So I said, 'You really are the limit, you know. You come here for a rest and I come in and I find you at this hour of the morning sitting up working away.' So she said—she did the Sunday School lessons for the Diocese—'Well, it's one way of keeping my father's memory alive.' She was devoted to her father.*[39]

When interviewed Old Girls and ex-staff had a great fund of anecdotes and descriptions of Miss Wilkinson. She was a gifted teacher. Rosemary Wilkins recalls her Scripture lessons on St John's Gospel and says, 'I can still remember some of her lessons quite clearly. She had good insight into the material.'[40] Mary Graham, who later became Headmistress of Moss Vale S.C.E.G.G.S., began at S.C.E.G.G.S. in 1937:

> *From that very first day at S.C.E.G.G.S. I found myself caught up in the spirit of the school and wanting to take part in everything. I think the daily chapel services had a lot to do with it, the reverence, the music, Miss Wilkinson's own deep faith which most certainly came across to us . . . Miss Wilkinson taught us scripture in my first year. We studied Matthew's gospel and there are bits of her teaching that have stuck in my mind to this day, nearly fifty years later. Talking about the beatitudes, she said that the meek are teachable and looking back on her life, could there be a better example than her own? On Jesus' commandment to love God and one's neighbour, she said that if we really did that there'd be no need for school rules. On the story of Martha and Mary she said that Jesus was really saying, 'Bread and cheese is all we want, Martha, come and let's be together.'*[41]

Joan Freeman wrote of her ten years at S.C.E.G.G.S.:

The school just suited me. I lapped up the basic academic training, which was indeed good and solid, but, even more importantly, the more subtle Christian background; provision for personal freedom; emphasis on self-discipline and the importance of intellectual honesty, personal training for life which I gained there: a good but not overpowering integrity, graciousness, kindness, generosity . . . all qualities which helped towards a satisfying fulfilment of life. 'Luceat Lux Vestra' was not just a motto. I felt it as a practical ideal, the spirit of which pervaded the school.[42]

Dorothy Wilkinson's personal stamp was evident. Mary Graham recalled her generosity and eccentricities:

One day I was talking to her in her study and she brought out a bag of chocolates. Another time, it was exam time in my Leaving year. I'd been charging down through the bush as usual to the Spit to get the tram, had tripped on something and had fallen headlong. Dirty and shaken I staggered home where my mother cleaned me up, did what she could for the grazes and sent me off with a note. I arrived very late of course and presented my note at the staffroom. The mistress there said I had better go to Miss Wilkinson. She read the note, looked at me and said I'd better have a glass of sherry. She produced a decanter of sweet sherry and poured me a small glass. I was finding it very difficult to get down. She noticed this and promptly got me a shredded wheatmeal which helped. She just kept me resting there for a time, then sent me off to the exam room with my original note which she had endorsed: 'Leave Mary for the full time unsupervised.' The invigilator read the note, looked at me and no doubt smelt the alcohol. She seemed to me to be rather dubious to follow instructions, but perhaps it was only her concern.[43]

Rosemary Wilkins said:

Sticky couldn't stand the smell of apples. If you had an apple anywhere near the place she'd make you banish it. If you were a day-girl and had your apple in a case in the classroom, she'd make you take it out . . . My parents thought Miss Wilkinson was marvellous and she was good with the parents. She used to have all the men dangling on a string. Men would do anything for her. My father, who was a busy man, a consulting engineer, used always to come and timekeep at the swimming sports. He was a very fussy man and I don't know how he stood being splashed by all the girls, but he always came, and a lot of the other men did too . . . She used to say something, and then she'd blink. She was a great blinker. She'd issue an ultimatum and then blink to make sure that was it.[44]

Miss Wilkinson's driving was legendary. Dorothy Shipley remembered: 'She was the most frightful driver. I remember I went along William Street and she'd zoom on the wrong side of cars, two of the wheels would be up on the pavement and you'd wonder whether you'd ever get there safely. But that was the way she went through life. She dived along and didn't spare herself in any way.'[45]

After finishing her formal education at S.C.E.G.G.S. Nancy Jackson spent some time there as general factotum. She recalled:

When Miss Wilkinson bought her car she wouldn't go out on her own. She was a very nervous driver. She was a very nervy sort of woman altogether. She had a great bun of hair. She had beautiful hair, an auburny colour. The bun was always a bit wispy and untidy. She didn't hold herself erect. She was always in a hurry and bent forward. She gave the impression of being quite small. One of my jobs was to go with Miss Wilkinson in her car. It was quite a terrifying experience. There was very little traffic of course, but she drove from school one day up to see her nephew who was boarding at Knox. I went with her and I left my suitcase in the car. I was sitting in the front beside her. She dropped me at home on the way back and I got out of the car and said to her, 'I'll just get my suitcase from the back', and she shot off like a bullet from a gun and left me standing on the road without my suitcase. I got it eventually but this was the type of driver she was. She didn't do anything by halves.[46]

Miss Wilkinson seemed to have the support and loyalty of her staff. One staff member who must be mentioned is Miss Capper, Miss Wilkinson's deputy from 1922 until 1939. Nicknamed 'Caps', she was described as a very down-to-earth, somewhat untidy person who hated the task of deputising in public when Miss Wilkinson was absent. She was universally liked and was a sort of Mr Chips. Another member of staff, Miss Stella Scroggie, who left in 1936, is remembered by many for her 'Afro' hairdo and her intelligent and unconventional teaching methods, which imparted a love of history to at least some of her pupils. She was more concerned to educate girls to think for themselves than to obtain good examination results.[47]

In 1938 another memorable history teacher arrived. Mrs Grace Davies, a good friend of Miss Wilkinson, was the widow of Archdeacon Davies, a former Principal of Moore Theological College. A Cambridge graduate, she was ahead of her time in using primary source material in her lessons.[48] Two members of staff left to become headmistresses: Miss Margaret Elliot was appointed Headmistress of 'Stratford' at Lawson in the lower Blue Mountains. Miss Constance Wood left S.C.E.G.G.S. in 1939 to become Headmistress of Tintern, Melbourne.

Girls from the 1930s distinguished themselves in various ways: two later became headmistresses: Una Fitzhardinge at St Catherine's Waverley (1949–54) and Mary Graham at S.C.E.G.G.S. Moss Vale (1953–59). Marion MacCabe, a Badham girl, had started a school at Gosford called Marshall Mount. It was purchased in 1931 by two Old Girls, Ruby Wheaton BA and Mrs K. M. Hamblin BA, DipEd, and was then moved to Lindfield.[49] Margaret Dovey, who later married Gough Whitlam, represented Australia in the breaststroke at the 1936 Munich Olympics. Helen Edwards became the first girl in New South Wales to become an air hostess in 1937.

Jean Curlewis, the writer, died in 1930.[50] An obituary in *Lux* said of her: 'With the death of Mrs Leonard Charlton (Jean Curlewis), the school has lost from the ranks of the Old Girls one of its most brilliant and charming personalities.'[51] The *Sydney Morning Herald*, in an article written by 'G.S.', noted: 'The obvious and the commonplace had no place in her work. Always she put the fresh point of view, the unexpected presentation. Jean Curlewis was a good Australian. She could interpret Australia to the Australians. She revealed qualities in our country that we did not know were present.'[52]

Joan Freeman, one of S.C.E.G.G.S.'s most brilliant Old Girls, almost had to leave S.C.E.G.G.S. in the Depression when her father, an accountant, lost his job:

The realisation that I would have to leave my beloved S.C.E.G.G.S., where I was firmly ensconced and preparing for the Intermediate Examination, was a bitter blow

Joan Freeman (Dr Jelley), 1935. Joan was Dux of the school twice, and in 1935 topped the state in the Leaving Certificate. After distinguishing herself at the University of Sydney, winning a number of awards for outstanding ability, she worked in nuclear physics for her PhD from Cambridge University. She headed a team of nuclear physicists at the Atomic Energy Research Establishment, Harwell, England and was awarded the Rutherford Medal in 1976.

> *to me and to my mother. But she had to go to Miss Wilkinson with heavy heart to explain the situation. What a transformation there was in her when she returned home from that interview! Miss Wilkinson had decided quite spontaneously that, in view of the promise I was showing, and the possible good publicity I might bring to the school, they could not afford to let me go. My mother was a very proud person, to whom the idea of charity was totally repugnant, but Miss Wilkinson, with her great capacity for understanding and tact, was able to persuade her that, from a purely business point of view, it would be a worthwhile investment on the school's part to keep me on without fees. It was a completely confidential and unofficial arrangement which no-one (except presumably the school Treasurer) ever knew about. But what a challenge for me! I* had *to justify the Head's faith in me.*[53]

Dorothy Wilkinson's faith was justified. Twice Dux of the school, Joan Freeman topped the state in the Leaving Certificate in 1935, winning the Aitken Scholarship, the John West Medal, the Graham Medal and the Fairfax Prize. She had gained four first class honours and two A's. Joan Freeman reported:

> *It was the first time any Girls' Grammar School had ever won this distinction. Miss Wilkinson was on top of the world about it, and proclaimed a special holiday for the school, in honour of the occasion. And the academic reputation of the school*

> *was certainly boosted. For me it was one of the most thrilling moments in my life—barely matched by the award of the Rutherford Medal of the Institute of Physics some 40 years later.*[54]

One subject that Joan Freeman needed at the University but was not offered at S.C.E.G.G.S. was physics. It was a prerequisite for Science at the University, so she studied it for the Leaving at Sydney Technical College. Neither did S.C.E.G.G.S. offer Leaving Certificate chemistry, although it was taught up to Intermediate standard. At a Council meeting in 1938 Mrs Trindall, a member of the Council, raised the possibility of introducing it into the Senior curriculum, and again in 1940 Miss Wilkinson promised to report back to the Council on the cost of equipment and the necessity for S.C.E.G.G.S. to offer matriculation chemistry. Matriculation level physics and chemistry were eventually introduced to S.C.E.G.G.S. in 1944. It was important for girls wishing to enter the Faculty of Medicine at the University, as chemistry was a compulsory subject in the course.

In addition to Joan Freeman's outstanding achievement, S.C.E.G.G.S. had many other successes. In 1933 fifteen girls sat for the Leaving Certificate and all were successful. In 1940 there were 30 Leaving Certificate candidates and 75 Intermediate candidates. Most years Miss Wilkinson would report that the examination results were excellent.[55] S.C.E.G.G.S. won the elocution shield at the Sydney Eistedfodd in 1934 and had many sporting victories, winning the coveted Tildesley Shield for tennis in both 1938 and 1939. At the All Schools Swimming Carnival in 1934 the Juniors won the cup and the Seniors came second; in September the same year both Seniors and Juniors won the All Schools Athletics and in 1937 S.C.E.G.G.S. won the Senior Cup at the All Schools Swimming Carnival.[56]

The editorial for *Lux* of February 1935 commented on a recent decision of the headmistresses of the independent schools to reduce competition in sport. They decided not to play any finals or keep records, to surrender all cups and trophies, and to discourage press publicity in connection with sports. Competitive sport seemed to divide schoolgirls into the elite, who participated in the top teams and won, and the losers, who became spectators only. The same issue of *Lux* contained Miss Wilkinson's Annual Report, in which she spoke of education for leisure:

> *Since machinery has come to stay, leisure will in the future belong to all, and Dean Inge tells us that 'on our good or bad use of it will depend to a very large extent our claim to be a really civilised and self-respecting nation. For the best things in life are not the expensive things—'not by bread alone but by every word'. . . When the curriculum is eased maybe we shall have time for 'silent reading' during school hours. Even next year we are planning a larger Reference Library where a whole class may browse at a time. By encouraging your girls in this way you are creating a port in time of sickness, a retreat from the hurry of modern life, and you are giving them here and now one of the two most valuable aids to education, a background on which to draw, and a vocabulary with which to express their thoughts.*
>
> *There is no need to emphasise sport as an occupation for leisure—certainly it is one of the best—especially when it brings us into contact with living people in a living world . . .*
>
> *Only the right use of leisure will keep for us our balance and perspective—else we shall be slaves of business, pleasure, sport.*[57]

Class IIIA (6th class) doing gymnastics, 1936. Left to right, above*: Carmen Clarke, Jill Bridgland, Nance Connor, Patricia Farrar;* below *Helen Kerr, Judith Bottomley, Josephine Hume, Shirley Dreverman.* Below *The senior and junior swimming teams, 1936.* From left*: Marjorie Wilkins, Margaret Dovey, Betty Smith, Barbara Thompson, Jean Hunter, Joan Baynes.*

From the outset of her time at S.C.E.G.G.S. Miss Wilkinson had activated a range of extra-curricular interests: sporting activities had been extended, special interest clubs formed and lunchtime music was always a special feature of her era. The emphasis on leisure activities was extended in 1936 to the creation of a 'hobby afternoon' on Tuesdays. Miss Enid Cambridge and Miss Howard Smith organised handcrafts including wool work, glove-making and linocuts. There was also a camera club, and a theatrical group performed scenes from *A Midsummer Night's Dream* with Miss Kent Hughes and Miss Walker.

A further extension of music education was the installation of a pipe organ. An organ fund had been set up in 1929 and the organ was built and ready to be shipped from Germany by 1934. The death of G. F. Hopkins, the organ builder, delayed the completion, however, especially since nobody knew exactly what remaining parts of the organ were still in bond. Before they could be released their quantity and specifications had somehow to be ascertained. The dedication of the organ in the school chapel took place on 25 October 1935, the Archbishop presiding and Victor Massey giving a recital. *The Sydney Church of England Grammar School 1895–1955* history of S.C.E.G.G.S. reports: 'All who heard him were delighted with its range and beautiful tone.'[58] Less than forty years later, it was no longer worth playing.

Miss Wilkinson did not often philosophise about educational aims and objectives. Her Principal's Report for 1935 gives an indication of her educational ideas:

> *From the children we ask a ready and intelligent obedience, and our Anglo-Saxon virtue of honesty—valuable asset for a gregarious people—and from the school itself, the minimum amount of dogma, which means for us the fundamentals of a British education. And after that—well, curricula are in the melting pot; at present we must at least meet the minimum demand of the business world . . . while even in this bread and butter world of ours a small percentage is fortunate enough to pass on to the University of whom a growing and strong minority are there to seek knowledge for its own sake.*
>
> *But to go back a little, one of the main duties of girls' schools, at any rate, is to the many who leave school at the age of sixteen or so, for whom the future would seem to offer a half-time position in an office, or even in their own homes. Especially for these we have been adding year by year, a variety of interests for their leisure time; the singing lessons under Miss Spencer, and our weekly concerts, have cultivated their musical sense and made them excellent critics, well able to enjoy the good and reject the bad . . .*[59]

Miss Wilkinson began her Principal's Report for 1937 with the words:

> *A School report can hardly begin without striking a note of gratitude to the NEF Conference. I expect His Grace has heard many such recently. Mine is a person alone:—I was so grateful for encouragement given by practical teachers like Happold, Rugg, and Zilliacus to schools struggling with many limitations. They bid one remember that a school is not great because it is doing its job. Zilliacus, especially with his bi-lingual pupils and a rigidly centralised scheme of national education, had faced and overcome odds which might have daunted even the bravest.*[60]

The initials NEF stood for New Education Fellowship which held a conference in each state in 1937. The Australian Council for Educational Research promoted the NEF conferences and encouraged educational reform, especially in the areas of curriculum change and the overhauling of the examination system.

Miss Wilkinson's reference to the NEF, which sounds rather cryptic today, demonstrates both an awareness of the wider educational scene and also a sense of frustration with existing conditions. The Depression years had imposed severe economic constraints, and added to these was an awareness that the educational system was ready for reform. In particular, the Leaving Certificate and matriculation requirements dominated the secondary curriculum in a way which is very similar to the contemporary problem of the domination of the Higher School Certificate in secondary school education in the 1990s. Furthermore, the examinations were external, and while they remained so, their effect was to ensure the continuation of traditional teaching methods. Radical change was therefore out of the question. This is why a visiting American Professor of Education stated in 1937: 'I see no hope for education in New South Wales until you dynamite the examination system'.[61] Although frustration arising from the constraints of the Depression years was widespread, it was not until after World War II that reform was practicable.

Like Edith Badham, Miss Wilkinson was basically educating the majority of her students to be wives and mothers. Unlike Miss Badham, she encouraged more of her students to attend the University on the one hand, and at the same time provided a spectrum of activities which were intended to educate the whole person. The branch schools and the Depression had meant that Dorothy Wilkinson's plans and ideas were not properly realised. The onset of World War II in 1939 marked the beginning of another decade of delayed dreams and 'making-do'.

— 10 —

Dorothy Wilkinson's last decade

WORLD WAR II dominated Dorothy Wilkinson's final years at S.C.E.G.G.S. As with all other private schools, the war meant stringencies and limitations, shortages, challenge, excitement and loss. *Lux* made constant reference to the war in editorials, and in lists of Old Girls and relatives on active service, killed or missing. There were descriptions of the war from Old Girls in England and details of the war effort at S.C.E.G.G.S. Original contributions to the magazine's literary section included such titles as 'A School Air Raid', 'To France', 'Sydney's Blackout', 'The Airman' and 'How to Finance the War'. A considerable number of Old Girls became involved in war work, many as nurses, in Sydney and with the Australian Imperial Forces (AIF) abroad.

Susan Davies, a fine violinist, was with an ambulance unit in London. Some with language qualifications were in the censor's office, many were with the Women's Royal Australian Naval Service (WRANS) and the (Women's Auxiliary Australian Air Force (WAAAFS). Joyce Whitworth was singled out for special mention in an Annual Report for being officer in charge of the Killara Training School, having gained 98 per cent in her examination. Joyce White (later wife of Frank Hutchens, the pianist) gained her advanced A Flying Certificate and subsequently was engaged in training recruits in signalling and wireless work.[1] The number of old S.C.E.G.G.S. girls involved in war work was much greater than in World War I, and this was true of women's involvement in the war from the wider community. While there were few women actively employed in World War I, there were a good many in World War II.

At school the girls were busy knitting, sewing and raising funds for the Mobile Kitchen, the Church of England National Emergency Fund (CENEF), and King George V Sailors' Home. In July 1941 *Lux* published a list of garments knitted at the school: for the Lord Mayor's Fund there were 45 socks, 19 mittens, 10 skull caps, 15 balaclavas and 26 mufflers. For British children and the Lord Mayor's Family Welfare Funds there were 5 jumpers, 1 pair of booties, 8 vests, 8 'modesties' and 1 suit. In addition Miss Ogilvie, the sportsmistress, had a special interest in raising money for War Savings Certificates, which were intended to be used as scholarships for the daughters of 'our gallant fighting men'.[2]

Miss Wilkinson introduced her Annual Report of 1939 with the words:

> *This is stock-taking time; the old order changing; men everywhere challenging fundamentals. We, therefore, as a typically British institution, and a Christian one cannot escape, unless, true to our own principles, we are sending out women of good will, able and ready to play their part in the great peace drama for which we are praying. In spite of (possibly because of) many limitations I believe we are; and this report is my attempt to face facts as I see them.*[3]

She recounted her delight at the comment of an educationalist friend, who told her that S.C.E.G.G.S. girls were everywhere recognised by their purpose in life. She continued:

> *S.C.E.G.G.S. stands to serve, and though her sphere of usefulness has varied from time to time, it has been an ever-widening one. To the ears of youth Duty may sound drab, and it certainly is often monotonous, but we today believe, perhaps as never before, that for individuals as well as for nations, that way lies our only chance of true and lasting happiness.*[4]

As in other schools and throughout the community, it was a period of idealism, lofty sentiment, moral reappraisal and exhortation. Brothers, fathers, fiances and husbands went on active service: some were killed and others were reported missing. At least one brother spent years in a Japanese concentration camp. There were contrasts with the S.C.E.G.G.S. experience of World War I: far fewer names were on the active service list.[5] Compared with nearly 500 by 1918, by the end of World War II there were about 121 names and, moreover, these included a number of women.

An editorial in *Lux* 1940 gives some indication of the way the war affected the school at first:

> *In these days of blaring wireless and shrieking posters, in a world which for many months has had its attention riveted on the conflict in Europe, in which seeming certainties have vanished overnight, and the things we valued most have turned to dust and ashes, it is hard to imagine a time when there will be no war. Yet such a time need not be consigned to some vague future if only we remember that winning the war is not our ultimate goal—it is but the first step in Britain's crusade to make the world safe for free peoples.*[6]

The war became immediate and menacing for Australians after the Japanese attack on Pearl Harbour on 7 December 1941. The subsequent invasion of South-East Asia culminated in the fall of Singapore on 15 February 1942 and reports of atrocities there heightened fear of the Japanese. When Darwin was bombed on 19 February, 8 ships were sunk, 23 aircraft destroyed and 243 people killed. It was the greatest crisis in Australia's history.[7] Although at the time people in Sydney had no idea of the extent of the bombing damage in Darwin, there was panic at the thought of a Japanese invasion and indeed four Japanese midget submarines entered Sydney Harbour and sank a ferry on the night of 31 May 1942.[8] Other Japanese activity along the north-east coast resulted in the sinking of 29 merchant ships, and the sinking of the hospital ship *Centaur*, incurring a total of 577 lives lost. This was the year of sirens, air-raid shelters, blackouts, sandbags and removed street-signs. Schools such as Ascham, Kambala, Shore and S.C.E.G.G.S. were thought to be particularly vulnerable in the event of a Japanese attack on Sydney Harbour. Ascham was made a Warden's Post in 1942, with the senior biology mistress in the role of senior warden. Although Kambala stayed on-site for the danger period, S.C.E.G.G.S. and Shore set up emergency branch schools in the Blue Mountains, and Ascham set up evacuation arrangements at Berridale and Blackheath. After the Battle of the Coral Sea (May 1942) and the Australian victory at Milne Bay, the Japanese were repulsed and by the end of 1942 the threat of invasion was believed to be over.[9]

As in all other schools, there was no building work, and a shortage of building materials existed during and after the war. Some schools faced extra burdens because of the war: PLC Croydon was requisitioned in 1942 by the military and had to struggle on using Meriden's facilities and moving into two houses in the area.[10] Bryden, the Headmaster of Knox, was summoned for a medical examination and it was feared he might be called up for active service. The Royal Australian Air Force (RAAF) also inspected the Knox site and warned that it might be requisitioned. Nothing came of these threats. Knox and Shore were among the many schools which built trench air-raid shelters on their playing fields.[11] S.C.E.G.G.S. built an air-raid shelter in the cellars of Barham, there was air-raid drill, the cloakrooms were sandbagged, and the upper-storey windows were blacked out.

The war affected school life in different ways. Tea, sugar, butter, meat and clothing were rationed from 1942 onwards. Paper was scarce and one reminder is the very slim editions of *Lux* from these years. At S.C.E.G.G.S. uniforms became darned and not always completely correct, and the boarders' meals occasioned more serious complaints than usual. The authorities had debarred the public from many areas around the Harbour and the art classes found it was difficult to find suitable spots for their outdoor sketching.[12] Inter-school sports meetings ceased.

In the boys' schools there was such a shortage of staff that there were no coaches available for many of the teams. Sydney Grammar, for example, had no-one to coach their First XV.[13] It was impossible to find ground staff or materials to maintain the sports fields and in addition some of these were requisitioned. The heads of schools affiliated with AAGPS decided to suspend all sporting fixtures for the duration of the war. Miss Wilkinson noted in her Annual Report of 1943 that the Tildesley Shield Tournament had to be abandoned through lack of tennis balls, and that the shortage of balls promised to be even more acute the following year.[14]

The state schools actively recruited women teachers and paid them better than did the private schools; S.C.E.G.G.S. experienced some staffing difficulties during the war but mostly, it seems, with domestic staff at North Sydney and at the emergency school at Leura.[15] Staff shortages existed partly because wartime industries offered attractive wages, whereas the salaries of the private schools lagged behind. A significant change during the war was the entry of married women into the workforce: at S.C.E.G.G.S. Mrs Sharland was one teacher who joined the staff as a wartime 'retread', and at least seven other married women were appointed during the war. The majority of staff members were single women nonetheless. Some S.C.E.G.G.S. girls were granted fee reductions and enrolments fell, especially in 1942.[16] Some girls transferred to

St Alban's Anglican church and hall, Leura. The Leura emergency branch of S.C.E.G.G.S. held classes here in 1942, when there was fear of a Japanese invasion of Sydney.

the Moss Vale branch from Head School, others went to Head School from the North Sydney school and some from Head School and other private schools attended the Leura emergency branch school in 1942.

The Leura emergency branch was opened for the beginning of first term, 1942. Accounts by Mrs Sharland[17] and a pupil from Wenona, Valerie Luker,[18] provide excellent information from the viewpoints of both teacher and pupil. Valerie Luker claims that the idea of the emergency branch was hatched by her parents, Miss Wilkinson and the local rector in her parents' sitting room at Leura.[19]

All the arrangements were made for the emergency branch in January 1942. The desks, tables, blackboards, chairs, lockers and other necessary furniture were sent by rail and stored in the church hall of St Alban's Anglican Church at Leura. In the first week there were 120 on the school roll, with 55 boarders.[20] The Chateau Napier accommodated the boarders. Art classes and the kindergarten were housed in the Chateau's tower room, named Paradise because of its superb views, and the primary school class was conducted in the ballroom. A mother of one of the girls opened a school hostel, capable of accommodating seventeen boarders. The Anglican church hall was the main classroom area, sectioned off by heavy stage curtains borrowed from Head School. After the first week the Methodist and Presbyterian church halls were also rented. Third year, with 25 girls, was housed in the Methodist hall, and the tiny adjoining kitchen was used as a chemistry laboratory, while the Presbyterian hall was appropriated for the dressmaking classes as they were able to use the sewing machines there belonging to the Comforts Fund.[21] As the year progressed, enrolments dropped: to 80 girls in second term and 60 in third. Girls came from a variety of other schools:

That afternoon (the day before school began in term one) Pat and I went to Leura Railway station to see the arrival of the main body of boarders from Sydney. From the railway bridge we watched a motley collection leave the train—the curious and the reluctant, the groups of friends familiar with each other's company and those obviously alone.

The royal blue tunics and black stockings of S.C.E.G.G.S. Darlinghurst dominated although there were some fawn stockings of S.C.E.G.G.S. Greenwich, now defunct.

Among the royal blue were the uniforms of Abbotsleigh, Ascham, PLC Croydon and others. We felt relief that Wenona uniforms would not be out of place, possibly proud that we were making our mark. By Easter the school had become a coherent organisation with a few traditions of its own . . . it would be quite usual to see three girls walking along the street engaged in happy chatter, one wearing a S.C.E.G.G.S. uniform, another Ascham and a third PLC's tartan.

School uniforms were something of a non-issue anyway . . . Mother had managed to obtain a S.C.E.G.G.S. tunic for me which replaced the Wenona one I had outgrown. To this was added my grey Wenona stockings, Wenona blouses and a plain dark green jumper. On a couple of occasions when I wanted to look very smart I borrowed a S.C.E.G.G.S. tie, wore a pair of fawn stockings I had had at Frensham junior school and my Sunday-best brown shoes. The effect was correct S.C.E.G.G.S. Greenwich.[22]

Schoolwork was kept parallel with Head School as far as possible, and for first term Miss Wilkinson divided her time equally between Leura and Darlinghurst. It must have been very difficult, for the trains were slow and crowded. For the last two terms Miss Spicer was appointed to Leura as Miss Wilkinson's deputy.[23] Of the teaching staff, six were lent by Head School, a full-time mathematics mistress was appointed and there were visiting members of staff for the extra subjects. In order to staff all the classes, teachers found themselves teaching unfamiliar or long-forgotten subjects. Mrs Sharland found it:

. . . rather in the nature of a cold plunge at first, but after years of teaching one's own subject exclusively the change provided new interests and a welcome break and public examination results have shown that the children did not suffer. Some, indeed, achieved better results than we expected, due perhaps in some measure to the more individual teaching possible in a small school.[24]

It seems that at one stage in 1942, Miss Wilkinson contemplated the establishment of a permanent school at Leura but the Leura emergency branch closed down at the end of 1942, despite the disappointment of a number of parents. Valerie Luker paid this tribute to Miss Wilkinson:

Much of the success of the school was due to the outstanding personality of Miss Wilkinson. She was not only an energetic and capable organiser, she was friendly and approachable. You did what she asked simply because she had asked it. A few days before the first term began, she collected me from home and took me to the tennis court adjoining the Methodist hall. Explaining that she thought the girls should have an opportunity to play tennis, she enlisted my help in marking the court. It was a hot February afternoon so after about ten minutes she decided to remove her navy blue and white silk dress. Her appearance was still decent but I marvelled that this remarkable Headmistress could work away so unselfconsciously at such a humble task wearing only a black milanese slip.[25]

From the staff's point of view, Mrs Sharland remembered that:

> *The year had its ups and downs, some difficult moments, many hearty laughs and much good companionship. Teaching behind curtains within earshot of at least three other colleagues and their classes was at first a somewhat shy-making affair, and it was difficult, for example, to create and maintain an atmosphere necessary to the appreciation of literature, when the congruence of triangles A,B,C, and D,E,F was being insisted upon next door, the mysteries of pollination being explained on the other side, while the respective merits of the Ablative Absolute and 'cum' with the subjunctive were being discussed a little farther away. Yes! it was difficult at first, and we found ourselves frequently lapsing into silence and 'giving the girls something to write', but very soon we got over it, and with occasional appeals to the more penetratingly-voiced of us, managed to lose our self-consciousness.*[26]

The North Sydney branch was a casualty of the war. It was closed in 1941 and although the minutes gave no reason for the decision, the disappointingly low enrolments and the financial losses no doubt explain all. Miss Wilkinson stated in her Annual Report of 1944 that the war was responsible. The closure was not a new idea—it had been suggested from 1938 onwards. The action was regarded as temporary, and meanwhile the Council did what they could to relocate the North Sydney staff. The financial situation for S.C.E.G.G.S. improved greatly after the closure: from a debit balance of £1937 for the current account in February 1941, the statements showed rising profit from June 1942. The Moss Vale debt was liquidated and at times the current account showed a credit balance of well over £3000. Standish, the North Sydney site, was sold in July 1945 for £13 000 to the Home Mission Society.

Although the North Sydney branch was never reopened, the Council bought Redlands, a school in Military Road, Cremorne, in March 1945. The school was more than 60 years old and claimed to be the oldest private school on the north side of the Harbour.[29] The Headmistress at the time was Miss G. A. Roseby, who had taken over the school in 1911. Before that she had been Headmistress of Ascham, and her cousins had been Headmistresses of Kambala. She agreed to stay on as Head, provided her sister also remained.

Although enrolments had fallen at Redlands during the threat of the Japanese invasion, numbers grew satisfactorily after the S.C.E.G.G.S. Council took control. By 1946 there were 266 girls enrolled, compared with 142 girls in 1941 and 102 in 1942 at the North Sydney branch. The Council paid £7680 for Redlands, plus £800 for goodwill and a further £2201 for furniture and fittings, totalling £10 681 for the purchase.[28] With a margin of more than £2000 from the sale of Standish, and the much healthier enrolments at Redlands, the Council had made a sound decision. The large catchment area for Redlands, which included all the Mosman peninsula, together with the school's good reputation and long tradition, meant that the Redlands venture would succeed where the North Sydney one had not. In August Miss Roseby resigned and the following November Mrs I. A. Humphrey was appointed as Headmistress of S.C.E.G.G.S. Redlands.[29]

At Moss Vale Miss Steel had resigned in 1943 and was replaced by Miss Baddams.[30] A tribute to Miss Steel in *Lux* in June 1945 made special mention of her sense of humour. She seemed capable, approachable and down-to-earth. The winters at Moss Vale took their toll on her health, and staff, pupils and Council regretted her departure. During the 1940s Moss Vale enrolments

S.C.E.G.G.S. Redlands 1945–1976. The school was founded in 1884; Miss G. A. Roseby had been Headmistress since 1911. The S.C.E.G.G.S. Council acquired the school as a going concern in 1945 to take over the work of S.C.E.G.G.S. North Sydney, which had been founded in 1911 and closed at Standish in 1942.

were quite satisfactory: mostly they were about 100, but in May 1942 they were up to 188 with transfers from the city schools.

Mrs Griffin had left S.C.E.G.G.S. in 1941 after twenty years on the staff. Miss Wilkinson praised her:

> *It is impossible to estimate what she has meant to S.C.E.G.G.S., her classwork being, as with all real teachers, only a part. Yet steady passes in a difficult matriculation subject (we have never had any anxieties about our Latin results since she came to us); accurate classical training as a foundation for modern languages, for science—the culture which Latin, and above all Greek, can give, Classical Honour students at the University, Vera Blackburn and Una Fitzhardinge especially, are no mean achievement. She built on Miss Badham's excellent foundations and did so worthily. Out of school she was always ready to help with the hockey team! To me personally her experience in education here was invaluable, we could discuss matters quietly, voicing our opinions and then sleeping on them—or she would throw out a suggestion at staff meetings which I might veto at sight and find myself adopting later.*[31]

Three members of staff who were to stay for a long time and exercise great influence arrived in 1937–38: Miss Ivy Vandervord, Miss Enid Cambridge and Miss Grace Spicer. Miss Vandervord joined the mathematics staff in 1937. She

Miss Ivy Vandervord has been part of S.C.E.G.G.S. since Miss Badham's time: first as a pupil, then as a member of staff under each of the other three Headmistresses.

had attended S.C.E.G.G.S. in Miss Badham's last year and had the distinction of having been on the staff under the next three Headmistresses, so that as pupil or teacher she was associated with the school under all its four Headmistresses. Miss Cambridge came as the art teacher in 1938, leaving 30 years later. In 1944 one of her paintings was purchased by the National Gallery. Her exhibitions were well received, with praise in the *Sydney Morning Herald* for her 'lyricism so characteristic of the best English watercolour tradition'. Miss Spicer came onto the staff in 1938 and later became Deputy Head. She was at S.C.E.G.G.S. for about 40 years. Mrs Sharland, the source of so much information on the Wilkinson years, was also remembered by Old Girls as an outstanding teacher, especially because of her authoritative, colourful personality and gift for reading literature with great panache in her beautiful BBC English voice.

During the war years, there were increasingly radical demands for change in New South Wales schools and although little change was implemented, there was a ferment of discussion. The leaving age was raised by the state from fourteen to fifteen in 1941, and enrolments rose. The examination system was relaxed to the extent that the high school entrance examination was abolished by 1943 and in 1944 the Intermediate Certificate was made an internal examination. Consequently more people stayed on to sit for their Leaving Certificate because it had become the only external examination, and the status it conferred was desirable for future employment. Indeed employers were demanding higher qualifications after the war.

The Leaving Certificate requirements were modified in a number of ways. In 1941 the maximum number of papers that could be taken was reduced from ten to eight. Mathematics and a foreign language were no longer required for matriculation by 1944, and there was a subsequent decline in the popularity of Latin and Greek.

Through the influence of the New Education Fellowship (see p. 112) Dewey's educational theories were being espoused. These stressed a pragmatic approach to education, the aims being personal and social—instead of moral and intellectual—development.[32] Problem-solving techniques, freedom for teachers and pupils, an emphasis on guidance rather than direction, and stress on child interest as an important motive for learning, were all part of the new approach. Initially the changes occurred in the primary school, where the examination system was not a force to be reckoned with. Two outcomes were the introduction of projects as a teaching device, and a new subject named social studies, which combined history, geography and economics in a study of humanity.

As at Shore and Kambala, examination results in the Leaving Certificate were extremely gratifying. If anything, standards were rising. S.C.E.G.G.S. was among the top ranking schools in its academic results. In her report to the Council Miss Wilkinson said in 1943:

> *I think the Head School record is educationally superior to that of Newington, Kings and St Josephs . . . but not as broadly based as that of Sydney Girls' High School at which the subjects were eight in number and of a comprehensive range, viz English, Latin, French, Mathematics, Modern History, Chemistry, Botany and Geology. On the other hand it is broader than Sydney Grammar School whose four subjects are English, Mathematics, Modern History and Geography.*[33]

She included a table (which is not entirely easy to understand) with an explanatory heading.

Miss Wilkinson's table showing the educational status of Head School.
The educational status of Head School (so far as such status can be related to a public examination) is shown to be high among all the schools, Girls' and Boys', sending candidates. Thus, A in an expert calculation by points allotted for each degree of pass attained by each pupil from Shore, Kings, Head School, St Joseph's and North Sydney High, with the order on the list was:

1	*North Sydney Boys' High* with an average of	*8.54*
2	***Head School***	***8.2***
3	*Shore & Grammar*	*8.0*
4	*Sydney Boys' High*	*7.78*
5	*Newington & St Joseph's*	*7.5*
6	*Fort Street Boys' High*	*7.4*
7	*Kings*	*6.6*

Miss Wilkinson concluded:

> *There is proof here that the Head School holds an honourable position among the secondary schools, State and Religious, of best repute in examination tests.*

It was the only school of those mentioned which had to arrange a refuge-school for a number of its pupils in 1942[34] under conditions likely to endanger its higher work. It was also the only school with two independent branch schools drawing from its supplies of income that were needed for its own development.[35]

The end of the war in the Pacific, on 14 August 1945, went almost unmentioned in *Lux.* It was overshadowed by the excitement of the S.C.E.G.G.S. Jubilee year and in particular the Jubilee pageant held in the Town Hall on 16 July 1945. Through 1945 the attendant celebrations were extensive and carefully planned. There were special services (one in the chapel and another in the Cathedral), an Old Girls' dance, a buffet tea in the gymnasium, and a pageant in the Town Hall on Monday 16 July 1945. A special edition of *Lux* the following March gave details of the celebrations with photographs. Letters from well-wishers and a list of subscribers to the Jubilee Fund were published. The Old Girls were in charge of the Jubilee Fund, with a £50 000 target, set up to fund the building of a library in the proposed new school wing. It would be called the 'Dorothy Wilkinson Library'.

A special booklet commemorating the Jubilee pageant was also published. It contained the text of the pageant, written by Bishop Pilcher. The Bishop helped with the music and wrote the words for at least one of the songs. Old Girls who saw the pageant remember it vividly: it made a very strong impact on them and the setting of the Town Hall must have heightened the grandeur of the occasion for the schoolgirls. The pageant was of famous women in history and the scenes were:

PART I
(BIBLICAL)

SCENE I: *Ruth and Naomi*
SCENE II: *The Queen of Sheba*
SCENE III: *Esther*
SCENE IV: *The Annunciation*
SCENE V: *The women at the tomb*

INTERVAL

PART II
(HISTORICAL)

SCENE VI: *Joan of Arc*
SCENE VII: *Florence Nightingale*
SCENE VIII: *Mary Reiby*
SCENE IX: *Daisy Bates*
SCENE X: *The Founding of the Church of England Girls' Grammar School*[36]

The presentation consisted of tableaux, with a lector explaining the import of each. The actresses (and occasional actor) had a few lines to say, and there was music and singing in each scene. Often the song was a well-known hymn. Apart from some dancing in the Esther scene, the presentation seems to have been rather static, relying for its effects on voice and visual impact. The language was formal and of course the extensive Biblical quotations were from the King James translation. Speaking of S.C.E.G.G.S. in the introduction to Scene I the lector stated:

The purpose of such a school is to train a womanhood which will serve God faithfully in Home and Church and State. The basis of character which is necessary for such service can only be found in Religion. Our Pageant therefore will begin by representing Five Scenes, *which will bring before us the characters and the work, and the high privilege of certain women of the Bible. In the latter part of the Pageant we shall witness the glory of the service rendered by women in more modern days.*

The tone was lofty and sententious. The climax of the evening was the final scene of the founding of the school with the school song 'Girls of the Grammar School' at the conclusion. This was not intended as a historical comment to the effect that the founding of S.C.E.G.G.S. was the crowning achievement of womanhood. Instead it was portrayed as the last in a chronological series of pioneering landmarks. Dorothy Wilkinson's role on stage was minor: the focus was upon Edith Badham and her plans for the school. Frank Hutchens, a regular visitor to S.C.E.G.G.S. and a well-known Sydney pianist, wrote from the Conservatorium of Music:

Dear Miss Wilkinson,
I should like to add my congratulations to the innumerable ones I am sure you are receiving on the great triumph and success of the pageant.
The whole idea showed imagination and a fine sense of colour and effect and the performance was so beautifully smooth and continuous. It must have entailed enormous work in preparation and you all so well deserve the unanimous appreciation. I was charmed with the girls' singing of my Anthem and would be grateful if you would tell them, at the same time extending my warmest thanks to Miss Spencer and Miss Schubach.
It was a great night for S.C.E.G.G.S.

Regards from,
Frank Hutchens.[37]

At the beginning of 1945, Dorothy Wilkinson's 25th year as Principal, Miss Wilkinson indicated that she was preparing to resign. She did not finally leave the school until May 1947. During that two-year period, her relationship with the Council seems to have been awkward and the appointment of a suitable successor a matter for dispute. For most of the school's history Principal and Council had worked well together, as far as can be ascertained. There had been the odd clash between Miss Badham and her Council in the early days as rights, duties and boundaries of power were defined. Although ex-officio Chairman of the Council, Archbishops Saumarez Smith and Wright had attended meetings of the Council only sporadically. Mowll, by contrast, attended most Council meetings in Miss Wilkinson's time. Mowll was a big man, a natural leader with a commanding presence and used to exercising authority. Once having decided upon a course of action, he generally got his way. He was both respected and loved, and his supporters worked tirelessly to implement his plans.[38]

Also on the Council were two of Mowll's right-hand men, T. C. Hammond and S. M. Johnstone. Both were Irish clergymen with powerful personalities. T. C. Hammond became Principal of Moore Theological College in 1935. A gold medallist from the University of Dublin, he was one of the most distinguished conservative Evangelical scholars within Anglicanism. Coming as he did from a polarised religious environment where Protestants were in a minority, he was a seasoned fighter in matters of faith. In his churchmanship he was opposed to compromise and is said to have advised Evangelicals that it was better 'to flog a dead horse than to be led by live asses'.[39]

S. M. Johnstone and T. C. Hammond were the major influences on Mowll after Mowll became Archbishop of Sydney. Mowll had indeed organised for Hammond to come to Sydney in the first place, and Johnstone actually lived at Bishopscourt with the Mowlls at one time. He was a good administrator, a capable historian, and could be ruthless. He did a lot of work behind the scenes. Johnstone was powerful on the S.C.E.G.G.S. Council as Secretary from 1939 to 1945 and he was appointed Deputy Chairman of the Council in 1946.

Mowll, Hammond and Johnstone were the three most powerful clergy in Sydney at the time. It was an unusually strong clergy cast. In addition to them there were some other eminent members of Council. W. J. Mann was a barrister and a leading layman, strong-minded, reputedly 'difficult', and at one time Chancellor of the Diocese. E. R. Holme was Professor of English Language at the University of Sydney and a respected figure in the University. Though not a Sydney Evangelical, he was also very active on the Shore Council. The presence of such men as these on the school Council indicates how important they thought the school was. Not only were they Council members, but their attendance at the Council meetings was punctilious. A. Prescott (Chairman of the Council from about 1960 to 1974)[40] stated in 1990 that the Archbishop regarded the Sydney Anglican schools as one of the three most strategically important places in the Diocese. The others were Moore Theological College and the Cathedral. Until he became Primate, Mowll regularly attended the council meetings of all the Anglican schools and took an active part in their business, especially when it touched upon matters of faith. Hammond and Johnstone shared his views.[41]

One of the contributing factors to their active interest in S.C.E.G.G.S. must have been that S.C.E.G.G.S. was one of the oldest Anglican girls' schools, with a reputation and tradition of being one of the foremost schools in Sydney. The school had become established financially and academically, and its Council had always numbered among its members University luminaries, leaders in society and respected churchmen. Sydney Evangelicals would have seen it as a strategically important site from which to promote the beliefs and practices of Evangelical Anglicanism. A number of daughters of the clergy attended, giving a personal dimension to this view. It was also the only Anglican girls' school in the centre of the city, so that attendance at meetings was not difficult for those working in the city. No other Anglican girls' school had the reputation and status that S.C.E.G.G.S. possessed at this time. It is likely that until the 1940s Headmistress and Council worked well together, and the gifts such men brought to school Council matters would have been of great benefit to Miss Wilkinson and the school. She seems to have earned their trust and respect and she was probably not unduly daunted by their formidable prestige. This changed to some extent in the 1940s.

Council minutes are very properly terse accounts of the bones of meetings, and tantalising for the hints dropped of personality clashes and heated debate. The kind of comment Beck would make, such as 'after lengthy discussion', prompts conjecture as to whether the discussion became argument and whether each strongly held position was stated vehemently. At a Council meeting in April 1942, Miss Wilkinson recommended that the Leura emergency branch school become an established day school. She had dealt with the practical problems, and a written statement was filed with the minutes. Aware of some opposition to her plan, she informed the Council that if they did not trust her judgment in this matter, she regarded it as a want of confidence in her as Headmistress. The end of the matter was that the Council unanimously supported the plan. As the year progressed, it was noted that the Leura school was not paying its way, and by October Wilkinson was recommending it be closed. The branch closed at the end of 1942.[42] Miss Wilkinson may have toyed with the idea of establishing a permanent school at Leura, encouraged by the initial success of the venture and stimulated by its challenge. In reality she was becoming weary after 25 years of headship and the difficulties attendant upon the running of Head School under wartime conditions. A permanent branch school at Leura was probably not financially viable and would have been an extra burden upon Miss Wilkinson, at least for a year or two, until the school was established.

There were some changes in membership of the Council and this in part explains Dorothy Wilkinson's difficulties with the Council in the 1940s. Mrs Swift (Mary Watson, Miss Badham's first pupil) resigned with accompanying expressions of regret from the Council. W. V. W. Thompson resigned at the same time, in 1941, and his resignation was merely noted.[43] T. A. Strudwick, a chartered accountant, replaced Thompson and subsequently became Treasurer. He was an asset to the Council as he was soon appointed to the Council's Executive Committee and Johnstone's Annual Report to the Synod noted that Strudwick had given 'valued advice'.[44] Some confidential correspondence between Holme and Johnstone reveals that both men thought the Council was both disorganised and unbusinesslike.[45] Johnstone felt that he had managed to inject some efficiency into the Council through the institution of the Headmistresses' monthly reports (not, he noted, something which endeared him to them), and also the formation of the Executive Committee. Overworked, stating he was 'too busy to pull his weight', and acknowledged as extremely busy by fellow Council members, Johnstone as Secretary found the volume of business generated by the three schools too much to handle. He had coopted Holme as Assistant Secretary although Holme doubted whether he had the necessary expertise. The time was ripe for the appointment of a full-time bursar, although this was not done until 1965.[46]

The appointment of Alwyn Prescott to the Council in 1944 was of particular significance. Alwyn Prescott was connected with S.C.E.G.G.S. from 1944 until 1974 and from the beginning was a very active Council member. He had graduated BE at the University of Sydney with first class honours in 1941, and lectured in the Faculty of Engineering subsequently. He decided to enter Moore Theological College and was ordained in 1943, although he did not graduate ThL until 1945. He was prized as a man with first-class talents, who had changed his career to become a clergyman, and was cultivated as a very promising man by Archbishop Mowll. For all his intellectual gifts, he was better at dealing with things than people and his logical, hardline, pragmatic approach earned him dislike. Certainly Miss Wilkinson's successor did not like him, and it is almost certain that Miss Wilkinson disliked him also. Within six months of his appointment to the Council, Prescott had replaced Johnstone as Secretary. He later became Chairman of the Council.

Over the following year there was a spate of resignations from the Council, and one from Miss Wilkinson. In October 1945 Strudwick resigned and there was some discussion about Lady MacCallum's resignation. She had recently celebrated her sixtieth wedding anniversary, which was followed shortly after by the death of her husband, Sir Mungo. She was now 82 years old[47] but did not resign, and although she ceased to attend Council meetings from this time, she took an active role in S.C.E.G.G.S.'s affairs, to the extent of hosting some S.C.E.G.G.S. Council committee meetings at her home.[48] It is possible that Lady MacCallum was asked to resign on the grounds of age, as a note in the minutes of October 1945 says:

> Resignation of Lady MacCallum
>
> *It was resolved to defer the receiving of the letter of Lady MacCallum to the next meeting. In the meantime Lady MacCallum would have* explained to her the reason for the Council's action. *(emphasis added)*

Strudwick resigned because of ill health. A resolution by Johnstone reads: 'Mr Strudwick joined the Council and became its financial adviser at a very critical period in the affairs of the School. By clear perception of the position and sound advice as to the remedy he rendered a service to the Council which it hereby gratefully records.'

In February 1946 G. Gelding, Mrs N. F. Babbage, Mrs Trindall and Dr McDouall resigned from the Council. No reasons were given. They were all the more dramatic because they included one very new appointee, and two very old and faithful supporters of the school. Gelding had been appointed to the Council in December 1945 and had been made Treasurer. He did not attend a single Council meeting. Trindall had been appointed to the Council in 1911, and the letter the Council sent her thanked her for her 35 years of service on the Council. McDouall had been a very active and dedicated member of Council since 1921. While it would seem that the resignations were triggered by some controversy in the Council, Prescott states that there was no dissension on the Council at that time.[49]

There are various possible explanations for this dramatic situation. Firstly Prescott, a young man of 29, was a new broom in the Council and wanted to get rid of the old-timers. He may have been behind Lady MacCallum's resignation. Certainly McDouall and Mrs Trindall were probably due to retire in his estimation. Holmes, for some reason, stayed on, although he was 74 in 1945.

Secondly, was the contention which arose over Miss Wilkinson's resignation (discussed further below). Here there were two possibilities: the decision to keep Miss Wilkinson on as Headmistress for 1946; or alternatively, they were distressed at the way Miss Wilkinson had been treated by the Council and resigned because of friction between Council members and Miss Wilkinson and consequent hurt feelings. There was certainly strong support for Dorothy Wilkinson to continue as Head from parents, staff and Old Girls, and one letter from a parent to the Council, for example, asked the Council to reconsider Dorothy Wilkinson's resignation, now that her health had improved.[50]

In addition, immediately after the war there was considerable change in membership of many institutions, committees and boards. While men were away on active service, those who would have retired in the normal course of events stayed on until the war ended. In 1946 new and younger people replaced older ones. Mrs Trindall and Dr McDouall were due for retirement, but their resignations may well have been precipitated by a crisis on the Council.

Dorothy Wilkinson's written resignation was presented to the Council at the February 1945 meeting. Her health was apparently poor but by August 1945 it had improved to the extent that she intimated that she was willing to stay on until an appointment had been made. Prescott's comments on Miss Wilkinson at this time were:

> *I greatly admired Miss Wilkinson but also found her difficult to work with. Her reports to the Council told them nothing and she did as she liked at school—she was greatly loved but at this time very erratic. She resigned as Headmistress; her position was advertised and the Council was about to appoint her successor, when she withdrew her resignation, as her health had improved as a result of a course of vitamin pills. She also made remarks to the Old Girls which were interpreted as meaning that the Council was trying to push her out!*[51]

A joint letter from members of the teaching staff was mentioned in the October minutes. It concerned Miss Wilkinson's resignation and indicated, as did other evidence,[52] that the staff, girls and Old Girls were very keen to see Miss Wilkinson stay on, that the successor did not have their support, and that they thought Miss Wilkinson had been treated badly by the Council. Although it is very unlikely that the Council had a particular person in view as Miss Wilkinson's successor, perhaps Miss Wilkinson's supporters saw that she was ill, upset and unhappy about leaving. That was enough for them: Miss Wilkinson should stay.

In November 1945 a special committee met at Lady MacCallum's house to work out a solution to the succession problem. The only applicant they seriously considered was Dr Hilda Rayward MA DipEd (Melbourne) DPhil (Munich). Rayward's credentials submitted to the S.C.E.G.G.S. Council were impressive. Her academic brilliance was unquestionable and she had testimonials from a Professor of Education, a former Director of Education in Victoria and one Headmistress. However, all of the references were out-of-date and some were twenty years old. A Headmistress writing in 1933 had described her as 'reliable, capable and loyal'. At the time when the Council was engaged in appointing Miss Wilkinson's successor, Redlands needed a new Headmistress also. Dr Rayward made it clear that she was interested only in the position at Head School, and the Council saw one solution as giving her that position, and asking Miss Wilkinson to take over Redlands 'and work it up as her last contribution to the success of the school'. Furthermore Dr Rayward would only take the position if she could begin immediately: she was not prepared to wait for another year. It is said that Miss Wilkinson did not like the Council's choice of successor, and so decided to stay on for 1946.[53] Miss Wilkinson stated firmly at the meeting that it was her own desire, and the desire of the staff and Old Girls, that she should continue for another year.[54] She implied that her resignation had not been official because the Council had not sent her a letter of acceptance. The dearth of applicants for Miss Wilkinson's job is difficult to account for, especially as little more than a year later there were five applicants for Headmistress of S.C.E.G.G.S. Darlinghurst.

Holmes summarised the Council's three possible options:

1 To appoint Dr Rayward as Headmistress and Miss Wilkinson as relieving Headmistress from 1 January 1946.
2 To appoint Dr Rayward as Principal and Miss Wilkinson as relieving Headmistress from 1 January 1946.
3 To ask Miss Wilkinson to continue as Principal until the end of 1946 and appoint Dr Rayward as Principal-elect, paying her a retainer fee.

Holmes and Stephens were inclined to think Dr Rayward would be a suitable appointment. After the interview Holmes recorded:

> *She was bright and interesting, she gave evidence of thinking about the educational problems of the moment . . . in all her talk she made no reference to any liking she had for work with girls . . . Her professional knowledge, interest and judgement were such as her career should imply, in* extent. *Whether there was any deficiency in* quality *could not be discerned . . . The chief difficulty with Dr R. appeared to be the increasing evidence that a movement of hostility to a change in the headship of the school is being promoted.*[55]

Rayward was not appointed and Miss Wilkinson stayed on as Principal until May 1947. Dr Rayward subsequently became Headmistress of Ascham in 1947, remaining there for four terms. She was, to quote a pupil of the time, 'a total disaster'. She was unable to impose discipline on the pupils and did not run the school: a mistress due to retire stayed on to keep the school going.[56] The 1986 Ascham history devotes only one line to her, and its authors said in a telephone conversation with this author that Dr Rayward was a Headmistress they would rather forget. Dorothy Wilkinson's judgment, painful as it was for her to act upon, had proved wise.

It is clear that the time had come for Miss Wilkinson to retire and that Council members such as Prescott thought she was a law unto herself and no longer very efficient. Her apparently erratic behaviour over her resignation was not what it seemed to Prescott. Her commitment to S.C.E.G.G.S. included a sense of responsibility to remain at the helm until the appointment of a suitable person to succeed her.

The process of finding a successor was left to the last minute: only in February 1947 was there a special meeting to consider the appointment of a new Headmistress. Two applicants out of five were interviewed: Miss Barbara Chisholm of Napier, New Zealand and Miss Merrillee Roberts of Sydney. Miss Chisholm was interviewed by W. H. W. Stevenson, Bishop of Nelson, and Miss Roberts by the Council. Miss Chisholm was thought to be 'very suitable from the point of view of school administration, but there was inadequate information re her religious standpoint'. On the other hand, Miss Roberts, 'while fully satisfactory on the religious and academic sides, had not as much experience in school administration as was desirable'. Although Roberts did not win the position, she subsequently became the first deputy to be appointed at S.C.E.G.G.S. Moss Vale.[57] Later she became Headmistress of Newcastle Girls' Grammar School, then Headmistress of Ascham from 1961 to 1972.

It was resolved to offer Miss Chisholm the appointment if she could begin duty not later than the beginning of second term. Hammond and Prescott did not oppose the appointment but were unhappy about appointing her before she could be interviewed by Council. Thus Chisholm was appointed, sight unseen and in a rush, on the recommendation of a New Zealand bishop. This was possible because Stevenson had been a Sydney Evangelical, and was the son-in-law of Archbishop Saumarez Smith, well-known to the Sydney clergy and a man whose word they were prepared to trust. He was also Alwyn Prescott's father-in-law. He summed up Chisholm with the words:

> *With regard to religion in the school she is enthusiastic on the matter of church schools because of their spiritual emphasis. She has taken scripture since she has been at Hamilton. She is also conscious of the need as far as possible of having a*

This photograph, taken at Speechday with Bishop Pilcher presenting a cup to Margaret Dowling, is one of the very few informal pictures of Miss Wilkinson. There are few photographs of her and there are few of the school in her time. She was continually on the move, and her warmth and spontaneity eluded capture by photography or painter's portrait.

staff that is definitely and actively Christian. I did not go into the matter of her academic attainments as I understand you were satisfied about them. To sum up I could have wished her to have had a more personal knowledge of Christ in her own experience. Unless you have someone else who can meet your need in this respect more than Miss Chisholm and at the same time has the necessary qualifications and experience on the scholastic side you could I think with confidence offer Miss Chisholm the post.[58]

Dorothy Wilkinson left S.C.E.G.G.S. at the end of term I in 1947, having done all she could to welcome and help her successor. Mrs Griffin wrote a vivid portrait of her when in 1945 it was thought Miss Wilkinson was about to leave:

As a member of the teaching staff for twenty years, I should have no difficulty in writing of Miss Wilkinson, but I find it difficult to recapture my own feelings as I try to recall the elusive spirit of the person who is Miss Wilkinson. Always there, but always flitting from one sphere of action to another, very hard to find in the flesh; but, when found, so ready and eager to listen to every difficulty, problem or suggestion; only an outline was needed, and then like a lightening flash, her whole energy was concentrated on the matter in hand; all the advantages and disadvantages were quickly assessed and with breath-taking speed everything burst into action and the project was a fait accompli.

With the Teaching Staff, Miss Wilkinson always maintained the friendliest relations; she received the best work from everyone because she expected the best. Though never appearing to investigate, she was fully aware of the effect and

> *influence of each member and kept her fingers on the pulses of the whole school. Miss Wilkinson has devoted the best years of her life and all her energies to the school, she has centered all her interests in it. Anyone connected with a large school knows that such a unity of purpose precludes the ordinary social contracts of life; this is a sacrifice which only becomes apparent when the life there draws to a close.*[59]

Dorothy Wilkinson lived only a few months after her retirement. On 18 September 1947 she was killed in an accident. As she was attempting to get off a moving bus, she fell and was run over by the back wheel of the bus. She was 64. The school was affected in much the same way as people were by the death of Queen Mary and King George VI. Some of the senior girls were grief-stricken.[60] A funeral service was held in St Andrew's Cathedral and a booklet commemorating her life and work was published. The resolution of sympathy in the Council minutes summed up her contribution to S.C.E.G.G.S.:

> *During her principalship, the enrolment of the school increased from some 250 to approximately 460 girls, while the sister schools of Moss Vale and North Sydney made considerable progress, progress in no small degree due to her advocacy of their needs. During her regime the school became recognised as one of the premier girls' schools of Australia, with a distinguished record in all spheres, old girls of the school having consistently won good places in the University examination lists.*
>
> *However, the greatest contribution that Miss Wilkinson made to the life of S.C.E.G.G.S. was her influence on the characters of the girls under her care. Her constant example of a strong religious faith, and its outworking in a sacrificial giving of herself in the service of the girls of the School could not but win for her the affection and profound respect of scholars, teachers and parents alike.*
>
> *During her Headmistress-ship, the School passed through certain periods of testing, in particular some acute years of depression, and the Second World War. As a result of the leadership which she gave, the school emerged from these trials stronger than before. So much did her work permeate every part of the School's activities, that it was said by at least one parent: 'Miss Wilkinson is S.C.E.G.G.S.' In the wider sphere she held office as Secretary and Treasurer of the Headmistresses' Association, and was a member of the National Council of Women. Truly the school motto was the watchword of her life 'Luceat Lux Vestra'.*[61]

Eulogies are rarely accurate. Balancing Dorothy Wilkinson's achievements and her great contribution to S.C.E.G.G.S. are the facts that after the extraordinary demands of running the school first in a severe depression, then during a five-year war, Dorothy Wilkinson was not fresh to meet the challenges of the postwar era. Prescott believes that the school was run down when Miss Chisholm took over, and that there was a lot of tidying up to do. The long preretirement period was at best a time of keeping the school machine ticking over, a time of keeping guard until the post could be relinquished.

— 11 —

Barbara Chisholm and the postwar years, 1947–1959

THE DEPARTURE OF Dorothy Wilkinson and the advent of the third Headmistress, Barbara Chisholm, coincided very nearly with the beginning of a new era: the postwar world. For Australia this period meant the strengthening of ties with America and the end of colonial dependency on Britain; of increasing urbanisation and industrialisation; of a participation in the technological revolution of which television, and Sputnik, and landing on the moon are the symbols; of a great influx of European migrants which altered the character and culture of the Australian people indelibly. In education this era was the prelude to the education revolution which formally took place with the implementation of the Wyndham Report in 1962. Initially it was a time of shortages, both of building materials and teaching staff. By the 1950s school populations rose considerably, and schools expanded, undertaking building projects that had not been possible since the 1920s. Inflation brought in its train demands for higher salaries, and school fees rose steeply. It was appropriate that such challenges and opportunities be met with a new school Principal: one with vitality, youth and a fresh approach.

Barbara Chisholm was 32 years old when she became S.C.E.G.G.S. Darlinghurst's third Headmistress. She came from an established New Zealand family, her maternal and paternal great-grandfathers having taken up land in the early days of settlement.[1] The family had not remained on the land and her father set up his own wholesaling firm despite his father's wish that he should be a Presbyterian minister. Her family had a keen interest in education and her mother strongly encouraged her three daughters to undertake tertiary education. Barbara Chisholm gained a BA at Canterbury University College in economics and history. After a spell of ill health which prolonged her student days, she was invited in 1940 to go temporarily to help in a Presbyterian girls'

Miss Barbara Chisholm, third Headmistress, 1947–1977.

boarding school, Solway College in Masterton, a large town in the North Island of New Zealand. The Headmistress, Miss Marion Thompson, deeply impressed her. Although old and almost blind she taught Barbara Chisholm to teach and made her enjoy it enough so that she wanted to continue. In 1943 she left Solway College and went to the Waihato Diocesan School as Senior Mistress, where she stayed until taking up her appointment at S.C.E.G.G.S. in 1947.[2]

Miss Chisholm's gifts were outstanding and it was only a matter of time before she became a Headmistress. At Waikato, even though she was scarcely 30, she was the chief support of the Headmistress and very possibly her successor. She recalls:

> *I was in a difficult position in the school I was with because the Headmistress was dying and the parents wanted to get rid of her and this was terrible and I didn't want to step into her shoes while she wanted another [year?]. She knew she had another couple of years, but she had cancer and it was very difficult, so I said to her, 'I think I'll apply somewhere else', She said, 'Don't leave me now', and when she talked it over she said, 'Oh yes, it would be a good idea.' So I applied for this in the September holidays, I think it was, and I didn't hear for weeks and weeks.*[3]

The manner of her appointment and her early experiences on her arrival were mostly unpleasant. There was no reply from the Council about her application until the Christmas holidays. This was probably due to inefficiency, and not to any sinister motive on the Council's part. She was then asked to travel to Nelson to be interviewed by the Bishop. The journey from Waikato in the North Island to Nelson in the South Island took two days and a night, and included a difficult trip by ferry across the Cook Strait. After that, because of travel restrictions, she had difficulty securing a return flight to Sydney for an interview with the Council: she managed to organise a flight across to Sydney but could get no assurance that there would be a flight home to New Zealand. She heard no more from the Council until the start of term in 1947, so she sent them a letter withdrawing her application. The Council then rang her to inform her that she was appointed, and she accepted. She finished her term with Waikato and began at S.C.E.G.G.S. after the May holidays.[4]

Her impressions of the Council at that time were that they were all old, with the exception of Prescott, and none had any real interest in education except Professor Holmes. Her comment on Alwyn Prescott and Dorothy Wilkinson was that Miss Wilkinson 'thought he was too young to have any opinions and he thought she was too old to be here'.[5] She was grateful for the trouble Holmes took to write to her before she left New Zealand about standards and trends in education, and about Sydney schools.[6] Lady MacCallum she described as the power behind the throne who no longer attended Council meetings but summoned people for an audience.

She travelled to Sydney by boat, sharing a cabin with a child, from whom she caught chickenpox. She was met at the wharf by a contingent of girls, staff, Council members and Miss Wilkinson. There was tea with Lady MacCallum one afternoon, then two days at Leura with Miss Wilkinson.[7] Miss Wilkinson did all in her power to make Miss Chisholm feel welcome. School records were few, so Miss Wilkinson had written Miss Chisholm long letters to help her understand the school before she arrived:

> *Miss Wilkinson broke her arm not long before she retired and her writing, which I gather had never been very legible, deteriorated, and she used to write me long letters about the school—twelve and fifteen pages, both sides of the paper often, and I used to leave them on the mantelpiece in my flat and read another line or two every time I went past, but she was wonderful, the things she tried to tell me.*[8]

Miss Chisholm inferred from this that Miss Wilkinson was doing all she could to ensure that Miss Chisholm would not experience the rejection she had suffered on her arrival as Edith Badham's successor 27 years earlier.

Barbara Chisholm's first reaction to S.C.E.G.G.S. was one of dismay:

> *I knew it was a city school with limited space but I was not prepared for the terrible shabbiness of the place or the complete lack of comfort for staff and boarders. I had been to a Church of England boarding school myself and had taught in another. Both had provided far better accommodation for boarders, and the Headmistress and staff had been able to live in some comfort and dignity. Not so at Darlinghurst. The staff bedrooms opened into classrooms and the Headmistress had a room a long way from anyone else—also among classrooms—and shared a bathroom, a long way from her bedroom, with the girls.*
>
> *I was to discover that though Darlinghurst was particularly bad, this lack of comfort for staff and heads was fairly common for N.S.W. independent schools for girls. Moss Vale was an outstanding exception—and a cause of dissatisfaction at Darlinghurst because it was almost always supported financially by Darlinghurst.*[9]

She had been told that she would have a 'flat near the church' so the reality of her living quarters was a shock.

She wrote her first report to the Council from her sickbed. The report began by asking for salary rises for the staff: she argued that the school's reputation would suffer if the right type of teacher were not attracted, and to do this it was necessary to pay better salaries:

> *The cook in one of our Church of England schools is paid £6 per week, clear. That is more than any member of this school is earning and I consider that her work is far lighter than that of the majority of teachers here. The teacher is constantly hearing of such things and yet is asked to believe that her work is considered of vital importance in the moulding of young people. The cook is obviously considered more valuable. I quote this case because it is a school council that is making the valuation.*
>
> *Not many young people grow up with a great desire to teach. Most of the outstanding teachers I have known have become teachers because they could not find any other employment. Not until they had taught for a time did the interest and enthusiasm which made them outstanding, develop. Nowdays there are many other avenues and unless we can make teaching attractive we have little chance of getting the best type of woman into our schools.*[10]

The report also criticised the school buildings: classrooms, absence of a library and an assembly room, lack of staffroom, and the general need for painting and repairs. There were comments such as: 'Some of the classrooms are terrible. One class is disturbed every time Charlie stokes the furnace.' 'The main linen cupboard is in a classroom.' 'The library, which should be one of the most important parts of the school, is a small collection of books housed in a not too watertight shack at the bottom of the garden.'

The solution to many of these problems she saw to be in more buildings: but buildings which did not interfere with the open space. To this end she strongly recommended leasing 'Molong', a property across the road, which could accommodate the boarders and resident staff. There was need for equipment: blackboards, typewriters, mapping equipment, science equipment, hundreds of books, a film projector, a 'radiogramophone' and a plentiful supply of good records. Miss Chisholm was asking for the same things as her predecessor. A circular letter signed by Miss Wilkinson as Secretary of the Headmistresses' Association of New South Wales to the Chairman of the Council, written during the war, shows that the Headmistresses, including Miss Wilkinson, were acutely aware of shortages and inadequate facilities. In it Miss Wilkinson asked specifically for higher salaries for teaching staff, a superannuation scheme and adequate buildings and equipment.[11]

Miss Chisholm's comment on her report and the Council's reaction was:

> *I didn't mince matters and heard later that there was a feeling that I should be asked to leave. Possibly this didn't happen because a certain group had quite unjustly blamed Miss Wilkinson for the state of the school.*
>
> *Why did I stay? Partly because I wasn't going to walk out on a challenge and partly because I developed chicken-pox shortly after my arrival and as a result found I had come among friends. Soon I came to value the spirit of the school—there is something about S.C.E.G.G.S. that is different from anything else I've known. The girls come from a great variety of backgrounds and areas and meet in friendliness and with a complete lack of snobbery. The academic standard has*

always been excellent and impressed me from the beginning and I found Old Girls, Staff (mostly!) and parents very helpful.[12]

A photograph in the March 1947 edition of *Lux* shows the new Headmistress with jet black hair, dark brown eyes and a face alight with a smile, but also energetic and determined. In those years the girls liked to believe she was a Maori princess. She was younger than all her staff and was patronised as a colonial by one English member of staff. For her first few years at S.C.E.G.G.S. she returned home for the long Christmas holidays. Lack of family in Australia and lack of opportunity to make friends outside the school made her situation as Headmistress a particularly isolated and lonely one.

Miss Chisholm's headship at S.C.E.G.G.S. was to be the longest yet: from 1947 to 1977. She continued the tradition which she found and admired there: the academic quality, the emphasis on the importance of each person at the school, the Christian values, and the spirit of service and communal responsibility. Changes she made were in the material resources of buildings and equipment, and in the curriculum. Her particular gifts were neither in the classroom as a teacher, nor in educational philosophy. Instead she was a capable administrator—shrewd, businesslike and practical—and was an outstanding Headmistress because her staff respected, trusted and liked her.

Barbara Chisholm's aims and educational values were stated at the end of her Annual Reports. In 1948 she said:

Above all, I want to carry on the great work of religious training for which this school has been noted. I have left mention of it till last because it is the most important part of our work. If girls can go out from S.C.E.G.G.S. realising that it is 'people' and not 'things' that matter, which count, they will give and find happiness in service.[13]

In 1951 she spoke of the school equipping girls to do their best to serve the community as leaders or as followers, with standards firmly based on the Christian faith so that they might 'know the good and have the courage to follow it'.[14] Year after year she emphasised the importance of Christian values:

More than anything else we wish to help them to realise that the Christian faith alone can give them a true standard of values in an unstable world. Religious belief cannot, of course, be forced, but we try to provide an atmosphere in which it can develop. We are very conscious of the difficulties with which children nowadays are faced and know that we can help them best by showing them that there is one unshakeable rock on which they can stand.[15]

In her monthly reports to the Council, there was always a section on religious activities (as requested by the Council). There were two sessions of morning prayers daily (one for seniors and one for juniors, because there was insufficient space for the whole school to assemble together) and on Wednesdays a service was taken by the school chaplain. From 1928 to 1955 the chaplain was the Rev. Clarence Lucas. He was replaced by Dr Archibald Morton who stayed until 1966. Both were incumbents of St John's Darlinghurst while chaplain at S.C.E.G.G.S. Apart from the Wednesday services, the chaplain would conduct confirmation classes and be present at official functions such as Speech Day. Confirmation classes were often very large: in 1954, for example, 52 girls were confirmed.[16] The chaplains had little real impact on school life: the girls saw them as distant figures who visited the school from time to time. Neither Lucas nor Morton seemed to be able to communicate with the S.C.E.G.G.S. girls on their own level.

There were two scripture lessons a week, some of which Miss Chisholm took herself. The Grace Johnstone Memorial Prize for gospel knowledge was offered annually.[17] There was a Crusader group in the school, Crusaders being an Evangelical Christian Union operating in private schools in Sydney. In an interview in 1985 Miss Chisholm said of the Crusader group:

> *I didn't initiate any sort of feeling against the Crusaders though I was a bit surprised that in a church school they didn't consider they got enough in daily chapel—we had daily chapel and two scripture lessons a week and three in some classes, and then they were intolerant to other people, and I didn't like that, because I was brought up in a High Church tradition . . .*[18]

Miss Chisholm's churchmanship marked her as 'different' in the Sydney Diocese where Low Church Evangelicals were in the majority. Although the Diocese contained examples of all shades of churchmanship, the Archbishop and the church leaders were all of the Evangelical tradition. The lines were clearly drawn and church party labels were more important then than they have since become. Archbishop Mowll, A. Prescott, the Begbies and Archdeacon Johnstone were strongly Evangelical church leaders and Chisholm's high churchmanship made her an outsider. This may have been acceptable to her in that it preserved her individuality and she could remain somewhat aloof from both Council and Diocese.

Despite her 30 years in Sydney, she did not seem to alter her position. As her views on the Crusader group indicate, for her the practice of Christianity was a private and personal matter. There was no room for the Evangelical stress on the 'horizontal' aspect of faith: that of fellowship and sharing the faith with other people, whether fellow Christians or those outside the faith. In addition to a private and personal expression of faith, the High Church was characterised by an observance of ritual (described by one S.C.E.G.G.S. teacher of the time, also High Church, as 'good manners in God's house') and strict adherence to the 1662 Book of Common Prayer. It was a very formal expression of faith. In the second half of the twentieth century the High Church of England has been in decline and has been replaced for the most part by the Anglo-Catholic tradition in all its gradations, from extreme Anglo-Catholicism (hardly different from Roman Catholicism) to middle-church Anglicanism.

Miss Chisholm's High Church position is very important because although it was in many ways similar to Edith Badham's, she was fostering a school tradition which was different from that desired by Evangelicals on the Council. For people like Mowll, Hammond, Johnstone, Prescott and the Begbies, a school was a mission field and a place to train up Christian pupils to be articulate, open and single-minded about their faith.[19] Under Barbara Chisholm, the services and ritual in chapel and church were the public expression of corporate Christianity. It was different from Miss Badham's time (there was no school chapel then, of course) because Edith Badham and Ernest Beck had a very long and close working relationship. A strong link which Miss Badham had with the Evangelicals was her extensive knowledge of the scriptures, which she taught and quoted with great effect.

While Miss Chisholm's churchmanship was not entirely satisfactory from the Sydney Evangelical point of view, she allowed Crusaders to operate in the school and in her cool and impartial but compassionate way, allowed staff and girls to express their individual brands of faith, provided it was not at another's expense. So, for example, she supported Mary Graham, an Evangelical, in her teaching career but opposed the religious enthusiasm which gave rise to clashes and tensions during Mary Guinness's time as Crusader leader.[20]

There were some changes to the curriculum. Miss Chisholm strongly supported the humanities, arguing that they were too often overlooked because they did not lead to lucrative employment. In her first Annual Report she said:

> *A child who learns to use words; who can write down what she knows clearly, and can follow an argument easily, has an advantage over the inarticulate child. The study of languages, particularly of Greek and Latin, develops the child's powers of expression and, therefore, helps it in any work it takes up later. We must do all we can to help the children to express themselves clearly both on paper and in speaking.*[21]

Speech training was introduced as a class subject and history became compulsory until the end of Fourth Year. Miss Chisholm took every girl in First Year for Latin, and one Old Girl remembers wanting to 'drop' Latin in Second Year and being forbidden by Miss Chisholm to do so. She finally managed to do so when Miss Chisholm went on a trip to England in 1954.[22] Ancient history was introduced in 1951. Until then it had not been a matriculation subject, so was of little use to those intending to go on to university.

Greek was gradually dropped from the curriculum: it was not generally popular and it was hard to find staff to teach it. Marie-Louise Alma recalls her father asking Miss Chisholm for Greek classes for his daughter. Miss Chisholm's response was: 'If you can find three other girls who will do Greek with her I'll engage someone part-time.'[23] When Una Fitzhardinge, an Old Girl who taught Greek at S.C.E.G.G.S., left to become Headmistress of St Catherine's in 1950, Mrs Griffin came back to take Greek. Later Mary Graham took Greek classes although she was still a beginner in the language herself. The two girls she taught for Leaving Certificate classical Greek both got A passes and the following year her student Ann Newton obtained first class honours and came third in the state.[24] Diana Bowman, S.C.E.G.G.S.'s fourth Headmistress, was one of the last girls to sit for Leaving Certificate Greek. By the end of 1957 Miss Chisholm noted in her Report to the Council that Greek would cease through lack of interest on the part of the girls.

As for other subjects, S.C.E.G.G.S. still did not offer Leaving Certificate physics, nor did it offer mathematics more challenging than general mathematics, although mathematics I and II had been offered in the 1940s. Wendy Kohn commented: 'It was not really what you would call an equal opportunity education. It was very much a "girl's education". I suppose it was as good as you would have got in a state school.'[25] That was not true. The selective schools were offering physics and mathematics I and II at the time[26] but S.C.E.G.G.S. girls had to take bridging courses before entering science-based courses at the University. Miss Chisholm's Annual Report of 1956 dealt with the academic standard at S.C.E.G.G.S. It was impressive:

> *I think that parents do not realise how good our record is. It is considered by competent authorities that in this country approximately 20 per cent of the children who enter First Year are capable of going on to Fifth Year. In fact, only about 10 per cent do so. At S.C.E.G.G.S. on an average, between 45 per cent and*

50 per cent of our First Year entry reaches Fifth Year standard and between 80 per cent and 90 per cent of our candidates pass the Leaving Certificate. Our average pass is approximately 40 per cent of the First Year entry—at least four times the average for the country. There are not too many schools with a better record—and remember that we have no difficult entry test: any girl who can pass the Sixth Class has a chance of getting into the school.

Last year one of our girls was among the first hundred in the state, fifth in the state in Ancient History and twentieth in Latin; another was third in Music and fifteenth in Latin. There were 8,500 candidates.

I hope I have not made you dizzy with figures . . .[27]

One problem Barbara Chisholm faced was staff shortages. She often had only one applicant for a position and had no choice but to appoint her. It was still possible to fire an unsatisfactory member of staff, as she did on at least one occasion not long after her arrival, but sometimes it was impossible to find anyone to fill a vacancy. At one time she was unable to secure a scripture teacher, and when Miss Chadwick left there was nobody to teach economics. Some of the staff were not good teachers, but there were some exceptionally good ones. Miss Chisholm herself did not possess any teacher training diploma, nor did she attach much importance to qualifications. Two long-serving and valued members of staff, Miss Spicer and Miss Ivy Vandervord, did not possess any formal qualifications for teaching, and Mrs Miller, who came to S.C.E.G.G.S. in 1956 and later became Deputy Head said:

Now I can remember when people used to say we should put people's qualifications in the school magazine, and I remember Barbara Chisholm saying, 'Not so long as we have Miss Vandervord and Miss Spicer on the staff, I won't humiliate them by doing this.'

Barbara was in some ways very astute . . . I think she was far more concerned with actual personal talent and ability than with things written on paper.[28]

Staff interviewed were unanimous in praise of Miss Chisholm as a Headmistress. They responded to her encouragement so that they gave her their very best. Mrs Miller commented, 'I think the thing that did impress me was that it was simply taken for granted that you were professional and that you did your job.' Mary Graham, as a teacher on the S.C.E.G.G.S. staff, and later as Headmistress of the Moss Vale branch, said that the amazing thing about Miss Chisholm was the way she had confidence in people. It enabled them to achieve things they would not otherwise have been able to tackle. She recalled the occasion when Miss Chisholm 'enthusiastically supported' her idea of applying for the job of Headmistress of Abbotsleigh. Archbishop Mowll asked Miss Chisholm if she thought Mary Graham could look after a school and Miss Chisholm replied, 'If I were going away, I'd be very happy to leave the school in her charge.' Mary Graham added:

I used to say it must have been the happiest staffroom in any school. I'd not taught in any other schools but I'd been in a lot of schools and I got to know a lot of the staffrooms.

There never seemed to be in any of them such harmony and calm. There is the feeling that the Head is the enemy in many schools.

Miss Chisholm trusted us and she gave us our heads.[29]

Mrs Miller described the relationships among the staff as 'friendly interaction' and the atmosphere as 'free and friendly'.

When Miss Chisholm arrived at S.C.E.G.G.S., Miss Oakey was Deputy Head or Senior Mistress. She became ill and died in 1950 and Miss Grace Spicer was appointed Senior Mistress. Miss Spicer remained at the school until 1971, a total of 33 years' service. She was a tireless and efficient Deputy, presumably not ambitious, and is chiefly remembered by the Old Girls for her habit of calling everyone 'girlie'. By contrast, Miss Chisholm knew everyone's name.

There were some outstanding teachers. Dr Helen Goldhammer, a Viennese Jew, came to Australia in 1939 and joined the S.C.E.G.G.S. staff in 1952 to teach chemistry. While at the school she was also a part-time research pathologist. She was a formidable and brilliant woman who expected very high standards and admitted that it was impossible for her to teach the girls in lower ability classes.

Mrs Enid Miller replaced Mrs Sharland in 1956 as Senior English Mistress. She was regarded by her students as an exceptionally able teacher. She was more sophisticated than some of the other staff, who had 'a kind of nurtured and institutionalised demeanour'.[30] Marie-Louise Alma, now a lecturer in English at Macquarie University, said of her:

> *She was absolutely illuminating. She had such extraordinarily high standards that you could not really come up to them. She just took it for granted and she went at the most tremendous pace. Nobody else had asked you to take notes. You had to get it all down. You had to remember it all. Very like university. It was very good and it was like a bolt from the blue.*[31]

Miss Cambridge taught art in such a way that it did not seem like instruction. An enthusiastic and eccentric figure, her clothes were 'vibrant pieces of art' which she silk-screened herself.[32]

Mary Graham was a significant teacher, although she was at S.C.E.G.G.S. Darlinghurst for only four years before taking up her appointment at Moss Vale. During her time as mistress in charge of Crusaders, the group flourished. She took a party of girls to Queensland and the Barrier Reef on her own, and Jane Wholohan remembers her with special gratitude. Jane was not sure what she would do when she left school. Miss Graham said she ought to become a teacher and that she should go to the University. When, halfway through Fifth Year, Jane found that she did not have the requisite number of subjects to matriculate, Miss Graham said that she would have to do ancient history honours. After she had finished her pass paper she would have to come back to school for an intensive program of study. Jane recalls:

> *I was literally locked up from before nine in the morning until well after school in the afternoon in a classroom where I was instructed and I read and I wrote, it seemed like forever. It was something like ten days.*
>
> *I ended up getting second class honours. So that really opened up that opportunity for me and I've always been tremendously grateful for the interest that she took. I went there a little reluctantly at first. She didn't suggest it to me, she told me that's what I was going to do. And I went home and I told Mum, 'That woman's not going to make me do that', but I was never game to tell her I wasn't going.*[33]

One teacher became a living legend: Miss Mary Flynn MA. She was appointed in 1948 to teach biology but she was the object of countless complaints from the parents because she simply could not teach, did not mark her examination papers, and fell asleep in class. The girls managed to pass biology by having outside coaching and by obtaining copies of the syllabus and teaching themselves. Miss Chisholm and other staff thought she was a clever woman who knew her subject, but she did not care about the girls. Miss Chisholm was well aware of the problem but on compassionate grounds could not bring herself to fire Miss Flynn until 1968.

Dr Goldhammer's assessment of the school's academic quality was that it was very good: practically everybody who went on to university finished their course there. Even a teacher like Miss Flynn was not entirely disastrous—the girls learnt to be independent and resourceful, and one Old Girl claims that Miss Flynn influenced her in her decision to become a teacher: 'she inspired me because she was so bad'.[34]

The S.C.E.G.G.S. schools' total population in 1947 was 858 and although numbers at Moss Vale stayed at about 120, enrolments at Darlinghurst and Redlands increased steadily. Both Darlinghurst and Redlands had waiting lists by this time. Council records from 1953 to 1970 are missing, but Miss Chisholm kept copies of all her Reports to Council, and these provide enrolment figures, but for Darlinghurst only. In 1947 there were 451 pupils and by 1959 there were 629: an increase of 28 per cent in just over a decade.

Miss Chisholm not only knew every girl's name but she knew their home situations as well. Dr Goldhammer remembers her saying from time to time in a staff meeting: 'Now go easy on—There's trouble at home', which was very much appreciated by the parents. Miss Chisholm was very aware of the parents and their importance in the school. She was concerned, for example, that the school buildings and grounds should look attractive for visiting parents. She also played with idea of a Parents' Association in 1955 but decided that since requests for one had ceased, she would continue instead with the established tradition of afternoon teas for mothers and the occasional meeting for a specific purpose.[35]

Although the staff and girls were impressed with her seemingly magical knowledge of the girls, she was also occasionally tough on the individual girl for the sake of the school's reputation. In one case the mother of a pupil came to the school on several occasions and made a scene. On one particular day she came to the school 'inadequately dressed and quite unable to control herself', and accused the staff of hiding her daughter. Miss Chisholm wrote to a welfare officer from a government department, saying that although the girl was a pleasant and intelligent child, for the sake of the other children she could not remain in the school if there were to be any more scenes.[36] From time to time there were expulsions for bad behaviour, but always after a series of warnings had been issued and both parents and girl interviewed. Miss Chisholm was cool, practical and fair, and her sense of humour was never far away.

Old Girls have provided a wealth of comment on the atmosphere of the school in the Fifties. Jane Wholohan said:

> *There was a lack of snobbery. We had a milk bar and I had to work there at nights and at the weekend and most of the people I was at school with came from families with professional or fairly well-to-do business backgrounds. But there was an acceptance of the fact that many of us came from quite different backgrounds and that we had different sorts of ability. It wasn't the only good that somebody was clever. The clever girls were accepted as being clever but there were girls who*

were good runners, or girls who were good singers or I can remember one girl who wasn't particularly bright—she was an average to slow student—but she was very good at knitting... My experience was one of acceptance and cooperation...
I think the idea was that one should strive to fulfil yourself. And to provide service was a strong ethos of the place.[37]

Marie-Louise Alma remembered the 'lovely warm atmosphere'. But Wendy Kohn had a different perspective. As a Jew, she did not fit in:

I was Jewish and that was a bit of an embarrassment. My father was very against it all but I loved all that chapel stuff because being an only child and rather introspective and liking music, it was right up my alley and I actually thought the religious part of S.C.E.G.G.S. was tremendous because for me that was a rebellion.

We didn't have a gardener or a car... I think those things mattered a lot in those days. It was a good thing that at that school there was such a mix of people from different backgrounds. There was definitely discrimination against people who didn't have as much and didn't do as much. It's funny how cruel kids can be. You can imagine what it was like having foreign parents. That was a real no-no. My mother used to work at the tuckshop a bit. She tried to be involved because she didn't work outside home. But my father, for example, wouldn't even come to speech days because of the religion. I have often wondered why they sent me there...

You had stereotypes. Girls were to be good at sport, everyone aspired to have curly hair, and I didn't. I had brown, straight hair and I wore glasses. There were some oddballs... these sorts of girls didn't really thrive at S.C.E.G.G.S. because we were a bit different—there was the stereotype of the blonde, blue-eyed, Bible-reading, hockey stick bearing good athlete who was just a little bit rebellious, but not too much, and I didn't fit that at all.[38]

In 1947 there was a case of a Jewish girl whose parents did not want her to attend scripture. Miss Chisholm insisted that she do so and the girl left S.C.E.G.G.S. at the end of the year.[39] At this time S.C.E.G.G.S. was in some ways a narrow-minded place. Racial and religious discrimination existed and the fact that at least one girl was aware of a stereotype means that there was room for social change within the school. While social background was no longer the barrier it had been in Miss Badham's day, the most acceptable girls were white Anglo-Saxon Anglicans.

An unavoidable part of school life was disciplinary procedure. Senior school discipline had two symbols: the card and the conduct bar. The card was to be carried at all times and signed by staff or prefects for infringement of rules. Three signatures ensured a detention. Rules included not talking while walking along a corridor, going up stairs one at a time, and wearing hat and gloves while in the street. Some of the girls thought the rules were petty and unenforceable. The conduct bars produced a great deal of competition and model behaviour. They were awarded for citizenship and good conduct: a white one first, then a blue one and finally a silver mitre. Mostly only the senior girls got the mitre. They were very special and never lost as it would have been a great disgrace to do so. Mary Guinness commented:

I wanted to get one and most people did. They weren't looked down on or pooh-poohed as something you didn't do. They definitely helped to keep the standard of conduct up.

I think in some ways too much was expected of us. I felt I was too serious... the responsibilities that were given to us were pretty big. As well as those conduct bars I was producing plays, running sports teams from the age of fifteen onwards and these are heavy responsibilities for somebody that young. And a lot was expected of house captains—I was captain of Docker.[40]

The Catherine Selby Prize was still coveted by all and a certain amount of anguish was experienced by those who felt they deserved it and did not get it, or by those who thought there had been injustice in the choice of the winner. Music and drama were important activities at S.C.E.G.G.S. Many Old Girls interviewed recalled their days in the choir. It was a very substantial commitment and Miss Spencer did not like girls missing practices, even if they had other duties which were more pressing. The choir only sang church music under the reign of Miss Spencer. Later Miss Schubach introduced secular music. The weekly concerts were still held. They were in the last period on Wednesdays and Old Girls and other musicians came to play for the school. Susan Davies, an Old Girl from Miss Badham's time, played the violin, and Lindley Evans gave a piano recital, for example. These were enjoyable occasions for many girls, but for the unmusical they were torture especially when, towards examination time, all the music students played their examination pieces.[41] An innovation from the beginning of Miss Chisholm's time was the annual competition of house plays, the girls from each house producing a play which was performed for the school. It increased the opportunity for girls to perform in a play and to learn some of the associated skills: lighting, set and costume design and people management.

The charity work which had always been a feature of the school was more energetic under Miss Chisholm. Every year harvest festival fruit, vegetables and groceries went to the Frances Newton Kindergarten, the Woolloomooloo Day Nursery, the Home of Peace and Deaconess institutions. The proceeds from the tuckshop went to the Woolloomooloo Day Nursery and there were frequent visits by missionaries and collections for missionary work. S.C.E.G.G.S. girls also raised money for a cot at Ashfield Babies' Home.

As soon as Miss Chisholm arrived she saw the need for more accommodation for classrooms, staff and boarders. Her hopes of buying or leasing Molong opposite the school came to nothing[42] and 'Arthursleigh', another property investigated by the Council in 1952, was also not purchased. Although Miss Chisholm had said at the beginning that she wanted more classroom space and boarding room accommodation, but not at the expense of playground, the 'yellow building' was erected in 1951 on part of the playground. It was officially opened by Sir John Northcott, the Governor of New South Wales, on 17 July 1952, the date of the school's fifty-seventh anniversary. The building had three storeys: two floors were for classrooms and the whole top floor comprised the Dorothy Wilkinson Memorial Library and two classrooms. Thereafter *Lux* contained long lists of books acquired over the year and some of the girls acted as most enthusiastic librarians.

Of great importance to Miss Chisholm was the provision of a private flat which was completed for her in a section of Barham in 1950. Earlier her bedroom had overlooked the volleyball court. In her November 1948 Report to Council she wrote: 'I should like very much to have wire put in the windows of the staff bedrooms. The mosquitoes are very bad indeed. In my room the wire would serve a double purpose as the wall below my window is a volley board and things in my room are always being knocked over and broken by balls.'

The new building (since called the 'yellow building'), was opened on Foundation Day, 17 July 1952.

The other major building plan which came to fruition was the swimming pool, completed by April 1957. It was a focus of great interest and excitement for the school community and Darlinghurst hosted an annual inter-S.C.E.G.G.S. Swimming Carnival where all the S.C.E.G.G.S. schools competed. A swimming pool was an unusual and somewhat odd building project. Few schools and even fewer private homes had swimming pools—their popularity lay in the future. Given the lack of space on the school site, it seems at first an even stranger project. It was really a response to the cramped site. If the girls could not have extensive playing grounds, at least they could have a pool, and that was something many other schools lacked. It was something of a status symbol and has always been, like the chapel, an important symbol at S.C.E.G.G.S. It represents sport, fun, freedom and the open air. The branch schools had extensive grounds, but only Head School had a pool. It was also an example of Miss Chisholm's innovative ideas. On many occasions under her headship, S.C.E.G.G.S. was the flagship of the independent girls' schools.

Parents worked hard to raise funds for the pool, and from their support in this project Miss Chisholm saw possibilities of enlisting their help in ongoing building plans. As in 1955 the idea of a Parents' Association came to nothing and when Miss Chisholm discussed it with other Headmistresses, they advised against such parental involvement in schools, no doubt because it was seen as a potential threat to the school's balance of power.[43]

The Council, like the staff, had grown old with Wilkinson and a number of Council members died in Miss Chisholm's first years at S.C.E.G.G.S. Archdeacon Johnstone died in 1949 and worked on Council business up to the time

The swimming pool has the city skyline as a backdrop. It was opened in March 1957.

of his death. Two longstanding members of Council died: Archdeacon W. L. Langley and W. J. G. Mann. Langley had been a member of Council from 1927 to 1941 and had replaced Beck as Secretary. Mann had served on the Council for 33 years: from 1915 to 1948. Lady MacCallum, a Council member to the last, died in 1952. A Council resolution recorded:

> *The Council of the Sydney Church of England Grammar School for Girls places on record its deep loss in the passing of Lady MacCallum, who had served as a member of the Council for 48 years, and as a member of its executive for many years. Her wise counsel and advice has had a profound influence on the schools in their development, as both in the meetings of the Council or as the private friend and confidante of many headmistresses she gave it gladly. Her name will always be associated with the Moss Vale School to which she was so generous as a benefactor.*[44]

The same Council meeting congratulated Professor Holme on his having received the honorary degree of Doctor of Letters from the University of Sydney in its centenary year. The Council considered that 'this is a well merited recognition of his distinguished services to education in this state, not only at the University itself but in connection with the Church schools of this city and in other ways.' Holme had retired from the Council in 1948. He had also been a very significant member of the Shore Council, having joined it in 1898, and with the exception of a short break from 1918 to 1921, serving on it until 1952. Between 1928 and 1945 he had been Chairman of the Shore Council.

R. C. Atkinson, a member of the Sydney Diocesan Standing Committee, joined the Council in 1948 but served only a short time as he died in 1951.

ALL SCHOOLS RUNNING

Back Row: J. Gamble, C. Windeyer, D. Bowman, M. Guinness, H. Economus.
Second Row: M. Ellis, H. Parradine, E. Coombes, J. Gyngell, J. Speers, J. Goodman.
Front Row: A. McNamara, R. Shawe.

The S.C.E.G.G.S. running team, 1954. The present headmistress is in the back row.

Drill display, 1956.

Neither the Archbishop nor Mrs Mowll had attended Council meetings regularly in the 1950s and in the Archbishop's place the Chairman was Dr F. G. N. Stephens until 1949, and subsequently Professor R. E. Smith. Stephens was a medical practitioner in Vaucluse whose three daughters had attended S.C.E.G.G.S., and Smith was Professor of Latin at the University of Sydney from 1946 to 1953.

Mrs Mowll died in 1957 and the Archbishop died of a heart attack in 1958. Obituaries in *Lux* said of Mrs Mowll:

> *She had been a member of the School Council for many years and her interest in all the school's activities, her understanding of its problems and her appreciation of its achievement meant a great deal to us all. She was a tremendously busy person; no good cause lacked her support, yet she always found time to be interested in the work and achievement of others.*[46]

Because Archbishop Mowll died in October, there was scant time to write an obituary for the annual issue of *Lux*. A short note near the front, framed in black, recorded his death and his involvement with the school over 25 years. In her Annual Report Miss Chisholm said: 'A few weeks ago Archbishop Mowll, President of the School Council, died suddenly. Most of you will remember his helpful words at many prize-givings, and I shall never forget his kindly interest in all our doings.'[47]

Mowll had become Primate of Australia in 1947. His increased responsibilities, his ecumenical interest in the World Council of Churches and his concern for mission meant that he was often absent overseas or visiting other dioceses. His attention was increasingly diverted from the Sydney Diocese and this included S.C.E.G.G.S. His band of supporters died or retired: Johnstone, Hammond (retired as Principal of Moore Theological College in 1953) and, not least, his wife Dorothy.[48] It was in the 1920s and 1930s that he had given S.C.E.G.G.S. his time and energies, and it was Miss Wilkinson, not Miss Chisholm, who therefore would have been most aware of and grateful for his substantial support.

New members of the Council included Miss Mason, W. R. Mason, L. R. M. Meyer, H. W. Brown, W. L. J. Hutchison, N. Girvan, Mrs Dillon and the Begbie brothers, first H. G. S. Begbie, then S. C. S. Begbie. H. G. S. Begbie was made an archdeacon in July 1949 and resigned from the Council soon afterwards. Both he and S. C. S. Begbie served as members of the Executive and Secretary to the Council whilst members. Two politicians were appointed to the Council: the Hon. H. V. Budd MLC and W. C. Wentworth MHR. Both attended meetings infrequently and neither was a member of the Executive. Barbara Chisholm valued the Begbies as particularly helpful and able members of the Council. She had succinct views on the Council members and the meetings:

> *Council meetings seemed to be taken up with the problems of the Moss Vale Farm! I am sure that having Darlinghurst, Redlands and Moss Vale run by one group of councillors was a mistake—a broad view was often taken when detailed examination of problems was necessary.*
>
> *The women on the Council were helpful to me but weren't allowed much voice in affairs—curtains and bedspreads were their domain. I was interested to find that boys' schools were not expected to run with so few businessmen or educationalists in the governing body.*[49]

It seems to have been an ineffective Council in the 1950s. There were a number of members who attended meetings rarely, others who never attended at all. Two of the latter were the Treasurer, B. G. Long, and T. C. Hammond. In April 1950 Smith wrote to them both to request that they attend meetings or tender their resignations.[50]

Miss Chisholm's request for higher salaries for her staff meant that three

Table 11.1 Revision of staff salaries at Darlinghurst, 1949

1. Minimum salary for any fully trained teacher: £260 pa
2. Annual increments to be £10 pa
3. Annual increments to be automatic up to £280 pa for fully trained primary teachers; to £300 pa for fully trained secondary teachers
4. Further special increments of £10 pa may be granted on the recommendation of the Headmistress
5. Senior Mistress: £350 pa minimum increasing to £450 pa by annual increments
6. The Council reserves the right to revise this scale at any time if special circumstances warrant
7. Salaries to the Matron-Housekeepers to be increased by a total of £110 pa, for 1949 only
8. The salary of the Headmistress to be increased by £50 pa

Source: S.C.E.G.G.S. Council minute book, Executive Committee, August 1948

Table 11.2 Increments in school fees per term for day girls, 1946–52

Year	Prep	Middle School	Junior	Senior
1946	£4 4s 0d	£9 9s 0d	£7 7s 0d	£11 11s 0d
1947	5 5s 0d	10 10s 0d	8 8s 0d	12 12s 0d
1948	6 15s 0d	12 0s 0d	9 18s 0d	14 2s 0d
1949	N/A	N/A	N/A	N/A
1950	7 7s 0d	N/A	11 11s 0d	16 16s 0d
1951	10 10s 0d	N/A	15 15s 0d	22 1s 0d
1952	13 13s 0d	N/A	18 18s 0d	24 3s 0d

Source: S.C.E.G.G.S. Council minute book, vol. 10, 1946–53

Table 11.3 Minimum weekly adult wage rates for males 1948–52

Year	£ Weekly	£ Annually
1948	12 4s 11d	177
1949	13 5s 0d	193
1950	14 5s 9d	207
1951	17 10s 0d	256
1952	21 6s 0d	309

staff members gained an increase of 10 per cent in 1947. At the end of the year the Executive Committee worked out a salary scale to be effective from 1 January 1949. The Headmistresses were requested to prepare lists of salary increases (see Table 11.1).

Mrs Miller recalled that she was very impressed with Miss Chisholm's efforts in these regards when she went for her interview for a position on the S.C.E.G.G.S. staff:

> *There are a number of things that really impressed me here. One was, partly that she was so friendly, but also everything was so clear about salaries. She said, 'What is your degree? Have you a Dip. Ed? How many years' teaching have you?'. . . looked it up on the scale and it was so cut and dried. Whereas before, more or less, it was a matter of guesswork [at some other schools].*[51]

As salaries rose, so too did school fees (see Table 11.2). From 1948 to 1952 minimum male salaries had doubled (see Table 11.3). In 1949 the minimum salary for a fully trained teacher at S.C.E.G.G.S. was above the minimum state award by almost one-third and there were allowances for annual increments in line with the state award increments for the first two years at least.

From 1946 to 1952, a period of six years, fees for day-girls and boarders more than doubled. In addition an enrolment fee of five guineas was payable from 1950. The fee rises were advised in a letter from the Chairman of the Council, regretting rising costs. In response parents sent letters to the school requesting fee reductions. Sometimes these requests were granted, and there were also half-fee concessions for the daughters of clergy and those in the teaching profession, provided they were Church of England. As enrolments rose, the finances of the school were very healthy, despite the new wage demands.

The fee increases were not designed merely to offset the salaries, however. The school had often hovered on the brink of zero profit and the new Treasurer, Wilfrid Hutchison, changed this. Prescott stated:

> *Under Mr Hutchison's leadership in the middle 1950s it was decided to increase fees with a view to making a certain surplus each year and that the surplus should be invested outside of the school Council in industrial shares and various other securities. This parcel was built up and by the end of the 1950s the Council was operating its schools on a very satisfactory basis with a surplus being generated each year and the reserve fund built up.*[52]

There are quite extensive financial records in the Diocesan Archives of the Council's investments. By 1959 they had invested £78 194 in shares.[53]

A letter from Hutchison dated 11 February 1959 detailed to a stockbroker the kind of shares S.C.E.G.G.S. wanted: gilt-edged securities, not government bonds, and definitely no shares in companies engaged in the sale of liquor and tobacco or gold and silver mining. He was dubious about investing in hire-purchase and finance companies. The money was spread across a great range of investments. More than 2000 shares were held with each of Woolworths, Lend Lease Corporation, Email, Elder Smith and David Jones; 1000–2000 shares were held with each of six other companies; 500–1000 shares were held with each of nine other companies and the most expensive parcels were smaller and spread among 32 companies.[54]

Not all the money invested belonged to S.C.E.G.G.S. From his position as Diocesan Administrator, Huchison persuaded various church bodies to invest through S.C.E.G.G.S. The money was lent out on interest bearing deposit at 3 per cent for S.C.E.G.G.S. to invest. In 1958 £50 000 was invested in this way by bodies including the Car Finance Board, the Property Trust, Moore Theological College, the Board of Education and the Finance and Loans Board.[55]

At the time it was highly profitable to S.C.E.G.G.S. In 1959, for example, Hutchison stated that shares which had cost S.C.E.G.G.S. £47 000 in 1955 were now worth £60 000. The financial crisis in the mid 1970s which almost closed S.C.E.G.G.S. arose from an ambitious financial project (see Chapter 14). Hutchison was still Treasurer and Prescott was Chairman of the Council when it happened. With hindsight it is possible to connect the disaster of the 1970s with the entrepreneurial activities initiated by the same people in the 1950s.

In 1950 there was a profit for the year of £5386. As always, Moss Vale barely balanced its budget and Darlinghurst made the most substantial profit. Of that total Darlinghurst contributed £5078, Redlands £659 and Moss Vale £1 1s 2d. In 1951 the Council took out a £75 000 loan with the MLC to fund the new building at Darlinghurst, and as yet there are no available records to ascertain cash flow for the remainder of the decade.

The Redlands branch school was a most successful venture. After initial costs when it was first taken over by the Council, it soon showed quite healthy financial returns and by 1953, 426 girls were enrolled. This was about four times the highest enrolment at the North Sydney branch. The Headmistress, Mrs Humphey, seems to have worked well with Miss Chisholm—indeed Chisholm left Mrs Humphrey to interview and appoint staff for her on occasions when she was absent on holiday in New Zealand. The absence of the Council minute books from 1953 to about 1977 presents difficulties in ascertaining the financial situation, examination results, enrolments and plans, especially for the branch schools.

At Moss Vale Miss Baddams resigned in July 1952 and Mary Graham replaced her as Headmistress. After two and a half years there, Miss Chisholm encouraged Miss Graham to take the whole of middle term off and go to England. Miss Chisholm took over the school in her absence, spending a few days every week at Moss Vale. The experience of travel was very beneficial to Miss Graham:

> *The first time I got outside my own country was a great eye-opener to me. The thing it did most of all for me was to reduce me—having had a bit of fuss made over me, people saying, 'A nice young Headmistress', 'What a clever girl', and all this rubbish. And being the Number One in a place goes to your head a bit, I suppose, if you are young and you are not as humble as you should be. But when I got over to see other countries and other places and other people, I realised how insignificant I was. I just got myself into a true perspective. And what a difference that made to the rest of my time there and the rest of my life.*[56]

It had been a hard two and a half years at Moss Vale: the staff situation was very difficult because salaries were poor, and while it was hard enough to recruit staff for city schools, it was even more difficult in the country because few people wanted to live in Moss Vale. The Headmistress did not have much choice in her appointments. In 1952 the farm at Moss Vale became a separate enterprise from the school. Recommendations for organising the farm were presented to the Council in 1952. These were prefaced with the observation that the present arrangements dated from a time when the farm was in a completely rundown condition and had no permanent manager in residence. The farm was now 'an appreciating asset' and had a manager in which the Council could feel 'complete confidence'. Henceforth the farm manager would be directly responsible to the Council and should keep separate accounts, but should supply on a commercial basis the vegetable and milk that the school needed.

One remarkable feature of the Headmistress's role in these years is that, by contrast with more recent years, she was expected to deal with a large range of household matters. At Moss Vale the Headmistress was to decide which vegetables the farm would grow for the school community, and no doubt a great number of other non-educational matters. At Darlinghurst Chisholm's monthly reports to the Council show that she supervised and initiated all repair and maintenance work, called for quotations, arranged for furniture to be re-upholstered, organised the purchase of a new stove and a new lawnmower, and arranged for the fitting of flyscreens. The list is very long.

The most important venture the Council made in the 1950s was the establishment of a new branch school at Wollongong. Although Canon Stewart had written to the Council in 1951 inviting it to purchase Roseville Girls' College,

S.C.E.G.G.S. 'Gleniffer Brae', the Wollongong branch, was founded in 1955.

the matter was not pursued. The Wollongong branch was opened in 1955 with Miss Kathleen McCredie as Headmistress. Prescott says:

> *It was a result of this vision of growing the numbers of schools to meet the educational needs of the girls of the Diocese and it was precipitated by the property that became S.C.E.G.G.S. Gleniffer Brae and which was owned by the Sid Hoskins family and becoming available for a girls' school. Originally this property was given to The King's School at Parramatta and The King's School council made the decision, having secured adjacent properties as well, to move The King's School to Wollongong to meet the growing need for a boys' school in Wollongong. However the result of the old boys' campaign against this action was that The King's School withdrew from the proposal and ultimately bought the present site in Pennant Hills Road and moved there . . . When that fell through the Hoskins family gave half the property that The King's School would have had to the Wollongong Council . . . and the other half to the church for the formation of a girls' school.*[57]

Wollongong was perceived by the Sydney Diocese to be a rapidly expanding city (in 1959 said to be the second fastest growing city in the world) close to the giant iron and steel industry at Port Kembla. No Anglican school existed there and it seemed that here was a strategic place to found a school committed to giving high quality Christian education. Four years later the Sydney Synod founded a boys' school in Wollongong: The Illawarra Grammar School with the Rev. R. F. Bosanquet as its founding Headmaster. Archdeacon Gordon Begbie, at that time Rector of St Michael's Wollongong, was influential in the founding of the two schools.

The site for S.C.E.G.G.S. Wollongong was the envy and despair of the Darlinghurst girls:

> *Acres of grassy terraces, lovely trees, and a wonderful view of Wollongong and the sea. The school itself has been the home of Sidney Hoskins, one time part-owner of the Australian Iron and Steel Works, now the famous Broken Hill Proprietary Ltd., with factories and subsidiaries all over the Commonwealth. Carved oak panelling lined the entrance hall, with smoothly sliding doors leading into the lounge and dining room, now the study used by the Headmistress.*
>
> *Trees everywhere, and wonder of wonders, everyone was allowed to climb them . . . Lunch could be eaten sitting on grassy lawns, and under shady trees.*[58]

S.C.E.G.G.S. Wollongong, known as 'Gleniffer Brae', began in 1956 with 78 pupils and numbers grew steadily. Miss McCredie was 28 when she became Headmistress. She had been in the New South Wales women's cricket team and endeared herself to the girls by playing hockey, tennis and cricket with them. Because she was young she attracted some excellent young staff members, among them Diana Bowman, who had been awarded a S.C.E.G.G.S. scholarship by the Council. The scholarship enabled Old Girls to attend university to gain teacher training. It had been Miss Chisholm's idea and its purpose was to attract able Old Girls into teaching at S.C.E.G.G.S. schools, as there was still a shortage of good quality staff. Wollongong had its share of eccentric and ineffective teachers, but because it was only two hours' distance from Sydney and offered more than a country town, staffing difficulties were not as acute as at Moss Vale.

In the 1950s S.C.E.G.G.S. experienced many of the same problems and trends of other schools, state and private. All private schools raised both salaries and fees. Both state and private schools had to deal with teacher shortages and poor quality staff. As jobs other than teaching became available, and were better paid, many left schoolteaching. The proportion of graduates teaching in state secondary schools fell from 84.6 per cent in 1944 to 42.1 per cent in 1959 and primary school teachers were encouraged to study for degrees at night in order to become secondary teachers.[59] The brighter students entering teacher training courses for primary school were diverted to junior secondary school courses. All schools experienced a boom in enrolments. All carried out building programs. Students were staying at school longer because employers were demanding higher levels of education. The technological revolution meant a greater emphasis on science subjects to the detriment of the humanities, history and languages in particular.

The curriculum and organisation of New South Wales education was long overdue for reform. The Wyndham Committee on Secondary Education worked from 1953 to 1957 and the recommendations of the Wyndham Report became the basis of the Education Act in 1961. Some of the changes it recommended had been implemented piecemeal during the 1950s: the rise of the comprehensive or area school; the decline of selective schools; the formation of special schools such as technical and domestic high schools; the expansion of junior high schools into comprehensive high schools. S.C.E.G.G.S. was immune from many of these changes as it already catered for a wide range of students, offering courses both for the academically bright and those who required practical, technical and non-academic subjects. In addition it had offered schooling for girls from kindergarten to Leaving Certificate since 1900. But staffing difficulties, expansion of the school community and changing curriculum demands were common to S.C.E.G.G.S. as to schools generally in New South Wales.

Like Miss Wilkinson a quarter of a century before, Miss Chisholm had arrived at S.C.E.G.G.S. appalled at the physical state of the school and challenged by its potential rather than by its actual state. She was critical of the disrepair of the buildings, shortage of accommodation for classrooms, staff and boarders; acutely disappointed at being provided with unsuitable living quarters; aware of the need for more buildings, more up-to-date facilities and more land. She found the Council mostly inept: inefficient, and for the most part lacking educational and professional expertise. She was concerned at the low salaries offered and worried by the implications for the quality of her staff.

In little more than a decade she managed to effect substantial change. Although on the debit side there was no further acquisition of land, and indeed more free land had been built upon, the school had a new building with two storeys of classrooms and a library. There were plenty of books in the library, and all kinds of equipment had been acquired to facilitate teaching. The swimming pool had enhanced the limited outdoor space and given a morale boost to the school community. Salaries had been increased satisfactorily and most of the new staff were good: some indeed outstanding. Above all, staff and student esprit de corps was excellent: something which is constantly mentioned in interviews and memoirs. There was little she could do about her Council: it included some very dedicated and helpful people, but lacked experts in a number of important areas. All were church appointees and while people of sterling character, were not all fitted to make a useful contribution in the deliberations on school policy and management. Educationally, the good academic tradition was continued: behind the best selective state schools for the moment, but leading the field with the best of the independent girls' schools.

— 12 —

The 1960s: years of change

IN RETROSPECT THE 1960s were golden years at S.C.E.G.G.S.: a decade of prosperity and challenge arising from educational, social and technological change. Often the challenges in the past had arisen from hardship: two world wars and two depressions had meant financial stringencies and limits to what was achievable. In secondary schools in New South Wales the major change was the introduction of the Wyndham Scheme which replaced an educational system in operation for 50 years. It was an earthquake in the secondary school system, causing shock waves in schools, churches and the general community. The 1960s saw the beginning of state aid and commonwealth grants to private schools, and there was unprecedented building activity.

Technological progress accelerated. While the Apollo 10 flight which put men on the moon represented its pinnacle achievement, the technological revolution meant increasingly sophisticated and costly equipment for schools. Photocopiers, language laboratories, television sets, video equipment, fordigraphs and 'teaching machines' (early computers which taught individual students at their own pace) were some of its products. Decimal currency replaced pounds, shillings and pence. The decade was one of experimentation where traditional moral and social values were questioned and often rejected. Student societies flourished. It was the era of the mini skirt, hippy culture, 'flower power', permissive sex and drugs. The controversial Vietnam War and conscription meant street demonstrations and student protest on university campuses where the slogan was 'Make love not war'. In popular music the Beatles, the Rolling Stones and folk singers like Peter, Paul and Mary, Joan Baez and Bob Dylan made the 1960s a halcyon age.

There was a rise in the quality of cultural life in Australia. In the art world private galleries multiplied and Australian artists like Nolan, Drysdale and Dobell gained both respect and good prices for their work. Writers showed increased professionalism and greater art: Patrick White, Morris West, Judith Wright, A. D. Hope and Donald Horne possessed widely divergent literary talent and, in some cases, even genius. In the performing arts, prominent Australians such as Charles Mackerras and Joan Sutherland still went to Europe and North America to work, but the Australian Broadcasting Commission (later Corporation) sponsored regular concerts and there were regular opera and ballet seasons. These were supported by the government through the Elizabethan Theatre Trust. Work was under way on the Sydney Opera House.

The Wyndham Scheme was enacted in the Education Act of 1961 and began to be implemented in the following year. Its main features were that an extra year was added to the secondary course; that there would be an external examination at the end of the fourth year (the School Certificate) and at the end of the sixth year (the Higher School Certificate); there would be a common core course and each subject would be offered at three levels: ordinary, credit and advanced. The aim was to maintain, even raise, standards. The Wyndham Scheme has been dubbed 'conveyor belt education' and replaced Peter Board's educational ladder.[1] It was an outworking of democratic principles whereby every child had the same opportunities and all moved forward at the same pace. The concept of absolute standards yielded to the view that standards were relative and it was a system of achievement by persistence rather than merit.

The hasty implementation of the Wyndham Scheme in 1962 meant that syllabi were drawn up in a hurry and there were ad hoc modifications as the year progressed. Because there were differences between individual schools, school principals were permitted to modify the curriculum. The initial plan was that all students in first year would take a common core of subjects: English, mathematics, science and social studies, and after that would take up additional elective subjects. French and other foreign languages were not to be introduced until second year. Science became an amalgamation of physics, chemistry, biology and geology. Social studies combined history and geography and were given greater weight in the curriculum. All students were to take mathematics until the School Certificate year. The senior curriculum became narrower than previously because science and mathematics taken together at the appropriate level constituted three subjects.

Major effects of the Wyndham Scheme were that schools, particularly state schools, grew much bigger. This was partly because of the extra school year added on to the secondary course, and partly because larger schools could more economically accommodate the curriculum demands. There was a need for more science laboratories and bigger libraries. Independent schools generally grew larger: the average enrolment of Anglican schools rose from 214 to 392 pupils between 1951 and 1967. Some schools closed: between 1951 and 1967 the number of Anglican schools fell from 45 to 33.[2] The Wyndham Scheme was a very expensive exercise and all schools had to contend with the increased burdens of financing the required new buildings. Many independent schools called in professional fundraisers to generate cash to pay for all the required resources. State schools, because of their size, became impersonal places where discipline was an increasing problem. A. Barcan, an educational historian, comments:

> *The remarkable thing is that whereas the basic pattern of Peter Board's scheme lasted nearly fifty years, the Wyndham System, which became operational with the first Higher School Certificate Exam in 1967, was to last merely seven. No sooner had the system come into existence than the social and educational environment which had produced it started to change remarkably.*[3]

Miss Chisholm's reports to the Council and her Annual Reports on Speech Day provide ample evidence of the difficulties the Wyndham Scheme imposed upon S.C.E.G.G.S. At the beginning of the 1962 school year there was no official notification from the Department of Education that the new course was in existence.[4] There were as yet no syllabi and there were no textbooks available. The insistence that every child do science and mathematics meant that the standard would have to be very low indeed to accommodate the weaker students.[5] At the 1963 Speech Day Miss Chisholm reported:

The girls in second year continue to be guinea pigs and I am afraid they will be all through their school days. Though we have a better idea now of what is required for the School Certificate examination we are still hampered by the lack of good books. There are difficulties, too, in teaching new groups of subjects. This is particularly the case in Science. There are no longer separate courses in Chemistry, Physics, Biology and Geology: they are all taught as parts of General Science. In theory this is a very good idea as it is now generally recognised that the sciences are interdependent. In practice, however, it is not easy to make twelve and thirteen-year-olds appreciate this. They tend to become muddled very easily and though they find the work most interesting they often have difficulty in learning the facts. It is interesting to note too, that there is now less time for science and mathematics on the timetable than there used to be in A classes, so that the girls going on to tertiary studies, are, at least in the early years of their secondary courses, having less of these subjects.[6]

The following year she noted that the new course still continued to present difficulties: lack of information and the late printing of books being the most trying. The matriculation requirements were still not known. The last Leaving Certificate examination was held in 1965 and this was also the first School Certificate year. There would be no possibility of girls' repeating the Leaving as the work for the new system was very different.[7]

The mathematics situation worried Miss Chisholm as there was a great scarcity of mathematics teachers and they were in greater demand under the new scheme. In November 1962 she was forced to appoint a mathematics teacher without university qualifications. As the Department of Education consistently paid higher wages, teachers were attracted to the state system. She decided to ignore the Wyndham Scheme's requirement that languages should not be introduced until second form:

I feel strongly that we should continue to offer languages and mathematics to every girl at the beginning of her secondary course. This will mean that children coming in from state schools will find it difficult to fit in, but we have so few of these that I do not think we should worry about them to the extent of altering our curriculum, I understand that most of the independent schools will do as I intend to do.[8]

Dr Goldhammer was very critical of the Wyndham Scheme. She refused to teach the biology component of the new science course and believed that the course was ill-conceived, with children being pitched into complicated scientific concepts before they were ready. Whole areas of important knowledge were omitted: there was, for example, no organic chemistry, and there was no attempt to correlate the various disciplines under the scientific umbrella.[9]

The greatest impact of the Wyndham Scheme upon S.C.E.G.G.S. was the need to build, to provide new equipment, and to pay for it all. For all independent

The Barbara Chisholm Assembly Hall was opened on 3 May 1966. The rear wall is decorated with colourful ceramic tiles made by students in the art department.

schools the 1960s was a great building decade and S.C.E.G.G.S. was no exception. A new assembly hall, the Barbara Chisholm Assembly Hall, was completed in 1966 with subsequent extensions comprising a tuckshop, squash court, change rooms and lecture theatre. The flats in the block on the corner of St Peter's Lane and Forbes Street had all been purchased by S.C.E.G.G.S. by 1962. The building was renamed Wilkinson House and served as accommodation for the boarders, freeing up other rooms for specialist classrooms.[10] A new science block containing extra classrooms was completed in 1967 and plans were under way for a new library which was completed in 1970. All this was funded in three main ways: by a fundraising campaign which raised £72 000 in 1964;[11] by a continuation of the Council's investment policy which had been initiated by the Treasurer Wilfrid Hutchison; and by commonwealth and state grants.

Commonwealth grants to schools were part of the wider issue of what came to be known as State Aid to schools. The financial burdens laid upon independent schools by the implementation of the Wyndham Scheme fell particularly heavily upon Roman Catholic schools. Most could not survive unless given financial assistance by the government. Roman Catholics campaigned aggressively for State Aid and in July 1962 actually closed their schools in Goulburn, sending their 600 pupils to state schools for a week.[12] The following year saw the beginning of State Aid. The state government granted scholarships for secondary students, free public transport, a textbook subsidy, and payment of interest on loans raised by private schools. The federal government made available commonwealth grants for capital projects. Between 1960 and

1965 State Aid to private schools became the policy of both state and federal governments.[13] S.C.E.G.G.S. received three grants: £16 000 in October 1965 for a science block; a further £23 000 in 1967; and in 1969 a grant of $47 000 to build a new library.

Although there is nothing to suggest that S.C.E.G.G.S. hesitated to accept government financial help, the State Aid issue was a vexed one for church schools. Most Protestant churches, including the Church of England, opposed State Aid. The Teachers' Federation and the Parents' and Citizens' Association did also. Their reasons were different. In the case of the churches, they feared that State Aid would lessen the independent schools' autonomy. In fact they were assured by the Minister for Education and the Prime Minister that they would not interfere with the schools' independence: the state government was responsible for the registration of schools, whereas the capital grants were federal.[14] The Parents' and Citizens' Association and the Teachers' Federation opposed State Aid on the grounds that the independent schools should rely on fees and parents' financial support since they represented a privileged section of the community. Taxpayers' money should be directed to state education, not to subsidising bastions of wealth and privilege.

The Presbyterian Church's General Assembly ruled that no Presbyterian school should accept State Aid although the Council of PLC Croydon continued negotiations for State Aid. By 1968 the ban had been lifted by the General Assembly.[15] The Sydney Synod of the Church of England established a committee under Bishop M. L. Loane to review the State Aid question. Archbishop Gough also appointed a commission under the chairmanship of Mr B. H. Travers, Headmaster of Shore, for the same purpose. Travers's committee recommended that Church of England schools accept the science grant provided that it did not commit the schools to accepting future forms of aid. The recommendation was accepted by the Standing Committee of Synod by a majority vote in August 1964. When Synod met three months later, it rejected the recommendation and reaffirmed opposition to all forms of State Aid, a view in accord with M. L. Loane's committee.[16]

Faced with such divergent opinions, school councils made up their own minds on the matter and by 1965 thirteen out of sixteen schools had decided to accept State Aid. It was a question of survival. While this involved the need to compete with other schools in the push to expand school facilities, the State Aid issue brought the independent schools closer together as they recognised the need to pool resources and discuss matters of mutual interest. By 1968 the Association of Independent Schools (AIS) had been formed as a forum for discussion of industrial and other educational matters. In 1970 the National Council of Independent Schools was formed. The Heads of independent schools had formed associations years before: Edith Badham had been the founding Head of the Association of Headmistresses in 1916[17] and L. C. Robson, Headmaster of Shore, had been one of the founders of the Australian Headmasters' Conferences in 1931. Now the bonds were strengthened. The Richardson Report, published in 1966, gave official Diocesan sanction to State Aid.

During the 1960s S.C.E.G.G.S. continued to expand, making the problem of accommodation for classes a recurrent theme. Enrolments rose from 640 in 1960 to 730 in 1969. There was talk of needing a new gymnasium, and the library housed in the top floor of the 1951 'yellow building' was already inadequate. Academically, the girls performed well in public examinations and an increasing number went on to university.

Miss Chisholm was proud of the girls' Leaving Certificate achievements when

Table 12.1 Leaving Certificate results at S.C.E.G.G.S., 1960–65

Year	Candidates	Passes	Matriculation	Commonwealth Scholarships
1960	57	52	43	12
1961	—	42	31	9
1962	—	56	41	10
1963	—	65	54	—
1964	—	73	—	10
1965	93	87	74	18

Source: *Lux*, 1961–66, Principal's Annual Reports; Chisholm's Reports to Council, 1961–66

she noted them in her monthly reports to the Council. There are no available figures for the total number of girls who sat for the examination, except for 1960 and 1965. The proportion of girls who matriculated was always about 75 per cent of those who passed, and in addition to those gaining Commonwealth Scholarships were a similar number who gained Teachers' College Scholarships (see Table 12.1). These were nearly as difficult to obtain as Commonwealth Scholarships by this time, according to Miss Chisholm. A significant number of S.C.E.G.G.S. girls came from families which emphasised academic success. This may have been an influential factor in the excellent academic achievements of S.C.E.G.G.S. girls.[18]

Barbara Chisholm drew particular attention to the high proportion of girls who completed their secondary schooling at S.C.E.G.G.S. In 1965 70 per cent of the girls who had been enrolled in First Year in 1961 passed the Leaving Certificate. This compared with 28 per cent in the state as a whole.[19] Again, this was probably due largely to the girls' home backgrounds. Those who went on to university nearly always completed their courses. By the mid 1960s there were five universities and one university college in New South Wales, and although records from *Lux* are not complete, they indicate that while most students attended the University of Sydney, increasing numbers attended the University of New South Wales. A few attended the Australian National University in Canberra, the University of Newcastle, the University of New England and Monash University in Melbourne. The number of girls going on to university increased: the 1961 *Lux* records 31; in 1965 there were 61. Although the majority still enrolled in Arts, others were enrolled in Medicine, Law, Pharmacy, Architecture, Veterinary Science, Agricultural Science, Social Work and Speech Therapy. Some achieved outstanding results. Felicity Baker won the University Medal in French in 1961 and was awarded the Hannah Fullerton Travelling Scholarship which enabled her to study at the Sorbonne. Subsequently she was awarded a Swiss government scholarship to spend time in Geneva completing her doctoral thesis on Rousseau. In 1967 Virginia Glover won the University Medal in Architecture and three other university prizes.

The Old Girls' notes at the back of the annual *Lux* record in addition other experiences of Old Girls: marriages, motherhood, travel, achievements and deaths. The 1960 edition notes that Anne Capper won the Ruth Fairfax Award for the most outstanding nurse of the year at St Luke's Hospital. In 1961 Hypatia Monk (Mrs W. C. Adams) and Mary Howell-Price (Mrs Holden) were awarded the MBE. Joyce Whitworth became the first Principal of the Australian Outward Bound School for Girls and in 1968 was awarded an MBE. In 1965 Dr Molly Devenish-Meares was elected a Fellow of the Royal College of Obstetricians and Gynaecologists and in 1965 Annette Bailey gained the Dame Constance D'Arcy Prize for Gynaecology in her final year of medicine at the

Blanche d'Alpuget attended S.C.E.G.G.S. 1950–1960.

University of Sydney. Diana Bowman was appointed as Headmistress of Girton Girls' School, Adelaide, in 1965. Many Old Girls became famous because of their husbands: Margot Budd (Mrs Doug Anthony), Margaret Dovey (Mrs Gough Whitlam), Helen Morris (Lady Cutler) and Mary Haydon (Lady Gunn).

A famous Old Girl who attended S.C.E.G.G.S. from 1950 to 1960 is the author Blanche d'Alpuget. In 1975 she won the Fellowship of Australian Writers' prizes for two short stories and was awarded a Special Purpose Grant by the Literature Board of the Australia Council. Her novel *Turtle Beach,* which was published in 1981, won several literary awards, including the *Age* Book of the Year Award and the South Australian Government's Bicentennial Award for Literature. *Robert J. Hawke, A Biography,* published in 1983, won the Premier's Award for non-fiction. Her other works include *Mediator,* a biography of Sir Richard Kirby (1977), and *Winter in Jerusalem* (1986).

Old Badham girls were now dying: it was a lifetime away since the school had been founded. Mary Watson (Mrs Swift), the school's first pupil, died in 1963. She had always occupied a special place in the school's collective affection. As she bore three sons, but no daughters, she did not send any children to S.C.E.G.G.S. but her grand-daughter attends S.C.E.G.G.S. Mrs Swift attended school functions and was given a place of honour at Speech Days. Midge Caird (Lady Bruxner) died in 1969. A number of loyal and outstanding ex-members of staff died also: in 1964 Miss Prosser, the sports mistress; Madame Pasley, who taught modern languages at S.C.E.G.G.S. from 1908 to 1942, and Grace Capper, a member of the staff from 1918 to 1939 and formerly Chisholm's deputy. Nona Dumolo, Badham's deputy and later first Headmistress of the North Sydney Branch, died in 1966; and Nancy Light, formerly on the staff and later Headmistress, for fourteen years, of the Waikato Diocesan School for Girls, Hamilton, New Zealand, was killed in a car crash in 1967.[20]

The death which made the most impression on the school community was that of Charlie Kelland in 1961. Charlie had been general factotum at S.C.E.G.G.S. for 36 years and died the week after S.C.E.G.G.S. had assisted at

Bellevue Hill Preparatory School, 1965–1983.

his fiftieth wedding anniversary celebrations. Miss Chisholm mentioned him frequently in her reports with appreciation and with concern for his well-being. He was almost indispensable to the school as his work ensured its smooth running in dealing with daily practical problems, taking a weight off Miss Chisholm's shoulders. The girls formed a guard of honour at his funeral at St Peter's Church, Darlinghurst. This emphasis on people which cut across traditions of status, wealth, education and class had characterised the S.C.E.G.G.S. family from the time of Miss Wilkinson onwards. It was evident also in the spirit of service encouraged by Miss Chisholm while the girls were at school, and in the community service carried out by many Old Girls in voluntary and paid capacities.

The Old Girls' Union was thriving. It had branches in Melbourne, Canberra and Queensland. In 1962 its Blue and White Ball had a record attendance of 1061 people. The school held an annual Open Day for the Old Girls and other functions during that year included theatre parties and an Annual Dinner in the gymnasium. Mrs K. A. Bennett, president for 21 years, retired in 1961 and Dorothy Shipley (Mrs Bremner) replaced her. Whereas the Old Boy network was of great value to Old Boys from independent schools in their business and career connections, there were not sufficient numbers of women in the workforce for the Old Girls' Union to serve such a purpose. The Union was a way of keeping in touch for the sake of friendship, and for the support of the school. With Dorrie Finck (Dr Holt) as their division chairman, the Old Girls were involved in the professional fundraising activities of 1964 where they worked with the parents to raise £72 000 for the new Hall.[21]

The school grew to its maximum size in the 1960s: the site could not support any more pupils. Three classrooms were vacated in 1965 when the lower primary school was moved to St Stephen's Anglican Church, Bellevue Hill. Miss Margaret Amiet was Mistress in charge and preschool boys were allowed to attend. There had been an infants and primary school at S.C.E.G.G.S. from the time it had moved to the Barham site in 1900, and during Wilkinson's time some primary classes had occupied St Peter's Rectory. Although the move to Bellevue Hill relieved the pressure on accommodation somewhat, there were several attendant problems which arose. The Bellevue Hill school was cut off from contact with the main school, and community perception of this was such that parents often sent their children on to other independent schools in the area when they entered fourth class. The Bellevue Hill school did not effectively act as a feeder for the main school. There was some difficulty over buildings and maintenance of the Bellevue Hill site. Since S.C.E.G.G.S. did not own the site, they could do little to improve the buildings or grounds, and the Bellevue Hill parish did not see such expenditure as their responsibility.

Girls attending the primary school at S.C.E.G.G.S. have recollections of a happy atmosphere with dedicated and kind teachers. Mrs Danby, who retired in 1969, was mentioned with affection by Old Girls. Gwynneth Thompson (Mrs Bowley), at S.C.E.G.G.S. for over 30 years, first as a pupil, later on as a member of the primary staff, then Head of the primary school, has written an account of the primary school during her time there. Miss Chisholm visited the primary classes every day, marking the roll and thereby learning every girl's name. The teachers took note of the Education Department's directives but did not always obey or agree with them: for example, when grammar went out of fashion in the mid 1960s, 'we kept on with basic grammar principles as we felt it important not only for English but also for Latin and French.' Class teachers did not teach every subject to their class (there were specialist teachers for art and sport, for example) and there were weekly outings to Rushcutters Bay tennis courts and Coogee swimming baths. Netball and hockey were played at Moore Park. There were inter-school sporting matches, trips to the Museum, the Mitchell Library, the Art Gallery and Taronga Park Zoo, to name just a few. Extra subjects offered included piano, organ and violin tuition, speech, tennis and remedial reading. Of Miss Chisholm, Gwynneth Bowley says:

> *Although extremely busy, her door was always open to both staff and girls. I can recall several instances of small primary school girls taking a deputation to her for something they considered unfair. It was dealt with with sincerity and understanding and the children were satisfied. She was held in great respect but not in fear or [seen as] unapproachable. No pressure was applied to staff, she seemed to give out confidence and trust to her staff so the end result was that most staff responded by doing a great deal extra for the pupils and the school.*[22]

Two staff members who had outlasted their contemporaries on the staff were Miss Spencer and Miss Ida Horrocks. Miss Spencer had led the choir since 1917 and retired, warmly thanked by Miss Chisholm, in 1968. Miss Horrocks, an Old Girl, played the piano accompaniment for the choir from 1921 until her departure in 1966. Two outstanding staff members joined S.C.E.G.G.S. in the 1960s. Miss Janet Lean came to teach geography in 1963 and has remained until the present time, becoming Deputy Head under Miss Chisholm's successor. Mrs Jo Karaolis came in 1967, left at the end of 1968 but returned to S.C.E.G.G.S. in 1978 when she became coordinator of history. She later became Headmistress of St Catherine's Waverley.

Janet Lean thought that many of the staff in 1963 were getting old and that the new syllabus called for younger, fresher people. It was a very formal staff from her point of view: 'the overwhelming thing was that nobody used a

Christian name at all'.[23] Staff conditions were 'appalling'. The staff shared a small room with a large table in the middle and around the wall were cupboards and shelves with an area three feet long by one foot deep (1m × 0.3m) for each person. Smokers were put in with the primary staff, who did not necessarily smoke. Miss Pauline McCann, a member of the mathematics staff, found it a cliquish staff. There was a set from which some were excluded, and this situation was exacerbated by poor official communication. Most communiques were given out at school assembly, which only the sports staff attended. For two years she was not informed that staff were expected to attend a staff meeting the day before the new term.[24] Hers was probably an exceptional situation as she lived in Wollongong and was a part-time member of staff. Janet Lean's comment on this was that communication was adequate: Miss Spicer came around to classrooms and staffrooms with memos. Before the advent of the photocopier there were few or no written memos, communication on noticeboards and by word of mouth being the norm.

One of the most colourful members of staff was Miss Enid Cambridge, the coordinator of art. Miss Cynthia Butterworth (Mrs Jackson) taught under Miss Cambridge and later succeeded her as coordinator. She recalled in an interview that Miss Cambridge ran quite a different department from the others at S.C.E.G.G.S. The art staff were a separate group from the other staff and mostly felt that the other staff looked down on them. They had no staff room of their own and were only allowed into the staff room to write reports. There were two small art rooms with large classes of up to 45 girls, but because there were about five art teachers they had to move to various classrooms around the school. The pottery room was a double garage underneath Wilkinson House, and it became intolerably hot in summer.

To reach one art room the art teachers found the quickest way was to climb through a window and walk across a roof. Despite the very inadequate conditions under which they worked, Cynthia Butterworth said that the art staff were very happy. Under Miss Chisholm they enjoyed great freedom: they appointed their own staff, had their own budget, and were virtually able to do whatever they wanted. Each art teacher had her specialty such as pottery, painting or craft. When a new person was required:

> *We would go up to the tech and find out who was available and at the end of each year when the students put on their exhibitions at East Sydney—part of their examination was to set up an exhibition—we would go up and see the design students' exhibition and choose who we would like to have . . . It worked well for us. We could interview the people and decide whether they could work with us.*[25]

Of Enid Cambridge, Cynthia Butterworth said:

> *She was a very stimulating person. I think the girls thought she was crazy most of the time. She was a painter. She was very, very inspiring. She taught me more than I learned in five years of college. I learnt everything from her. Everything. She never tired, she was enthusiastic all the time—she had no family, which helped, and living on her own, the hours just didn't mean anything. She totally threw herself into teaching.*
>
> *We had these huge art exhibitions at the end of each year which we all dreaded. We'd take over the whole of the gymnasium and we'd have a man called Karl who was the school carpenter . . . and he would virtually devote the whole week to Miss Cambridge. It used to take us about a week to hang everything. We'd mount all the*

Table 12.2 Comparison of teachers' salaries, 1964

Year	4 years' training		2 years' training	
	S.C.E.G.G.S. £	Department of Education £	S.C.E.G.G.S. £	Department of Education £
1	1300	1600	960	1180
2	1350	1700	990	1260
3	1400	1800	1020	1340
4	1450	1900	1050	1420
5	1500	2000	1080	1500
6	1550	2100	1110	1580
7	1600 maximum	2175	1140 maximum	1660
8		2250		1725
9		2325		1790
10		2400		1855
11				1920
12				1985

Source: Chisholm's Report to Council, September 1964

> *girls' work, all the best stuff would be mounted at night after classes. We'd always have dinner with the boarders and then work on into the night. The exhibition would be on Saturday, and then we'd pull it down on Sunday afternoon. It was an annual occurrence while she was there. When she left I took over, and we fell by the way. I think we had one [more exhibition] in the assembly hall after that.*[26]

A continuing concern for Miss Chisholm was staff salaries. Jo Karaolis recalled:

> *While I was teaching during this period [1967–68] there was a move to start a union for teachers in independent schools and I remember that most of us felt that this was inappropriate and we dreaded the effect it might have on the teaching profession. Miss Chisholm rather angrily spoke to us one lunchtime and told us that we had no right to expect the same salary as teachers in Government schools because we did not have to do after-school sport or make other special contributions. I don't think in those days we even did grounds duty.*[27]

Denise Reading, a Latin teacher on the staff, was impressed by the sacrificial team spirit and love for the school which characterised the staff. Staff at other schools in her experience were not so altruistic.[28] Miss Chisholm knew it was important that the staff be paid adequately in order to attract the best people to the school, and also to counteract incipient unionism. In her monthly Report to Council in November 1961, she stated that S.C.E.G.G.S. was not keeping pace with other independent schools. Again in 1964 she drew Council's attention to Department of Education salary scales (see Table 12.2).

In effect the Department's increments for those with four years' training were double those of S.C.E.G.G.S. In addition the ceiling was reached after seven years at S.C.E.G.G.S. compared with ten years in a state school.[29] The discrepancy was even wider for those with two years' training. Two traditional arguments in favour of lower pay at independent schools were that lower pay would attract the dedicated teachers and that conditions were much better at private schools (classroom discipline, in particular). Miss Chisholm was not happy to use the same salary categories as the Department because, in doing so, people with qualifications would always take precedence over people who were of far greater value to the school.

Miss Chisholm had little use for qualifications *per se*, and in the same way was sceptical of the contemporary view that current educational methods were obsolete:

> *The introduction of the scheme based on the Wyndham Report and the current controversy over State Aid for Independent Schools have led to more discussion than usual about education. There have been many suggestions that present teaching methods are obsolete—that we are teaching children by horse and buggy methods in a space age—and that we are burdening them with facts that will be of little use to them. Machines for teaching a variety of subjects have been produced and some are being displayed in Sydney now. Science and mathematics should, according to the critics, be the chief subjects taught and the wonderful things of literature, the great lessons of history and the pleasures of language study should be abandoned as useless.*
>
> *All this seems to me to be great nonsense. The children are people, not embryo technicians and our aim should not be to concentrate on things which will be useful to them in their future careers, but to teach them to be useful to others, to have enquiring minds, a right sense of values and the ability to continue learning after their formal education is over.*[30]

In addition to the stresses of running a school and the additional strain of implementing the Wyndham Scheme, Miss Chisholm had personal difficulties. She now had a flat in Wilkinson House, which was an improvement on her previous accommodation, but she found the noise from the garages below made it difficult to relax or work on weekends. In the end the Council took over the garages and they became the pottery rooms for the art department. She had a rather nasty accident in May 1966 when investigating a fire under the new hall. She fell over in the dark near the swimming pool, breaking her wrist in two places and chipping a front tooth.[31]

In 1969 Miss Chisholm took three months' leave and travelled overseas where she enjoyed a holiday as well as investigating education in England, Scotland and Holland. The trip was a stimulating and refreshing experience. She returned with some new ideas and some old ones reinforced. The main impressions she gained were that girls at the top of the school benefit from 'a move from the traditional classroom'; that some teaching machines would help in the teaching process, especially if the school employed a technician to prepare material for the machines and look after them; and finally that one more foreign language should be introduced at S.C.E.G.G.S. An innovation was her intention to begin French classes in the primary school and she would introduce it into fourth class the following year.

Although by this time she had been at S.C.E.G.G.S. for over twenty years, Miss Chisholm was open to new ideas and influences, and keen to investigate resources offered by technological advances. Some innovations she made were the establishment of a video department under the Rev. Colin Clark, and the appointment of a school counsellor in 1965.[32] In 1961 Miss Chisholm had appointed the first trained librarian to take charge of the Library part-time. By 1965 this position was full-time, with part-time assistants.

Other innovations were of special interest to the girls. The sixth form did not have to wear school uniform:

> *When they introduced that, in the* Sun *there was a wonderful cartoon that showed two little girls in school uniform and a girl getting on a bus in a huge hat and*

A parade in front of the 'yellow building' to show uniform through the school's history was a part of the 75th Anniversary celebrations in 1970. From left to right*: summer uniform 1970; Gai Brakell in swimming costume, 1930s; Class 1 girl, 1900s; Deborah Vine Hall models 1895 uniform; Edwina Olding in Year 12 'civvies' style of 1970.*

> *pearls trying to say, 'Schoolchild's concession, please.' You couldn't wear trouser suits—that was a bone of contention. You couldn't wear the clothes you really wanted to wear. There were so many provisos—you could only wear four different outfits the whole time.*[33]

Miss Chisholm commented: 'A few sixth form girls have come to school in ordinary clothes and have caused very little stir. I have limited the number of dresses they wear and most have been very suitably dressed. The girls concerned are really much more interested in the 40 hours voluntary social work I expect them to do this year.'[34]

In addition to this involvement in community service, S.C.E.G.G.S. girls also participated in quiz shows on television. One show was called 'Top of the Form' and was filmed in the new Barbara Chisholm Hall in 1967. S.C.E.G.G.S. also participated in the program 'It's Academic' and the S.C.E.G.G.S. team won its first heat. The excitement generated was good for morale and television provided a free advertisement for the school.

In sport there were some resounding successes. Jane Cortis was selected to swim for the Empire Games in 1962 and again for the Olympics in Tokyo in 1964. In 1966 the Senior A basketball team was undefeated and the following year the hockey team was undefeated until its last match, against Abbotsleigh, which resulted in a 6–4 loss. Comfort came from the knowledge that those four goals were the only ones scored against Abbotsleigh in five years.[35] For the

Table 12.3 Enrolments at S.C.E.G.G.S. branch schools, 1964

Head School	709
Redlands	641
Moss Vale	225
Wollongong	269

Source: Diocesan Archives, St Andrew's House, Box 132

Table 12.4 Finances for the four S.C.E.G.G.S. schools, March 1964

Head School	£21 500	credit
Redlands	11 750	credit
Moss Vale	814	credit
Wollongong	4 121	debit

Source: Diocesan Archives, St Andrew's House, Box 132

most part S.C.E.G.G.S. did not shine at sport because of the difficulties attending all sporting activity. The S.C.E.G.G.S. site contained only three tennis courts and a swimming pool, and all other sport entailed travel to other locations such as Rushcutters Bay and Moore Park.

Another branch school was acquired by the Council in 1967: Loquat Valley. This school was situated at Bayview and was acquired from Gordon Taylor, who had founded it. The new Headmistress was Mrs Prescott, wife of the Rev. Alwyn Prescott. By 1970 the school had 71 pupils. The other branch schools were apparently thriving (see Table 12.3). The Council's finances were also showing a healthy profit in early 1964 (see Table 12.4). The minutes show a net profit of £29 926. The credit balance in the bank was short-lived as the following November the Council was planning to borrow £50 000 to finance the construction of new assembly halls at Darlinghurst and Redlands.

The Loquat Valley School was the last branch school to be acquired by the S.C.E.G.G.S. Council. It was purchased in 1967 and was a primary school. Mrs Millicent Prescott was its Headmistress.

Miss Turnbull, Principal of the Moss Vale branch, resigned in 1965 because she was planning to marry. She had survived a tragic incident at the school when, in November 1961, a man had entered the chapel during morning prayers and shot and killed a schoolgirl, Wendy Luscombe. Miss Turnbull had grappled with the man and had been shot herself.[36] She was awarded an MBE in 1962 for her bravery. Her successor was Miss Horniman.

The S.C.E.G.G.S. Council was very large, comprising about seventeen members, with Prescott as Chairman. Miss Chisholm felt that there was an anomaly in the fact that while the S.C.E.G.G.S. group of schools was bigger than any other girls' school in New South Wales, the Sydney Diocese did not appoint people with the necessary expertise to deal with such a responsibility: 'they left it in the hands of the people they felt they owed something to because they had been good Sunday School superintendents.'[37] While there were people of undoubted financial expertise on the Council, there seems to have been a number of appointments which justified Chisholm's criticism. A recognition of the need for professional assistance to manage the S.C.E.G.G.S. finances was made by the appointment in 1965 of Mr S. R. P. Furley as Administrative Officer of the Council.[38]

The Sydney Diocese published a report on Diocesan activities in 1964. It was called *The Report of the Commission appointed by the Archbishop of Sydney.* The commissioners asked a series of searching questions of church schools, including: What are the functions of church schools? How necessary are they? Do independent schools play a special part in the community? Is the charge of snobbery justified? Why do boys' schools produce so few candidates for the ministry? What was their financial position? Should some be closed? Are new church schools necessary?

The Report provided a synopsis of the replies from the schools. Shore and Abbotsleigh were identified with some of the responses and conclusions: S.C.E.G.G.S. was not specifically referred to. Matters addressed were the aims of church schools, academic education and vocational training, the role of sport, whether church schools promoted snobbery, and whether church schools had a special part to play in the community. Their independence from the state system was seen to be very significant in catering for individual needs, setting high standards and being free from departmental bureaucracy and its constrictions.

The nature and composition of school councils were discussed. While small councils of 5–9 people were seen as the ideal, the importance of paying very close attention to appointments to such councils was acknowledged, because every member had to be active and well-informed. It was considered very important that there should be 'senior men of affairs in business and administration on the councils of girls' schools'.[39] Because most councils included Synod appointees as well as representatives from other school constituencies, it was unlikely that a small council would contain the requisite number of active and well-informed people. In this situation, where the council was not self-perpetuating but appointed externally, a larger council was likely to be more suitable as from it would generally come an executive to do much of the continuous work for which the council was responsible.

The conclusions reached in the report were that while the academic and sporting aspects of school life were of a high standard in church schools, the quality and impact of Christian teaching was less satisfactory. Related to this was the concern that 'the flow of young masters and mistresses who are dedicated Christians is causing concern in some circles . . . the Commission suggests that the Church should constantly place the vocation of teaching before young people.'[40]

For S.C.E.G.G.S. it was a timely review, although S.C.E.G.G.S.'s responses to the questionnaire are not known. In many ways S.C.E.G.G.S. was marked out as a school which promoted and taught Christian values and behaviour: the presence of 30 daughters of the clergy at one time in the 1960s underlines that fact. On the other hand some of the concerns noted in the report related directly to S.C.E.G.G.S. There was a definite problem with staffing, and in choosing a teacher Miss Chisholm would have opted for a competent teacher above a practising Christian. Similarly the chaplains who served at S.C.E.G.G.S. were not ideally suited to the job of pastoring schoolgirls, although the role of school chaplain was viewed in the report as of very great importance. The school Council was weak: few members possessed the kind of business expertise and experience which the report recommended. In the report's section on school finances, it said of schools: 'Their problem is essentially economic and financial. Their purpose is not economic or financial but the financial means to the desired ends must be found.'[41]

Every school was involved in the difficult task of paying for buildings and paying staff salaries while keeping fees at a reasonable level and raising the extra finance by fundraising campaigns. S.C.E.G.G.S.'s solution to the financial problem in the early 1970s makes the reading of warnings and concerns expressed in the report over councils and financial mismanagement sound like prophecy.

13
The 1970s: education in crisis

BARBARA CHISHOLM HAD been Headmistress of S.C.E.G.G.S. Darlinghurst for almost 25 years in 1970. Her dark hair was now silver but her monthly reports to the council reveal a woman of energy, dedication and great enthusiasm. The next few years were full of innovation, change and experiment, stimulated partly by her overseas trip and also by opportunities provided by the commonwealth government. Miss Chisholm's enthusiasm is highlighted by hints of her exasperation with the Council for showing little active involvement in school activities and changes.[1] Council meetings were not held at the school, the Council was very large[2] and S.C.E.G.G.S. Darlinghurst was only one of five schools for which the Council was responsible.

There may have been individual members of Council who saw the need for active and regular support for Miss Chisholm and her work at the school, but the S.C.E.G.G.S. school empire needed reorganising: it had long ago become unwieldy. One of the consequences arising from the size of the Council and the enormity of its task was a reduction in the individual Council members' sense of responsibility and accountability. There is in such organisations a subconscious assumption that someone else is shouldering the responsibility and knows what is going on. It was, therefore, a potentially dangerous situation.

The circumstance which gave rise to Miss Chisholm's repeated invitations for the Council to visit the school was the installation of audiovisual equipment in the newly opened library. The previous library on the top floor of the 1952 'yellow building' was no longer adequate, and the space was needed for classrooms. A government grant of more than $22 000 helped towards the cost of the new library, which was built on the southern side of the 'yellow building'. In June 1971 the library won the Grolier Award 'for the NSW School Library which has made the most progress in the past year'[3] and in the first three months of its use there were more than 1000 visitors to the school to inspect the library and audiovisual equipment. On one occasion 120 graduates from the University

The Audiovisual Studio in 1970. From left: *Sophie Inwald, Hilary Kramer and Darien Smith.*

of Queensland visited S.C.E.G.G.S., and on 6 June 1970 100 librarians came to inspect the library. Miss Chisholm greatly enjoyed acting as hostess.

The library was the first of its kind to be built in Australia, with fully-integrated audiovisual equipment wired up to the classrooms. The teachers incorporated its facilities into their programs, and the equipment was generously donated by Phillips. The Rev. Colin Clark set up the equipment and was put in charge. It was used enthusiastically by the staff and girls. The reason for its success was partly Clark's expertise, but also Miss Chisholm's infectious enthusiasm. The audiovisual equipment is mentioned frequently in her reports to the Council and she spoke of it at length in an interview.[4]

The value of the audiovisual system was that films on educational topics could be shown on a television monitor, a much more convenient method than the film strips and 8 mm film using a projector and screen. In addition the girls could do their own filming, and they also worked experimentally using video cameras. History, geography and English benefited in particular from the equipment. Conscious of its cost, Miss Chisholm was glad when the school could lend it to other organisations. It was offered in 1971 for the video coverage of the Sydney Diocesan Synod and for Children's Book Week coverage.[5] She was keen to encourage the S.C.E.G.G.S. schools to share their equipment and insisted that her staff ensured that any equipment they requested would be used effectively.[6] On these grounds she dismissed the request for a computer, which would have cost $4000.[7]

Although the audiovisual project was her chief innovation, there were a number of others. An orchestra was formed, Indonesian and Japanese were introduced, lunchtimes were lengthened three days a week so that there was more time to spend in club activities. The girls now ran the Wednesday and Friday assemblies[8] and there were changes and experimentation in class structure and teaching methods. First year was no longer streamed, and open plan teaching was tried. As had always been the case, the staff were given considerable freedom to take initiative and encouraged to try out new ideas.

The educational scene in New South Wales during these years was one of accelerating change. Education was in a state of crisis, and independent schools were particularly vulnerable for financial reasons. Changes in the curriculum, the impact of feminism and the withdrawal of State Aid were the major factors. Changing federal governments, changing Directors-General of Education; commissions, committees and reports on education; and significant changes in society meant that new policies, recommendations and remedies were tried. A committee set up by the Department of Education and chaired by Dr John Vaughan produced a statement at the end of 1973 which officially consigned to the dustbin the educational aims enunciated in the 1957 Wyndham Report. Barcan comments that the new educational aim formulated by this committee 'was appropriate to an age of relativism, of personal rather than social concerns, of moral flexibility'.[9] The committee stated: 'The central aim of education, which, with home and community the school pursues, is to guide individual development in the context of society through recognisable stages of development towards perceptive understanding, mature judgement, responsible self-direction and moral autonomy.'[10]

The Whitlam Labor government came to power in 1972 and remained in office until December 1975. During this period there was a great deal of extra money available for some areas of education: the distinction would no longer be between state and non-state schools, but between 'rich' and 'poor' schools. According to Dr Ian Paterson, Headmaster of Knox Grammar School, by 1972 half of the $100 million spent on schools by the federal government went to Catholic and independent schools.[11] The purpose behind the grants was to support the Roman Catholic education system. Paterson stated:

> *Numbers in the Teaching Orders fell dramatically in the early 70s; Catholic schools could not cope with demands for a wide curriculum; nor was their maintenance adequate. The surge of new enrolments with the War's Baby Boomer's children could not be handled without massive spending. Indeed the Catholic school system was in imminent danger of collapse.*[12]

The Karmel Report, issued in 1973, classified schools into categories A to H, with those in most need of funds in category H. Aid to schools in category A was to be phased out during 1974 and 1975. The Labor government cut aid immediately, however, and following a public outcry the matter was reassessed. Anglican schools had been hardest hit. The original method of assessing aid had been very crude: the main factor used was pupil–teacher ratio. The Schools Commission was appointed as a statutory body in January 1974 and a compromise was reached whereby all independent schools received a basic level of aid. Paterson noted: 'The fact is that no Catholic school has ever qualified for placement in the higher Categories due to the bias of the formula. By its mathematics, schools like Riverview and St Josephs simply are not "wealthy" so fall into lower categories for funding at higher levels.'[13]

The reaction of the S.C.E.G.G.S. school Council to the Karmel Report was reported in the minutes of 18 June 1973:

> *STATE AID*
> *Considerable discussion took place as to the most effective procedure to be adopted in opposing the section of the Karmel Report on education dealing with the withdrawal of subsidies to non-government schools. It was suggested that the Committee's findings, particularly as varied by Cabinet, are a camouflage for government prejudice against a particular section of the community. It was also suggested that the proposed actions of the Government might be challenged under the structure of the constitution, as it would appear that differentiation between various sectors of the community would be implemented.*[14]

The only school of the S.C.E.G.G.S. group to receive aid under the Karmel Report was Darlinghurst. It was placed in the second highest category: B. Its aid was to fall from $104 to $65 per secondary student annually. The other schools were placed in Category A. The situation had changed by the beginning of the following year. Council minutes for January 1974 show the classification for the S.C.E.G.G.S. schools as: Darlinghurst—D; Loquat Valley—B; Redlands, Wollongong and Moss Vale—A.

Quite separate from the strains imposed by the Karmel Report, S.C.E.G.G.S. was entering a period of acute financial crisis (discussed in detail in chapter 14). The accounts for each school were in disarray, and Moss Vale and Wollongong were operating at a deficit. The immediate impact of the Report on the S.C.E.G.G.S. schools was an increase in fees of 12 per cent for the beginning of 1974.[15] Financial anxiety had caused significant fee rises earlier: at the beginning of 1972 they had risen by 20 per cent. The circumstances on that occasion were a rise in teachers' salaries: they now had to be paid in accordance with the Assistant Masters and Mistresses Association (AMMA) award.[16] The Report was also the death knell for the Moss Vale school. The Chairman of the Council stated in August 1973 that:

> *... the future of Moss Vale as a school in the S.C.E.G.G.S. group had been discussed in the light of continuing losses together with the projected loss of per capita subsidies. All aspects had been carefully considered and it was proposed that should certain investigations now proceeding fail, a recommendation be made to the Council that Moss Vale be withdrawn from the group.*[17]

The Moss Vale loss for 1971 had been approximately $50 000.[18] The Report thus precipitated an action long contemplated by the school Council: the closure of Moss Vale.

For all private schools the Karmel Report meant that the future hung in the balance. An economic recession and declining enrolments made times tough for all private schools in the 1970s. Paterson described the situation:

> *By the late 60s and early 70s society was dislocated and undermined by the deep distrust of traditional authority and values that came with the continuation of the Vietnam War. Those were tough times for independent schools—many closed their boarding establishments; others became co-educational to survive; others amalgamated for economies of scale; and others simply disappeared. Enrolments dropped as independent schools were vilified and mocked as institutions designed to embalm distinctions of social class. Budgets were carefully cossetted—indeed, at Knox, for a time we had the students sweep and clean classrooms each day to save costs.*[19]

But for S.C.E.G.G.S. the Report simply exacerbated an existing financial crisis. The enormity of S.C.E.G.G.S.'s other financial crisis meant that in effect the Karmel Report and its consequences were of secondary importance. It was eclipsed by the far more major and dramatic matter which from 1974 to 1976 consumed the school.

In the end, S.C.E.G.G.S., like the other independent schools, learnt cunning in playing games with bureaucracy and in the art of extracting State Aid. The initial form to be completed and returned by each school was designed to encourage the schools to boast of their prosperity.[20] Because schools were then graded into a category according to assets and pupil–teacher ratio, those schools which seemed best-endowed were penalised. It became important to demonstrate need rather than achievement. Boarding schools were initially not included in the assessment. Boarding schools demonstrated that they were performing a service to the community and pointed out that the boarders were a drain on the financial resources of the school. Rarely did boarding do more than cover costs and the boarding accommodation could have been used much more profitably for further classrooms, thereby expanding the school population. The original A–H categories were changed to levels ranking schools from 1 to 12. S.C.E.G.G.S. Darlinghurst was in Category 3 in 1977 and Category 2 in 1978.[21]

The State Aid issue raised a good deal of public debate in the 1970s. 'DOGS' (Defence of Government Schools) was an aggressive voluntary organisation which attacked independent schools and promoted the view that they were costly, unnecessary and elitist. In particular they opposed State Aid to private schools as a misappropriation of taxpayers' money. Their arguments were seen as emotive rather than rational by many supporters of private schooling. Simple arithmetic indicated two things: first, that the cost to the state of providing government schooling for the children currently attending private schools would greatly exceed the total amount of State Aid granted. Second, the argument could just as easily be turned on its head: why should private school parents support public education through the tax they paid (often the very people on the upper end of the tax scale) when they were also paying for their own children's education?

Figure 13.1 Enrolments in New South Wales schools, Kindergarten–Year 12, 1978

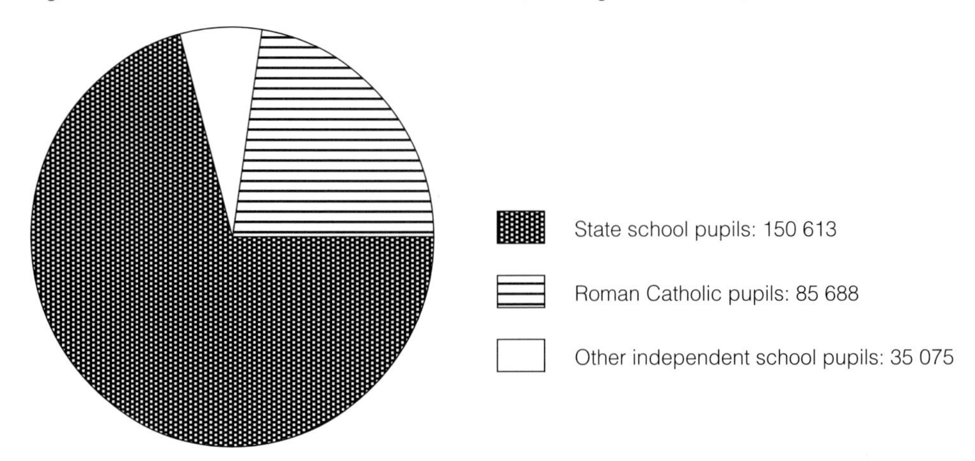

Source: *Australian Students and their Schools*, Schools Commission, Canberra, 1979

State Aid, both state and federal, has continued to be granted to independent schools since the 1970s, but the threat of its withdrawal hangs heavily over them. The establishment of school foundations or trusts with accompanying Development Offices in the 1980s was designed to provide the schools with adequate financial resources should the state and federal programs discontinue their grants. One major social change in the 1970s was the onset of radical feminism which was linked with changes in women's roles in the community. Betty Friedan's book *The Feminine Mystique*, published in 1963 in the United States, explored the idea of 'the problem that has no name'. She meant by this that a great number of women were unfulfilled and disappointed because the traditional role of wife and mother was simply not adequate. She argued that most women knew they had a problem but were unable to articulate what it was and therefore were unable to deal with it. Her solution was 'educational shock treatment': the provision of educational opportunities to develop and expand women's potential.

The book which launched radical feminism in Australia, however, was Germaine Greer's *The Female Eunuch* published eight years later. Greer claimed that her book was part of the second feminist wave:

> *After the ecstasy of direct action, the militant ladies of two generations ago settled down to work of consolidation in hosts of small organisations while the main force of their energy filtered away in post-war retrenchments and the revival of frills, corsets and femininity . . . Evangelism withered away into eccentricity.*
>
> *The new emphasis is different. Then genteel middle-class ladies clamoured for reform, now ungenteel middle-class women are calling for revolution. In the old days ladies were anxious to point out that they did not seek to disrupt society or to unseat God. Marriage, family, private property and the state were threatened by their actions, but they were anxious to allay the fears of conservatives, and in so doing the suffragettes betrayed their cause and prepared the way for the failure of emancipation. Five years ago it seemed clear that emancipation had failed: the number of women in parliament had settled at a low level; the number of professional women had stabilised as a tiny minority; the pattern of female employment had emerged as underpaid, menial and supportive. The cage door had been opened but the canary had refused to fly out. The conclusion was that the cage door ought never to have been opened because canaries are made for captivity; the suggestion of an alternative had only confused and saddened them . . .*
>
> *The castration of women has been carried out in terms of a masculine–feminine polarity, in which men have comandeered all the energy and streamlined it into an aggressive conquistadorial power, reducing all heterosexual contact to a sado-masochistic pattern.*[22]

In Australia a number of feminist books appeared including Miriam Dixson's *The Real Matilda: Woman and Identity in Australia, 1788 to 1975*, and Anne Summers's *Damned Whores and God's Police*, in which she rewrote Australian history in aggressively feminist terms. Both books argue that women have been oppressed and downgraded in a male-dominated society in the home, the workforce and in politics. In a chapter entitled 'Suburban Neurotics' Summers argues that the stereotyping of women still existed at the time of writing (1975) and claimed that 'women are kitchen creatures and childraisers'.[23]

Discussion of women's rights and their social role had been lively since Edith Badham's day. What was new now was the widespread dissemination of

Table 13.1 Percentage of women in the workforce

1947	3.4
1954	7.0
1961	9.6
1966	14.1
1971	18.0

Source: A. Summers, *Damned Whores and God's Police*, Penguin, London, 1975, p. 431

radical and aggressive feminism. It resulted in the Anti-Discrimination Act of 1977, which supported the rights of women to equal opportunities in the workforce; increasing flexibility in wife–husband, mother–father roles; and an emphasis on the rights of woman to a career. At the same time as these shifts of attitude in the community were occurring there was a rise in the divorce rate, a rise in the number of women in the workforce (see Table 13.1), a rise in the phenomenon of 'latchkey' children, and a demand for more day-care centres. Another major shift in attitude was the rise of overt homosexuality, including lesbianism.

For the S.C.E.G.G.S. Darlinghurst community these influences were significant. Miss Chisholm had employed a full-time school counsellor since 1965. Schools were taking on more of the traditional duties of parents and family, and were expected to do so. They provided counselling and help in 'life education', which included areas such as sex education and help with family relationships. In the area of career aspirations, girls were encouraged at S.C.E.G.G.S. to aim for tertiary study and to take up a career. Staff members like Dr Goldhammer were feminist in the sense that they encouraged girls to consider themselves every bit as competent as males. Dr Goldhammer was emphatically against what she called 'women's lib', however, as she argued that the women's movement made women who wanted above all to be wives and mothers feel inferior. It was wrong to demote the traditional roles. She recalled the occasion when she reprimanded a girl for being late to her chemistry class. The girl's response was, 'Dr G., did it ever occur to you that boys don't like clever girls?'

In her Headmistress's Report for 1973 Miss Chisholm argued for 'old-fashioned education':

> *This year I visited schools in the United States, Canada, Denmark and England . . . In the United States pupils seemed too often to be working their way through reams of standardised tests—moving from A to B in infinitesimally small steps—or following such general courses that there was nothing to get their teeth into.*
>
> *It is a pity many Australian writers and lecturers seem to follow the American pattern so closely. We hear so much about developing the personality of children, which, if parents and teachers are not careful, can produce very self-centred people; about giving them a broad outlook, which is often very hazy; of developing their powers of criticism—apparently without 'burdening' them with facts on which to base their criticism; of preparing them for 'real life' whatever that is, and of 'relevance'. 'Relevance to what?' one may ask. Topics, projects, activities—not necessarily related, are advocated. Schools which try to organise knowledge for the pupils are castigated for teaching 'dull facts' and told that the acquisition of knowledge is a waste of time as it will soon be outdated. I am afraid I am old-fashioned. I do not believe that children are sent to school to find out everything for themselves but to be taught by experts who will try not only to give them knowledge*

Mrs Lesley Rowan and a geography class, 1970.

and a respect for learning, but also to show them how to do their own research efficiently, joyfully and confidently.[24]

In an earlier report she outlined the role of a school: 'It is the ability to put their knowledge to good use, to discover new things for themselves and to make a useful contribution to the community which distinguishes the pupils of a good school.' With wry perception she criticised the Education Department in a number of areas. The popular emphasis on egalitarianism was detrimental to education:

Everyone must go through the same system and there must be a uniform end product. We shouldn't dream of having the same approach in other fields: we don't expect everyone who can keep afloat to swim in an Olympic team, or everyone who can play five-finger exercises to become a concert pianist. No one will spend his money training a draught horse for the Melbourne Cup but most will expect their children to be champion scholars. We don't seem to like to admit that some people are cleverer than others.[25]

The school gained only provisional registration in February 1970:

We had nine inspectors here on 18th and 19th. We shall be given only provisional registration because we are not teaching needlework in Form 1. I am loath to introduce this again as it is an unpopular subject, so I have written to the Secondary Schools Board to ask if we may follow the Boys' Craft Syllabus instead of the Girls'. This would allow us to do Pottery and Graphic Arts which the girls love.

> *The Home Science inspector was annoyed that we haven't facilities for cooking classes.*
>
> *As a group we felt they had little to offer in the way of advice and one or two of their suggestions were silly—for instance they said we should vary the subjects offered more frequently. I pointed out that when we had good members of staff we didn't send them off somewhere else so we could make changes and that we didn't expect them to teach subjects other than their own.*[26]

A personal accolade was her appointment in March 1970 to the Council of Macquarie University. She was awarded the MBE in 1972 and the OBE in 1977 for services to education. There were also personal links with the University of Sydney, as in Miss Badham's and Miss Wilkinson's time. For example, a regular visitor to the school was Sir Herman Black, later Chancellor of the University of Sydney, and Professor John Ward. Professor Ward, later Vice-Chancellor of the University, had two daughters at the school and his wife Pat was a member of staff. At one time Professor Ward was Chairman of the Parents and Friends at S.C.E.G.G.S. Darlinghurst.

There were various celebrations to mark the school's seventy-fifth birthday. A new edition of the 1955 school history was written by an Old Girl, Gillian Appleton. There was a special anniversary service and a uniform parade which was a great success. Girls saw what a contrast there was between their own uniforms, with hemlines well above the knee, and the decorously long skirts of the uniforms worn at the turn of century. In 1971 the terrace house in Victoria Street where S.C.E.G.G.S. began in 1895 was under threat of demolition,[27] but was saved by the 'green bans' of the Builders' Labourers' Federation. Formerly 65 Victoria Street, it became 55 Victoria Street and it was later purchased and beautifully restored by Rebel Penfold-Russell, the daughter of an Old Girl, Rada Penfold-Hyland.

One of the significant staff changes in these years was the retirement of Miss Spicer in 1971 after 40 years at S.C.E.G.G.S. Her position as Senior Mistress was taken by Mrs Enid Miller. Miss Nancy King also retired after 28 years of French teaching. Miss Grace Spicer died in 1973 and in the same year Bishop Gordon Begbie and Canon Morton died. Bishop Begbie had been a most helpful, kind and active council member, and Canon Morton had been school chaplain for eleven years (1955–66).

In 1973 the primary school moved into two terrace houses situated on the Bourke Street school boundary. They were renamed Begbie Terrace and provided a bright, warm and homely atmosphere for the younger S.C.E.G.G.S. girls. Although S.C.E.G.G.S. Darlinghurst had a new library, most of the school facilities and buildings left a great deal to be desired. There were now parking problems for the staff vehicles, not to mention those of parents attending a school function. Most parts of the school looked dingy: carpeting and painting were required. The Bellevue Hill site needed a great deal of attention.[28] There was an urgent need for new classrooms and new art rooms.[29] Sadly for Head School, there would be little money to spend on such things for nearly a decade.

The early 1970s was a period of multifarious problems for the S.C.E.G.G.S. group of schools. Three out of the five schools had serious problems with leadership, only Loquat Valley and Darlinghurst being exempt from such difficulties. Enrolments fell in 1972: by 16 per cent at Moss Vale and by 6 per cent at Redlands. Some of the Redlands girls transferred to Darlinghurst, but there was an overall loss of 48 girls from the S.C.E.G.G.S. schools. While the

Begbie Terrace, part of the primary school.

major factor was cited as the fee rise of 20 per cent, a contributing reason was the unhappiness of the school communities under their Heads. In the case of Moss Vale, the Council committed little to the minutes but stated in September 1971:

> *It was noted that enrolments were declining and losses increasing and the Finance Committee considered that this school should be closed down unless a solution could be achieved very quickly. It was felt that an effective approach to the problem was not likely under the present headmistress. It was further suggested that the Rev. Colin Clark and his wife might provide the answer as Acting Principal and Senior Mistress.*[30]

Some suggestions to attract more pupils, made by Miss Horniman, were that the school give driving lessons, and that a course of Asian studies be implemented.[31] She resigned in July 1972 and Colin Clark became Headmaster of Moss Vale from September 1972, remaining there until the school closed.

The situation at Redlands is not clear from the minutes, but one parent stated she had withdrawn her daughter from the school because the syllabus was 'too narrow'. The problem seems to have been the management style of the Headmistress, Mrs Humphrey.

At Wollongong the Headmistress, Mrs Woodhouse, gave the Council an ultimatum in October 1972. Her solicitor stated:

> *It is not simply that Mrs Woodhouse wants her husband on the staff, but that, if this doesn't happen, she will resign. She needs to have her husband's company on social occasions, holidays and excursions. She needs him as a science teacher and as a support in the school and the community. She overworks (16–18 hours per day). There has been a huge increase in paper work.*[32]

There was a serious clash with a member of staff. The request to appoint her husband to the staff was unanimously opposed by the Council. Mrs Woodhouse resigned in September 1973 and the Council asked Diana Bowman to consider taking up the position. When she indicated that she was not willing, Mrs Marrott, the ancient history teacher, became Acting Head. Dr Ruth Shatford was appointed as Head, but the school closed in 1974 before she could begin her work there.

Nineteen seventy-four marked the end of an era. The closure of two schools and the dismantling of the S.C.E.G.G.S. operation were imminent. Financial losses incurred by the branch schools were a contributing factor to the dramatic events of the next few years.

— 14 —

The S.C.E.G.G.S. financial crisis, 1970–1977

BY 1970 S.C.E.G.G.S. Darlinghurst was 75 years old. The school enjoyed a high reputation because of its academic record, enterprising educational activities and the calibre of S.C.E.G.G.S. girls. Miss Chisholm was one of the most experienced and respected Headmistresses in Sydney, highly regarded by her peers. Despite such success, in the last years of Miss Chisholm's term as Headmistress, S.C.E.G.G.S. Darlinghurst was nearly closed. The cause was a financial crisis and the result was the end of the S.C.E.G.G.S. school system. The S.C.E.G.G.S. crisis served as a warning to all Sydney independent schools and is indelibly recorded in the S.C.E.G.G.S. Darlinghurst collective memory, promoting caution and conservatism in all financial enterprises in the years which have since elapsed. One of the bitter fruits of the experience was a souring of relationships with the Sydney Anglican Church.

The events of mid 1974 to December 1976 are too recent to reveal fully all that took place. Access has been granted to files relating to S.C.E.G.G.S. which are still confidential. But the crisis of the S.C.E.G.G.S. schools stirred up deep emotions and partisanship at the time, some of which still lingers on. A full coverage of the facts would clear some misunderstandings; it would also do some harm.

A letter from Archbishop Loane to the Chairman of the Council, the Rev. Alwyn Prescott, written on 20 June 1974 advised him that there was urgent need for an independent inquiry into the finances of S.C.E.G.G.S. At a special meeting on 16 August the Standing Committee agreed to set up a panel of inquiry because the Archbishop was concerned about three things: the failure of the S.C.E.G.G.S. schools to operate at a profit; a development project planned by the S.C.E.G.G.S. Council at a time of great economic uncertainty; and alleged misuse of funds by the Treasurer, Geoffrey Glanville.

The panel of inquiry's brief was to consider:

- first, the administrative structure of the S.C.E.G.G.S. operation with particular reference to the competence of the present Council, the central office system and the relationship of the five Heads to the Council;
- second, the financial state of S.C.E.G.G.S., including the liquidity of the Council and its capacity to meet its commitments, the financial viability of the schools, the position arising from the actions of the Treasurer, Glanville, and the position arising from the development project (see below);
- whether Redlands and Loquat Valley schools should be given a separate council each.[1]

The panel of inquiry consisted of A. E. Davis, Honorary Secretary of The King's School Council and formerly Senior Partner in Henry Davis, York and Co.; J. M. Dixon, Chairman of the Shore Council and formerly Director and Deputy General Manager of CSR; W. J. Pickard, Bursar of The King's School; and Mr R. H. Y. Lambert, a partner in Binder, Hamlyn and Co.

The crisis was precipitated by the discovery that the Treasurer of the Council, G. Glanville, had taken $200 000 from S.C.E.G.G.S. and used it for private investment. He could not repay it. After his action was discovered, he fled to Brazil where he was held in custody. The Council was unaware of the gravity of the S.C.E.G.G.S. financial situation until Glanville's activities were known. In addition to being Treasurer, Glanville was the solicitor for the Council and advised on purchases of property. In time his advice had proved disastrous and in any case it was quite improper for the Council to have placed such power and responsibility in the hands of one man.

The project to which the Archbishop's letter referred was a large-scale commercial and residential property development. From the middle of the 1960s the question became vital as to whether the Darlinghurst school should stay on its existing site or move to a larger site in an outer suburb such as Campbelltown. When the decision to remain was made, it was on the grounds that a change of site would destroy the character of the school, which drew from all parts of the Diocese.[2] Instead a program of purchasing properties around the school began. The aim was to acquire all the land in the block bounded by Bourke, Liverpool and Forbes Streets, and St Peter's Lane, the lane itself and the St Peter's site.[3] If the proposal at the time to widen William Street had been implemented, the school would have had a frontage to William Street. High-rise commercial buildings were planned for part of the site in the belief that the revenue from these would finance the purchase and provide a long-term endowment for the school. A similar policy of territorial expansion was initiated in relation to the Redlands site, and adjoining property was acquired mainly by means of borrowed moneys.[4]

It is not clear who initiated the idea of commercial development by the S.C.E.G.G.S. Council. A letter dated 1 September 1990 from the Rev. A. Prescott says:

> *I am not sure whose idea it was to develop towards William Street, but I think it probably came from Stuart Furley or Geoff Glanville as they were principally involved in property matters. I am not sure of dates, but advice was obtained concerning the possible relocation of the school vis a vis developing at Darlinghurst. The real estate man advocated relocation and indicated that the site would bring a*

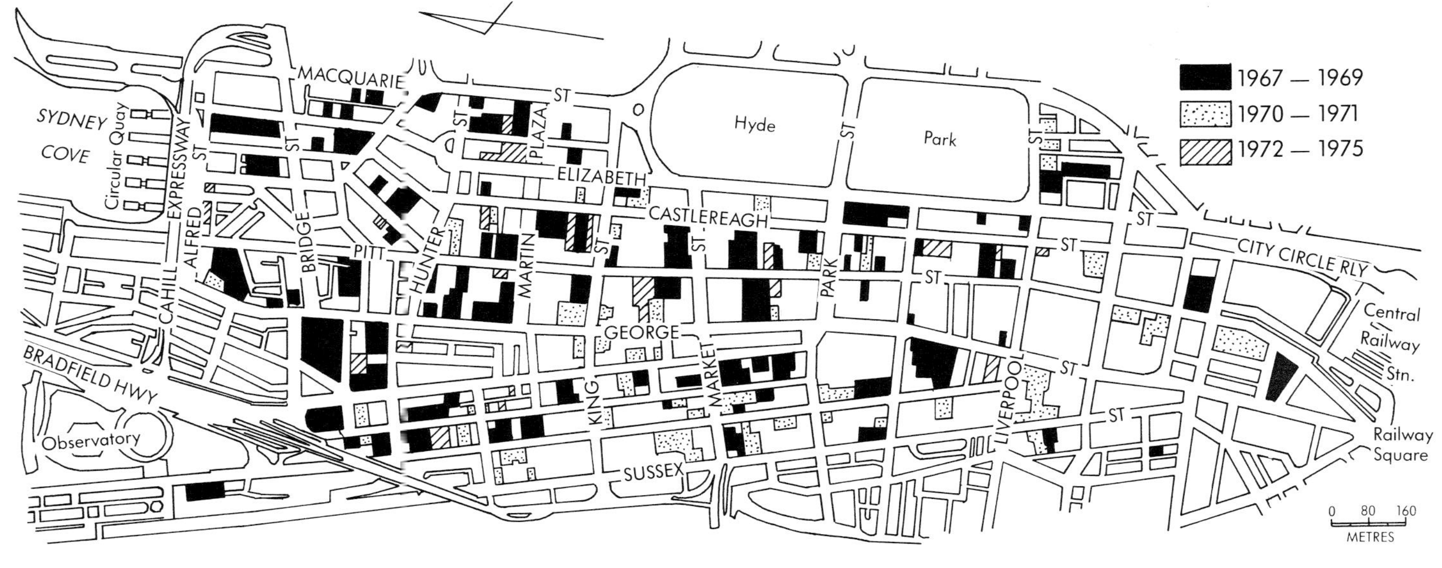

City of Sydney development application approvals, 1967–74. S.C.E.G.G.S. was one of many intending to engage in a large-scale development at this time.

good price as a development site. The School Council considered this proposal and rejected it.

Discussions (informal) were held with City Council officers early on in our thinking, and the City Council inadvertently made our ideas public when they published their William Street Boulevarde plan and showed a block 'S.C.E.G.G.S. Development' including properties not then owned by S.C.E.G.G.S.—a mistake which would have cost S.C.E.G.G.S. dearly in the acquisition of the William Street properties. I do not know the date of the formal application but it was during the purchase of the properties around S.C.E.G.G.S.

The chronological sequence of events is clear from the Council minutes. On 21 June 1971 Furley, in consultation with Prescott and Glanville, was authorised to purchase real estate offered by Home Units Australia for $1.8 million. On 28 August 1971 application for approval of the development was lodged with the Standing Committee and it was decided to lodge a Development Application with the City Council. In September Furley reported that he had received an offer of £25 million sterling loan from an overseas source. Furley was also in touch with the ABC (Australian Broadcasting Commission) as a possible tenant.[5]

At the meeting of 22 September 1971 a debate with far-reaching consequences took place. Mr W. A. Cale, an estate agent on the school Council, suggested that the Council should have the services of a solicitor specialising in international banking to act in conjunction with the William Street project.[6] He advocated an approach to Mr Adrian Henchman, a partner of Allen, Allen and Hemsley. Glanville's response to the proposal was that *he* wanted to be the Council's legal representative. He claimed that to go elsewhere for such legal advice was a slur on his professional capacity and he promised to seek other opinions when they were warranted. The Council resolved that Glanville be retained as the Council's solicitor.

By the end of the year the Council had engaged in further large-scale borrowing: a $90 000 loan from the Bank of New South Wales in October and, on 15 November 1971, $4 million from Bill Acceptance Corporation Ltd. (BAC). A valuation by Raine and Horne estimated that the value of the school site—$35 per square foot (gross $5.5 million) at the time—would rise to $100 per square foot ($26 million gross) with rezoning. On 17 January 1972 another loan from BAC was secured. The school Council also agreed to a loan of $500 000 with the Bank of New South Wales to offset the debit in the current account and cover additional purchases. By February 1972 most of the site between Liverpool Street and St Peter's Lane had been bought by S.C.E.G.G.S.[7]

From this point on, there began to be difficulties. The Development Application was not approved. By March it had been passed on to the State Planning Authority to gain consent for rezoning. In April Cale brought to the Council's attention two newspaper articles warning of a glut in office space. He advised the Council to let one-third of the space to the ABC to minimise financial risk. By September the delay in the Development Application was explained by the information that the City Council was planning to build a railway station at Kings Cross on the projected Eastern Suburbs railway line, and that the S.C.E.G.G.S. development would mean that the new station would be unable to handle the volume of passengers.[8] Approval was never granted. In September 1973 interest rates rose to 11.5 per cent and by the following June they had reached 14 per cent.

The S.C.E.G.G.S. development scheme was very much part of a development boom from the late 1960s to 1974. Figure 14.1 shows the extent of Development Application approvals by the City of Sydney during this period. There were 4.5 million square metres of new projects planned between 1967 and 1975.[9] In addition the state government gave approval for extensive redevelopment of the Woolloomooloo area. However, beginning with an action in 1971 to defeat a redevelopment project in Hunters Hill, part of which was to be developed into townhouses, the Builders' Labourers' Federation (BLF) placed 'green bans' on a number of projects which violated environmental standards or gave offence to local residents. Unionists opposed the development in the Woolloomooloo area, with green bans introduced by the BLF in 1973. Chaos followed and a large number of developers and investors fell into receivership as a result. For example, Regional Landholdings, the biggest developer in the area, sustained a loss of about $20 million.[10]

The glut of office space which resulted from the redevelopment in the central business district meant a fall in rental value. In about 1970 the rental for the most expensive space in the city was $161 per metre but by 1974 this had fallen to as low as $65 per square metre. Falling rentals and rising costs led to forced sales and lower prices.[11]

By mid 1974, the total liabilities of the S.C.E.G.G.S. Council amounted to $7.5 million.[12] A total of 53 properties adjoining the school had been acquired, some at grossly inflated prices. The scheme ran into difficulties when property values fell and the Council found itself unable to cover running costs of the school, unable to sell the properties for what they had paid, unable to meet interest costs on the borrowings and having to borrow further money to finance their operating loss.

The Rev. A. Prescott, Chairman of the Council at that time, recalled later:

> *The crisis arose as a result of three things. The first was that at a certain period of the Whitlam era interest rates went sky high and financing which was proper and prudent when the interest rates were around 6 per cent became quite impossible when the interest rates rose to over 20 per cent as they did just about the time the crisis came to a head. The second factor that was militating and beginning to cause worries was the beginning of the 'Green Movement' which was showing up with Jack Mundey and the Builders' Labourers' Federation putting a ban on certain building operations in the Darlinghurst area. And the third factor was the activities of the Treasurer, Mr Glanville.*[13]

The finances were in such disorder that it took months to unravel the true state of affairs. A budget summary drawn up in August 1974 by the Executive Officer, Furley, showed that while Darlinghurst had made a profit of $84 000 in the first part of 1974, three other schools had operated at a loss, Moss Vale losing $74 000, Redlands $68 000 and Gleniffer Brae $12 000. Later figures disclosed that the situation was much worse because of losses over the previous years, and that Darlinghurst was also incurring a substantial cash deficit.[14] The loss on educational operations in 1974 was of the order of $300 000.[15]

The panel of inquiry made a number of recommendations and stated:

> *We feel the greatest sympathy for the members of the S.C.E.G.G.S. Council who have given devoted service in the management under extremely difficult conditions of five schools and who are now involved in a grave situation, largely as a result of accepting in good faith the advice of a professional man who has betrayed their trust.*[16]

"As from today, we'll have education instead of property development. First lesson: How not to develop property."

The panel recommended the formation of a management committee to control the finances, the employment of a firm of accountants, a salvage operation which would include a meeting with the major creditors, and the sale of the Moss Vale and Wollongong schools. At a special meeting of the Standing Committee the recommendations were adopted.

Back in December 1973 W. G. S. Gotley, the Diocesan Secretary, had written to Furley stating that the development scheme seemed feasible and it was understood that Prescott had undertaken fully to inform the Standing Committee of the proposals and the basis of financing before proceeding with the project.[17] In the event, however, a number of transactions had been entered into without either the Archbishop or the Standing Committee being informed.

The position became public when the matter was reported to the Diocesan Synod. The Archbishop gave a clear and factual account of events and concluded with the following comments:

> *The position as disclosed is one of enormous complexity, and it will take many months before the problems are resolved. It is believed that the Schools have a continuing future though not necessarily in their present form. Certain reorganization will be essential . . .*
>
> *There are doubtless many questions that will arise for which no clear answer can be furnished at the moment. The Committee of Management, with their legal and financial advisers, have spent many hours and have worked almost daily in order to arrive at these first essential decisions. I must express my gratitude to them, as well as the hope that the critical situation which developed so suddenly will be successfully overcome. It will be the earnest desire of all members of this Synod that these Schools, with their girls and staff, will have God's blessing in a strong and stable future.*[18]

Public reaction was immediate. A Molnar cartoon in the *Sydney Morning Herald* showed a classroom scene with the caption: 'As from today we'll have education instead of property development. First lesson: How not to develop property.'[19] An Emeric cartoon in the *Sun-Herald* depicted a removalist's van taking furnishings from a dilapidated S.C.E.G.G.S. to a prosperous state school.[20] An article entitled 'A Church with Mammon Trouble' said: 'A Red Sea of ink has risen over the church leaders as they approach a Promised Land of Riches beyond their dreams. They have left their run too late: the luxuriant business jungle before them has withered.'[21] The writer Ian Moffitt was reminded of a Pro Hart painting which showed religious leaders building a mighty tower while Christ staggered neglected down a side street under His cross.[22]

Some of the issues to be dealt with were: to what extent was the Diocese responsible for the debts incurred by the Council? Would it be possible to honour the debts incurred? Were any of the schools financially viable? If so, could any of the schools be kept open? An immediate settlement of the debts was urgent because of snowballing interest and the threat of imminent action by the creditors. For the Archbishop a major concern was that if the creditors were not paid there would be a heritage of bitterness and hostility towards the church for the next 100 years.[23]

The S.C.E.G.G.S. Council met for the last time on 11 September 1974. It had managed the school for 79 years. It was replaced by a Management Committee consisting of S. Atkin, Archdeacon E. D. Cameron, G. Christmas, J. E. M. Dixon and N. Malone. N. M. Cameron, a partner of Allen, Allen and Hemsley, was retained as legal adviser and the daily management of the schools was placed in the hands of R. Moore of Price Waterhouse & Co., Chartered Accountants.[24]

At a meeting in October 1974 the Standing Committee acknowledged that many people saw S.C.E.G.G.S. as part of a single church entity and that the church therefore had moral obligations to students, staff and suppliers of the S.C.E.G.G.S. schools. All obligations up to 31 January 1975 should be met.

Accordingly $312 000 was made available as an interest-free loan to meet current debts.[25] The Executive Officer was dismissed and despite Miss Chisholm's displeasure, Moore from Price Waterhouse became a familiar figure at the S.C.E.G.G.S. schools as he set about reducing running costs. Economies at Darlinghurst included reducing the salary bill by cutting back on ancillary staff and changing the pupil–teacher ratio from 1 teacher:14.5 students to 1:15.5. Fees rose by 7.5 per cent.[26]

The Management Committee spent the remainder of 1974 and 1975 negotiating the settlement of the S.C.E.G.G.S. debt and operating the schools to break even or produce a profit. Darlinghurst concluded the end of the 1975 financial year with a slight surplus. The Moss Vale school was closed at the end of 1974 and The Illawarra Grammar School (TIGS) took over the management of Gleniffer Brae as a coeducational institution. The Loquat Valley school continued under the management committee until the end of 1975 and was sold to a diocesan body called the Council for the Promotion of Sydney Church of England Diocesan Schools in 1976. Redlands continued with greatly diminished numbers through 1975, and a council of parents was invited to manage the school.[27]

Such rationalisation of the S.C.E.G.G.S. schools caused great sadness to the school communities involved. The Darlinghurst school was perceived by many to be the cause of the financial crisis because of the development project linked to the school site, and it emerged as the only school relatively unscathed. Parents, staff and students from Moss Vale and Wollongong mourned the loss of schools which were far more than mere educational establishments: they were communities with traditions. There was a strong sense that they had been expendable because they were not on the scene of action where the decisions were made. Moss Vale had long been regarded as a financial drain on S.C.E.G.G.S. but the much younger Wollongong school, with its superb site and potential for future prosperity, was different. One of its disadvantages was that its founding Headmistress, Kathleen McCredie, had left in 1969 to become Headmistress of Abbotsleigh. At the time of its closure the school was run by an acting Head—had Miss McCredie been still there, it is probable that she could have rallied the parents to a rescue operation, similar to the ones at Redlands and Darlinghurst.[28] There were certainly parents ready to give financial support to keep the school open. Dr Ruth Shatford had been appointed by the Council to the position of Headmistress of the Wollongong school from the start of 1975 and the closure meant that she found herself without employment. She subsequently became Headmistress of Tara Anglican School for Girls at Parramatta.

All the properties purchased specifically for the Darlinghurst development plans were mortgaged, and since there was no intention of proceeding with the development, they were gradually sold. Small portions of land at Moss Vale and Wollongong were also sold in 1975. Properties which had originally cost the council $2.27 million were valued at a total of $700 000 in April 1977.[29] Inflated purchase prices together with the subsequent dramatic slump in property values from 1974 meant that the money borrowed for the purpose of acquiring the properties was never recovered.

Negotiations with the major creditors were complex and time-consuming. The small secured creditors had been paid off by the sale of much of the property adjoining the Darlinghurst school site. There were four major creditors, two of whom—Beneficial Finance Limited and Mutual Life Corporation—were amply secured. The other two creditors were BAC and the Bank of New

South Wales. Negotiations with BAC were delicate and dragged on for more than two years.

The Council had overrun its overdraft limits with the Bank without reference to the Diocese in any way. The Bank seems to have assumed that the Diocese would provide security for and sanction further loans. However, although the S.C.E.G.G.S. account was in disorder ($250 000 was borrowed 'for essential needs' in early 1974), the Bank did not inform the Diocesan authorities.[30]

By 1976 BAC was facing a liquidity problem and pressuring the S.C.E.G.G.S. Management Committee. Legal action was threatened. Throughout 1975 and 1976 a number of proposals were put to BAC but with no conclusion. BAC would not accept that the Diocese would close the Darlinghurst school if pressed and expected the Diocese to pay the debt, although it was clear that legally the Diocese was in no way responsible for the debts incurred by the S.C.E.G.G.S. Council.[31]

On 23 September 1976 BAC informed the Chairman of the Management Committee, Bishop (formerly Archdeacon) Cameron, that there would be no further correspondence between them and another letter written on the same day threatened that BAC would take steps to enforce their rights at the end of seven days.[32] This meant that litigation would begin and, in the opinion of the Management Committee, make the continuation of the schools impossible. Accordingly on 26 October a letter to parents at the Darlinghurst school included the following statement: 'Under the circumstances the Standing Committee considers that it is unable to offer education to children and employment to staff and must therefore regretfully advise you that the school operating under its control at Darlinghurst will be closed at the end of the current term.' Staff at the schools were also given formal notice of termination of employment.

A defunct school was of no use to BAC because it was unsaleable. It was in everybody's interests to keep the school open. The decision to close the S.C.E.G.G.S. schools effectively stimulated the action necessary to save them. This happened in two ways. First, BAC decided to accept an offer of settlement which until then it had rejected. Second, the school community was mobilised and at Darlinghurst a 'Save S.C.E.G.G.S. Fund' was set up. Money raised by parents and Old Girls, together with a grant from the Diocese of $500 000, meant that enough funds were available for a settlement to be negotiated.

The details of the settlement, of which N. M. Cameron was the chief architect,[33] were that S.C.E.G.G.S. would settle the debt to BAC, reckoned at $4.5 million plus interest, by paying $3.4 million by 31 December 1977.[34] The money was raised from four sources: the Diocesan S.C.E.G.G.S. Assistance Fund grant of $1 million; 'Save S.C.E.G.G.S. Fund' 's raising of a further $1 million; and the sale of the commercial land adjoining the Darlinghurst and Redlands schools, together with money recovered from the Law Society in respect of the Glanville matter, amounted to $1.4 million.

The Darlinghurst school site was sold to a newly formed company called 'SCEGGS Darlinghurst Ltd' for $1.5 million. Of this, $1 million came from the 'Save S.C.E.G.G.S. Fund' and $500 000 from the Diocese. The balance of the Diocesan S.C.E.G.G.S. Assistance Fund, namely $500 000, was paid direct to BAC.

The agreement was signed on Christmas Eve 1976. It was the best solution, for it ensured the continuation of the Redlands and Darlinghurst schools and the Diocese was seen to honour its debts.

The initiative of parents was vital to the rescue operation. They first met on

10 November and from this meeting a committee was formed with E. Davis, a solicitor, as chairman. The Old Girls and parents set about raising money in every possible way:

> *We . . . had organised a loan with the Bank of New South Wales, as it was then, to provide the funds to buy the school until such time as we got the money . . . At the meeting the parents resolved the Committee would form a new Board and we would buy the school. We then went on a massive fundraising exercise for the balance of the money. We had some things which upset the church, like we had an art union. We sold wine—we had an arrangement with Penfolds and Peter [Burger] who was then working for Penfolds, got a thousand dozen bottles of wine. We had fetes . . . the school did a walkathon in Centennial Park, the girls walked up and down Macquarie Street to all the doctors, we had dinners by the thousand and we had a fairly massive fundraising which only yielded from memory another two or three hundred thousand dollars, so that by the time we settled the purchase of the school we were still short.*[35]

The rescue of S.C.E.G.G.S. gave a great sense of purpose to the S.C.E.G.G.S. community. The parents and Old Girls saw it as a crusade and out of the crisis came a strong sense of a common bond and renewed awareness of the value of the school. In her November report to Council Miss Chisholm said: 'I have been deeply moved by the support we have received from other schools and from many people who have no connection with the school. The girls have become very united and the spirit of the school has never been stronger. Only twenty-eight girls left as a result of the troubles.'

The response from other members of the community revealed the high esteem in which Miss Chisholm and S.C.E.G.G.S. were held. The Headmaster of Shore, B. H. Travers, offered to accommodate the S.C.E.G.G.S. girls at Shore. The offer was highly valued because of Shore's reputation for being a stronghold of male education. In addition Shore sent a gift of $1000 to the S.C.E.G.G.S. fund. A letter from Professor Ken Cable, Chairman of St Catherine's Waverley, assured S.C.E.G.G.S. of the 'best efforts and support of St Catherine's'. Yvonne Bowers, a pupil at the time, recalls: 'The sight of Miss Barbara Chisholm, our Headmistress, toiling through rain and mud with the rest of us in the Walkathon in Centennial Park reminds me of the kind of woman she was and the example she set us all.'[36]

The previous two years had been an enormous strain for Miss Chisholm. Mrs Miller recalled in an interview that the announcement of the closure of Darlinghurst was an 'absolute shock'. The Darlinghurst staff had thought that Redlands was in danger of closing but that Darlinghurst would thereby be safe, and that all the visits from 'financial people' had nothing to do with them.[37] The strain of keeping all the worries a secret must have been very hard, particularly for a Headmistress contemplating retirement after a long period of service. Once the S.C.E.G.G.S. difficulties were known, the main problem, apart from attending numerous committee meetings, was maintaining morale at the school.

Reactions to the way the Anglican church handled the S.C.E.G.G.S. troubles were frequently critical and often diametrically opposed. The mopping-up operation was a thankless task and most of the opprobrium stirred up by the crisis fell upon the men who bore no personal responsibility for the situation. Two churchmen who received little thanks and much hostility, and whose waking hours were mainly consumed by the worries of the S.C.E.G.G.S. matter,

The spectacular climax to the "Save SCEGGS Appeal" — boys and girls of leading Sydney schools working together to support their sister school, SCEGGS

Some of the highlights: the internationally acclaimed Scots' College Pipe Band; schoolgirl gymnastic displays; massed boys' and girls' choirs; 200 beautiful girls marching to the music of pipe and brass bands.

Bring the kids to see what kids can do in this magnificent display At the Sydney Sports Ground, Wednesday, March 30 at 7.30 p.m.

Admission: Adults $3.00 — Children 50c

A unique evening's entertainment compered by show business personality, Gary O'Callaghan.

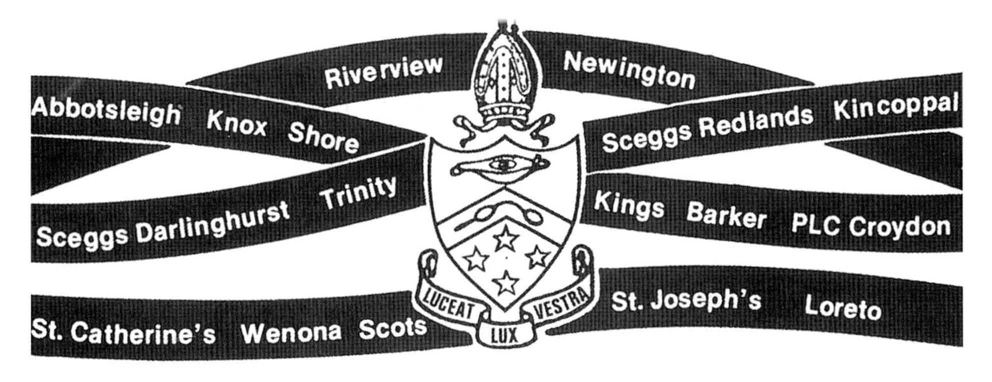

One of the many events organised by the 'Save S.C.E.G.G.S.' group. It shows the number of schools rallying to S.C.E.G.G.S.' aid.

were Archbishop Loane and Archdeacon (now Bishop) Cameron. Their tireless efforts and genuine concern to find an honourable solution are largely unknown and for the most part unacknowledged by the S.C.E.G.G.S. community. Correspondence received by, and replies to letters from Archbishop Loane and Bishop Cameron show that they took the letters very seriously, replying with courtesy and explaining as helpfully as was possible. One reply from the Archbishop ran: 'There can be no doubt that many of the criticisms that could be made in this situation would be at least partly justified and very difficult to refute . . . the Management Committee and the Diocese as a whole is, I am sure, sensitive to this situation and to the point of view expressed in your letter.'[38]

The following selection from the correspondence relating to S.C.E.G.G.S. indicates the diversity of strongly held views. (One solution might have been to send correspondent A a letter from correspondent B to show that the situation was far from straightforward.)

A letter from an Anglican staff worker asked, 'How can the Church of England justify its donation of $500 000 during this period of high unemployment and Christmas appeals to assist the poor?'

Letters from Old Girls and parents included the following opinions:

> *It appears to me that your willingness to protect the school's creditor is greater than your school spirit . . .*

> *The policy of the Church of England is that they do not allocate profit from one area to another. They can pull down a building a few years old to erect an office block and shopping mall. Where did the finance come from?*[39]

> *Boys' schools seem to get by. Is it discrimination against the girls?*

Finally, a letter from DOGS ran:

> *17 October 1974*
>
> *Dear Sir,*
>
> *In view of the large amounts of public money contributed to your schools in State Aid over the last few years, what contribution will you make in return (when properties, schools and equipment etc are sold) to the taxpayers and ratepayers, who have been subsidising your schools all this time?*

Although the Standing Committee was unanimously in favour of assisting S.C.E.G.G.S. financially, the same was not true of the Sydney Synod. The issues raised in the first letter were related to a host of questions concerning the right use of church money and the priorities for spending it. Many members of Synod had no connection with the private school system and little sympathy with supporting what were seen as privileged institutions for a particular social class. It caused a genuine crisis of conscience for some and at least one well-known and respected member of the Synod, E. Newman, resigned and left the Anglican church in consequence.[40]

There was one area in which Synod could be said to be responsible for the whole S.C.E.G.G.S. disaster. The S.C.E.G.G.S. Council had ultimately been the Synod's responsibility: it appointed most of the Council members. Poor Synod appointments to Council and the lack of accountability on the Council's part and oversight of the Council's operations were the responsibility of the Synod.

In addition, the unwieldy nature of the S.C.E.G.G.S. system cried out for a major overhaul. In this sense, then, every Synod member and every Council member bore some responsibility for the very unfortunate events set in motion by a fraudulent Treasurer and an economic recession.

It is likely that the crisis sped up a process of disintegration of the S.C.E.G.G.S. group of schools which had already begun. The probability is that Redlands would have become a separate school in its own right within ten years as would, in time, Gleniffer Brae at Wollongong. Moss Vale would have had to close sooner or later. The long-term effects of the crisis were not all bad: the old Council was replaced by far more streamlined and efficient separate governing bodies for Darlinghurst and Redlands. The Moss Vale school, for so long a financial liability, was finally closed. It was a solution which nobody had dared implement but which had been frequently mooted. The tragedy was that the Wollongong school was closed down permanently.

Many of the students from Gleniffer Brae joined TIGS, as it became coeducational at this time. There is a tradition kept alive in the TIGS community of S.C.E.G.G.S. and its Old Girls. This has become active with the establishment of an Alumni Association where a newsletter and various functions foster old ties. TIGS has always suffered from the same financial difficulties experienced by the two S.C.E.G.G.S. country schools. The catchment area is limited, alternative education offered by Wollongong schools is highly regarded, and it has been a struggle to raise standards and provide competition for the very able students the school would like to attract. Its present Headmaster, the Rev. Peter Smart, was formerly Headmaster of Tamworth Grammar School, which flourished under his leadership.

Since 1976, Redlands, renamed 'Sydney Church of England Co-educational Grammar School' (S.C.E.C.G.S.), has prospered. Its present Headmaster, Mr Peter Cornish, and school Council have a reputation for bold entrepreneurial activities. It owns properties at Belrose and Jindabyne and in 1989 the school purchased the site of Cremorne Girls' High School for $15.5 million in order to accommodate a baccalaureate college in which overseas students were actively encouraged to enrol. Enrolments in 1989 were 1054 pupils, soaring to 1369 by late 1990.

Loquat Valley school celebrated its forty-third year in 1990. Its present Headmaster is Mr Stephen McGrath. It is a coeducational preparatory school, taking children from Kindergarten to Year 6, and acted as a feeder school for the Peninsula Grammar School for boys and St Luke's Girls' College until the end of 1992. All three schools were part of the Sydney Anglican Schools Corporation.

The loans crisis at S.C.E.G.G.S. raises a difficult question. How far was the whole crisis the result of the unwieldy structure of the S.C.E.G.G.S. group of schools? A complex number of factors contributed to the crisis. Would it have happened if Darlinghurst had been the only school run by the Council? The answer may well be 'no'. If there had been no other schools bleeding away the profits and keeping Darlinghurst the Cinderella of the group, then perhaps there would not have been the desire to shore up a financial base. The S.C.E.G.G.S. schools were only as strong as the weakest member. If the Council had concentrated its energies and attention on the efficient running of one school rather than five, then defects in the system would have been more obvious sooner. If the Council had been smaller and each member had been expected to have first-hand knowledge of the school (or all the schools), then a corporate sense of responsibility would have been much stronger. For some

Council members, the job was probably a sinecure. If the appointments to the Council had been more related to the school community and its needs, and less orchestrated by a remote Synod, those appointed to the Council would have been chosen for their particular contribution, and would have been more aware of the needs of the school (or schools). All this is speculation. It is certain, however, that the crisis sped up the inevitable process of the disintegration of the S.C.E.G.G.S. empire.

The final task of the Management Committee was to hand over management of S.C.E.G.G.S. Darlinghurst to the new company, SCEGGS Darlinghurst Ltd. Under its Articles of Association the new company was limited by guarantee and its members consisted of two Old Girls, representatives of the parents and up to four Diocesan representatives. The new Board elected David Clark, Managing Director of Hill Samuel, as the Chairman. Parent representatives on the Board were Ted Davis (solicitor), Fred Waring (property executive), Peter Burger (property executive) and Tony Walker (company secretary). The Old Girls elected Denise Fleming (company executive) and Diana Bowman (educationalist). The three church representatives were Bishop E. D. Cameron, Kathleen McCredie (Headmistress of Abbotsleigh), and N. M. Cameron (solicitor). By contrast with the old Council, this Board was small and had a significant number of legal and financial experts.[41]

The formal announcement of the purchase of the school site by SCEGGS Darlinghurst Ltd was made on 30 March 1977. The purchase completed the process whereby the school passed from the ownership of the Sydney Anglican Diocese to a company limited by guarantee. There has been, since that time, a view that the church mismanaged the school's affairs and the parents and Old Girls would be more efficient and successful, especially as, from this group's perspective, it was they who effected the rescue of the school.

The two main tasks of the new Board of Directors were to run the school on a sound and profitable financial basis, and to find a successor for Barbara Chisholm. Enrolments by August 1977 were at 499, 200 pupils fewer than in 1970. In the following year numbers rose steadily, and by continuing to exercise strict economy the Board ran the school at a profit. Miss Chisholm was persuaded by the new Board to remain on for a further year. During that year the post was advertised. There were thirteen applicants and from a shortlist of four, the Board appointed Diana Bowman to begin as Head in 1978.[42]

— 15 —

S.C.E.G.G.S. in the 1980s

THE 1980s WERE a decade of accelerating social change and economic prosperity. Secondary schools became more lavishly furnished and equipped, their administrative bureaucracies mushroomed and the computer, facsimile machine and photocopier revolutionised teaching and office practices. Social dislocation, evidenced by an increase in crime, suicide, homelessness and divorce threw a heavy burden on schools in providing resources traditionally provided by the home. Teacher morale began to fall, aggressive teacher unions dictated policy through their members to Heads and councils, and fewer students trained to become teachers. University quotas increased pressure on students at the Higher School Certificate examination and scaling procedures in the marking meant that brighter students generally concentrated on mathematics and sciences rather than the humanities. Students became more inclined to choose a career—not from a sense of vocation, but on the basis of what income it would produce. The process of secularisation continued and in curricula and career choices the philosophy was often pragmatic: if it works, do it.

Diana Bowman took up her position as Headmistress of S.C.E.G.G.S. in 1978. She was its first Australian-born Head. An Old Girl of S.C.E.G.G.S., she distinguished herself at sport, in particular athletics and swimming, as captain of Beck House and a prefect, and in the Leaving Certificate of 1954, where she gained first class honours in Latin and A's in French, mathematics and classical Greek.[1] The bank or secretarial work were the career choices her family expected of her, and none of the family had gone on to tertiary education. Miss Chisholm instituted the S.C.E.G.G.S. scholarship with the Council for her. This enabled her to do an Arts degree and a Diploma of Education, her part of the agreement being that she would teach in a S.C.E.G.G.S. school for three years on completion of her training.[2]

She taught at Moss Vale for two practica during her student days, then was appointed to Gleniffer Brae where she taught Latin as her main subject. Subsequent appointments were to Hornsby Girls' High School, then as

Diana Mildred Bowman, fourth Headmistress of S.C.E.G.G.S., 1978– .

Headmistress of Girton, an Adelaide girls' school, in 1965. Her first headship came after five years' teaching experience. Both Heads under whom she taught (Miss Kathleen McCredie at Gleniffer Brae and Miss Molly Cahill at Hornsby Girls' High) took a personal interest in her and her teaching career. They gave her responsibility, encouraged her to experiment, and gave her confidence in her teaching ability. She says of them, 'They were both inspired women and they inspired others.'[3] After three years at Girton, she resigned and from then until her appointment as Head of S.C.E.G.G.S., she taught at Drummoyne Boys' High School and Ravenswood Girls' School. She won a postgraduate award to undertake a master's degree full-time at the Canberra College of Advanced Education. It was while she was engaged in these studies that she was appointed Headmistress of S.C.E.G.G.S. Darlinghurst.[4]

In the 1980s S.C.E.G.G.S. pulled out of the financial slough of the mid 1970s crisis, and became a thriving, prosperous and highly respected school. Under the headship of Diana Bowman, the school regained capacity enrolment (more than 730 pupils) and developed long waiting lists to the year 2000 and beyond. The S.C.E.G.G.S. Board, with Mr Sam Cullen as Chairman, ensured that finances were healthy and conservative. Parents sent their children to S.C.E.G.G.S. for three main reasons: for its atmosphere of care and friendliness; for its social mix of girls from all over Sydney which resulted in a lack of elitism; and for its fine academic record.[5] The school continued to be in the vanguard of education in a number of areas, and Diana Bowman became foremost of a new breed of Heads in her professionalism in a job which now demanded considerable administrative skills as well as leadership in education. Schools had become increasingly complex.

According to Dr Ruth Shatford, Head of Tara, three major factors have shaped education in the 1980s: the predicament of youth, the predicament of the economy and the influence of the teacher unions.[6] A report published in 1988 by the Commission for the Future[7] outlined the changes sweeping society and the effects on young people. Suicides doubled between 1968 and 1988; heroin claimed five times as many young people in 1988 as in 1978; the incidence of reported rape rose more than 150 per cent in the decade after 1975, as did robbery, burglary and other theft. Serious assault increased fourfold. The report stated:

> *. . . the figures point unequivocally to an alarming escalation in the social and psychological problems facing young Australians today. Behind these problems are increases in family conflict and breakdown, increasing poverty, high youth unemployment, soaring youth homelessness and growing educational pressures. Underlying these developments are social, economic and technological changes that may, in themselves, be imposing a growing psychological stress on children and young adults—a stress that finds bleak expression in the fear and pessimism with which many of them regard the future.*[8]

Schools have had increasing demands made upon them to provide personal and career counselling services, and education has been seen increasingly to provide the key to employment and wealth. One result of parental pressure for students to obtain tertiary education has been a higher retention rate at school.

The first careers adviser was appointed at S.C.E.G.G.S. at the beginning of the 1980s. It was not a full-time post. In 1987 a new course called 'Life and Careers' was introduced, with Mrs Kay Ward as the first professional full-time counsellor at the school.[9] She coordinated the course, which was designed for Years 7 to 10. The course covered career awareness, knowledge and understanding of the world of work, job investigation and decision-making and, finally, finding a job.[10] The course was designed to help girls think about career prospects and initiate them into the world of work.

The state of the national economy was the second factor to shape education by the late 1980s. The educational catchword was 'relevant', and school curricula were expected to provide vocational training and to assist in pulling the country out of its debt-ridden state. Dr Shatford states: 'Whereas once our ideal for education would have been a liberal and liberalising education based on a desire for giving personal fulfilment to the individual, there seems to have been in many quarters an abandonment of this ideal in favour of a blatant instrumental approach to education.'[11]

A statement made by John Dawkins, the Federal Minister of Employment, Education and Training, enunciated this view when he spoke of: '. . . maintaining a higher education system that is able to take a long term and independent approach in pursuing its teaching, scholarly and research functions and using higher education to address Australia's pressing economic and social problems and to meet the nation's increasing need for an educated and skilled population.'[12]

In her Headmistress's Report for 1987, Diana Bowman said:

> *I share the concern of many that in the creation of the new Commonwealth Department of Employment, Education and Training the Government seems to be*

embracing a purely utilitarian concept of education. I am not questioning the claims of employers that many unemployed young people lack the skills and self-discipline necessary to make them employable, but education does not create jobs—the most it can do is enable the better-educated student to beat others to the job that is available. It is not the false assumption that education is the handmaiden to employment that worries me so much as the narrow and short-sighted conception of education that it involves.

Life is rich and it is complex. If all we do is equip our students for whatever employment they can find when they leave, then we cannot claim to be doing much for them. We certainly cannot justify keeping them at school for twelve years: the kind of employment skills they need could be taught in half that time. Our task is also to deepen their appreciation of life, to introduce them to the great store of knowledge that man has acquired, to extend their understanding of themselves and their society, to make them compassionate towards others and responsive to opportunity. It will be most unfortunate if the Government in its present concern to be seen doing something for the youth unemployment interferes with our broader task or further muzzles our endeavours.[13]

The third major factor was the influence of teacher unions, which became more militant, more radical and more wealthy. The level of membership rose significantly and unions became wealthier with the imposition of a substantial annual levy. They became a significant force in the trade union movement, their chief aim being to raise salaries and thereby to extend career opportunities. The ITA (Independent Teachers' Association) became a force to be reckoned with for all Heads of independent schools.

The cost of salary rises meant increased costs in running independent schools. These costs were met with fee rises and the establishment of school foundations, a concept borrowed from schools in the United States. A consequence of rising fees and the pressure upon parents to contribute to a foundation was a further polarisation of education around those able to afford private school fees and those whose incomes were insufficient. More mothers went back to work in order to help meet the burden of school fees. Independent schools became increasingly costly: something affordable for the wealthy only. S.C.E.G.G.S.'s school fees rose between 10 per cent and 14 per cent annually, since the rate of inflation was about 7 per cent. In years when teachers' wage demands rose significantly, the fees rose correspondingly. On the other hand, S.C.E.G.G.S. continued to provide fee concessions and scholarships to a number of its students. The cost to the school in 1988 for fee concessions was approximately $100 000: about 3.5 per cent of the annual budget. Daughters of clergy received a 75 per cent discount, while daughters of staff received discounts of between 25 per cent and 50 per cent. In addition eight academic scholarships and one music scholarship provided a 100 per cent discount of fees.[14]

These factors combined to alter the educational process in secondary schools in a great many areas. The role of the Head changed, as did that of the school council. Staff, students and parents developed different expectations and relationships. The school facilities, buildings and programs altered. Government influence through funding, curriculum policy and the public education system affected policies in the independent schools.

The role of the Head changed in that more importance was placed on the Head as educator and administrator and less on the Head's role as moral and spiritual leader.[15] Councils now looked for a person with proven administrative ability and strong involvement in educational issues, such as experience as a curriculum coordinator. The former type of Head could provide Christian leadership, was unmarried and 'expected to give her all in a spirit of service'. Such Heads were Miss Kathleen McCredie at S.C.E.G.G.S. Wollongong and Abbotsleigh, and Miss Mary Graham at S.C.E.G.G.S. Moss Vale.[16] Terms such as 'stress management', 'time management' and the Head's 'mental and physical health' were never considered. According to Miss Bowman, the Head of the old order, to be successful, would have to know each pupil personally, have control over all decision-making and have knowledge of plumbing, architecture, gardening and cooking. (The introduction of bursars and maintenance managers changed the latter aspect of a Head's role.) Between 1978 and 1989 15 of the 58 independent girls' schools in New South Wales had a change of Head.[17]

Characteristics of the new Heads included higher educational qualifications, residence away from the school, and spouses and families. Heads were better paid, with better superannuation and conditions. They could train on the job through curriculum development courses run by the AIS, and a financial management course offered by the University of New England.

A major change in the Head's duties was the need to be an administrator. This came about for a number of reasons. One was the need to keep extensive records in order to satisfy government requirements for funding.[18] Other reasons include: the added work required for school assessments, the increasing rigidity of school inspections and the need to provide each Year 12 student with a portfolio upon leaving the school. At S.C.E.G.G.S. this includes a work experience certificate, a community services record, a record of co-curricular achievements (sporting and drama activities, for example), academic results and a reference. Diana Bowman added that the availability of government money in the early 1980s (S.C.E.G.G.S. received $500 000 for its building work at that time) made extra work for the Head with the planning and building of new facilities. In addition she observed that Heads had become more accountable to parents, to employers in the community and to the government.[19]

Mrs Joy Yeo, Head of Roseville Girls' College, saw the greatest change in the role of the Head as the increase in the complexity of the job. She described it as an 'extraordinary juggling situation' where the demands and needs of six groups had to be satisfied: the school council, the staff, the parents, the pupils, the Education Department and the local community. Heads were expected more than ever before to be able to understand principles of business administration. All these generalisations have been true of S.C.E.G.G.S., and Diana Bowman stated:

> *I don't think Heads have as much time as they would like to spend with their staff or their students—I see this as a change in their role. In my own role of Head I have tried to maintain personal contact with each staff member. It becomes more and more difficult because of other pressures. It was interesting that these characteristics—encouragement, support in failure, experimentation, personal interest, respect and affection (possibly all embodied in the word 'love') were put to Heads at the NCIS (National Council of Independent Schools) Conference, 1990 as necessary characteristics of a good leader whether in business or education.*
>
> *That is one great advantage of S.C.E.G.G.S. We are small enough to have a climate where these can flourish—provided the caring environment is established and maintained. As a Head 25 years ago I had a much greater involvement with the boarders. I ate with them, I slept in the boarding house, I took them on outings,*

I took them to Church. I do very little of this now. I taught ten Scripture periods a week, I was the disciplinarian. There were numerous public roles expected of a Head in Adelaide—not so much now.

When I accepted the job at Girton I had to take a smaller salary than I was being paid at Hornsby Girls' High School. Dedication was the key word. Money was 'filthy lucre'. Heads were a Protestant extension of the Catholic religious of that time—the pleasures of this world were for those outside![20]

Diana Bowman made time for being in the classroom, teaching Latin or religious education to Year 7. One result of this was that she learnt the names of all the girls, as well as keeping in touch with the practical and changing issues relating to classes, staff and students. A Head who is no longer working at the coalface becomes remote, inaccessible and out of touch.

During the 1980s, school Heads became more supportive of one another, less competitive. As the ITA grew in strength and the demands of the curriculum grew, the Heads grew closer, pooling advice and experience. They relied more heavily on AHISA (Association of the Heads of Independent Schools of Australia) and AHIGS (Association of the Heads of Independent Girls' Schools), founded in 1985, and they formed their own registered union APIS (Association of Principals of Independent Schools). Diana Bowman was President of AHIGS in 1987 and 1992.

School councils changed. They had greater responsibilities than previously. These included oversight of the school Foundation and other fundraising entities, government funding requirements, industrial implications relating to awards and staffing conditions, legal accountability, and dealings with local councils. Although council members were increasingly selected for their specialist skills and expertise, there still lingered an awareness that school councils were 'the greatest weakness that besets Australian independent schools'.[21] Miss Coral Dixon, Head of Ravenswood School for Girls, said in an interview:

A very wise senior Headmaster told me that if my council was not hand-picked within five years I had failed as a Head. And I think you do, as a Head, have quite a bit of influence . . . you do have the opportunity to note people of talent, to influence your chairman, to say 'We need a person of their skills'. . .

I think everyone must keep their role very clearly in mind and the Head needs to be very aware that he or she was appointed by that council and unless the partnership between Head and Council works, the school will not succeed and the Head may not survive. So it is the *crucial relationship and I think the Head is very vulnerable—probably has less security of tenure than any member of staff, from the junior groundsman up.*[22]

The S.C.E.G.G.S. Board is unusual because of its composition. It is small by comparison with many other school councils, and its members are elected by three different groups: the Anglican Synod (up to four representatives), company members of SCEGGS Darlinghurst Ltd (up to six representatives) and the Old Girls (two representatives).

There is a danger that elections will occur along party lines, that personal ambition, pressure groups or special interest groups will dictate policy rather than making the good of the school the overriding goal in all elections. It is also possible that Board issues could be debated along personal and party lines rather than what is most beneficial for S.C.E.G.G.S. There is the possibility that the Board will not have the right balance of expertise to enable it to make informed and wise decisions. In the 1980s the Board was subject to such pressures from time to time, but the Chairman and Headmistress made it clear on any such occasion that the good of the school must come first. The new Board was still in its first decade in the 1980s and traditions of Board policy had to be rethought and reformed as a result of the demise of the old Council.

The work of the Board grew during the decade. Industrial matters, the question of establishment of a school Foundation, and matters of fundraising lengthened the Board agenda. Subcommittees became more important to discuss and research matters subsequently raised at Board level. There continues to be a significant number of legal and financial experts on the Board as well as those with business experience. Complementing these are men and women from medical, educational, sociological and church professional backgrounds. The Board's profile, on recommendation from fundraising and development experts, was raised. One innovation was that teaching departments attended Board meetings in 1990 to meet the Board and to describe the work of their department to the Board and answer questions Board members might have.

Public perception of education changed during the 1980s. Dr Shatford noted a pattern which has emerged in senior administration in both state and commonwealth governments. It is that of establishing a pool of senior managers who can be assigned to a particular task or role on the basis of their managerial, financial and policy skills rather than their expertise in a particular area, such as education. Non-educators seem to have been appointed as chief schools' officers:

> *Careful financial control and good management along the best lines of business practice seem to be valued in these appointments more than educational experience and insight and identification with the teaching profession. Prior to the 1980s the position of Director-General was usually held by an educator who had gained promotion through the system, having begun as a humble classroom teacher. He was always seen as an apolitical administrator who, in his most senior years in the service, acted as educational spokesman . . . [the] appointment is now seen as being very much more political.*
>
> *Hedley Beare, Professor of Education at the University of Melbourne, has said that 'making educational pronouncements as a professional is now a hazardous act; the chief executive is regarded as a manager and it is the Minister who makes the pronouncements, educational as well as political. The office may be known as that of 'permanent head' but impermanence seems to be a common characteristic of its holders. During the 1980s of the 24 people who have occupied the eight positions in the states and territories equivalent to that of Director General, almost half of them have been reassigned, retired early, or have moved to another posting. By changes of appointments and changes in the title of the chief executive, governments seem to signal their discontent with the existing situation in education under their control. It seems that ministers have great faith in organizational restructuring as a means of implementing their policies.*[23]

Significantly, problems with members of staff were labelled 'industrial' problems, and business terminology was used for organisational structures in education. According to Dr Shatford 'Education has entered the marketplace in Australia.'[24] Schools had always to be viable economic enterprises, but in the 1980s school councils saw themselves as responsible for multimillion dollar businesses. The uncertain future of recurrent government funding led to

Barham in the 1990s, still shaded by its Moreton Bay figtree.

fundraising, establishment of school foundations and similar trust funds and one result was the aggressive competition for the dollar.

The development officer was an innovation. His/her job was 'friend-raising and fundraising'. With the development officer (a concept borrowed from America) came ancillary staff, glossy publications, aggressive promotion of the school and its needs directed towards former pupils and the parent community. Development officers were regarded with suspicion by teaching staff, especially as their salaries were sometimes higher than both that of the Head and the Deputy Head.[25]

Government funding during the 1980s took two forms: per capita grants according to the school's level on a wealth scale, and interest subsidies. Under the Hawke government grants were fixed for four-year terms, enabling schools to budget several years ahead. Grants in the top school categories fell behind, eroded by inflation (see Table 15.1). The interest subsidies were of great benefit to schools. They provided up to 12 per cent of interest repayments on loans for buildings equivalent to those in government schools. I. Paterson commented: 'The extent of this generous subsidy, during the Golden Age of the 1980s, can be judged from its blow-out from $3.1 million at the start of the decade to $17.5 million by the end. The Government could not sustain this 179 per cent growth rate in real terms.'[26]

State education was in disarray in the 1980s. The major causes of the problem were a choked bureaucracy and a radical Teachers' Union. The independent schools profited from the growing disaffection with state education: schools grew larger and waiting lists longer. Booking a baby into a school at birth was not always a guarantee of entry, such was the demand for private education. New schools were set up. It was a period akin to that earlier time from 1833 to 1866 when financial aid from the government encouraged rapid growth in church schools.[27] As the interest subsidy figures quoted above indicate, schools

Table 15.1 Commonwealth and state funding for S.C.E.G.G.S., 1985–89

Year	Per capita rate		Total received
	Primary $	Secondary $	$
1985	373	592	346 759
1986	397	630	392 640
1987	412	654	413 284
1988	424	672	429 380
1989	458	726	501 471

Source: S.C.E.G.G.S. Bursar's files

engaged in a great deal of building. Most buildings were specialist buildings: computer classrooms, music buildings, sporting complexes and swimming pools. S.C.E.G.G.S. built art and primary classrooms, and was among the first schools to set up a classroom of computers.

It was an era of affluence for schools: carpets were laid where lino or bare boards sufficed earlier. S.C.E.G.G.S. was carpeted throughout, the heating upgraded, the staff were given their own desks, more staffrooms and rooms for specialist teaching were provided. The library became computerised. In 1989 the school subsidised meals for the staff, which they ate in a refurbished dining room. As one school acquired a classroom full of computers or a new gymnasium, other schools followed suit. There was a sense in which Heads were in competition for their schools to have the most up-to-date facilities: sporting grounds, campsites away from the school site and modern attractive buildings. Parents expected the school to provide facilities which matched those of neighbouring independent schools. Fees would not cover the cost of such enterprises and the Development Office and school Foundation worked to fund the projects. Opinions vary as to whether all these facilities improved the educational product. In the area of computers, for example, some Heads saw them as a current and expensive fad, a concession to parent pressure; others saw them as essential to the business of educating young people to handle technology wisely and competently in a technological age.[28]

One of the phenomena of the decade was an expansion of school administration. While the primary school section of independent schools remained small, with the primary school Head still teaching classes and without secretarial help, the administration of secondary schools grew enormously. Paterson commented:

> *Schools now explode with Directors of studies, Admission Registrars, Property Managers, Counsellors, Development Officers and the like each of which require back-up secretarial and clerical help. In turn the capital investment per office worker has come close to trebling in real terms in the last decade, with its computers, word processors, copying machines and facsimile machines . . .*
>
> *We have come a long way since the time when Dr McKenzie's*[29] *secretary was also the Admissions Registrar with only an accountant, his clerical assistant and a telephonist to make up the entire administration team for a school of 900 boys. Birtles, Head of Brisbane Boys' College, stayed up late at night to write out accounts for parents in longhand and without assistance.*
>
> *For the 1990s we need to question the size of our administrations. The explosion of administrative staff has been a consequence of the Golden Age, and I suspect there is ample fat to exorcise.*
>
> *I believe it was Thring of Uppingham, over a hundred years ago, who said 'The*

watchword of administration must be SIMPLIFY'. Today we are into complexity—we have this incessant desire to record everything, preferably on computer. Teachers and administrators continue to overwhelm me with the beautiful necessity of being able to track a boy's medical record, his home situation, his reports, his detentions, his sports, his visits to the school counsellor by a press of a computer button. To what end I ask? Would it not be more beneficial simply to speak to the boy; to spend time with him? At times, I am convinced that computers are the modern day equivalent of the Ford Edsell car—a great and clever idea that was to be the ideal consumer car, but it was a flop in the market. Do we really *need computers? I feel like Martin Luther at the University of Wittenberg challenging the Roman Catholic Church. Given the capital costs are the efficiency savings worth it? Frankly, I suppose not. In fact, we have a whole new type of capital cost that is eating away constantly at our finances.*

Schools must be simpler *places, where the purposes are clear and understood, and wherein the complexities of society are reduced to child-manageable proportions. The more we bureaucratise our schools, the more impersonal and institutional they will become.*[30]

At S.C.E.G.G.S. administration mushroomed. New in the 1980s were: a full-time computer expert with two additional office assistants, an office administrator, an enrolment registrar, an additional secretary in the general office and another in the Bursar's office.

In the area of the curriculum there were some changes. The School Certificate, taken at the end of Year 10, became an internal examination and therefore of not much value either to employers or as a motivating goal within the school. The Higher School Certificate became more of a burden than previously. Where the other states of Australia began to opt for assessments instead of an external examination, in New South Wales the examination remained, with the final student result out of a possible aggregate of 500 consisting partly of marks gained from assessments. The method of scaling the raw marks and the different scaling methods and requirements of each university made the two final years of school very stressful for the majority of students.

The quotas introduced by the universities, the University of Sydney in particular, meant that only students with very high marks were eligible to enter certain faculties: Arts/Law, Economics/Law, Medicine and Veterinary Science. As a result some students enrolled in the prestigious faculties because they were eligible on the basis of their marks rather than because they were suited to the career for which the faculty prepared them. Less prestigious courses, such as Arts, attracted fewer bright students. Students were inclined to concentrate on mathematics and the sciences because scaling procedures in the HSC favoured these subjects. Many had overspecialised in their last two years at school. The complaint of educators is expressed by Miss Bowman: '. . . the HSC. I believe that non-government schools are grossly constrained by this monster that the Department of Education has created. Do we educate or do we train for the HSC? Whether the former or the latter, parents believe non-government schools can beat this monster more effectively.'[31]

Another curriculum change was the requirement that the school give more attention to individuals and minority groups through means such as special remedial programs, gifted and talented programs, school counselling and by taking on exchange students. School camps became an integral part of the curriculum. These camps were designed to foster skills in outdoor living and environment awareness. Year 7 S.C.E.G.G.S. girls went away for a week-long camp to Littledale at Cootamundra, and more recently to one at Nambucca Heads. Year 9 girls went to Vision Valley. Such is the popularity of the camp program that the girls asked for one annually, not just for those in Years 7 and 9. The carefully structured programs provide activities which are designed to promote skills in leadership, management and team work.[32]

The White Paper, 'Excellence and Equity', issued by the then Minister for Education and Youth Affairs, Dr Terry Metherell, in November 1989 made a number of significant changes to the curriculum.[33] Based on the Scott and Carrick Reviews (Scott on educational organisation, and Carrick on curriculum) the White Paper was designed to be implemented in schools in 1992. Its main thrust was to strengthen the core curriculum while identifying 'Key Learning Areas' which would broaden education. The key areas were: English, mathematics, science and technology, creative and practical arts, personal development, health and fitness and, lastly, human society and its environment (including modern languages). The Paper reflected the government's concern with the state of the national economy:

> *Australia must have a well-educated community with the skills to underpin our national development. Schooling cannot be oblivious to the major economic and technological challenges that face Australia. Australia is a debtor nation facing the task of restructuring its economy and greatly increasing its productivity and competitiveness. That urgency has to be reflected, in part, in our schools.*[34]

In 1987 S.C.E.G.G.S. introduced the semester system. This enabled students to enrol for a single semester course, and at the same time the syllabus was expanded to include textiles and design, computer studies, Asian studies, drama, and life and careers. Girls had a greater range of subjects to choose from and were more motivated because there were more subjects available to interest them.

The earlier part of this chapter referred to the predicament of the youth in the 1980s. The Commission for the Future's report on social and psychological problems faced by young people in Australia states:

> *Those who think they can, are determined to make it. They are working harder. They may have no more respect for the system than did the young of the 1960s and 1970s but they no longer want to change it: they just want to ensure that they come out on top . . .*
>
> *The likely outcome of these changes will be a society increasingly divided into winners and losers, with all that follows from that: two communities that view each other with resentment, suspicion, even fear; a society that has to live with both increasing lawlessness and unrest, and the increasingly authoritarian measures needed to maintain law and order.*[35]

In schools pupils changed in some ways. More mothers going out to work changed their perception of women's role, at home and in the community. They were more likely to envisage a career as well as or instead of a husband and family than their counterparts in the 1970s. Increasing numbers of de facto relationships and a rise in the rate of divorce meant the breakdown of traditional family relationships and this, coupled with the fact of working mothers, meant that schoolchildren had to be more independent. The pressures on children increased: the influence of drugs and the pressure of the peer group were notable. The media exerted pressures also: television, videos, cinema and magazines were designed to attract a teenage clientele. For many children visual entertainment replaced reading as a leisure activity and source of information. Another characteristic of the 1980s was a perceived rise in the incidence of some illnesses: anorexia, PVS (post viral syndrome), glandular fever and leukaemia.[36]

School Heads see that many parents abdicated their responsibilities in the 1980s: Miss Bowman says the schools have taken over many of the traditional roles of parents. Schools now teach social skills, drug and alcohol prevention, sexuality and even parenting. Both Miss Dixon and Dr Shatford claim that a significant amount of time is taken up with family problems:

> *I know that being a Head in the late 80s and early 90s so much of your time is taken up with really serious social problems and one might expect that in a well-heeled suburb in the upper North Shore all was rosy behind the family front door but there are enormous family problems and very often the family will turn to the Head for advice and for someone to weep with and to point them in the right direction.*[37]

Similarly Dr Shatford said that parents have been shaken, have lost direction and now look to the school to help them. She has decided it is appropriate to offer advice on public occasions such as parent–teacher evenings on how to handle their teenage daughters. A favourite message is 'Parents unite!' to those who have Year 8 daughters claiming that their parents are the only ones not allowing something. She states that parents are very grateful for advice and strategies on dealing with their daughters' behaviour.[38]

Parents at S.C.E.G.G.S. were encouraged to contact the school when in need of help or counselling. In addition, parenting evenings were run by the Parents' and Friends' Association. Topics such as drugs and alcohol, AIDS and anorexia were dealt with and were welcomed by the parents. Miss Bowman commented that broken families have become more accepted in the community and de facto parents were coming openly to school functions by the end of the decade. A new question was asked not infrequently: 'Can I bring my four parents?' Another sign of change was that the parents' religion was often left a blank on the school enrolment form.[39]

An important aspect of S.C.E.G.G.S. and a number of other independent schools was its boarding house. Some closed down in the decade while others, like S.C.E.G.G.S., kept theirs open. The boarders continued to be a minority at S.C.E.G.G.S.: there were between 60 and 70. During the rural recession of the early 1980s there were fewer country girls and more Asian boarders at S.C.E.G.G.S. The trend in the latter part of the 1980s was for parents to transfer their enrolments from Year 7 to Year 10 or 11. This gave rise to problems for senior girls entering the restricted environment of a school after the freedom they had enjoyed at home: some had been used to frequenting pubs and discos, to going out freely in the evenings and to driving their own vehicle. S.C.E.G.G.S. was a great culture shock to them. A few girls ran away, but these were mostly those who had been sent to school to take them out of a home with family problems.[40]

The location of S.C.E.G.G.S. made boarding life increasingly difficult: the active prostitution in the street gave girls an unbalanced view of normal city life; security problems increased and there were incidents of break-ins. Greater

The latest building at S.C.E.G.G.S. with the city in the background. The three levels above the Library contain an auditorium, Discovery Room and classrooms. Built during 1991, it was dedicated 19 March 1992.

surveillance was necessary. A boarding administrator was appointed in 1989 which transferred much of the responsibility for the boarders from the Head. Finding staff for boarding houses was a problem for S.C.E.G.G.S. as in all girls' schools, although S.C.E.G.G.S. reduced the difficulty by offering higher pay and shorter hours than some of the other Sydney girls' schools. Whereas in boys' schools, the position of housemaster was a promotion, and a house and adequate living facilities were traditionally offered, girls' schools did not offer attractive accommodation or job opportunities for boarding house staff. Consequently the divorced, the widowed and older single women were the people who, because of personal need, applied for positions in the boarding house. Miss Bowman maintained that boarders were a very good influence in school life: they shone at school camps where team work and self-reliance were important, and the country and overseas boarders introduced a different perspective from that of the city-dwelling day-girls.[41]

A general perception from people running schools is that the more fees parents pay, the more influence they will expect to possess. Higher fees will involve greater parent participation. S.C.E.G.G.S. has been run by a Board composed partly of parents since 1977, but more Heads and councils are aware that the consequence of parental financial investment in the school through payment of fees and their contribution to fundraising programs, is a recognition that parents are indeed in a client relationship with the school and their wishes must therefore be taken into account. This has always been a delicate issue in church schools, especially those with greater social status. The problem is one of who initiates policy. As long as parents' fees are the lifeblood of the school, then the parents must be kept satisfied. In the case of some church schools, this has meant a dilution of the Evangelical Christianity of its founders in favour of a more socially acceptable and formal Christian tradition. The kind of pressure parents could exert was also seen in the area of curriculum policy, where computers were introduced into schools in the 1980s as they were seen by many parents as indispensable for career opportunities.

The decade of the 1980s was a low point for teachers: possibly their lowest since the founding of the colony. Few students in 1990 opt for a teaching career: only one student at S.C.E.G.G.S. considered teaching as a career option in 1989.[42] The fact that the requirement for entering teacher training at university is the lowest of all faculty quotas has reinforced the popular view that teaching is for those who cannot gain entry into any other tertiary training. Dr Shatford describes the phenomenon:

> *There has been a marked decline in teachers' professional confidence and status in the community signalled to the community by a comparatively low rate of salaries held down by a combination of wage indexation, a wage freeze and currently, an income and prices accord. The political debate on schooling has moreover been peppered with such terms as output, performance, competence, merit in teaching, educational efficiency and centres of excellence, all indicative of the demands of an ever-increasing kind being made upon our teaching force . . . Teaching as a career is now seen in the community as unstable as an occupation and carrying an uncertainty of employment and poor prospects of career advancement.*[43]

While Dr Shatford's assessment is undoubtedly one side of the coin, Heads see their own staff in more positive terms. Miss Bowman states:

> *Teaching is much more specialised than it was ten years ago. The dedication and even competitiveness of the S.C.E.G.G.S. staff are catching. I have never worked with a more competent, dedicated and sensitive staff. An 'average' teacher would stand out as being quite inadequate at S.C.E.G.G.S. There is a very strong drive in each one of them to succeed. There is not an iota of complacency among the staff.*[44]

Likewise Dr Paterson is optimistic about teachers: he believes that the 'yuppie' materialist syndrome of the 1980s has proved 'impoverished in spirit, in meaning, in fulfilment'. He thinks that many will trade high salaries, stress, and constancy of work for the attraction of long holidays, lower income and the rewards that flow from teaching and the relationships established in the classroom.[45] One characteristic of the 1980s was certainly the drain of good people away from teaching to industry, particularly those in the fields of mathematics, science, economics and commerce. Some of the boys' schools, Sydney Grammar for example, paid salaries comparable with industry to retain these valuable staff members. There has been great pressure upon Heads and school councils to maintain excellence in the face of decreasing choice of staff available.

Despite problems arising from low salary, low morale and pressures from the teacher unions, the quality of teachers in independent schools in the 1980s was higher than ever before. Diana Bowman stated: 'It is almost inconceivable at S.C.E.G.G.S. that any teacher would teach in two departments (I taught five subjects in my Wollongong days). So specialised are the objectives of the syllabus that staff can afford only to be committed to one discipline.'[46]

At S.C.E.G.G.S. teacher training was an absolute prerequisite. In-service training, including staff weekends away for curriculum development, were part of the S.C.E.G.G.S. program. Whereas 'in-service training' was seen to be an optional extra for teachers in the 1970s, it became part of the requirement for teachers in the 1980s. The state government issued a ruling in 1989 that 1 per cent of the school's budget was to be spent on in-service training. For S.C.E.G.G.S. in 1989 that represented approximately $30 000.[47]

Despite enormous changes in society, in technology, in career opportunities and in the curriculum, schools remained places where human relationships and values were paramount, and where teaching was most effectively carried out face to face. In financial terms the decade of the 1980s was one of prosperity and expansion. The independent schools experienced a boom as confidence in the state system eroded and as education was perceived to be vital in preparation for adult life. Tougher entry requirements into desirable university faculties, strong awareness that worthwhile careers were those which earned the most money, and that this in turn depended on top HSC performance, led to increased pressure on schools to 'deliver the goods'. Private schools were seen to be able to do this best, and to be worth the financial investment required.

Falling teacher morale and disintegration of the family, together with tough demands by teacher unions, placed much greater stress upon school communities. For school principals it meant some loss of authority over staff, greater difficulty recruiting staff and the pressure of providing resources once given by families. Heads were increasingly made aware that the school was a community not an institution, that education meant more than teaching a syllabus. Accelerating rates of technological change had wide-ranging effects: from the indispensable photocopier, computer and facsimile machine to unprecedented expansion of career options. Two major determinants of education in the 1990s will be the quality of teachers and the availability of finance to sustain the independent school tradition.

— 16 —
A final word

IN 1992 S.C.E.G.G.S. was 97 years old. It was founded as a Church of England school which would provide good secondary education for girls and was the first of its kind in Sydney. For the length of its existence, for almost a century, the original aim has been pursued, so that today the school's educational reputation is one of excellence. The connection with the Anglican church has changed. While no longer an Anglican school run by the Synod of the Sydney Diocese, the school continues to have a strong commitment to Christian education and firm links with the Anglican church.

What constitutes a good education for girls has changed significantly over the last 95 years, and it is this single factor which, more than any other, accounts for changes at S.C.E.G.G.S. When Edith Badham began her time as Principal, her purpose in educating her girls was to produce young ladies of good character. 'All the learning of the Egyptians is as nothing compared with good character,' she had said. A classical education was offered, as well as a wide range of 'accomplishment' subjects, and religious instruction was an important part of the curriculum. Learning and clear thinking were very important, but not as important as character training. Only the outstanding students were encouraged to sit for public examinations and to take up tertiary studies. The aspiration of most of Edith Badham's pupils was the traditional combination of marriage and raising a family. A career was very rare indeed. Miss Badham was training her girls to be good wives and mothers.

World War I ended the old order. Many girls never married because so many young men of their generation did not return from the battlefields. Many entered the workforce. Dorothy Wilkinson arrived at S.C.E.G.G.S. shortly after the war ended and, while maintaining Miss Badham's classical curriculum and the religious instruction, she encouraged S.C.E.G.G.S. girls to go to the University. In her time S.C.E.G.G.S. girls graduated as doctors, scientists, architects and lawyers, as well as qualifying as teachers. Training for leisure in sporting, cultural and hobby activities was emphasised.

Through Miss Wilkinson's time until after World War II, when Barbara

Chisholm was Head, education at S.C.E.G.G.S. was on a par with other independent girls' schools but lagged behind the selective high schools in terms of the subjects offered. Mathematics I and II, physics and chemistry were not offered, so that girls entering Science and Medicine at the University were at a disadvantage.

It was under Diana Bowman that S.C.E.G.G.S. girls were first offered an education which was 'non-sexist'. The sciences and mathematics were traditionally considered male subjects and girls had elected not to study them and had been discouraged from doing so. Miss Bowman has encouraged S.C.E.G.G.S. girls to pursue options which until recently have been traditionally male. There is now a strong feminist tradition at S.C.E.G.G.S. and girls are encouraged, indeed expected, to pursue tertiary studies and a career.

Since 1945, the pace of secularisation has quickened and the social order of the 1990s is a sharp contrast to that of 1895. In the wider community absolute values, the concept of revealed truth and the whole Christian tradition are no longer generally accepted. Relative standards and diversity of religion are the characteristics of the new secularism; its twin gods are materialism and individual fulfilment. Religious instruction is still given at S.C.E.G.G.S., although it does not continue beyond Year 10. S.C.E.G.G.S., like all schools, has perforce taken on not only religious education but also personal education and counselling, which were formerly the prerogative of parents. Education at S.C.E.G.G.S. in the 1990s is concerned with developing the whole person—spiritual, academic, social and physical—in order to enable each girl to realise her potential and to equip her for life in the community, whether in a professional career or in any other vocational field.

A good education in the 1990s is more complex than it was in 1895. Opportunities, pressures and the complexity of the social order make it indefensible to train girls simply to be women of good character and clear judgment. The school must now equip girls to compete with men in the workforce and, in addition, act as homemakers and parents.

A number of factors have shaped S.C.E.G.G.S. into the unique school that it is today. The most important of these influences are its Anglican tradition and roots, its four Headmistresses, its location, its branch schools and the school community—the Council, staff and girls who have been its life. The Anglican nature of S.C.E.G.G.S. has made it an institution of the Sydney Diocese with its religious instruction, the form of worship, church dignitaries and the formal relationship to the Synod all helping to shape the school's religious tradition and underpinning its aims. The Anglican church was both a help and a hindrance, a foundation and an obstruction to S.C.E.G.G.S. The name of the church gave S.C.E.G.G.S. immediate status and respect, as did the association with archbishops, bishops, archdeacons and notable lay folk. From the beginning S.C.E.G.G.S. was more than a finishing school or a dame school—it was designed to be an important Anglican girls' school. The drawbacks to the Anglican connection were the arm's length appointments to Council and the consequent lack of expertise which led to mismanagement in the areas of branch school policy and financial planning. Since 1976 the Anglican influence has been limited to some representation on the Board. Nevertheless under the present Head the Anglican tradition is strongly upheld.

S.C.E.G.G.S. is unusual in that there have been only four Headmistresses at the school in 95 years. The first three served for at least a quarter of a century each. Each Head has been an exceptional person. Each has served the school with single-minded devotion and wisdom. Each has been Head there long enough to conserve the tradition and to exercise a distinctive influence. One common emphasis of each Head has been the worth of every individual at the school. The school has been remembered with affection by every generation of staff and Old Girls as a place where each person is valued. In consequence, quite a number of staff members have given extraordinarily long terms of service and many Old Girls have returned to teach or have sent their own daughters to S.C.E.G.G.S.

The location of S.C.E.G.G.S. has been very important. The various suggestions to move the school from Darlinghurst have been abortive because it was recognised that the school would thereby lose its distinctive character. The disadvantages of the site are its size, the attendant problems of vice in the Darlinghurst locality and the expense of acquiring surrounding property. The advantages are that the school is a catchment area for most of Sydney, so that among its pupils there is a mixture of social class, suburban attitudes, race and family background. The girls' education is richer because the school is socially multifaceted.

The branch schools were a very significant influence on S.C.E.G.G.S. from 1906 to 1974. They were a financial drain on the Darlinghurst school and a distraction for the Council, with the result that the Darlinghurst school was neglected. Under different management, with separate governing bodies, the branch schools would not have detracted from the Darlinghurst school. Each school was a response to local needs and indeed met them, thereby serving the local community. Redlands was a very successful school while Loquat Valley and Gleniffer Brae were potentially so. From the point of view of Darlinghurst, however, the branch schools were burdensome and harmful.

The financial crisis of the mid-1970s was of cataclysmic importance for S.C.E.G.G.S. It was certainly not just a minor interruption to the school's smooth running. The events of those years were unique to the Sydney school and it is amazing that S.C.E.G.G.S. survived the experience. The final outcome was beneficial to S.C.E.G.G.S. The branch schools were sold or closed and the Council reconstituted, thereby enabling the efficient operation of one school instead of five.

Changes over the years at S.C.E.G.G.S. were frequently responses to external pressures and challenges. Two depressions and two world wars during the school's first 50 years meant physical restrictions and financial stringencies. Plans and innovations were curtailed and, for Miss Wilkinson in particular, there were many frustrations and disappointments. The postwar years for S.C.E.G.G.S. have been ones of greater affluence and enterprise, especially since the establishment of SCEGGS Darlinghurst Ltd.

Other external changes have been in the area of educational philosophy. Three major reports have challenged S.C.E.G.G.S. Reforms under Peter Board were a challenge to S.C.E.G.G.S. to reassess the curriculum and to prepare more students for tertiary study. The Wyndham Report increased the cost of school operation by widening the curriculum and adding on another year at school. The Karmel Report increased the financial burden of private school education by decreasing State Aid. In each case S.C.E.G.G.S. was not markedly affected. Changes introduced by government authority were frequently things that S.C.E.G.G.S. already had in operation or, with some relatively minor adjustments, could implement. On each occasion, there was some criticism and lack of cooperation from the current Head.

Technological change has meant the proliferation of form-filling and paperwork, but also variety and increased professionalism in teaching. Social change

S.C.E.G.G.S. girls near the lawn between Barham and the 'yellow building', 1993.

has included the breakdown of the family, the increase of secularism, decline of moral standards, and a changing role for women. Education at S.C.E.G.G.S. has perforce responded by providing staff and curricula to address the needs which have been created.

In the face of such change, what has remained constant at S.C.E.G.G.S.? In some ways, S.C.E.G.G.S. in 1992 is not much different from S.C.E.G.G.S. in 1900. The locality is the same, the range of schooling offered is almost identical, the Anglican chaplain continues to be the Rector of St John's Darlinghurst, the girls come from all over Sydney and many of the same subjects are taught. Differences include a different Headmistress, albeit still a Greek scholar, a Board of Directors not an Anglican Council, a sevenfold increase in pupil numbers, less playground space, a wider variety of sports, computers and audiovisual equipment in the classrooms and girls whose aims may no longer be marriage and motherhood but tertiary education and a professional career.

One important characteristic of S.C.E.G.G.S. has not changed. The teaching process still depends on the interaction of teacher and pupil. It is still based on the communication of knowledge and skills and the most important ingredient in the learning process is the ability of the teacher to teach. Nothing has replaced the teacher–pupil relationship, and the basic chemistry of the teaching and learning process remains unchanged.

Postscript

During 1993 some notable events have taken place in the S.C.E.G.G.S. community, some of which will be very influential in the years to come. First, two people must be mentioned. Susan Davies (Dr Peterson), an Old Girl from Miss

Wilkinson's time and an accomplished violinist, was awarded her doctorate from the University of Western Australia earlier this year. At the age of 80 she is the oldest person to become a Doctor of Philosophy at the University. Janet Lean, Deputy Head of S.C.E.G.G.S. since 1979, will retire at the end of 1993. Miss Lean has been an able administrator, a good friend to other members of staff, and a source of strength in the S.C.E.G.G.S. community. She helped set up the Audiovisual Department and managed it until her appointment as Head of the Social Sciences Department in 1974; she introduced the school's outdoor education programme and established tutor groups for senior students and leadership training for prefects. She has made an outstanding contribution to the school.

After a gap of more than 70 years, rowing has been reintroduced as a sport at S.C.E.G.G.S. Two parents, Susan Hayes and Ric Macready, reintroduced rowing with a camp at Balmain Rowing Club before school started in 1993. The girls train on Saturday and Sunday mornings, using the club's equipment and coaching facilities. They have already rowed in a number of regattas, gaining second and third places on some occasions. S.C.E.G.G.S. will shortly take delivery of its first boat, a coxed sweep oar four to be named the 'Edith Badham'.

On 28 July 1993, contracts were exchanged for the sale to S.C.E.G.G.S. of St Peter's Anglican church and the other properties on the site bounded by St Peter's Lane, Forbes Street, St Peter's Street and Bourke Street. This is the biggest single purchase of land that the school has made since it purchased Barham. The site will be a great asset to S.C.E.G.G.S. as it will provide much-needed space for the development of school resources: the extension of the school's site opens up a wealth of possibilities. The historic church building is a distinctive landmark and is constructed of picked sandstone with a slate roof of three gables. It is classified as an historic Gothic Revival building and has a simple interior and beautiful stained-glass windows.

The architects Devine Erby Maslin (DEM), have drawn up a conservation plan for the St Peter's site and also a masterplan for the use of the whole school site. The plan includes relocation of the boarding facilities onto the St Peter's site, the building of a Gymnastics Hall, a Sports Hall and a new swimming pool. S.C.E.G.G.S. is indeed on the brink of a new and challenging era. May this school set on a hill ever live out its motto 'Luceat Lux Vestra'.

Appendices

Appendix 1 Statement to Synod by the President, the Most Rev. M. L. Loane, Archbishop of Sydney, 14 October 1974

The Council of the Sydney Church of England Girls' Grammar School was constituted by Ordinance of Synod. This Ordinance gave the Council wide powers of management over the finances and property of the school; this power was later supplemented by various mortgaging Ordinances. The Council itself became a Body Corporate by Act of Parliament in 1938. At that time it was responsible for the management and control of the school at Darlinghurst (founded in 1895), the school at Moss Vale (founded at Bowral in 1906), and the school at North Sydney. The latter was closed down in 1942, but Redlands at Cremorne was acquired in its place in 1945. Since then the Council also became responsible for the operation of the school at Wollongong (founded in 1955), and the school at Loquat Valley (founded in 1967). The Council consists of 19 members, of whom four clergy, six women, and eight laymen are elected by Synod, and one woman is elected as an Old Girls' representative. The Council is an independent and autonomous body. It is required to submit an annual report and an audited copy of its financial statements to Synod each year. Apart from this, in normal circumstances, it functions without reference to Synod or Standing Committee.

In August, 1971, Standing Committee received a letter from the Chairman of the Council which stated its desire 'to develop and extend both the Darlinghurst and Cremorne schools.'

On August 3, 1972, a conference took place between the Finance Committee of Standing Committee and representatives of the Council.

This meeting was arranged as it had come to the notice of the Finance Committee of Standing Committee that the Council had borrowed large sums of money without first seeking the approval of Standing Committee. The representatives of the Council gave assurances to the Finance Committee that, in substance, there was no need for concern.

This position was unaltered at the beginning of this year as far as Standing Committee was concerned. However on March 28th, 1974, the Chairman of the Council informed me that the auditors had prepared the balance sheet for the year ended December 31, 1972, but were unwilling to sign it unless the Council were to pass certain resolutions. The Chairman thought that the Council would have to decline to pass such resolutions. As a result, he and the Executive Officers of the school had at once begun to carry out an investigation. It soon appeared that a sum in excess of $100 000 could not be accounted for. This led to the immediate resignation of the Honorary Treasurer who was also the Solicitor for the Council, and the matter was reported to the Law Society.

On June 19th, I was advised of the probable intention of the Council to close the School at Moss Vale as from the end of this year. This was subsequently confirmed at a special meeting of the Council.

As Archbishop of Sydney, I hold a nominal position as President of the Council. This has always been a titular office. I do not attend meetings of the Council, nor do I receive minutes of the Council meetings. However, in view of these developments, on June 19th, I took the unusual step of writing to the Chairman of the Council. I said that the misuse of funds and the closure of the School at Moss Vale, added to the problems inherent in the current economic climate, forced me to the conclusion that there was an urgent need for an independent inquiry into the Council's financial situation. The Executive Committee of the Council concurred with this statement. I then appointed a Panel of Inquiry, consisting of Mr A. E. Davis, the Hon. Secretary of The King's School and formerly the Senior Partner in Henry Davis, York & Co; Mr J. M. Dixon, the Chairman of Shore, and formerly a Director and Deputy General Manager of The Colonial Sugar Refinery Co.; Mr W. J. Pickard, the Bursar of The King's School; and Mr R. H. Y. Lambert.

This Panel undertook as far as possible a thorough examination of the commitments of the Council, and submitted a written report to me on August 14th. This report stated that the position was so complex, both legally and financially, that in its opinion a Committee of Management should be appointed to control all financial operations of the Council, and that other steps should be taken to ensure as far as possible the continuance of the schools.

A special meeting of the Standing Committee was held two days later, on August 16th, to receive this report and act on its recommendations. As a result, a Committee of Management was appointed, consisting of Archdeacon E. D. Cameron (Chairman), Messrs. J. M. Dixon, S. Atkin, N. Malone and G. R. Christmas, and an Ordinance was passed to give this Committee special powers.

The Committee of Management immediately resolved to seek the help of Messrs. Allen, Allen and Hemsley on all legal issues and of Price Waterhouse & Co., in unravelling the financial problems. Price Waterhouse were not able to submit a complete statement until Thursday, October 3rd. This showed that the total liabilities of the Council now amount to $7.5m.

A special meeting of the Standing Committee was held on Friday, October 11th, to receive the report and confirm the decisions of the Committee of Management. The position as disclosed is one of enormous complexity, and it will take many months before the problems are resolved. It is believed that the Schools have a continuing future though not necessarily in their present form. Certain reorganization will be essential. Standing Committee was informed that the accumulated trade debts amount to $312 000. It was resolved to authorise an immediate advance from the Finance and Loans Board to discharge these debts and to instruct the Finance Committee to recommend a programme of repayment from sources which will not affect parochial assessments or deprive parishes of prospective assistance. The Committee of Management will furnish Standing Committee with a monthly report and will take all appropriate measures to ensure the continuance of Christian education through these Schools.

There are doubtless many questions that will arise for which no clear answer can be furnished at the moment. The Committee of Management, with their legal and financial advisers, have spent many hours and have worked almost daily in order to arrive at these first essential decisions. I must express my gratitude to them, as well as the hope that the critical situation which developed so suddenly will be successfully overcome. It will be the earnest desire of all members of this Synod that these Schools, with their girls and staff, will have God's blessing in a strong and stable future.

Appendix 2 Survey of Old Girls

The following questionnaire was sent out to S.C.E.G.G.S. Old Girls during the years 1985 to 1989. No particular age group was targetted in the survey. Four hundred and fifty-eight forms were returned completed.

Survey questions

1. Was your mother an Old Girl of S.C.E.G.G.S.?
2. List any other relatives who attend/attended S.C.E.G.G.S.
3. In which suburb/town/city did you live while attending S.C.E.G.G.S.?
4. How did you travel to school each day?
5. Were you a day girl or boarder?
6. What was your school house?
7. i) What was your father's occupation while you were at S.C.E.G.G.S.?
   ii) Was your mother employed then? If so, give details.
8. Do you hold any degrees, diplomas or personal certificates [gained] after you left S.C.E.G.G.S.?
9. What were your main occupations in the first five years since leaving S.C.E.G.G.S.?
10. What have been your subsequent occupations?
11. Please list any hobbies or details of personal interest.

This survey was designed to assist the S.C.E.G.G.S. Archives in addition to the present history. Some questions were of importance only to the Archivist and the results of these are not recorded below.

Table A Results of Question l
Those having as mother an Old Girl of S.C.E.G.G.S. (expressed as a percentage of respondents by years of attendance category)

Years	%
1900–20	10
1921–47	7
1948–77	23
1978–90	20

Table B Results of Question 2
Old Girls with children attending S.C.E.G.G.S. (expressed as a percentage of respondents by years of attendance category)

Years	%
1900–20	6
1921–47	16
1948–77	8
1978–90	N/A

Table C Results of Question 3
School entrants by geographical background (expressed as a percentage of respondents by years of attendance category). Note that insufficient responses were received for 1978–90 to provide a meaningful breakdown.

Region	1900–20 %	1921–47 %	1948–77 %
Sydney			
City	8	6	2
City East	23	35	13
City North:			
North Sydney	—	5	1
Mosman area	8	9	5
Northern beaches	—	—	2
North Shore line	4	9	8
Other		2	2
City North-West	13	7	13
City South-West	—	1	18
City South	4	9	14
Country			
Newcastle area	—	2	—
Gosford area	—	—	—
Bathurst area	15	2	4
Southern highlands	5	—	—
Goulburn area	—	2	5
Blue Mountains	—	1	—
Wollongong area	—	1	2
Distant country	15	8	7
Interstate	5	—	2
Overseas	—	1	2

Table D Results of Question 4
Mode of travel (expressed as a percentage of respondents by years of attendance category). Some columns total more than 100% owing to multiple responses i.e. some used more than one form of transport.

Mode	1900–20	1921–47	1948–78	1978–90
Tram	45	35	13	—
Ferry/bus	16	26	60	55
Train	19	13	26	12
Walked	13	3	2	—
Car	3	2	4	50
Aeroplane	—	—	—	—
Coastal steamer	3	—	—	—

Table E Results of Question 7(i): actual responses
Father's occupation (actual responses by years of attendance category). Note that insufficient responses were received for 1978–90 to provide a meaningful breakdown. The list of occupations is not complete, but indicates the range of occupations and the changes in fathers' occupations between 1900 and 1977.

Occupation	1900–20	1921–47	1948–77
Advertising	—	1	—
Architect	—	—	1
Army	—	1	—
Auctioneer	1	—	—
Accountant	—	9	10
Bank manager	2	7	9
Bank teller	1	1	3
Barrister	1	1	3
Bishop	—	—	1
Building contractor	—	1	3

Table E (Cont.)

Occupation	1900–20	1921–47	1948–77
Butcher	—	—	2
Caravan park proprietor	—	—	1
Church work	—	—	3
Civil engineer	1	2	—
Clergyman	1	11	3
Clerk	—	—	4
Commercial traveller	—	1	1
Company director	—	11	18
Company manager	—	5	7
Company representative	2	1	—
Company secretary	1	1	1
Computer engineer	—	—	1
Dentist	—	1	1
Dispensing chemist	1	1	3
Doctor	1	13	19
Engineer	—	—	14
Executive	—	—	3
Farmer	2	—	5
Geologist	—	—	1
Grazier	7	24	14
Gentleman of leisure	1	1	—
Hairdresser	—	—	1
Headmaster	—	2	—
Horse trainer	1	—	—
Hotelier	—	—	2
Importer	1	2	1
Journalist	1	—	1
Judge	—	1	—
Manufacturer	—	—	2
Master mariner	—	—	1
Mechanic	—	—	1
Merchant	2	1	—
Newsagent	—	—	1
Plasterer	—	—	1
Poultry farmer/orchardist	—	1	2
Professor	1	—	4
Property developer	—	—	1
Public relations	—	—	2
Public servant	—	1	3
Racing	—	1	—
Radio announcer/commentator	1	1	1
Real estate	—	1	2
Retailer	—	—	1
Retired	—	3	—
Sales manager	—	2	2
Sawmiller	—	—	1
School master	—	2	5
Shopkeeper	—	1	3
Small business	—	1	7
Solicitor	5	1	3
Stock & station agent	1	1	1
Stockbroker	—	1	—
Surveyor	2	—	—
Taxi driver	—	1	—
Timber & shipping agent	1	—	—
University lecturer	—	—	2
Wool broker	1	—	1
Other	—	65	27
Total responses:	39	182	209

Table F Results of Question 7(i): categorised

Father's occupation (responses from Table E by category of type of occupation, expressed as a percentage). Note that insufficient responses were received for 1978–90 to provide a meaningful breakdown.

Category	1900–20	1921–47	1948–77
Blue collar	0	0	5
Business	20	6	13
Church	3	6	3
Education	3	2	5
Executive	3	9	14
Farmer	23	13	9
Finance	7	9	10
Government employment	0	1	1
Professional	30	10	21
Other	11	44	19

Table G Results of Question 7(ii)

Mother at work (actual responses by years of attendance category)

1900–20	1921–47	1948–77
2[a]	6[b]	10[c]
9.5%	12%	33%

Notes: [a] Out of 21
[b] Out of 51
[c] Out of 31

Table H Results of Question 8

S.C.E.G.G.S. girls completing tertiary education (expressed as an actual number and as a percentage of responses)

1900–20	1921–47	1948–77	1978–90
9[a]	103[b]	191[c]	11[d]
50%	57%	90%	100%

Notes: [a] Out of 22
[b] Out of 180
[c] Out of 213
[d] Out of 11

Appendix 3 School songs

Girls of the Grammar School

Girls of the Grammar School, girls old and new,
Gathered or parted, all the world through,
Still to the motto that binds us keep true—
Luceat Lux Vestra.

Your lamp may light you to hard mental toil,
Your distaff reel with science's great coil;
Often maybe you'll burn youth's midnight oil—
Luceat Lux Vestra.

Your lamp may kindle a glow warm and clear,
Light of the hearth and home, keep that light pure,
Kindle at that bright source lights far and near—
Luceat Lux Vestra.

You, whose lamp shines to us now from afar,
Bright still and clear your light, e'en as a star,
Still you are joined to us—over the bar—
Luceat Lux Vestra.

Life-giving, far and near, our light is one,
Pledge of our union through years yet to come;
Light from our God above, our risen Sun,
Luceat Lux Vestra.

The lyrics were written by Mrs Julia Jackson (nee Badham, stepsister of Edith Badham) in 1913. There are two tunes: the first was written by Nelson Illingworth (Director of the New South Wales Conservatorium 1916–20) in 1913; the second was written by Bishop Charles Venn Pilcher in 1937 and is the one used in more recent years.

A breeze from the Harbour blowing

A breeze from the Harbour blowing,
The Southern Cross on high,
A queenly city glowing
In the gold of a sunlight sky;
Praise on them all bestowing
Raise we our joyful cry.

All our life before us,
Eager its joy to prove.
Hope shining o'er us,
Bright as the skies above;
Swell, swell the chorus
In praise of the school we love.

Here's to the best we aspire,
Be it work with hand or brain;
We have learned, if we win, to aim higher,
If we lose, to press forward again;
And in all that we strive to desire,
The glory instead of the gain.

Not for all to be clever—
All may be true and kind,
Faithful in high endeavour,
Each to the cause combined,
Holding aloft for ever
The lamp of a stainless mind.

Pain may be ours, or pleasure,
Yet through each future year,
Whether in toil or leisure,
Whether with smile or tear,
Still shall the memory treasure
Thoughts of our school days here.

The lyrics were written in 1912 by Major Thomas Austin Anderson (later Brigadier-General Anderson and husband of Old Girl Ethel Mason) and sung to the tune of the 'Eton Boating Song'.

Appendix 4 Heads, Office Bearers and Branches

Headmistresses of S.C.E.G.G.S.

Miss Edith Annesley Badham	1895–1920
Miss Dorothy Irene Wilkinson BA, MA, DipEd	1920–47
Miss Barbara Mary Chisholm BA, OBE	1947–77
Miss Diana Mildred Bowman BA, DipEd	1978–

First Assistants (also known as Senior Mistresses and Deputy Headmistresses)

Miss Janet Uther	1895–1901
Miss Isabella Langley	1902–04
Miss Constance Smith	1905–06
Miss Nona Dumolo	1907–10
Miss Clarinda Murray	1911–13
Miss Emma Noad	1913–21
Miss Elsie Capper	1921–39
Miss Dorothy Oakey	1940–47
Miss Una Fitzhardinge	1948–49
Miss Grace Spicer	1950–71
Mrs Enid Miller	1972–78
Miss Janet Lean	1979–

Chairmen of Council

The Archbishop of Sydney was the President of the Council, according to the Ordinance to regulate the Constitution of the Council, drawn up in 1895. In his absence the meeting was chaired by a male member of the Council.

Archbishop William Saumarez Smith	1895–1909
Archbishop John Charles Wright	1909–33
Archbishop Howard West Kilvinton Mowll	1934–58

After Archbishop Mowll, the subsequent Archbishops did not attend Council meetings and the Chairmen included the Rev. Gordon Begbie and the Rev. Alwyn Prescott. Council minutes are missing from 1953 to 1976 and the facts relating to office bearers in these years are therefore not easy to ascertain.

From 1974 to 1976 Archdeacon (later Bishop) Ewan Donald Cameron was Chairman of the Management Committee after the dissolution of the S.C.E.G.G.S. school Council in September 1974.

From 1977 the school was governed by a company limited by guarantee, SCEGGS Darlinghurst Ltd, and the following were Chairmen of the Board of Directors:

Mr David Clark	1977–79
Mr Samuel Cullen	1979–92
Mrs Marcia Cameron	1992–

Chaplains

Rev. Canon Arthur Wellesley Pain	1895–97
Rev. Canon Ernest Claude Beck	1897–1928
Rev. Clarence Arthur Leopold Lucas	1928–55
Rev. Canon Archibald Wentworth Morton	1955–66
Rev. Bernard William James Gook	1967–74
Rev. Thomas Wallace	1975–76

Rev. Jack Richards	1977–83
Various visiting chaplains	1984–85
Rev. Jonathan Charles Holland	1985–88
Rev. Dr William Lawton	1989–

Old Girls' Union Presidents

Miss Edith Badham (Headmistress 1895–1920)	1909–20
Mrs F. G. Sargood (Lilian Christian 1895–19?)	1920–24
Mrs D. Maughan (Jean 'Muffie' Barton 1895–1900)	1924–25
Miss Beulah Bolton (1903–07)	1925–28
Mrs H. V. Vernon (Mary Stephens 1895–97)	1928–33
Mrs M. F. Bruxner (Winifred 'Midge' Caird 1895–1900)	1933–40
Mrs K. A. Bennett (Kathleen King 1904–11)	1940–61
Mrs T. Bremner (Dorothy Shipley 1929–37)	1961–66
Miss Joan Stevenson (1934–40)	1966–70
Mrs P. B. Reed (Joan Kennedy 1937–42)	1970–72
Mrs I. A. Coull (Pamela Hall 1950–53)	1972–76
Mrs S. G. Macintosh (Valda Joy 1933–39)	1976–78
Mrs P. S. Roberts (Lyn Iceton 1945–48)	1978–83
Mrs I. A. Coull (Pamela Hall 1950–53)	1983–88
Mrs P. H. Burger (Margaret Hall 1957–60)	1988–

Branch schools and their Headmistresses

Moss Vale (originally Bowral) branch
Founded 1906. Settled permanently at Bong Bong in 1930.

Headmistresses:

Miss Isabella Langley	1906–1906
Miss Constance Smith	1907–26
Miss Muriel Hammond	1926–39
Miss M. J. Steel	1939–44
Miss Violet Thanie Baddams	1945–52
Miss Mary Graham	1953–59
Miss Jean Turnbull	1960–65
Miss Valerie Horniman	1965–72
Rev. Colin Clark	1972–74

Hunters Hill branch
Founded in 1912 and closed in 1915.

Headmistress: Miss Galloway 1912–15

Redlands (formerly North Sydney) branch
Founded in 1911 at North Sydney. Closed in 1941. 'Redlands' was purchased in 1945. In 1976 the school was sold to a company formed by the parents.

Headmistresses:

Miss Nona Dumolo	1911–25
Miss Ella Slack	1924–33
Miss E. Arundel	1934–41
Mrs I. A. Humphrey	1944–73
Mrs Foote	1974–76

Wollongong branch: 'Gleniffer Brae'
Founded in 1955 and closed in 1976.

Headmistresses:

Miss Kathleen McCredie	1955–69
Mrs Woodhouse	1970–74
Acting Headmistress: Mrs Marrott	1975–76
Headmistress-elect: Dr Ruth Shatford	

Loquat Valley branch
A primary school taken over from the school founded by Gordon Taylor. Opened as S.C.E.G.G.S. in 1967. Sold in 1976.

Headmistress: Mrs A. Prescott 1967–76

Notes

Chapter 1

1 A. Barcan, *A History of Australian Education*, Oxford University Press, Melbourne, 1980, p. 9
2 *Proceedings of the Synod of the Diocese of Sydney*, Presidential Address, August 1892, p. 31
3 Barcan, p. 2
4 ibid. p. 53
5 C. Turney (ed.), *Pioneers of Australian Education*, vol. 1, University of Sydney Press, Sydney 1969, p. 136
6 G. Sherington, *Shore: A History of Sydney Church of England Grammar School*, Allen & Unwin, Sydney, 1983, p. 5
7 S. M. Johnstone, *The History of the King's School Parramatta*, The Council of The Kings' School, Sydney, 1932, pp. 23–6
8 ibid. p. 19
9 Turney, p. 1
10 *Australian Record*, 11 February 1893, p. 9
11 Sherington, p. 6
12 Turney, p. 100
13 C. Turney, *Grammar: A History of Sydney Grammar School 1819–1988*, Allen & Unwin, Sydney, 1989, p. 21
14 A. Barcan, *A Short History of Education in NSW*, Martindale Press, Sydney, 1965, p. 114
15 N. Kyle, *Her Natural Destiny*, NSW University Press, Sydney, 1986, pp. 19, 69, 100
16 Turney, *Pioneers*, pp. 128–9
17 *Votes and Proceedings of the Sixth Synod*, 1884, p. 23 and 1885, p. 25
18 *Votes and Proceedings*, 1884, p. 23
19 ibid. p. 24

Chapter 2

1 *Sydney Morning Herald*, 29 July 1889, p. 91
2 ibid.
3 *Australian Record*, Editorial, 11 February 1893, p. 9
4 *Australian Record*, 23 June 1893, p. 11
5 *Votes and Proceedings of the Seventh Synod of the Diocese of Sydney*, 1886, p. 23
6 *Australian Record*, 27 January 1894, p. 7
7 *Australian Record*, 11 February 1893, p. 9
8 *Votes and Proceedings of the Synod of the Diocese of Sydney*, 1891, Appendix no. XXI, p. 123
9 ibid. p. 122
10 S. Judd and K. Cable, *Sydney Anglicans*, Anglican Information Office Press, Sydney, 1987, p. 131
11 *Votes and Proceedings*, 1891, Appendix B, p. 94
12 C. Badham, *Letters and Speeches*, The University of Sydney, 1890, p. 33
13 F. Crowley (ed.), *A New History of Australia*, Heinemann, Melbourne, 1984, p. 218
14 *Proceedings of Synod*, op. cit.
15 ibid. July 1893, Appendix XXIII, p. lxii
16 Lilith Norman, *The Brown and Yellow*, Oxford University Press, Melbourne, 1983, p. 12
17 J. Milburn, Girls' Secondary Education in NSW 1880–1930, MEd. thesis, University of Sydney, 1965, p. 54
18 ibid. p. 54
19 ibid. pp. 64–5
20 ibid. p. 68
21 National origins of Headmistresses and Principals: In Roman Catholic schools: Irish, 69 per cent; Continental, 19 per cent; English, 12 per cent; In Protestant Schools: English, 67 per cent; Continental, 21 per cent; Australian, 12 per cent. Milburn, pp. 38–9
22 C. Fairfax Simpson et al., *Ascham Remembered 1886–1986*, Sydney, 1986, p. 1
23 Judd and Cable, p. 124
24 ibid. p. 126
25 *Votes and Proceedings of the Synod of the Diocese of Sydney*, 1884, p. 24
26 *Votes and Proceedings*, 1885, p. 25
27 *Votes and Proceedings*, 1886, p. 23
28 Sherington, *Shore*, p. 20
29 *Votes and Proceedings*, 1891, p. 24
30 ibid. p. 124
31 *Votes and Proceedings of the Sydney Diocesan Synod*, 1892, p. 31
32 ibid. p. 3
33 ibid. p. 166
34 *Australian Record*, 11 February 1893, p. 9
35 *Australian Record*, 25 November 1893, p. 12
36 K. Cable, unpublished biographical notes
37 P. Egan, A History of St John's Parish and Church at Darlinghurst, MA (Pass) project, University of Sydney, 1985, p. 52
38 ibid. p. 53
39 *Lux*, vol. 25, no. 1, 1928, p. 1
40 *Votes and Proceedings of the Sydney Synod*, 1894, Appendix XXIV, p. lxxiv
41 ibid. p. lxxiv
42 S.C.E.G.G.S. Council minute book, vol. 1, November 1894
43 ibid.
44 S.C.E.G.G.S. Council minute book, vol. 1, May 1894
45 S.C.E.G.G.S. Council minute book, vol. 1, April 1895

46 S.C.E.G.G.S. Council minute book, vol. 1, 5 December 1894
47 S.C.E.G.G.S. Council minute book, vol. 1, 16, 26 April 1894
48 25 April 1895, in S.C.E.G.G.S. archives
49 S.C.E.G.G.S. Council minute book, vol. 1, May 1895
50 University of Sydney archives: graduates' card index
51 S.C.E.G.G.S. Council minute book, vol. 1, 14 June 1895
52 Badham family, History of the family of Professor Charles Badham, 1984 (unpublished)
53 S.C.E.G.G.S. Council minute book, vol. 1, 24 June 1895

Chapter 3

1 *Sydney Church of England Girls' Grammar School 1895–1955*, Council of Sydney Church of England Girls' Grammar School, Sydney, 1958, p. 22
2 Interview with Mary Watson's three sons, Dick, Peter and Snow, 31 March 1987
3 Letter from Mary Watson to the S.C.E.G.G.S. Council, c.1950, S.C.E.G.G.S. archives
4 Wilma Radford, Charles Badham and his Work for Education in NSW, MEd. thesis, University of Sydney, 1969, p. 34
5 ibid. p. 10
6 ibid. pp. 22–6
7 NSW Legislative Assembly, *Votes and Proceedings*, 1872, vol. 1, pp. 686–7
8 Tangible memorials to the famous man are the Badham Room, the Badham Building and the Badham Bursary at the University of Sydney
9 C. Badham, *Speeches and Lectures*, University of Sydney, Sydney, 1890, p. 33
10 Badham, Family history, op. cit.
11 Radford, p. 83
12 J. Milburn, Girls' Secondary Education in NSW 1880–1930, MA thesis, University of Sydney, 1965, p. 39
13 Marjorie Hesslein interview, 15 March 1985
14 Dorothea Baltzer interview, 13 November 1984
15 ibid.
16 *Australian Economist*, 23 April 1895, p. 1
17 E. A. Badham, 'Nursery Rhymes' quoted in Badham family history
18 C. Badham, p. 7
19 Principal's Annual Report, *S.C.E.G.G.S. 1895–1955*, p. 29
20 ibid. p. 29
21 C. Badham, p. 61
22 Sydney Girls' High School, PLC Sydney, MLC Burwood, St Catherine's Waverley
23 Milburn, p. 62
24 S.C.E.G.G.S. 1896 Prospectus, S.C.E.G.G.S. archives
25 Principal's Annual Report 1896, p. 28
26 Milburn, p. 35
27 Principal's Annual Report 1896, p. 29
28 Sherington, *Shore*, p. 34
29 S. and A. Coupe, *Walk in the Light*, MLC School in association with Ayers and James Heritage Books, Melbourne, 1986, p. 17
30 A. Nobbs, *Kambala: The First Hundred Years 1887–1987*, Kambala Centenary History Committee, Sydney, 1987, p. 17
31 L. Norman, *The Brown and Yellow*, Oxford University Press, Melbourne, 1983, p. 14
32 Principal's Annual Report 1896, p. 29
33 *Lux*, March 1946, p. 9
34 *Australian Economist*, 23 April 1895, p. 483

Chapter 4

1 S.C.E.G.G.S. Council minute book, vol. 1, May 1895
2 An amendment to the Ordinance in 1910 made provision for such a contingency
3 E. A. Badham's General Remarks, S.C.E.G.G.S. archives
4 S.C.E.G.G.S. Council, S.C.E.G.G.S. Council minute book and the official Prospectus differ on the membership of the first Council. Archdeacon Langley and Dr J. C. Corlette are not listed on the Prospectus but are in the S.C.E.G.G.S. Council minute book, vol. 1, 6 June 1895
5 *Sydney Church of England Girls' Grammar School 1895–1955*, Council of Sydney Church of England Girls' Grammar School, Sydney, 1958, p. 24
6 *Votes and Proceedings* 1897, p. 87
7 S.C.E.G.G.S. Council minute book, vol. 2, March 1897
8 ibid. March 1897
9 *Votes and Proceedings*, 1895, pp. 172–3
10 *Votes and Proceedings*, 1896, p. 159
11 *Votes and Proceedings*, 1897, p. 159
12 ibid. p. 159
13 Prospectus 1896, S.C.E.G.G.S. archives
14 L. Norman, *The Brown and Yellow: Sydney Girls' High School 1883–1983*, Oxford University Press, Melbourne, 1983, p. 15
15 Sherington, *Shore*, p. 34
16 S.C.E.G.G.S. Council minute book, vol. 2, May 1895
17 S.C.E.G.G.S. Council minute book, vol. 2, January 1896
18 ibid. February 1896
19 Norman, p. 14
20 Sherington, p. 38
21 See for example, S. & R. Coupe, *Walk in the Light*, p. 13
22 S.C.E.G.G.S. Council minute book, vol. 2, June, 1896
23 ibid. 8 May 1896
24 *Votes and Proceedings*, 1897, p. 159
25 S.C.E.G.G.S. History, 1955, pp. 131–2
26 *Votes and Proceedings*, p. 159
27 *Votes and Proceedings*, p. 153. Numbers dropped back to about 80 in 1899
28 S.C.E.G.G.S. Council minute book, vol. 2, May 1899
29 S.C.E.G.G.S. Council minute book, vol. 2, January 1900
30 ibid. February 1900
31 The origin of the name 'Barham' was the subject of correspondence between Canon Beck and James Watson, a prominent local historian and father of S.C.E.G.G.S.' first pupil. It was thought initially that the house was named after one of the towns of that name in Huntingdon, Kent or Suffolk. Two ships in the British navy bore the name, and further research revealed the existence of a Charles Middleton who became an Admiral of the British Navy and was created Lord Barham. Charles Middleton had been Comptroller of the Navy and 'had the arranging of matters in connection with the dispatch of the First Fleet and Governor Phillip'. There was a tenuous family connection with Admiral Barham because Edward Deas Thomson's grandfather, John Thomson, married three times and his second wife, Janet, was the aunt of Admiral Charles Barham. Barham was known as 'Barham Hall' in the nineteenth century.
32 F. MacDonnell, *The Glebe: Portraits and Places*, Ure Smith, Sydney, 1975, pp. 76–9
33 *Australian Dictionary of Biography*, vol. 2, 1788–1850, Melbourne University Press, Melbourne, 1967, pp. 523–7

34 G. Farwell, *Squatters Castle: The Story and Times of a Pastoral Dynasty*, Lansdowne Press, Melbourne, 1973, pp. 282, 290, 293, 301
35 S.C.E.G.G.S. Council minute book, vol. 2, January 1900, 9 February 1900
36 'The Story of Barham', anonymous and undated, S.C.E.G.G.S. archives
37 Belinda Patton and Ed Jurkiewicz, Conservation Study of Barham, November 1986, S.C.E.G.G.S. archives
38 James Broadbent, Ian Evans, Clive Lucas and Max Dupain, *The Golden Age of Australian Architecture—the work of John Verge*, David Ell Press, Sydney, 1978, p. 43
39 ibid. p. 43
40 P. Egan, A History of St John's Parish and Church at Darlinghurst, MA (Pass) project, Sydney, 1985, p. 18
41 S.C.E.G.G.S. Council minute book, vol. 2, February 1900
42 Badham Family History (unpublished), notes on Julia Badham

Chapter 5

1 Interviews with Old Girls Sarte Russell and Dorothea Baltzer, who were at S.C.E.G.G.S. in the early years, make this very clear
2 John Charles Wright, Archbishop of Sydney from 1913 until 1933.
3 J. Milburn, Girls' Secondary Education in NSW 1880–1930, MA thesis, University of Sydney, 1965, p. 54
4 Questionnaires in S.C.E.G.G.S. archives. See also Appendix 2 Table (vi)
5 S.C.E.G.G.S. archives, Letter dated 6 August 1899
6 Letter dated 3 September 1899
7 Ruby Bulkeley interview, 3 July 1985
8 Kate Waddy letter, 4 February 1900
9 Mary Beith interview, 28 October 1985
10 Kate Waddy letter, 6 August 1899
11 ibid. 11 March 1900
12 ibid. 12 November 1899
13 ibid. 11 March 1900
14 N. Kyle, *Her Natural Destiny: The education of women in NSW*, University of NSW Press, Sydney, 1986, p. 138
15 ibid. p. 109
16 Milburn, op. cit., pp. 12–16
17 Baltzer, op. cit.
18 ibid.
19 S.C.E.G.G.S. Council minute book, vol. 2, 24 November 1899
20 Salary information for the decade is omitted from histories of Kambala, MLC Burwood, Wenona and Sydney Girls' High School.
21 Turney, *Grammar*, p. 117; see also Sherington, *Shore*, p. 54
22 *Lux*, vol. 15, no. 3, p. 15
23 Bulkeley interview
24 Evelyn Olding interview, October 1984
25 In November 1898 one candidate out of ten passed her piano examination, S.C.E.G.G.S. Council minute book, vol. 2, 25 November 1898
26 Olding interview
27 ibid.
28 S. Braga, *Barker College, A History*, Ferguson, Sydney, 1978, pp. 114–17
29 Turney, p. 70
30 ibid. p. 71
31 *Lux*, vol. 1, no. 1, 1900, p. 19
32 Isobel Jefferson interview, March 1985
33 Olding interview

34 C. Fairfax Simpson et al., *Ascham Remembered 1886–1986*, The Fine Arts Press, Sydney, 1986, p. 4
35 *Votes and Proceedings*, 1897, p. 160
36 Marjorie Hesslein interview, March 1985

Chapter 6

1 S.C.E.G.G.S. Council minute book, vol. 2, August 1900
2 ibid.
3 S.C.E.G.G.S. Council minute book, vol. 3, February 1900
4 ibid. November 1906
5 ibid. November 1910
6 S.C.E.G.G.S. Council minute book, vol. 4, October 1912
7 ibid. July 1912
8 ibid. April 1912
9 Eric C. Moroney, *Schools of Hunter's Hill 1857–1981*, Hunter's Hill Historical Society, Sydney, 1980
10 S.C.E.G.G.S. Council minute book, vol. 4, September 1915
11 ibid. August 1914
12 ibid. February 1913
13 ibid. April 1914
14 ibid. 1915
15 Moroney, p. 12
16 They were: Wyanoke Private School (1911–1917), Narrawa Private School (1912–13), Binstead Girls' Grammar School (1913–17), Malvern Preparatory School (1912–14), Girrahween School (1905–57), Marist Convent School (1908–)
17 *Lux*, vol. 12, no. 1, July 1913, p. 9
18 *Votes and Proceedings*, 1892, p. 166
19 ibid. p. 192
20 About three times per year from 1912–18
21 S.C.E.G.G.S. Council minute book, vol. 4, March 1915
22 S.C.E.G.G.S. Council minute book, vol. 3, May 1908
23 ibid. May 1911
24 S.C.E.G.G.S. Council minute book, vol. 4, 1914
25 S.C.E.G.G.S. Council minute book, vol. 3, July 1911
26 S.C.E.G.G.S. Council minute book, vol. 4, October 1911
27 S.C.E.G.G.S. Council minute book, vol. 3, August 1909
28 ibid. September 1909
29 ibid. October 1910
30 ibid. vol. 4, August 1911
31 *Lux*, vol. 3, no. 4, 1905, p. 15
32 *Lux*, vol. 12, no. 1, 1913, p. 9
33 Marjorie Hesslein interview, March 1985
34 *Lux*, vol. 3, no. 2, 1904, p. 7
35 ibid. vol. 5, no. 1, 1906, p. 10
36 ibid.
37 Ruby Bulkeley interview, 31 July 1985
38 *Lux*, vol. 4, no. 1, 1905, p. 10
39 ibid. p. 11
40 Dorothea Baltzer interview, November 1984
41 Evelyn Olding interview, October 1984
42 Mary Beith interview, October 1985
43 Olding interview
44 Sixteenth Annual Report to the Synod, S.C.E.G.G.S. Council minute book, vol. 4, August 1911

Chapter 7

1 A. Barcan, *A History of Australian Education*, Oxford University Press, Melbourne, 1980, p. 20
2 A. Barcan, *A Short History of Education in NSW*, Martindale Press, Sydney, 1965, p. 211
3 Barcan, *A History*, p. 208
4 ibid. p. 231
5 Grace Newbury
6 E. Badham, 'Registered Schools and the Syllabus', 1914, S.C.E.G.G.S. archives
7 Sherington, *Shore*, p. 92
8 F. Crowley (ed.), *A New History of Australia*, Heinemann, Melbourne, 1984, p. 348
9 *Lux*, vol. 13, no. 3, p. 1
10 Sherington, *Shore*, p. 91
11 *Lux*, vol. 13, no. 4, January, 1915, p. 31
12 Dorothea Balzer interview, November 1984
13 S.C.E.G.G.S. Council minute book, vol. 5, July and August 1916
14 Marjorie Hesslein interview, March 1985
15 ibid.
16 ibid.
17 Mary Beith interview, October 1985
18 *Lux*, vol. 14, no. 6, July 1916, p. 2
19 S. Judd and K. Cable, *Sydney Anglicans*, Anglican Information Office, Sydney, 1987, p. 187
20 ibid. p. 187
21 S.C.E.G.G.S. Council minute book, vol. 4, October 1915
22 Annual Report to the Synod 1917
23 S.C.E.G.G.S. Council minute book, vol. 5, October 1919
24 ibid. July 1917. Also Annual Report to the Synod 1917
25 ibid. November 1918
26 ibid. April 1919
27 ibid.
28 ibid. April, June and August 1919
29 S.C.E.G.G.S. Council minute book, vol. 4, August 1909
30 S.C.E.G.G.S. Council minute book, vol. 5, April 1919
31 ibid.
32 ibid. July 1919
33 S.C.E.G.G.S. Council minute book, vol. 5, October 1919
34 24th Annual Report to the Sydney Synod 1919
35 *Lux*, vol. XVII, no. 4, January 1920, p. 1
36 *Lux*, vol. 1, no. 2, 1900, p. 13
37 *Lux*, vol. 1, no. 5, 1901, p. 16
38 *Lux*, vol. 2, no. 5, 1904, p. 2
39 *Lux*, vol. 15, no. 4, 1918, p. 17
40 *Sydney Church of England Girls' Grammar School 1895–1955*, Council of Sydney Church of England Girls' Grammar School Sydney, 1958, p. 125
41 Eleventh Annual Report to the Sydney Synod 1906
42 *Lux*, vol. 14, no. 2, 1915, p. 6
43 *Lux*, vol. 11, no. 2, 1912, p. 15
44 Freda Du Faur, *The Ascent of Mount Cook and Other Climbs*, Capper Press, Christchurch, 1977, p. 37
45 B. Niall and F. O'Neill, *Australia Through the Looking Glass: children's fiction 1930–1980*, Melbourne University Press, Melbourne, 1984, pp. 110–14
46 *Lux*, vol. 11, no. 1, 1912, p. 12
47 *Lux*, vol. 17, no. 4, 1920, p. 1
48 Obituary in Memorial Edition of *Lux*, vol. 18, no. 1, June 1920, p. 7

Chapter 8

1 S.C.E.G.G.S. Council minute book, vol. 5, May 1920
2 ibid. Special Meeting September 1920
3 ibid. October 1920
4 G. Sale, *The History of Casterton School*, Casterton School, United Kingdom, 1983, p. 35
5 ibid. pp. 87, 89
6 Casterton School Register, Casterton archives
7 Letter dated 10 February 1989, from Trevor Sorell, Alumni Secretary, Launceston Church Grammar School
8 S.C.E.G.G.S., *In Memoriam, Dorothy Irene Wilkinson, Headmistress, Sydney Church of England Girls' Grammar School, 1921–1947*, 1949
9 B. Rait, *The Story of Launceston Grammar School 1846–1946*, W. R. Rolph and Sons Pty Ltd, Launceston, 1946, p. 104
10 *Lux*, vol. 18, no. 3, January 1921, p. 2
11 *Lux*, vol. 36, no. 2, October 1939, p. 4
12 *Lux*, vol. 18, no. 4, June 1921, p. 24
13 W. Sharland interview, October 1984
14 ibid.
15 S.C.E.G.G.S. 'In Memoriam Issue', article entitled 'From the Press'
16 S.C.E.G.G.S. Council minute book, vol. 5, November 1920
17 Her maiden name was Lily Christian. *Lux*, vol. 19, no. 1, 1921, p. 42
18 S.C.E.G.G.S. Council minute book, vol. 5, November 1920
19 ibid. October 1920
20 ibid. November 1920
21 ibid. September and October 1921
22 ibid. February 1920 and vol. 6, February 1930
23 ibid. vol. 6, September 1921
24 ibid. July 1923
25 ibid. June 1925
26 S.C.E.G.G.S. Council minute book, vol. 6, August 1923
27 ibid. June 1924
28 ibid. February 1925
29 ibid. September 1926
30 S.C.E.G.G.S. Council minute book, vol. 6, September 1926
31 ibid. February 1929
32 ibid. November 1922
33 ibid. December 1922
34 ibid. December 1921, February 1923, October 1925, September 1926
35 S.C.E.G.G.S. Council minute book, vol. 6, table containing figures for 1922–29
36 ibid. 1928
37 Esther Tuckey, *Fifty Years at Frensham*, Winifred West Schools, Mittagong, 1964, p. 1
38 S.C.E.G.G.S. Council minute book, vol. 6, July 1922
39 ibid. February 1925
40 ibid. April 1926
41 S.C.E.G.G.S. Council minute book, vol. 6, February 1925
42 ibid. March 1928
43 ibid. December 1929
44 S.C.E.G.G.S. Council minute book, vol. 6, April 1930
45 ibid. February 1931
46 Survey of Old Girls
47 *Lux*, vol. 18, no. 4, June 1921, p. 25
48 ibid. p. 3

49 *Lux*, vol. 27, no. 21, June 1930, p. 31
50 *Lux*, vol. 23, no. 1, February 1926, p. 3
51 *Sydney Church of England Girls' Grammar School 1895–1955*, p. 120
52 Milburn, Girls' Secondary Education, thesis, p. 211
53 *Lux*, vol. 18, no. 4, June 1921, p. 2
54 For example *Lux*, vol. 24, no. 1, 1927, p. 20
55 S.C.E.G.G.S. Council minute book, vol. 6, April 1923
56 *Lux*, vol. 23, no. 3, September 1926, p. 8
57 *Lux*, vol. 23, no. 1, February, 1926, pp. 10–11
58 Sir David Griffin recollections, March 1986, S.C.E.G.G.S. archives
59 S.C.E.G.G.S. Prospectus 1927, S.C.E.G.G.S. archives
60 Barcan, *A Short History*, p. 255
61 Barcan, *A History*, p. 244
62 ibid. p. 255
63 The theory was named after J. F. Herbart, the German philosopher, psychologist and educationalist who died in 1841. It was developed and modified by educationalists in the United States and England in the late nineteenth century.
64 See Chapter 8. Also Annual Report 1914 and E. Badham, 'Registered Schools and the Syllabus', in S.C.E.G.G.S. archives.
65 Milburn, pp. 172–3
66 S.C.E.G.G.S. Council minute book, vol. 6, November 1925
67 S.C.E.G.G.S. Council minute book, vol. 6, August 1925
68 Sheila Joy interview February 1986. Sheila Joy spoke of a 'nervous collapse'

Chapter 9

1 A. Nobbs, *Kambala: The First Hundred Years 1887–1987*, Globe Press, Sydney, 1987, p. 69; J. McFarlane, *The Golden Hope: Presbyterian Ladies' College, Sydney 1888–1988*, Globe Press, Sydney, 1988, p. 77; B. Mansfield, *Knox: A History of Knox Grammar School 1924–1974*, John Sands, Sydney, 1974, p. 30; S.C.E.G.G.S. Council minute book, vol. 7, 1931–1940
2 S.C.E.G.G.S. Council minute book, vol. 7, September 1932
3 L. Norman, *The Brown And Yellow*, p. 97
4 S.C.E.G.G.S. Council minute book, vol. 7, December 1933
5 ibid.
6 S.C.E.G.G.S. Council minute book, vol. 7, December 1933
7 ibid.
8 S.C.E.G.G.S. Council minute book, vol. 7, July 1935
9 ibid. December 1936
10 S.C.E.G.G.S. Council minute book, vol. 6, February 1931
11 S.C.E.G.G.S. Council minute book, vol. 7, August 1939
12 ibid. July 1936
13 ibid. April 1933
14 ibid. February 1935
15 ibid. February 1934, July 1935
16 *Lux*, vol. 32, no. 1, February 1935, pp. 10–11
17 S.C.E.G.G.S. Council minute book, vol. 6, December 1929
18 S.C.E.G.G.S. Council minute book, vol. 7, February 1938
19 *Lux*, vol. 34, no. 1, February 1937, p. 13
20 S.C.E.G.G.S. Council minute book, vol. 7, June, October, November 1936
21 S.C.E.G.G.S. Council minute book, vol. 8, Executive Committee, p. 81
22 S.C.E.G.G.S. Council minute book, vol. 7, February 1940
23 S.C.E.G.G.S. Council minute book, vol. 7, Head School Report, April 1940
24 ibid. August 1940
25 ibid. vol. 7, November 1937

26 ibid. November 1938
27 ibid.
28 ibid. October 1935
29 ibid. November 1937
30 ibid. May 1938
31 ibid. May 1936
32 ibid. June 1932
33 ibid. November 1939 and November 1940
34 ibid. November 1936
35 M. MacCallum, *Plankton's Luck: a life in retrospect*, Hutchinson, Melbourne, 1986, pp. 19–22
36 MacCallum, pp. 22–3
37 S.C.E.G.G.S. Council minute book, vol. 4, April 1915 and vol. 5, July 1916
38 S.C.E.G.G.S. Council minute book, vol. 5, October 1915 and August 1916
39 W. Sharland interview, October 1984
40 Rosemary Wilkins (Mrs Cameron) interview, June 1984
41 Mary Graham (Mrs Blomfield) interview, August 1985
42 Joan Freeman (Mrs J. Jelly), Reminiscences of S.C.E.G.G.S. (unpublished), S.C.E.G.G.S. archives
43 Graham interview
44 Wilkins interview
45 Dorothy Shipley (Mrs Bremner) interview, undated
46 Nancy Jackson (Mrs Anderson) interview, June 1984
47 ibid.
48 Sharland interview
49 *Lux*, vol. 28, no. 1, February 1931, p. 25
50 Daughter of the author Ether Turner (Mrs Adrian Curlewis)
51 *Lux*, vol. 27, no. 2, June 1930, p. 38
52 ibid. p. 3
53 Freeman interview
54 ibid.
55 S.C.E.G.G.S. Council minute book, vol. 9, February 1941
56 ibid. March 1937
57 *Lux*, vol. 32, no. 1, February 1935, pp. 13–14
58 *Sydney Church of England Girls' Grammar School 1895–1955*, p. 86
59 *Lux*, vol. 33, no. 1, 1936, p. 9
60 *Lux*, vol. 35, no. 1, February 1938, p. 10
61 Barcan, *A History*, pp. 249–50

Chapter 10

1 *Lux*, March 1942, p. 4
2 *Lux*, February 1941, pp. 2–3
3 *Lux*, vol. 26, no. 3, February 1940, p. 3
4 ibid.
5 *Lux*, March 1944, p. 14. Note: *Lux*, July 1940, vol. 38, no. 4 is the last numbered volume of *Lux*
6 *Lux*, vol. 38, no. 4, July 1940, p. 1
7 F. Crowley (ed.), *A New History of Australia*, Heinemann, Melbourne, 1984, p. 464
8 One of the submarines was blown up at Bottle and Glass rocks at Vaucluse, according to Old Girl Vashti Farrer
9 Crowley, p. 467
10 J. McFarlane, *The Golden Hope: Presbyterian Ladies' College 1888–1988*, Globe Press, Sydney, 1988, pp. 89–90

11 B. Mansfield, *Knox 1924–1974*, John Sands, Sydney, 1974, p. 64; Sherington, *Shore*, p. 64
12 *Lux*, August 1942, p. 3
13 Sherington, p. 156
14 *Lux*, March 1944, p. 3
15 S.C.E.G.G.S. Council minute book, vol. 9, November 1941
16 S.C.E.G.G.S. Council minute book, vol. 8, Executive Committee, February 1940
17 W. Sharland, *Australian Teacher*, vol. 2, no. 1, June 1943, pp. 29–33
18 Now Dr Havyatt
19 V. Luker, 'S.C.E.G.G.S. in the Mountains—recollections of a Wenona girl who attended S.C.E.G.G.S. at Leura in 1942' (unpublished), in S.C.E.G.G.S. archives
20 S.C.E.G.G.S. Council minute book, vol. 8, Executive Committee, February 1942
21 Sharland interview, p. 30
22 Luker, pp. 3–4. Other material gained from interviews supports the Luker material but is of no independent value
23 S.C.E.G.G.S. Council minute book, vol. 9, April 1942
24 Sharland, p. 31
25 Luker
26 Sharland, p. 32
27 *Sydney Morning Herald*, 29 May 1945
28 S.C.E.G.G.S. Council minute book, vol. 9, May 1946
29 ibid. November 1945
30 ibid. October 1943
31 *Lux*, March 1942, p. 4
32 Barcan, *A Short History*, pp. 258–9
33 S.C.E.G.G.S. Council minute book, vol. 9, February 1943
34 She had forgotten that Shore had set up an emergency branch at the Mt Victoria Hotel in 1942 and Ascham had also set up emergency branches
35 S.C.E.G.G.S. Council minute book, vol. 9, February 1943
36 'Luceat Lux Vestra! a pageant in commemoration of the jubilee of the Sydney Church of England Girls' Grammar School, 1895–1945', Sydney, 1945, S.C.E.G.G.S. archives
37 *Lux*, March 1946, p. 9
38 K. Cable and S. Judd, *Sydney Anglicans: A History of the Diocese*, Anglican Information Office, Sydney, 1987, pp. 228–9
39 ibid. pp. 233–4
40 S.C.E.G.G.S. Council minute books are missing from 1953–70: unable to verify exact date
41 Transcript of Prescott tape, January 1990
42 S.C.E.G.G.S. Council minute book, vol. 9, October 1942
43 ibid. April 1941
44 ibid. 1942
45 St Andrew's House archives, Box 699, File 1, letters dated 6 March 1944 and 29 February 1944
46 St Andrew's House archives, Box 132, File 1, Executive minutes, 22 January 1965
47 *Sydney Morning Herald*, 18 July 1952. The obituary states that she died 'in her ninetieth year'
48 S.C.E.G.G.S. Council minute book, vol. 9, November 1945
49 Letter from Prescott to M. H. Cameron, 4 October 1989
50 Diocesan archives, St Andrew's House, Box 88, Archdeacon Johnston's files
51 S.C.E.G.G.S. Council minute book, vol. 9, November 1945: Holmes' report of a conversation with Dr Rayward, Professor Stephens and himself

52 An undated letter from 34 members of staff (including all the senior mistresses) and from a parent bear witness to this. Box 88, Diocesan archives
53 Telephone conversation with Caroline Fairfax-Simpson (Co-editor of *Ascham Remembered 1886–1986*, The Fine Arts Press, Sydney, 1986), September 1989
54 S.C.E.G.G.S. Council minute book, vol. 9, November 1945
55 Fairfax-Simpson conversation. Corroborated by Mary Maltby, S.C.E.G.G.S. archivist
56 Prescott letter
57 Letters to Smith, 1 November 1949 and November 1950, Box 88, St Andrew's House archives
58 Letter in S.C.E.G.G.S. Council minute book, vol. 9
59 *Lux*, June 1945, pp. 13–4
60 Diana Bowman's recollection. In 1978 Diana Bowman became the fourth Headmistress of S.C.E.G.G.S.
61 S.C.E.G.G.S. Council minute book, vol. 10, May 1947

Chapter 11

1 Barbara Chisholm letter to Marcia Cameron, 15 June 1983
2 Barbara Chisholm letter to Marcia Cameron, 17 October 1983
3 Chisholm interview, November 1983
4 ibid.
5 ibid.
6 Chisholm letter to Marcia Cameron, January 1984
7 Wilkinson account in *Lux*, September 1947, p. 87
8 Chisholm interview, July 1985
9 Chisholm letter, January 1984
10 Chisholm's Report to Council, June 1947
11 Diocesan archives, St Andrew's House, Box 699, File 1
12 Chisholm letter, January 1984
13 *Lux*, March 1949, p. 4
14 *Lux*, December 1951, p. 21
15 *Lux*, 1956, p. 19
16 S.C.E.G.G.S. Council minute book, vol. 10, June 1954
17 ibid. March 1951 and Executive Committee, June 1951. Note: *Lux* became an annual publication in December 1952.
18 Chisholm interview, June 1985
19 Transcript of Prescott tape recording sent to Marcia Cameron in response to questions, January 1990
20 Interviews with Mary Guiness (Mrs Jones), June 1985 and Mary-Louise Alma (Dr Claflin), June 1985
21 *Lux*, March 1948, p. 8
22 Guinness interview
23 Alma interview
24 Mary Graham (Mrs Blomfield) interview, August 1985
25 Wendy Kohn (Mrs McLeod) interview, September 1984
26 Such selective girls' high schools were: North Sydney Girls' High, Sydney Girls' High, Fort Street Girls' High and St George Girls' High
27 *Lux*, 1956, p. 19
28 Enid Miller interview, August 1984
29 Graham interview
30 Vashti Farrer (Mrs Waterhouse) interview, September 1984
31 Alma interview
32 Jann Nicholson (Mrs Davies) account 'Memories of Schooldays at S.C.E.G.G.S. Darlinghurst 1951–56', S.C.E.G.G.S. archives
33 Jane Wholohan interview, September 1985

34 Guinness interview
35 Chisholm's Report to Council, February 1955
36 Chisholm's Report to Council, November 1947
37 Wholohan interview
38 Kohn interview
39 Chisholm's Report to Council, November 1949
40 Guinness interview
41 Nicholson account
42 S.C.E.G.G.S. Council minute book, vol. 10, February 1950
43 Chisholm's Report to Council, October 1948
44 S.C.E.G.G.S. Council, S.C.E.G.G.S. Council minute book, vol. 10, July 1952
45 Sherington, *Shore*, p. 175
46 *Lux*, 1958, p. 3
47 *Lux*, 1959, p. 9
48 Cable and Judd, *Sydney Anglicans*, pp. 262–3
49 Chisholm letter, January 1984
50 Diocesan archives, Archdeacon Johnstone's papers, Box 88, File April 1950
51 Miller interview
52 Prescott tape transcript
53 Diocesan archives, Box 132, File 2
54 ibid.
55 ibid.
56 Graham interview
57 Prescott tape transcript
58 *Lux*, 1957, p. 11
59 Barcan, *A History*, p. 302

Chapter 12

1 Barcan, *A History*, pp. 323–4
2 ibid. p. 321
3 ibid. p. 304
4 Chisholm's Report to Council, February 1962
5 *Lux*, 1963, p. 36
6 *Lux*, 1964, p. 3
Shades of Badham's comments on the introduction of Peter Board's scheme in 1941 (see Chapter 8): 'We do not yet know what the matriculation requirements will be . . .'
7 *Lux*, 1966, p. 3
8 Chisholm's Report to Council, February 1962
9 Dr Helen Goldhammer interview, November 1984
10 Chisholm's Report to Council, November 1961
11 Chisholm's Report to Council, July 1964
12 Barcan, *A History*, p. 317
13 Barcan, *A Short History*, pp. 286–7
14 J. MacFarlane, *The Golden Hope. Presbyterian Ladies' College Sydney, 1888–1988*, The Council of PLC Sydney, Sydney, 1988, p. 120
15 ibid.
16 Sherington, *Shore*, pp. 214–15
17 D. E. and I. V. Hansen, *Feminine Singular: A History of the Association of the Heads of Independent Girls' Schools of Australia*, Hyland House, South Yarra, 1989, p. 7
18 Jo Karaolis' account written in response to questions from author, March 1990
19 *Lux*, 1967, p. 3
20 *Lux*, 1967, p. 52
21 *Lux*, 1964, p. 51 and 1962, p. 55

22 Gwynneth Bowley's written account, 'The S.C.E.G.G.S. primary school' (undated)
23 Janet Lean interview, December 1984
24 Conversation with author, April 1990
25 Cynthia Butterworth (Mrs Jackson) interview, September 1984
26 ibid.
27 Karaolis account
28 Denise Reading account in response to survey of S.C.E.G.G.S. staff, March 1990
29 Chisholm's Report to Council, October 1969
30 *Lux*, 1963, p. 3
31 Chisholm's Report to Council, May 1966
32 ibid. May 1966; Chisholm interview, November 1983
33 Jean Pender and Anne Robinson (Mrs Judd) interview, 1984
34 Chisholm's Report to Council, June 1966
35 Diocesan archives, Box 132
36 Diocesan archives, Box 132, November 1961
37 Chisholm letter to author, January 1984
38 Diocesan archives, S.C.E.G.G.S. Council minute book, January 1965
39 Report of the Commission appointed by the Archbishop of Sydney 1964, p. 227
40 ibid. p. 153
41 ibid. p. 183

Chapter 13

1 See Chisholm's Report to Council, August 1970, for example
2 *The Yearbook of the Diocese of Sydney 1970.* There were 4 clergy, 8 laymen, 6 women, 1 Old Girl and the Archbishop as ex officio President: total, 20
3 Chisholm's Report to Council, June 1971
4 Chisholm interview, November 1983
5 Chisholm's Report to Council, July 1971
6 ibid.
7 ibid.
8 *Lux*, 1973, p. 7
9 Barcan, *A History*, p. 361
10 ibid. p. 362
11 I. Paterson, 'The Future Funding Prospects for Schools', paper presented at the Thirteenth Fundraising Convention, February 1990, Sydney
12 ibid.
13 ibid.
14 S.C.E.G.G.S. Council minute book, vol. 11
15 S.C.E.G.G.S. Council minute book, Executive Committee, vol. 12, September 1971
16 ibid. November 1971
17 ibid. August 1973
18 ibid. September 1971
19 Paterson
20 Conversation with Professor K. Cable, August 1990, re St Catherine's response to the Karmel Report
21 D. Bowman's Report to Council, May 1978
22 G. Greer, *The Female Eunuch,* MacGibbon and Kee, London, 1970, pp. 11, 12, 16
23 A. Summers, *Damned Whores and God's Police,* Penguin, London, 1975, p. 428
24 *Lux*, 1974, p. 5
25 *Lux*, 1970, p. 5

26 *Lux*, 1971, p. 11
27 Chisholm's Report to Council, March 1971
28 Chisholm's Report to Council, October 1971
29 ibid. July and September
30 S.C.E.G.G.S. Council minute book, vol. 11, September 1971
31 S.C.E.G.G.S. Council minute book, vol. 11, October 1971 and March 1972
32 S.C.E.G.G.S. Council minute book, Executive Committee, vol. 12, October 1972

Chapter 14

1 Diocesan archives, St Andrew's House, E. D. Cameron's papers, Standing Committee file, Box 1180
2 N. M. Cameron interview, August 1990
3 Transcript of Prescott tape recording sent to author in response to questions, January 1990
4 ibid.
5 S.C.E.G.G.S. Council minute book, Executive Committee, vol. 12, September 1971
6 ibid.
7 ibid.
8 Prescott letter to author, 1 September 1990. S.C.E.G.G.S. Council minute book, vol. 12, September 1972
9 M. T. Daly, *Sydney Boom, Sydney Bust: The City and its Property Market 1850–1981*, Allen & Unwin, Sydney, 1982, p. 65
10 ibid. p. 66
11 ibid. p. 67
12 E. D. Cameron Report on S.C.E.G.G.S. to the Standing Committee, 1974–1976, p. 1
13 Prescott letter
14 Cameron Report, p. 2
15 N. M. Cameron interview
16 Diocesan archives, St Andrew's House, Box 1184, Standing Committee File, August 1974
17 Diocesan archives, St Andrew's House, Box 1179, E. D. Cameron files, no. 11, p. 13
18 *The Yearbook of the Diocese of Sydney*, Sydney, 1975, p. 250. See Appendix 1 for full text
19 *Sydney Morning Herald*, 18 October 1974
20 *Sun Herald*, 20 October 1974
21 The *Australian*, 17 October 1974
22 ibid.
23 Diocesan archives, St Andrew's House, Box 1180, M. Loane to E. D. Cameron
24 E. D. Cameron Report, p. 1
25 ibid.
26 Diocesan archives, Box 1179, Management Committe minutes, November 1974
27 E. D. Cameron Report, p. 1
28 K. L. McCredie's own view in conversations with author
29 Diocesan archives, Box 1180, Price Waterhouse Report, April 1977
30 Diocesan archives, Box 1179, E. D. Cameron's summary of the proceedings of S.C.E.G.G.S. Council, June–December 1976
31 ibid. Allen, Allen and Hemsley advice to the Standing Committee, 19 May 1976
32 ibid. File 1
33 ibid. N. M. Cameron's proposal to E. D. Cameron 28 June 1990. Also numerous verbal statements to this effect by E. D. Cameron to author

34 Deed made 24 December 1976 between S.C.E.G.G.S Council and BAC and ANZ Bank. Original in Allen, Allen and Hemsley files
35 E. Davis interview, June 1990
36 Yvonne Bowyer recollections—included with answers to the survey of Old Girls (undated)
37 Mrs Miller interview, January 1984
38 Diocesan archives, Box 1180
39 This was a reference to the demolition of St Andrew's Cathedral School and the erection of St Andrew's House: an office block with the school occupying the top floors
40 N. M. Cameron interview
41 Diocesan archives, Box 1179, Board minutes, December 1976
42 ibid. September 1977

Chapter 15

1 *Lux*, 1954, p. 33
2 D. Bowman, 'Characteristics of the 1980s', August 1990
3 ibid.
4 ibid.
5 Enrolment survey of parents, August 1990
6 R. Shatford: 'Australia Today', a paper delivered to Harvard University in August 1990
7 Commission for the Future, document entitled 'Casualties of change—the predicament of youth in Australia', quoted in Shatford's paper
8 Shatford paper, p. 5
9 *Lux*, 1987, p. 9
10 S.C.E.G.G.S. Staff Handbook, 1989, p. 19
11 Shatford, p. 10
12 ibid. p. 12
13 *Lux*, 1987, p. 9
14 S.C.E.G.G.S. Board minutes, January 1988
15 Bowman, 'Characteristics'
16 ibid.
17 ibid.
18 Joy Yeo interview, August 1990
19 Bowman, 'Characteristics'
20 ibid.
21 *Independence*, Journal of the Association of the Heads of Independent Schools of Australia, vol. 15, no. 1, June, 1990, quoted by Coral Dixon in interview, August 1990
22 Coral Dixon interview, August 1990
23 Shatford, p. 22
24 ibid.
25 Dixon
26 I. Paterson paper, 'The Future Funding Prospects for Schools with particular emphasis for the period post 1992', February 1990, p. 21
27 ibid. p. 19
28 Peterson; R. Shatford interview, August 1990
29 A former Headmaster of Knox
30 Paterson, pp. 20–1
31 Bowman, 'Characteristics'
32 ibid.
33 *Excellence and Equity: NSW Curriculum Reform*, November 1989, NSW Ministry of Education and Youth Affairs
34 ibid. p. 10

35 Commission for the Future
36 Bowman, 'Characteristics'
37 Shatford, p. 14
38 Shatford interview
39 Bowman, 'Characteristics'
40 Conversation with D. Bowman, November 1990
41 ibid.
42 ibid.
43 Shatford, p. 14
44 Bowman, 'Characteristics'
45 Paterson
46 Bowman, 'Characteristics'
47 S.C.E.G.G.S. Board minutes, budget figures, October 1989

Bibliography

Archival sources

Diocese of Sydney Archives, St Andrew's House: Boxes 88, 132, 699, 1178, 1180

S.C.E.G.G.S. archives, Forbes Street, Darlinghurst: letters; photographs; school prospectuses; S.C.E.G.G.S. Council minute books, 1895–1953, 1970–90; Headmistresses' reports to the Council; *Lux*, 1900–88; maps, deeds, contracts; occasional pamphlets e.g. on deaths of Edith Badham and Dorothy Wilkinson; articles e.g. by Edith Badham; survey forms containing information on staff and Old Girls (see Appendix 2) and accounts of school life; memorabilia—prizes, uniforms, badges, pockets, ribbons; register of staff and Old Girls

University of Sydney Archives, University of Sydney: newspaper cutting books—*Sydney Morning Herald*, 1890–1910; card index of graduates

Written accounts

There are numerous written accounts of S.C.E.G.G.S., ranging from single paragraphs to many pages. They are mostly written by Old Girls and former members of staff and usually describe the time they were at S.C.E.G.G.S. Some were written as a response to the survey of Old Girls and former staff and some were sent to the Archives, possibly when the writers were aware that a school history was being contemplated. Some were written at the request of the author. All are lodged in the S.C.E.G.G.S. Archives.

D. Bowman, S.C.E.G.G.S. and education in the 1980s, August 1990; interview February 1986

B. Chisholm (former Headmistress), written account in response to questions from M. H. Cameron, January 1984; letters, December 1989 and June 1983; interviews, November 1983, February 1984 and July 1985

J. Karaolis, S.C.E.G.G.S. during her time on the staff, February 1990 (J. Karaolis was at S.C.E.G.G.S. 1967–68, and history coordinator 1978–87; she became Headmistress of St Catherine's, Waverley, in 1988)

V. Luker, The Emergency Branch at Leura, October 1988

Rev. A. Prescott (former Chairman of Council), letter, September 1990; transcript of tape sent to M. H. Cameron in reply to a number of written questions, January 1990

Interviews

S.C.E.G.G.S. Old Girls

Note that A denotes attendance during Badham era, B during the Wilkinson era, C during the Chisholm era, and D during the Bowman era.

Alma, Anne-Marie (Dr Claflin), July 1985 (C)
Baltzer, Dorothea, November 1984 (A)
Beith, Mary (Mrs d'Arcy Irvine), October 1985 (A)
Bulkeley, Ruby, July 1985 (A)
Burton, Doris (Mrs Plomley), 1984 (A)
Ebsworth, Margery (Mrs Guy Ebsworth), November 1984 (A)
Farrer, Vashti (Mrs Waterhouse), September 1984 (C)
Finkh, Dorrie (Dr Holt), July 1985 (B)
Fitzhardinge, Una (Mrs Richard Fitzhardinge), June 1985 (B)
Freeman, Joan (Dr Jelly), 1989 (B)
Graham, Mary (Mrs Blomfield), August 1985 (B)
Guinness, Mary (Mrs Jones), June 1985 (C)
Halloran, Audrey (Dr Muller), July 1985 (B)
Hesslein, Marjorie (Mrs Ferris), March 1985 (A)
Hicks, Vanessa (Mrs Winship), July 1985 (C)
Jackson, Nancy (Mrs Anderson), June 1984 (B)
Jefferson, Isobel, March 1985 (A)
Joy, Sheila, February 1986 (B)
Kohn, Wendy (Mrs McLeod), September 1984 (C)
Langford, Mrs, 1984
not an Old Girl herself, Mrs Langford was interviewed on behalf of her mother, Vera Henrietta 'Ettie' Black (Mrs Chandler) (A)
Mills, Alyson (Mrs Wheeler), March 1985 (B)
Olding, Evelyn (Mrs Bryden-Brown), 1984 (A)
Pender, Jean (Mrs Maddox), 1984 (C)
Robinson, Anne (Mrs Judd), 1984 (C)
Russell, Charlotte 'Sarte', May 1985 (A)
Shipley, Dorothy (Mrs Bremner), undated (B)
Stephens, Teodora (Mrs Paige), 1984 (A)
Tivey, Jane (Mrs Davis), June 1984 (B)
Watson, Bronwyn (Mrs Sarno), July 1985 (C)
Wholohan, Jane, September 1985 (C)
Wilkins, Rosemary (Mrs Cameron), June 1984 (B)
Willson, Ruth, March 1985 (B)
Wilson, Joan, March 1985 (B)
Wilson, Mollie (Mrs Alexander), March 1985 (B)
Woodd, Iris (Mrs Carter), November 1984 (A)

S.C.E.G.G.S. staff

Mrs G. Bowley (Head of primary school 1973–76), May 1985
Miss D. Bowman (Headmistress 1978–), February 1986, and informally on many occasions
Miss B. Chisholm (Headmistress 1947–77), November 1983, February 1984, July 1985
Miss S. Elliott (music coordinator 1983–89), April 1985
Dr H. Goldhammer (science teacher 1952–72), November 1984

Miss J. Lean (S.C.E.G.G.S. 1963– ; Deputy Head 1973–93), December 1984
Mrs E. Miller (S.C.E.G.G.S. 1956–78; Senior Mistress 1972–78), November 1984
Mrs W. Sharland (English mistress 1941–55), October 1984
Miss I. Vandervord (Old Girl; mathematics teacher 1920–83), October 1985

Other interviews

Mr Neil Cameron, partner of Allen, Allen and Hemsley and Deputy Chairman of S.C.E.G.G.S. Board until 1979, June 1990 and other conversations on numerous occasions
Mr E. Davis, parent of S.C.E.G.G.S. girl and chairman of 'Save S.C.E.G.G.S.' campaign, June 1990
Miss Coral Dixon, Headmistress of Ravenswood School for Girls, Gordon, August 1990
Dr R. Shatford, Head of Tara Anglican school, Parramatta, August 1990
Mary Swift's three sons: Dick, Peter and Snow Watson, March 1987
Mrs J. Yeo, Headmistress of Roseville Girls' College, August 1990

Unpublished work

Badham, E., Registered Schools and the Syllabus, 1914
Badham, V., History of the Family of Professor Badham to mark the Centenary of his Death, 1984
Cable, K., Some Reflections on School Councils, n.d.
Cameron, E. D., Report on the Financial Crisis at S.C.E.G.G.S. 1974–1976, n.d.
Carrick, J. L., Funding for Non-Government Schools, n.d.
Egan, P., A History of St. John's Parish and Church at Darlinghurst, MA thesis Sydney University, 1985
Milburn, J., Girls' Secondary Education in NSW 1880–1930, MEd. thesis, Sydney University, 1965
Paterson, I., The future funding prospects for schools, February 1990
Radford, W., Charles Badham and his Work for Education in NSW, MEd. thesis, Sydney University, 1969
Rawlinson, R., School Governance and Councils
S.C.E.G.G.S. Staff Handbook 1990
Shatford, R., Australia Today, 1990

Published work

A Decade of Change—Women in New South Wales 1976–1986, NSW Women's Advisory Council to the Premier, Sydney, 1987
Austin, A. G., *Select Documents in Australian Education*, Pitman, Melbourne, 1966
Australian Students and their Schools, Schools Commission, Canberra, 1979
Badham, C., *Letters and Speeches*, University of Sydney, Sydney, 1890
Badham, E. A., *A Trip to Java*, F. Clark, n.d.
——*Java Revisited and Malaya*, F. Clark, Sydney, n.d.
Barcan, A., *A History of Australian Education*, Oxford University Press, Melbourne, 1980
——*A Short History of Education in NSW*, Sydney, 1980
Barlow, L., *Living Stones, Convent of the Sacred Heart*, Kincoppal–Rose Bay School, Rose Bay, Sydney, 1982
Braga, S., *Barker College, a History*, Ferguson, Sydney, 1978
Broadbent, J. et al., *The Golden Age of Australian Architecture—the Work of John Verge*, David Ell Press, Sydney, 1978

Burrows, D., *History of Abbotsleigh*, Council of Abbotsleigh, Sydney, 1968
Chambers, C., *Lessons for Ladies, a social history of girls' education in Australasia, 1870–1900*, Hale and Iremonger, Sydney, 1986
Coupe, S. & R., *Walk in the Light. A History of MLC Burwood*, MLC School in association with Ayers and James Heritage Books, Sydney, 1986
Crowley, F. ed., *A New History of Australia*, Heinemann, Melbourne, 1984
Daly, M. T., *Sydney Boom, Sydney Bust. The City and its Property Market 1850–1981*, Allen & Unwin, Sydney, 1982
Du Faur, F., *The Ascent of Mount Cook and Other Climbs*, Christchurch, 1977
Emilson, S., *Frensham—an Historical Perspective*, Winifred West Schools Ltd, Mittagong, 1988
Fairfax-Simpson et al., *Ascham Remembered 1886–1986*, The Fine Arts Press, Sydney, 1986
Farwell, G., *Squatters Castle, The Story and Times of a Pastoral Dynasty*, Lansdowne Press, Melbourne, 1985
Ferguson, A. (ed.), *High: the Centenary History of Sydney Boys' High School*, Sydney, 1983
Gardiner, L., *Tintern School and Anglican Girls' Education 1877–1977*, Tintern Church of England Girls' Grammar School, Melbourne, 1977
Greer, G., *The Female Eunuch*, MacGibbon and Kee, London, 1970
Hansen, D. E. & I. V., *Feminine Singular: A History of the Association of the Heads of Independent Girls' Schools of Australia*, Hyland House, South Yarra, 1989
Heath, P. J., *The Daring of Your Name: A History of Trinity Grammar School, Sydney*, Allen & Unwin, Sydney, 1990
Jobson, S., *Frank Hutchens*, Wentworth Books, Sydney, 1971
Johnstone, S. M., *The History of the King's School, Parramatta*, The Council of the King's School, Sydney, 1932
Judd, S. and Cable, K., *Sydney Anglicans: a History of the Diocese*, Anglican Information Office, Sydney, 1987
Kyle, N., *Her Natural Destiny*, NSW University Press, Sydney, 1986
Latham, C. E. & Nichols, A., *Trinity Grammar School: A History*, Council of Trinity Grammar School, Sydney, 1974
MacCallum, M., *Plankton's Luck: A Life in Retrospect*, Hutchinson, Melbourne, 1986
MacDonnell, F., *The Glebe: Portraits and Places*, Ure Smith, Sydney, 1975
MacFarlane, J., *The Golden Hope: Presbyterian Ladies' College 1888–1988*, Globe Press, Sydney, 1988
Mackenzie, J. and Dickson, I., *Life at Firbank 1909–1959*, Melbourne Firbank Old Grammarians Association, Melbourne, 1960
MacKenzie, N., *Women in Australia*, Cheshire, Adelaide, 1962
McKeown, P. J. ed., *Deo, Ecclesia, Patriae: 50 years of Canberra Grammar School*, Australian National University Press, Canberra, 1979
Mansfield, B., *Knox 1924–1974*, John Sands, Sydney, 1974
Metherell, T., *Excellence and Equity: NSW Curriculum Reform*, Department of Education, 1989
Newth, M., *St Andrew's Cathedral School: a Pictorial Review*, Ambassador Press, Sydney, 1980
Niall, B., & O'Neill, F., *Australia Through the Looking-glass: Children's Fiction 1930–1980*, Melbourne University Press, Melbourne, 1984
Nobbs, A., *Kambala: The First Hundred Years 1887–1987*, Kambala Centenary History Committee, Sydney, 1987
Norman, L., *The Brown and Yellow*, Oxford University Press, Melbourne, 1983
Rait, B., *The Story of Launceston Grammar School*, W. R. Rolph and Sons, Launceston, 1946
Report of the Commission appointed by the Archbishop of Sydney, Sydney, 1964
Sale, G., *The History of Casterton School*, Casterton School, Casterton, 1983
S.C.E.G.G.S., *Luceat Lux Vestra! A pageant in commemoration of the Jubilee of the Sydney Church of England Girls' Grammar School 1895–1945*, 1945

S.C.E.G.G.S., *'In Memoriam, Dorothy Irene Wilkinson, Headmistress, Sydney Church of England Girls' Grammar School, 1921–1947*, 1949
Sherington, G., *Shore: A History of Sydney Church of England Grammar School*, Allen & Unwin, Sydney, 1983
Storey, B., *History of North Sydney Girls' High School 1912–1977*, Management Development Publishers Pty Ltd, Sydney, 1982
Summers, A., *Damned Whores and God's Police—the Colonisation of Australia*, London, Penguin, 1975
Sydney Church of England Girls' Grammar School 1895–1955, Council of Sydney Church of England Girls' Grammar School, Sydney, 1958
Sydney Church of England Girls' Grammar School 1895–1970, Council of Sydney Church of England Girls' Grammar School, Sydney, 1972
The Australian Dictionary of Biography, vol. 2, 1788–1850, Melbourne University Press, Melbourne, 1966
Tuckey, E., *Fifty Years at Frensham*, Winifred West Schools, Sydney, 1964
Turney, C., *Grammar. A History of Sydney Grammar School 1819–1988*, Allen & Unwin, Sydney, 1989
——*Sources in the History of Australian Education 1788–1890*, University of Sydney Press, Sydney, 1975
——ed., *Pioneers of Australian Education*, vol. 2 Sydney, 1972
Votes and Proceedings of the Diocese of Sydney 1889–1898
Votes and Proceedings of the NSW Legislative Assembly 1872
Yearbooks of the Diocese of Sydney 1960–1974
Zainuddin, A., *They Dreamt of a School. The Centenary History of MLC Kew 1882–1982*, Hyland House, Melbourne, 1982

Magazines and newspapers

Australian, 1974
Australian Economist, 1895
Australian Record, 1893–94
Cosmos Magazine, 1895
Independence, the Journal of the Association of the Heads of Independent Schools in Australia, 1990
Lux, S.C.E.G.G.S. school magazine
NZL Quarterly Magazine, 1923
Sun-Herald, 1974
Sydney Morning Herald, 1890–1910

Index

Page references in italics refer to illustrations

215

KLONIE
BARHAM
S.B
215